IN THE GRAVEYARD
OF EMPIRES

ALSO BY SETH G. JONES

The Rise of European Security Cooperation

IN THE GRAVEYARD
OF EMPIRES

America's War in Afghanistan

SETH G. JONES

W. W. NORTON & COMPANY

New York   London

Unless otherwise noted, all maps were created by Carol Earnest.

Book design by Charlotte Staub

ISBN 978-0-393-06898-6 (hardcover)

W. W. Norton & Company, Inc.
500 Fifth Avenue, New York, N.Y. 10110

W. W. Norton & Company Ltd.
Castle House, 75/76 Wells Street, London W1T 3QT

*To those
struggling for peace
in Afghanistan*

CONTENTS

LIST OF MAPS AND GRAPHS

CHRONOLOGY

1839–1842 First Anglo-Afghan War, which results in a crushing defeat for the British. The departing force is reduced from 16,000 to one British soldier.

1878–1880 Second Anglo-Afghan War culminates in the Battle of Kandahar, in which British forces decisively defeat Ayub Khan in September 1880.

1893 Sir Henry Mortimer Durand, British foreign secretary of India, signs an agreement with the Afghan ruler, Amir Abdur Rehman Khan, separating Afghanistan from British India on November 12. The demarcation is known as the Durand Line.

1919 Third Anglo-Afghan War, which leads to the Treaty of Rawalpindi on August 8, recognizing Afghan independence.

1929 King Amanullah Khan, who had led Afghanistan to independence and attempted to modernize the country, is overthrown by Habibullah Kalakani, a Tajik. Kalikani is overthrown several months later, marking the start of a dynasty spanning five decades by the Pashtun Musahiban family. The first leader is Muhammad Nadir Shah.

1933 Upon the assassination of Muhammad Nadir Shah, his son, Zahir Shah, takes over at the age of nineteen, beginning one of Afghanistan's longest periods of stability in recent times. For thirty years, however, Zahir Shah remains in the background while his relatives run the government.

1963 Zahir Shah takes control of Afghanistan and introduces an era of modernity and democratic freedom.

1973 On July 16, Zahir Shah is overthrown in a coup d'état engineered by his cousin, Daoud Khan, with support of the Afghan army.

1978 Afghan army and air force officers engineer a bloody coup on April 27 in the Afghan lunar month of Sawr, and Daoud Khan is assassinated. Power is transferred to Nur Mohammad Taraki, who establishes the Democratic Republic of Afghanistan.

1979 Nur Mohammad Taraki is arrested by his deputy, Hafizullah Amin, and executed. As instability grips the country, Soviet forces invade on Christmas Eve. On December 27, Soviet Special Forces and KGB storm the Presidential Palace, kill Hafizullah Amin, and install Babrak Karmal as president.

1986 Soviet Premier Mikhail Gorbachev announces a partial withdrawal of Soviet troops from Afghanistan. In November, the Soviets replace Babrak Karmal with Muhammad Najibullah, former head of the Afghan secret police.

1989 On February 15, the last Red Army units roll across the Termez Bridge from Afghanistan and return to the Soviet Union.

1992 The United States ends arms shipments to the Afghan government and militia groups. Afghan groups conduct Beirut-style street fighting in Kabul, destroying parts of the city. Over the next several years, fighting in Kabul reduces the city to rubble.

1994 Taliban forces take control of the southern town of Spin Boldak in October and capture Kandahar in November, beginning the Taliban takeover of most of Afghanistan.

1995 Taliban forces advance northwest and northeast from Kandahar, capturing Herat in September and moving toward Kabul.

1996 Mullah Muhammad Omar removes the cloak of the Prophet Muhammad from the *Khirka Sharif* shrine in Kandahar in April and appoints himself *Amir al-Mu'minin* (Commander of the Faithful). Kabul falls to the Taliban in September.

1998 Taliban forces conquer Mazar-e-Sharif in August and kill Iranian diplomats, leading Iran to mobilize nearly 200,000 troops for an invasion. But the United Nations helps broker a settlement. Also in August, the United States launches cruise missiles against al Qa'ida training camps in Khowst Province after al Qa'ida attacks the U.S. embassies in Tanzania and Kenya.

2000 Taliban forces capture the northern city of Taloqan and take control of most of Afghanistan.

September 2001 The commander of the Northern Alliance, Ahmed Shah Massoud, is assassinated by al Qa'ida operatives on September 9. Two days later, al Qa'ida operatives hijack commercial planes in the United States and crash them into the World Trade Center in New York City and the Pentagon in Washington, DC. A fourth plane crashes in a field in Shanksville, Pennsylvania. On September 26, a CIA team led by Gary Schroen, code-named Jawbreaker, lands in Afghanistan and begins the U.S. effort to overthrow the Taliban.

October 2001 The United States begins its bombing campaign against the Taliban on October 7.

November 2001 U.S. and Afghan forces conquer the northern city of Mazar-e-Sharif on November 10, followed by Taloqan (November 11), Bamiyan (November 11), Herat (November 12), Kabul (November 13), Jalalabad (November 14), and Kunduz (November 26). At the end of November, the United States begins planning the war in Iraq.

December 2001 Afghan political leaders sign the Bonn Agreement on December 5, establishing a timetable for the creation of a representative government. The southern city of Kandahar falls to U.S. and Afghan forces on December 5–6, largely completing the overthrow of the Taliban regime. The United States narrowly misses killing

Osama bin Laden during fighting in Tora Bora, near the Afghanistan-Pakistan border.

March 2002 U.S. and Coalition forces launch Operation Anaconda against al Qa'ida fighters and other militants in the Shah-i-kot Valley from March 2 to 16.

April 2002 In a speech at the Virginia Military Institute on April 17, President Bush urges a "Marshall Plan" for Afghanistan, calling for financial assistance.

June 2002 Afghanistan holds an emergency *loya jirga*, which leads to the selection of Hamid Karzai as head of a transitional government.

August 2002 Insurgents orchestrate a series of offensive operations in such provinces as Kandahar and Khowst. These attacks mark the beginning of the Taliban-led insurgency against Hamid Karzai's government.

March 2003 Khalid Sheikh Muhammad, one of the prime organizers of the September 11 attacks, is captured in Pakistan on March 1. U.S. forces invade Iraq on March 20.

July 2003 U.S. and Afghan forces launch Operation Warrior Sweep in Paktia Province.

August 2003 U.S. Special Operations Forces and Afghan soldiers engage in intense fighting in Deh Chopan, Zabol Province.

November 2003 U.S. and Afghan forces launch Operation Mountain Resolve in Nuristan and Kunar Provinces.

December 2003 Afghanistan holds a constitutional *loya jirga*, which discusses a new constitution. In early January, after several weeks of debate, it approves the constitution.

April 2004 The Pakistani government reaches an agreement with the Taliban and local tribal leaders known as the Shakai Agreement. The Pakistani army promises to stay in cantonment areas, local militants agree not to attack Pakistani government officials, and all foreigners are required to register with the government. The agreement breaks down shortly thereafter.

June 2004 Pakistani forces conduct an operation in the Shakai Valley after alarming intelligence reports indicate that a force of more than 200 Chechens and Uzbeks, some Arabs, and several hundred local supporters are gathering in the area.

July 2004 The nongovernmental organization Médecins sans Frontières (Doctors without Borders) withdraws from Afghanistan, citing a deteriorating security environment.

October 2004 Afghans hold presidential elections and elect Hamid Karzai as president. NATO completes Stage 1 of its expansion into northern Afghanistan.

September 2005 Afghans hold parliamentary elections for the Wolesi Jirga (House of People) and Meshrano Jirga (House of Elders). NATO completes Stage 2 of its expansion, moving into western Afghanistan.

March 2006 U.S. and Afghan forces launch Operation Mountain Lion in Kunar Province.

May 2006 U.S. and Afghan forces launch Operation Mountain Thrust, the largest offensive since the fall of the Taliban, to quell the Taliban insurgency in southern Afghanistan.

July 2006 NATO completes Stage 3 of its expansion, moving into southern Afghanistan.

September 2006 Operation Medusa begins in Kandahar Province against dug-in Taliban forces. It involves forces from such NATO countries as Canada, the United States, and the Netherlands. Afghan and U.S. forces initiate Operation Mountain Fury against insurgents in Paktika, Khowst, Ghazni, Paktia, and Lowgar Provinces. In addition, the governor of Pakistan's North West Frontier Province reaches an agreement in Miramshah with a tribal grand *jirga*, in which the Taliban promise not to use the area to conduct attacks in Afghanistan. Over the next few months, however, the United States estimates that cross-border infiltration increased by between 300 and 400 percent in some areas.

October 2006 NATO completes Stage 4 of its expansion into the east, and Afghanistan is now divided into five geographic commands: Regional Command Central, North, West, South, and East.

November 2006 At NATO's summit in Riga, Latvia, tensions surface over military contributions in Afghanistan. France, Germany, Spain, and Italy remain reluctant to send their troops to southern Afghanistan. The Netherlands, Romania, and smaller nations such as Slovenia and Luxembourg agree to ease their restrictions on deployment.

January 2007 British Royal Marines begin Operation Volcano to clear insurgents from firing points in the village of Barikju in northern Helmand Province. This effort is followed by Operation Achilles, a major offensive that starts in March and ends in late May.

July 2007 The U.S. National Intelligence Council publicly releases its estimate of *The Terrorist Threat to the U.S. Homeland*. The document concludes that al Qa'ida remains "the most serious threat to the Homeland" and that it has "a safehaven in the Pakistan Federally Administered Tribal Areas (FATA)."

December 2007 On December 27, former Pakistani Prime Minister Benazir Bhutto is assassinated during her election campaign. In testimony before the House Armed Services Committee, U.S. Secretary of Defense Robert Gates sharply criticizes some NATO countries for not supplying urgently needed soldiers and other aid as violence escalates in Afghanistan.

April 2008 President Hamid Karzai escapes an assassination attempt on April 27, as gunmen open fire during a military parade celebrating the nation's victory and liberation from the Soviet occupation.

June 2008 During fighting along the Afghanistan-Pakistan border on June 10, U.S. forces kill nearly a dozen Pakistani Frontier Corps soldiers who are shooting at them.

July 2008 The Indian Embassy in Kabul is bombed on July 7, killing more than fifty people. In leaks to several newspapers, U.S. government sources acknowledge that Pakistan's intelligence service is involved in the attack. On July 13, insurgents launch a coordinated attack on a U.S. vehicle patrol base in Wanat, as heavily outnumbered U.S. and Afghan soldiers bravely fend off the assault.

August 2008 A United States AC-130 gunship accidentally kills Afghan civilians on August 22 in the Shindand district of Herat Province. In an unprecedented move, President Hamid Karzai flies to Herat to meet with locals and condemn the "the unilateral operation of the Coalition Forces." Pakistani President Pervez Musharraf resigns on August 18.

September 2008 U.S. Special Operations Forces conduct a helicopter-borne assault in South Waziristan, Pakistan. On September 20, a truck bomb explodes outside the Marriott Hotel in Islamabad, killing more than fifty people, including two Americans.

November 2008 On November 26, approximately ten terrorists from Lashkar-e-Taiba conduct a coordinated attack on several sites in Mumbai, India. After telephoning Indian Prime Minister Manmohan Singh, Afghan President Hamid Karzai calls for a regional fight against terrorism.

February 2009 President Barack Obama announces a nearly 50 percent increase in U.S. forces to Afghanistan, sending an additional 17,000 Marines and Army soldiers. Militants wearing suicide vests attack three Afghan government buildings in the heart of Kabul, killing at least twenty people.

INTRODUCTION

I SPENT THE MORNING of September 8, 2006, with several Afghan friends in a guesthouse in Kabul, Afghanistan's capital, sipping a warm cup of *sher chai*, a traditional Afghan drink prepared using black tea, cardamom, and milk. The house was constructed of concrete, with whitewashed walls and a small leafy courtyard. There was a meticulously crafted assortment of red and pink roses around the perimeter, and a small vineyard with green grapes on one end. Like much of the capital city, this house had been rebuilt after the overthrow of the Taliban regime in 2001. Just five years after the American invasion, Kabul was a vastly different city, awash in electronics equipment and sprinkled with new Internet cafés. The streets were clogged with bright yellow taxicabs, watermelon carts, bicycles, and cars imported from Europe and Asia. Young boys and girls shuffled to school along the congested sidewalks. Construction projects dotted the city. Several new banks and an upscale indoor shopping mall named Kabul City Center were going up downtown. Economic growth was up 8.6 percent that year alone.[1]

But there were ominous signs that the new order was teetering. At 10:20 a.m., a piercing noise shattered the morning lull. A suicide bomber had driven a dark Toyota Surf into a convoy of U.S. soldiers. I was in the vicinity of the attack, which occurred near Massoud Square, bordering the main gate of the U.S. Embassy. The square had been named for Ahmed Shah Massoud, military leader of the United

Islamic Front for the Salvation of Afghanistan (or Northern Alliance), who was assassinated by al Qa'ida suicide bombers two days before September 11, 2001.

The attack wounded twenty-nine people and killed sixteen. Two of the dead were American soldiers. One was Staff Sergeant Robert Paul, an Army reservist from The Dalles, Oregon, who was part of the 364th Civil Affairs Brigade. In an obituary, his grieving family wrote, "He never turned down an opportunity because he always wanted to make a difference in everything he did."[2] The other American killed was Sergeant 1st Class Merideth Howard, an Army reservist from Waukesha, Wisconsin, whose husband mourned her death by blasting her remains skyward in two fireworks displays. A few months earlier, an Army crew filming a segment on U.S. reconstruction efforts in Afghanistan showed Sergeant Howard handing out hundreds of backpacks. "Most of the kids are in school, even if it's just a few hours a day," she said. "And that's what we're trying to do, is just help them out as much as we can."[3]

The rest of the dead were Afghan civilians unfortunate enough to be in the blast zone. One was an elderly man selling used clothing from a dilapidated, rusty pushcart. Among the others were a half-dozen municipal street sweepers finishing their morning cleaning, and two gangly boys selling water. At the bomb site, I could see thick black smoke curling up the charred trees nearby. The blast had torn a six-foot-wide crater in the road and left scattered over a wide area a gruesome and disquieting collection of items: Muslim prayer caps, khaki-colored military hats, shoes, and body parts. The explosion, which also had ripped apart an armored Humvee, was the largest suicide bombing in the capital up to that point. I tried not to be discouraged, but the trends suggested a growing insurgency.

Two days later, on September 10, another suicide bomber assassinated Hakim Taniwal, governor of Paktia Province. I had been scheduled to visit him later that week. He was a genteel, bespectacled sociology professor who had fled from Afghanistan to Pakistan in 1980, moved to Australia in 1997, and then returned home to Afghanistan in 2002 to help rebuild his shattered country. Afghan President Hamid

Karzai had asked his close friend Taniwal to come to Paktia, a rugged
province in the foothills of the Hindu Kush mountains in eastern
Afghanistan, which had become a hotbed of insurgent activity. Australia's minister of foreign affairs, Alexander Downer, who knew Taniwal,
described him as a scholarly, soft-spoken man of integrity, and "a good
man, with a reputation as a highly capable administrator."[4]

Taniwal's family had begged him not to return to Afghanistan, but
he felt an overwhelming sense of patriotism and couldn't miss the
opportunity to help rebuild his homeland. Ghulam Gul, the suicide
bomber, crept up to Taniwal's car and blew himself up as the car
pulled away from the governor's office in Gardez. The next day,
nearly a thousand mourners attended Taniwal's funeral, including the
Afghan ministers of interior, refugees, communications, and parliamentary affairs. The outpouring of grief and the admiration for Taniwal were palpable. But in a shocking display of irreverence, another
suicide bomber blew himself up at the funeral, killing at least seven
people and wounding up to forty. Five of the dead were policemen
and two were children. The Taliban decision to target a funeral, one
of the most solemn occasions in Islam, defied basic human dignity.
President Karzai denounced the attack as a "heinous act of terrorism
. . . against Islam and humanity."[5]

Afghanistan, one U.S. soldier remarked to me at the time, was
beginning to feel like Iraq in 2003. Kabul—and indeed Afghanistan
more broadly—had a strange *fin de siècle* air. What had happened?
Why did an insurgency develop in Afghanistan?

Downward Spiral

As horrible as they were, the September 11, 2001, attacks provided
the United States with an opportunity to eliminate al Qa'ida from
Afghanistan. And the United States jumped at the chance, launching
within weeks the most significant and expensive counterterrorism
effort in the history of the United States. In an emotional address to
a joint session of Congress nine days after the attacks, President

George W. Bush pledged to begin a global "war against terror": "The leadership of al Qa'ida has great influence in Afghanistan and supports the Taliban regime in controlling most of that country. In Afghanistan, we see al Qa'ida's vision for the world." Afghanistan would be the first battleground. "Our war on terror begins with al Qa'ida, but it does not end there. It will not end until every terrorist group of global reach has been found, stopped and defeated."[6]

Overall, the United States spent more than $430 billion for military and diplomatic efforts over the first five years and deployed military forces to the Middle East, Africa, and Asia.[7] This amount was larger than the annual gross domestic product of 89 percent of the world's countries.[8] Afghanistan was where much of the planning and training for the September 11 attacks took place and, at least initially, it was the central front of America's "war on terror." And rightly so. Following his capture, Khalid Sheikh Muhammad, head of al Qa'ida's military committee and Osama bin Laden's principal operative for the attacks, boasted: "I was Emir [commander] of Beit al Shuhada [the Martyrs' House] in the state of Kandahar, Afghanistan, which housed the 9/11 hijackers. There I was responsible for their training and readiness for the execution of the 9/11 operation."[9]

In 2001, U.S. Special Operations and CIA forces, along with Afghan indigenous troops backed by U.S. airpower, combined to overthrow the Taliban regime in less than three months while suffering only a dozen U.S. fatalities.[10] Some argued that the operation revitalized the American way of war.[11] Indeed, it was a remarkably effective campaign. Approximately 100 CIA officers, 350 Special Forces soldiers, and 15,000 Afghans—running as many as 100 combat sorties per day—defeated a Taliban army estimated at 50,000 to 60,000 plus several thousand al Qa'ida fighters.[12]

Despite the idealism of the initial campaign and the success of military operations, the United States squandered this extraordinary opportunity. America was a global superpower with the resources and talent to effectively overthrow governments and replace them with new ones. But it failed to seize the moment. By 2006, tensions had escalated dramatically and Afghanistan was leveled by a perfect storm of political upheaval in which several crises came together: Pakistan emerged as a sanctuary for the Taliban and al Qa'ida, allowing them to conduct a greater number of operations from bases across the border; Afghan governance became unhinged as corruption worked its way through the government like a cancer, leaving massive discontent throughout the country; and the international presence, hamstrung by the U.S. focus on Iraq, was too small to deal with the escalating violence. The simultaneous pressures came to a head in 2006, when the Taliban, Gulbuddin Hekmatyar's Hezb-i-Islami, the Haqqani network, foreign fighters, criminal groups, and a host of Afghan and Pakistan tribal militias began a sustained effort to overthrow the U.S.-backed Afghan government.

This book has much to say about insurgencies. For our purposes, an insurgency is a political-military campaign by nonstate actors seeking to overthrow a government or secede from a country through the use of unconventional—and sometimes conventional—strategies and tactics.[13] Insurgencies can involve a wide range of tactics and forms of protest, from small-scale marches to large-scale conventional violence.[14] The Afghan insurgency quickly made the leap to extreme violence. Insurgents in both Afghanistan and Pakistan imported suicide bombing, improvised explosive technology, and global communications strategies from Iraq and other battlefields, such as Hizbullah in Lebanon. Al Qa'ida succeeded in reestablishing its base by skillfully exploiting the weakness of the Pakistani state in the Pashtun tribal belt. Instead of defeating al Qa'ida and the Taliban in 2001, the U.S.-led Coalition merely pushed the core leadership of al Qa'ida and the Taliban out of Afghanistan and into Pakistan. This outcome was not inevitable. Rather, it was the result of America's inability to finish the job it had started and to provide the requisite attention and resources.

By 2006, a full-bodied insurgency had developed in Afghanistan. The overall number of insurgent-initiated attacks increased by 400 percent from 2002 to 2006, and the number of deaths from these attacks increased more than 800 percent during the same period.[15] Many of the attacks were against Afghan government officials, though others targeted civilians and Coalition forces. The increase in violence was particularly acute between 2005 and 2006. The number of suicide attacks quadrupled, remotely detonated bombings more than doubled, and armed attacks nearly tripled between 2005 and 2006.[16] The following year would bring more of the same, as insurgent-initiated attacks rose another 27 percent.[17]

The rapid growth of Afghanistan's insurgency led to a series of recriminations by U.S. soldiers and their NATO allies. Some U.S. soldiers began referring to NATO's International Security Assistance Force (ISAF) by a range of derogatory names such as "I Suck at Fighting," "I Saw Americans Fight," or "I Sunbathe at FOBs." The latter was a reference to the small, heavily fortified forward operating bases (FOBs) established in rural areas. American soldiers dismissed many of their NATO allies for hunkering down in their FOBs and blamed the escalation of violence at least partly on the reluctance of NATO countries to fight.

I had spent time with soldiers and civilians from most NATO countries in Afghanistan while conducting research on the security situation in the country, examining the state of the Afghan police, army, justice system, and insurgent groups. In the early years after the U.S. invasion, I could travel around the country fairly easily by vehicle, since the security situation was relatively stable. While I sometimes wore local dress and grew a beard, I felt safe in most areas. The American journalist Sarah Chayes, who had been a correspondent for National Public Radio in Afghanistan during the 2001 war, put it eloquently: "Kandahar, in those days, shimmered with a breathless hope. Afghans, even there in the Taliban's former den, were overcome by the possibilities opened up by this latest 'revolution,' as they referred to it. . . . They were hungry to participate again in the shaping of their national destiny, the way they had back in the golden age before the Communist coup and the Soviet invasion."[18] But by 2006, security for foreigners—and even local Afghans—in rural areas of the east, south, and central regions began to deteriorate, making it more difficult to move around by car. I increasingly used airplanes or helicopters to travel from Kabul to dangerous parts of the south and east.

As road travel became more dangerous, crime also developed into a major problem. Interfactional fighting arose among warlords. The deteriorating security situation was worst at the local level, where Afghan security forces could not protect rural villagers. A report by the National Directorate of Security, Afghanistan's intelligence agency, concluded that Taliban cells knew who was collaborating with NATO and Afghan government forces: "Individuals who flirt with the government truly get frightened as the Afghan security forces are currently incapable of providing police and protection for each village. . . . When villagers and rural communities seek protection from police either it arrives late or arrives in a wrong way."[19]

These challenges were somewhat predictable. To paraphrase Thomas "Tip" O'Neill, the longtime Speaker of the U.S. House of Representatives, all politics in Afghanistan are local. Past empires that have dared to enter Afghanistan—from Alexander the Great to Great Britain and the Soviet Union—have found initial entry possible, even easy, only to find themselves mired in local resistance. Aware of this history, the United States had the resources, manpower, and strategic know-how to create a new order. And it was on the right track, at least initially. But the moment was fleeting. Despite the impressive gains in security, infrastructure, and democracy, the United States shifted resources and attention to Iraq and allowed the Taliban, al Qa'ida, and other insurgent groups to rebuild in Afghanistan and Pakistan. The lessons from past empires provide a stark lesson.

Graveyard of Empires

Around 330 BC, Alexander the Great and his army suffered staggering losses in fierce battles against Afghan tribes. His astonishing conquest of Eurasia became bogged down in Afghanistan and India. Over the next two thousand years, the region was deeply problematic for major empires from the West and the East—from the Arab armies to such legendary conquerors as Genghis Khan, Timur (more commonly known as Tamerlane), and Babur.

The modern Afghan state was founded in the mid-eighteenth century by Ahmed Shah Durrani, who united the region's disparate Pashtun tribes and conquered major portions of modern Afghanistan, Pakistan, northeastern Iran, and western India. By the nineteenth century, Russia and Britain became intimately intertwined in what would become the Great Game, using Afghanistan as a buffer state in the struggle between their empires. Between 1839 and 1919, the British fought three brutal wars in Afghanistan to counter Russian influence in the region. Rudyard Kipling's searing experience in Afghanistan and British India inspired his poem "Young British Soldier," which echoes the din of battle:

> *When shakin' their bustles like ladies so fine,*
> *The guns o' the enemy wheel into line,*
> *Shoot low at the limbers an' don't mind the shine,*
> *For noise never startles the soldier.*
> *Start-, start-, startles the soldier . . .*
>
> *If your officer's dead and the sergeants look white,*
> *Remember it's ruin to run from a fight:*
> *So take open order, lie down, and sit tight,*
> *And wait for supports like a soldier.*
> *Wait, wait, wait like a soldier.* [20]

The British tried a number of strategies against Pashtun tribes during the Anglo-Afghan Wars. One was "butcher and bolt," the practice of slaughtering unruly tribesmen and then moving quickly to pacify new areas. But they were unable to conquer the country, leading Winston Churchill to refer to the tribesmen as "a brave and warlike race."[21] The Soviet Union suffered a similar fate. The Soviet invasion of Afghanistan in 1979 was met with fierce resistance from the Afghan population, and thousands of Russian soldiers and mujahideen (Muslim fighters involved in jihad, or holy war) died in the conflict. Pakistan's Inter-Services Intelligence Directorate (ISI), with assistance from the U.S. Central Intelligence Agency and Saudi intelligence, provided substantial assistance to the mujahideen and such Afghan leaders as Gulbuddin Hekmatyar and Jalaluddin Haqqani, some of whom would later take up arms against the United States and other Coalition forces after the September 2001 terrorist attacks. When the Soviets withdrew in February 1989, the country was devastated. An estimated one million Afghans had been killed, more than five million had fled abroad, and as many as three million people were forced to leave their homes to avoid the bloodshed.[22]

After the 2001 overthrow of the Taliban regime, British military forces in Afghanistan were given a pointed reminder of their country's role in Afghanistan's history. British soldiers in Helmand Province, a hotbed of the insurgency in southern Afghanistan, occupied a cluster of dusty, crudely constructed forts, on the banks of the Helmand River, which their forebears in the British military had built more than a century earlier. "You can't hold it against them for wanting to repel the invaders," said British Warrant Officer 2 Jason Mortimer, who manned a sandbag-lined bunker in the ruins of one of these old forts in 2008. Afghan fighters, he recalled, sent the British "packing with a bloody nose" after the Anglo-Afghan Wars.[23]

U.S. military and diplomatic officials were also well aware of Afghanistan's history. In late 2001, General Tommy Franks, head of U.S. Central Command, said, "Secretary [Donald] Rumsfeld and I agreed that we should not flood the country with large formations of conventional troops. . . . We don't want to repeat the Soviets' mistakes."[24] Nevertheless, U.S. policymakers gravely underestimated the gritty resolve of the Afghans. Though most of the landscape is barren and parched, and though its people appear unobtrusive and primitive, this region has nurtured a proud warrior culture that has repelled invading armies for more than two thousand years. Indeed, the central tragedy of the American experience in Afghanistan is the way this history was disregarded. The United States began its operations with a good plan, competent people, and significant support from local Afghans, but it was unable to take advantage of the opportunity. The "light footprint," as it was known, was a blessing during the overthrow of the Taliban regime, but it became a curse once the insurgency began to overwhelm what few U.S. resources existed on the ground. As one senior U.S. administration official told me, "We seized defeat from the jaws of victory."[25]

Debating Afghanistan

So why did an insurgency occur? There are two common schools of thought. Some argue that Afghanistan's ethnic makeup was largely responsible for the insurgency. Afghanistan has four major ethnic groups: Pashtun, Uzbek, Tajik, and Hazara, as well as a range of minor ethnic groups. The long-standing ethnic fissures in Afghanistan, says this camp, made violence inevitable. The last decade of fighting had pitted Pashtun groups from southern Afghanistan against Uzbek, Tajik, and other groups from northern Afghanistan, fueling long-held grudges and sparking further conflict. Others have argued that Afghanistan's insurgency was caused by a series of economic developments broadly subsumed under the umbrella term *greed*. Building on a body of economic literature, this argument assumes that violence generates profits for opportunists, making insurgents indistinguishable from bandits or criminals. Afghan insurgent groups were motivated by the potential for profit from the cultivation, production, and export of poppy, much like the way that cocaine profits fueled the rise of the Revolutionary Armed Forces of Colombia (FARC). After the U.S. invasion, Afghanistan cornered the global opiate market. In 2007, the United Nations Office on Drugs and Crime (UNODC) announced: "No other country in the world has ever produced narcotics on such a deadly scale."[26]

A careful examination of Afghanistan since 2001, however, shows that these arguments are fundamentally flawed. None of them can adequately explain why an insurgency developed. Rather, two factors were critical.

One was weak governance, which provided an important precondition for the rise of an insurgency. The inability of the Afghan government at all levels to provide key services to local Afghans, especially in rural areas, gutted support for the national government and forced citizens to look elsewhere for security. Governance, as used here, is defined as the set of institutions by which authority in a country is exercised. It involves the ability to establish law and order, effectively manage resources, and implement sound policies. By all accounts, Afghan leaders at all levels failed to provide good governance. Riddled with corruption and incompetence, institutions such as the Afghan National Police were unable to secure a monopoly of the legitimate use of violence, while national and local officials were unable to effectively manage resources and implement sound policies. In addition, insurgent groups were able to tap into a broad array of resources from individuals in neighboring governments and the international jihadi community.[27] Perhaps most important, outside actors helped undermine the provisional Afghan government. Many looked to the United States for help, but American and other international assistance was among the lowest of any state-building mission since World War II, a startling statistic, given that the Afghan mission was launched on the heels of the September 2001 terrorist attacks.

The second motivating factor for insurgent leaders was religious ideology. Taliban leader Mullah Muhammad Omar and al Qa'ida leaders such as Ayman al-Zawahiri and Osama bin Laden advocated jihad to recover "occupied" Muslim lands. They demanded a return to a radical interpretation of Islam stripped of local customs and cultures. The Taliban leaders saw themselves as the cleansers of a social and political system gone wrong in Afghanistan, and an Islamic way of life that had been compromised by corruption and infidelity to the Prophet. Al Qa'ida leaders were motivated by an ideology grounded in the works of Sayyid Qutb, a leading intellectual in the Egyptian

Muslim Brotherhood, and other Islamist thinkers, and they advocated the establishment of a radical interpretation of *sharia* (Islamic religious law). In sum, there was both a "supply" of rural villagers disgruntled by a failing government and a "demand" for recruits by ideologically motivated leaders. Afghanistan's insurgency was caused by the synergy of collapsing governance and a virulent religious ideology that seemed to fill the void. But understanding this phenomenon required getting out into rural areas and talking to local Afghans and international and Afghan forces operating there. The insurgency in Afghanistan, it turned out, was much more about what happened in local villages and district centers than what happened in Kabul.

The Research Approach

My goal in Afghanistan was specific: to understand the motivations of key actors and to assess what factors contributed to the rise of Afghanistan's insurgency. I chose to examine Afghanistan because it is a case of such intrinsic importance to the United States. The attacks in Washington, New York, and Pennsylvania on September 11, 2001, were planned in Afghanistan, and many of the hijackers went through training in Afghanistan. Even after the overthrow of the Taliban regime, core al Qa'ida leaders continued to reside along the Pakistan-Afghanistan frontier.

It is also important to understand what this book does *not* try to do. It is not a broader effort to build and test a theory of why insurgencies begin. Rather, it is a study of the specific aspects of insurgency in Afghanistan. This book also does not pretend to offer a comprehensive analysis of Afghanistan across such areas as politics, economics, education, and health care. Many nations, international organizations such as the United Nations, and nongovernmental organizations logged countless hours trying to build Afghanistan's fragile infrastructure and institutions. As Nobel Prize–winning economist Amartya Sen has argued, many of these areas are interrelated: "Political freedoms (in the form of free speech and elections) help to promote economic security. Social opportunities (in the form of education and health facilities) facilitate economic participation. Economic facilities (in the form of opportunities for participation in trade and production) can help to generate personal abundance as well as public resources for social facilities."[28] These aspects are certainly important, but the focus in this book is on the deteriorating security situation and the key factors that contributed to it.

Discovering Afghanistan proved a fascinating journey. Afghanistan sometimes gets an unnecessarily bad rap. In James Michener's novel *Caravans*, for instance, the main character, Mark Miller, was stationed in Kabul at the U.S. Embassy in the aftermath of World War II. His description of the city was overwhelmingly negative: "Kabul provided positively nothing for foreigners: no hotels that we could use, no cinema of any kind, no newspapers, no radio with European programs, no restaurants available to visitors, no theaters, no cafés, no magazines."[29] Michener, who had traveled through Afghanistan in 1955, hit on the perfunctory, stereotypical image of Afghanistan, which was sometimes repeated by foreigners after the U.S. invasion. But I found it a mesmerizing and deeply complicated country.

Over the course of several years' research, I combed through thousands of primary and secondary sources. I visited Afghanistan multiple times every year between 2004 and 2009, and I conducted thousands of interviews in Afghanistan, Pakistan, India, the United States, and other NATO countries. Within the Afghan government, for example, I interviewed officials in the Presidential Palace, National Security Council, Ministry of Interior, Ministry of Defense, and National Directorate of Security (Afghanistan's intelligence service). Within the United States government, I interviewed individuals in the White House, Department of State, Department of Defense, Central Intelligence Agency, Drug Enforcement Agency, U.S. Agency for International Development, Federal Bureau of Investigation, and other government agencies with a presence in Afghanistan. I spent time with soldiers and civilians from virtually all NATO countries in Afghanistan, from the Canadians and British in the south to the Germans and Norwegians in the north. I also conducted interviews with staff from the United Nations and a variety of nongovernmental organizations.

The book includes information from original interviews with key U.S. policymakers, such as Secretary of State Colin Powell, Deputy Secretary of State Richard Armitage, CIA Station Chief in Islamabad Robert Grenier, Commander of U.S. forces in Afghanistan Lieutenant General Karl Eikenberry, U.S. Ambassador to Afghanistan Ronald Neumann, U.S. Ambassador to Afghanistan Zalmay Khalilzad, Commander of U.S. forces in Afghanistan Lieutenant General David Barno, and countless others. It also includes original interviews with key Afghanistan policymakers, such as Foreign Minister Abdullah Abdullah, Minister of Interior Ali Jalali, and Afghan Ambassador to the United States Said Jawad.

In addition to interviews, I compiled and reviewed thousands of government documents from the United States, Afghanistan, and Coalition countries such as Germany and the United Kingdom, as well as transcripts and videos from the Taliban, Hezb-i-Islami, al Qa'ida, and other insurgent groups. I was fortunate to have access to a trove of documents that have not yet been published, such as the Afghan National Directorate of Security's *Strategy of Insurgents and Terrorists in Afghanistan*, the Afghanistan National Security Council's *National Threat Assessment* from various years, and the Afghanistan Ministry of Defense's *The National Military Strategy*.[30] The book also includes recently released declassified material from the Central Intelligence Agency, Defense Intelligence Agency, State Department, Soviet Politburo, and other sources about Afghanistan's descent into war from the 1970s through 2001. The use of such material helps capture more accurately the course of events—and their causes—over the past several decades.

A Road Map

This book proceeds somewhat chronologically. It follows the gradual collapse of governance in the late 1960s and 1970s that culminated in the Soviet invasion of 1979, which led a band of Americans such as U.S. Congressman Charlie Wilson to increase U.S. assistance to the Afghan mujahideen as they drove the Red Army out of the country. In June 1993, CIA Director James Woolsey told a small gathering at CIA headquarters that honored Charlie Wilson, "The defeat and breakup of the Soviet empire is one of the great events of world history."[31] This book continues with an examination of CIA and other U.S. government assessments of the bloody Afghan civil war in the early 1990s, the rise of the Taliban regime in the late 1990s, and the Taliban's fateful alliance with Osama bin Laden and al Qa'ida.

With the September 11, 2001, attacks in the United States, the story transitions to the overthrow of the Taliban regime that year by an eclectic mixture of Northern Alliance forces, CIA operatives, U.S. Special Forces, and staggering U.S. airpower. It follows the discussions in the U.S. government about establishing a "light footprint" in Afghanistan, as Pentagon, State Department, CIA, and White House officials debated whether or not to engage in nation-building. It also tracks the exodus of Taliban and al Qa'ida fighters into neighboring Pakistan, and the establishment of a sanctuary for many of these fighters in Pakistan's Baluchistan Province, Federally Administered Tribal Areas, and North West Frontier Province.

The book then moves to the rise of Afghanistan's insurgency and the collapse of Afghan governance. It outlines Afghan difficulties in establishing law and order in rural areas as well as challenges in delivering essential services to the local populations. Weak governance, it turns out, has been a critical factor in the rise of most insurgencies over the past fifty years. The next chapters explore the proliferation of violence beginning in 2006, catalyzed by what Lieutenant General Eikenberry referred to as a "perfect storm" of crises. The book also explores the role of outside actors in aiding insurgent groups, including al Qa'ida and Pakistan's Inter-Services Intelligence Directorate and Frontier Corps.

To better appreciate Afghanistan's complex history, which has seen the ruthless destruction of foreign armies, our story begins with

Alexander the Great's audacious sojourn into Afghanistan—one of the most notable failed attempts to conquer the region. What becomes eerily apparent, however, is how quickly the United States ran into challenges similar to those faced by past empires. "Ambushes, assassinations, attacks on supply convoys, bridges, pipelines, and airfields, with the avoidance of set piece battles; these are history's proven techniques for the guerrilla," wrote Mohammad Yousaf, who ran Pakistan's ISI operations in Afghanistan during the Soviet War.[32] Indeed, Afghanistan's rich history serves as a springboard for understanding the American experience in a country that since antiquity has been called a graveyard of empires.

IN THE GRAVEYARD
OF EMPIRES

FIGURE 1.1   Map of Afghanistan

CHAPTER ONE

Descent into Violence

AFGHANISTAN'S STRATEGIC LOCATION, wedged between Persia, the weathered steppes of Central Asia, and the trade routes of the Indian Subcontinent, has long made it alluring to great powers. When Alexander the Great began his march into Afghanistan around 330 BC, locals witnessed a forbidding sight. Riding ahead of the invading force were scouts armed with *sarisas*—pikes up to twenty feet long, weighted at the base and projecting fifteen feet in front of the mounted cavalry. Agile soldiers armed with javelins surveyed the heights on both flanks. The core of Alexander's army was a thick column of horsemen and foot soldiers that snaked along Afghanistan's windswept roads. Some soldiers wore plumed helmets, purple tunics, and glistening armor. Alexander had begun his Asia campaign four years earlier, and the invasion of Afghanistan was a key part of his quest. His army had already swept through what is now Turkey, Syria, Lebanon, Israel, Egypt, Iraq, and Iran before arriving at the edge of Afghanistan.[1]

One of the most interesting accounts of the campaign was provided by the Roman historian Quintus Curtius Rufus. He described Alexander gathering his soldiers together before their march into Afghanistan and addressing them with bravado:

> In a new, and if we wish to confess the truth, insecure empire, to
> whose yoke the barbarians still submit with obdurate necks, there is

3

need of time, my soldiers, until they are trained to milder disposi-
tions, and until better habits appease their savage temper. Do you
believe that so many nations accustomed to the rule and name of
another, united with us neither by religion, nor customs, nor community of language, have been subdued in the same battle in which
they were overcome?

It is by your arms alone that they are restrained, not by their dis-
positions, and those who fear us when we are present, in our absence
will be enemies. We are dealing with savage beasts, which lapse of
time only can tame, when they are caught and caged, because their
own nature cannot tame them. Then you will hurry to recover what
is yours, then you will take up arms. But how much better it is to
crush him while he is still in fear and almost beside himself.[2]

Rufus wrote that the address was received with great enthusiasm
by Alexander's soldiers.[3] The great Hellenic army entered Afghanistan from what is today Iran. They paused to found a garrison city,
Alexandria-in-Areia, near Afghanistan's western city of Herat, then
marched south to the lower Helmand River Valley. The Helmand
River, the longest in Afghanistan, stretches more than 700 miles from
the Hindu Kush mountains in the north to the Helmand Valley in the
south. Its waters, used by local farmers for irrigating crops, left
behind rich soil to feed the orchards and date-palm groves that lined
its banks. In this period, the valley was fertile and well populated,
and Alexander's army halted there to await the end of Afghanistan's
bitter winter before proceeding north. In the early spring, the army
marched to the Kabul Valley, trekking across melting snow and ice,
but the persistent, biting cold took its toll.

Rufus wrote: "The army, then, abandoned in this absence of all
human civilization, endured all the evils that could be suffered, want,
cold, fatigue, despair. The unusual cold of the snow caused the death
of many, to many it brought frost-bite of the feet, to very many blind-
ness of the eyes."[4]

But in the Kabul Valley, the army finally found sustenance. Alexander's Afghan campaign continued until the spring of 327 BC, when
the army crossed the Hindu Kush into India. The Hindu Kush moun-

tains form part of a vast alpine zone that stretches across South Asia. To the east, the mountains intersect with the Pamir range near the borders of China, Pakistani-controlled Kashmir, and Afghanistan. They then continue southwest through Pakistan into Afghanistan, where they eventually descend into a series of minor ranges in western Afghanistan. Historically, the high passes of the Hindu Kush have been of great military significance, providing access to the northern plains of India for such conquerors as Alexander, as well as invaders such as Genghis Khan, Timur, and Babur. And they inspired the British travel writer Eric Newby, who wrote, during his trek through the Hindu Kush, "Here on the Arayu, one of the lonely places of the earth with all the winds of Asia droning over it, where the mountains seemed like the bones of the world breaking through, I had the sensation of emerging from a country that would continue to exist more or less unchanged whatever disasters overtook the rest of mankind."[5]

Afghanistan was one of the most difficult campaigns that Alexander the Great ever fought. His adversaries were not conventional European armies but tribesmen and horse warriors who inhabited the steppes and mountains of the region. Both sides fought barbarously. Alexander's army was technically superior to the local forces they faced, but it needed to clear and hold an expansive territory. The solution was to fight on multiple fronts in a constant war of attrition against the local Afghans, and to deal ruthlessly with the locals. The army sacked rebellious cities, killed or enslaved their inhabitants, and doled out savage reprisals. If not genocide, it was certainly mass killing.[6] Despite the bloodletting, his army failed to subjugate Afghanistan's population, and his tenuous grasp on the region collapsed after his death in 323 BC.

Alexander's march was eventually followed by the Islamic conquest of Afghanistan, which began around 652 AD, two decades after the death of the prophet Muhammad in Medina, when Arab armies from the Middle East captured Herat. But they failed to convert the recalcitrant mountain tribes, and their revolt preserved the loose conglomerate of Buddhists, Zoroastrians, Hindus, and others that had dominated before the rise of the Caliphate. In 1221 AD, Genghis Khan and his Mongol army swept through Afghanistan and northern India, leaving behind a trail of devastation and creating an empire that stretched from China to the Caucasus. They depopulated territory, slaughtering civilians in an attempt to eliminate the possibility of rebellion, and they decimated cities such as Herat.

Marco Polo, the Venetian trader and explorer, trekked across Afghan mountains later in the century, remarking that "this kingdom has many narrow passes and natural fortresses, so that the inhabitants are not afraid of any invader breaking in to molest them. Their cities and towns are built on mountain tops or sites of great natural strength. It is a characteristic of these mountains that they are of immense height."[7] In 1383, the conqueror Timur began his Afghan conquest, again with the capture of Herat. He was the last of the mighty Mongol rulers to achieve a vast empire with territory stretching from present-day India to the Mediterranean Sea. The poverty, bloodshed, and desolation caused by his campaigns gave rise to haunting legends that inspired such works as Christopher Marlowe's *Tamburlaine the Great*. Early in the sixteenth century, the Mughal emperor Babur left present-day Iran and crossed the Amu Darya River, which would later serve as the border between the Soviet Union and Afghanistan. Babur, a descendant of Genghis Khan, captured Kabul in 1504 at the age of twenty-one. In 1522, he captured Kandahar and repeatedly tried to invade India, but he was never able to establish a firm foothold. He left behind traces of Persian culture—from language to music, painting, and poetry—that one can still see in Afghanistan.

In the nineteenth century, the British fought three brutal wars in Afghanistan to balance Russian influence in the region. Britain had drawn the line against Russia at the Amu Darya River, and its leaders made clear they would contest any Russian move to the south. But Britain paid a heavy price for its interest in Afghanistan. The first Anglo-Afghan War, which lasted from 1839 to 1842, ended in a humiliating British defeat. The departing British force, numbering

16,000 soldiers, was systematically reduced to *one* as British forces were ambushed in biting cold and knee-deep snow. William Brydon, the lone survivor, later recalled: "This was a terrible march, the fire of the enemy incessant, and numbers of officers and men, not knowing where they were going from snow-blindness, were cut up."[8]

In 1878, the British invaded again, launching the second Anglo-Afghan War. Roughly 33,500 British troops began a swift assault on three fronts, but cholera shredded the British ranks and many were felled by heat; daytime temperatures in the shade rose to over one hundred degrees. Some British commanders did not even visit their soldiers in the hospital to avoid the utter shock of what they would see.[9] On July 27, 1880, Afghans loyal to Ayub Khan defeated the British army during the Battle of Maiwand. Despite a decisive victory at the Battle of Kandahar in September 1880, however, the British pulled out of the country following intense domestic opposition to the war. After the fighting ended, Lieutenant General Sir Frederick Roberts remarked: "It may not be very flattering to our *amour propre*, but I feel sure I am right when I say that the less the Afghans see of us the less they will dislike us. Should Russia in future years attempt to reconquer Afghanistan, or invade India through it, we should have a better chance of attaching the Afghans to our interests if we avoid all interference with them in the meantime."[10] His words were prophetic.

In 1917, however, the Russian civil war triggered the collapse of Nicholas II's regime, ensuring that Russia would pose no strategic threat for the foreseeable future. British leaders began the third Anglo-Afghan War in 1919 and later that year signed the Treaty of Rawalpindi, which recognized Afghan independence on August 8, 1919. British policymakers had long seen Afghanistan as a strategically important buffer state to protect British interests in India from Russian expansion. During the eighty years of hostility, the British had grappled with a growing revolt from Pashtuns in southern and eastern Afghanistan, who took power once Afghanistan became independent. Characterized by their own language (Pashto) and the practice of Pashtunwali—a legal and moral code that determines social order and responsibilities and governs such key components as honor, solidarity, hospitality, mutual support, shame, and revenge—the Pashtuns would play a major role in Afghan history in the twentieth century.

In 1919, King Amanullah Khan tried to modernize the country, but he was overthrown in 1929 by Habibullah Kalakani, a Tajik. Kalakani was ousted a few months later after Pashtuns rebelled, and members of the Pashtun Musahiban family then founded a dynasty that would rule Afghanistan for nearly five decades, from 1929 to 1978. The first of their leaders was Muhammad Nadir Shah, who had grown up in British India, served as a general in the army, and spent part of his adult years living in southern France before becoming king. But he was assassinated in 1933, and his son, Muhammad Zahir Shah, took his place at the age of nineteen. For several years Zahir Shah remained in the background while his relatives ran the government. One of the most prominent was Daoud Khan, a cousin and brother-in-law of Zahir Shah, who was educated in France and became prime minister in 1953. Daoud Khan was an advocate of Pashtun irredentism, including the creation of a greater "Pashtunistan" in the Pashtun areas of Afghanistan and Pakistan. But Zahir Shah eventually took control of the government in 1963 and catapulted the country into a new era of modernity and democratic freedom.

Collapse of the State

In 1967, Ronald Neumann left the University of California–Riverside with a master's degree in political science and headed to Afghanistan, where his father, Robert Neumann, was the U.S. ambassador. The elder Neumann had been a tenured professor at the University of California when President Lyndon B. Johnson nominated him to the post. "My father had a profound impact on my interest in foreign affairs," Ronald Neumann later recalled. "Because of him, I made up my mind in the tenth grade to go into the Foreign Service."[11]

It was Ronald Neumann's first trip to Afghanistan, and the last he would take before following in his father's footsteps as U.S. ambassador to Afghanistan nearly four decades later. With his wife, Neumann traveled the country. They drove from Herat to Kabul, along part of the same route that Rory Stewart would later memorialize in his 2001 best seller *The Places in Between*.[12] Neumann went on a hunting expedition for the famous Marco Polo sheep in Badakhshan, Afghanistan's mountainous northeast in the heart of the Hindu Kush. After returning from his trek across the region in the late thirteenth century, the Italian explorer had described these 300-pound beasts as "wild sheep of enormous size" with horns "as much as six palms in length."[13] "It was an exotic adventure, a throwback in time," said Neumann.[14]

He also drove through the Salang Tunnel, linking northern and southern Afghanistan through the Hindu Kush mountains. In 1955, the Afghan government and the Soviet Union signed an agreement to build the tunnel, which was opened in 1964. The tunnel was the highest road tunnel in the world until 1973, when the United States built the Eisenhower Memorial Tunnel—just slightly higher and slightly longer—in the Rocky Mountains. For travelers at this time, the tunnel was one of the marvels of the country, if not all of Central Asia.

The country that Ronald Neumann toured in 1967 had enjoyed several decades of stability and a relatively strong government. American and European tourists poured into Kabul each year. The Afghan capital was the Central Asian hotspot for young backpackers, who flocked to the city's coffee and carpet shops. King Zahir Shah had introduced a representative form of government, for which he received mostly high marks from the U.S. government. In a secret Eyes Only 1970 memo to President Richard Nixon after meeting with the king, Vice President Spiro Agnew described him as "a quiet, rather intense person, with great dedication to his country" who "appears to be very well versed in world affairs."[15] He was in his mid-fifties, and mostly bald, with a neatly trimmed mustache, and he often felt more comfortable donning a pressed Western suit rather than wearing traditional Afghan clothes.

The king had summoned a *loya jirga* (grand assembly) in 1964, one of the freest and most influential ever convened by the Afghan state.

The *loya jirga* wrote a constitution that set up a bicameral legislature and an independent judiciary. It also established a system of checks and balances based on the separation of executive, legislative, and judicial powers. U.S. State Department reports lauded Zahir Shah's "blueprint for democracy" and noted that he had effectively maintained stability throughout the country.[16] While the central government was weak, Zahir Shah's regime was nonetheless able to establish law and order by dividing up responsibilities. In urban areas, such as Kabul, the government provided security and services to the Afghan population. But in rural areas, tribes, subtribes, clans, and other local entities ensured order. In cases where major disputes arose in rural areas, the government's security forces would sometimes intervene. Consequently, the formula for peace and stability involved a power-sharing arrangement between the center and the periphery.

By the early 1970s, however, there were signs of growing economic and political instability. In August 1971, Ambassador Robert Neumann held a tense meeting with Zahir Shah. Responding to rising tensions, Neumann "decided to hit him hard re lack of progress in country, particularly deteriorating economic conditions." He warned Zahir Shah that the political environment was becoming venomous and Afghans were becoming restless. "In my four and one-half years here I had never heard so many exp ressions at all levels of society about a feeling of hopelessness that [the] new government could accomplish any thing."[17] There were also reports of corruption in the government and tribal unrest, which were undermining popular support.[18] Public opinion began to turn against Zahir Shah, who was increasingly perceived as overly discrete and out of touch. In his end-of-tour memo, Ambassador Neumann reflected on the king:

> The adjectives—indirect, cautious, furtive, clever, et al—which come to mind when one thinks of the King well represent the difficulty which observers here, both Afghan and foreign, face in trying to assess both the man and his creature. He has written no memoirs or autobiography, his public pronouncements are infrequent and generally anodyne, and in his contacts with a wide cross section of Afghan

society, he prefers to listen rather than to declaim, a preference which frequently leads to confusion about his views.[19]

In 1972, U.S. officials in Afghanistan and their intelligence contacts began hearing about a possible coup. In one meeting, Wahid Abdullah, director of information in the Afghan Ministry of Foreign Affairs, asked Ambassador Neumann how the United States would respond to a takeover by Muhammad Daoud Khan. Daoud, who had been Afghanistan's prime minister from 1953 to 1963, was known for his progressive policies, especially in regard to women's rights. Wahid Abdullah was eager to gauge the U.S. reaction, and he remarked somewhat cryptically that "[Daoud] knows I am here."[20] A takeover seemed imminent. In April 1972, the State Department received word that a possible coup might occur within a "couple of weeks," possibly led by Daoud.[21] Throughout 1972 and 1973, both American and Soviet intelligence services collected information about a possible coup.[22]

On June 26, 1973, Zahir Shah was flown to London to be treated for hemorrhaging in one eye caused, one State Department assessment reported, "by a volleyball."[23] After receiving treatment, Zahir Shah then went to Italy for a short vacation. His "vacation" turned out to be far longer than anyone expected. His next trip back to Afghanistan would be in April 2002, three decades later, after the overthrow of the Taliban regime. On July 16, 1973, Daoud engineered a coup d'état with support from the Afghan Army. The United States reaction was mixed. In a report to Henry Kissinger, for example, the U.S. National Security Council concluded that Daoud had provided Afghanistan "with strong leadership" during his tenure in the 1950s, and had "made strenuous efforts to modernize the economy and armed forces." However, it also noted that Daoud had turned to the Soviet Union for economic and military assistance and warned that he "may well lean a bit more toward the Soviets."[24]

At the time, Afghanistan was mostly a backwater of U.S. foreign policy. "There was little intrinsic U.S. interest in Afghanistan," acknowledged Graham Fuller, who was the CIA station chief from 1975 to 1978. "But it was a rich opportunity for recruiting Soviet diplomats and KGB personnel, as well as Chinese officials." Fuller had received bachelor's and master's degrees in Russian and Middle Eastern studies from Harvard University and had studied there with the respected Russian historian Richard Pipes and the future national security adviser, Zbigniew Brzezinski. While he had never worked in Moscow or behind the iron curtain, Fuller had become increasingly drawn to the vulnerability of the Soviet Union. "I was interested in understanding the soft underbelly of the Soviet Union, which is why I wanted to serve in Afghanistan." Indeed, over the course of the 1970s, the CIA grew more concerned about Daoud's ties with the Soviet Union and the Afghan Communist parties. "We knew that Daoud had close connections to the Soviets," said Fuller. "And Moscow's involvement in Afghanistan would become progressively more acute."[25]

The Sawr Revolution

Daoud's coup was a turning point for Afghanistan. After fifty years of relatively stable Pashtun leadership, suddenly the national power structure had been shaken. Governance deteriorated over the next decade as Daoud attempted to impose strong central control, and Moscow, which had been providing military aid since at least 1955, grew increasingly alarmed about intelligence reports of instability in Afghanistan.[26] In April 1978, a leading Communist activist, Mir Akbar Khyber, was assassinated. Some 15,000 demonstrators joined his funeral procession, demanding justice, and the security situation intensified. Daoud responded by arresting Marxist leaders, but his crackdown triggered a violent response. Army and air force officers engineered a bloody coup on April 27, 1978, in the Afghan lunar month of Sawr (Taurus); Daoud was assassinated during the coup. On April 30, military officers handed over power to a Revolutionary Council headed by Nur Mohammad Taraki, who promptly signed

Decree No. 1 and proclaimed the establishment of the Democratic Republic of Afghanistan.[27] Moscow provided immediate aid to try to stabilize the situation, including armored personnel carriers, combat radios, Kalashnikov rifles, and Makarov pistols.[28]

In the United States, there were mixed reactions to Daoud's overthrow. "One of the first intelligence reports I sent back to Washington was to provide a background of the people who constituted the new government," recalled the CIA's Fuller. "They were members of the Communist party, and we had pretty good biographies on them. But the State Department and U.S. Agency for International Development hit the roof," because U.S. laws prohibited them from providing assistance to Communist parties. "They had to stop a lot of their funding to the Afghan government. But I was calling it as I saw it; the Soviets were on the march."[29]

Taraki was born to a poor peasant family in Ghazni Province in July 1917. In the mid-1940s, he founded the left-wing party *Weesh Zalmayan* (Awakened Youth). In 1953, he left Afghanistan for Washington, DC, where he served as press attaché in the Afghan Embassy. When Zahir Shah appointed Daoud as prime minister, Taraki publicly resigned his post and held a press conference accusing the Afghan government of being "a bunch of feudal lords." According to one report, the former press attaché was soon called back, and, "upon his return to Kabul, he telephoned the despotic Daoud from the Kabul Cinema, telling him 'I am Noor Mohammad Taraki. I have just arrived. Shall I go home or to the prison?' "[30] Taraki was allowed to go home, but he was kept under police surveillance. In 1965, he helped found the People's Democratic Party of Afghanistan, which split into two groups in 1967: *Khalq* (Masses), headed by Taraki; and *Parcham* (Banner), headed by Babrak Karmal.

The Khalq faction advocated an immediate and violent overthrow of the government and the establishment of a Soviet-style Communist regime. The Parcham faction supported a gradual move toward socialism, arguing that Afghanistan was not industrialized enough to undergo a true proletarian revolution such as that called for in *The*

Communist Manifesto. Bitter resentment between the Khalq and Parcham factions would later contribute to the collapse of the Democratic Republic of Afghanistan and the Sawr Revolution.

In many ways, Babrak Karmal was the antithesis of Taraki. He was born into a wealthy family in a small village outside of Kabul, and his father was a well-connected army general. He attended law school at Kabul University and quickly gained a reputation as an activist in the university's student union. A Soviet dossier on Karmal hinted that he was sometimes more show than substance. "He is a skilled orator, emotional, and inclined to abstraction to the detriment of a specific analysis," but he had "a poor grasp of economic issues which interest him at a general level."[31] Karmal became increasingly involved in Marxist political activities, which led to his imprisonment for five years. His pro-Moscow leftist views strengthened while in prison through interaction with several other inmates, such as Mir Muhammad Siddiq Farhang. After his release, he ran for office and was elected to a seat in the lower house of the National Assembly, where he would be a controversial figure for many years. When he died in 1996 at the age of sixty-seven, the Afghan radio station Voice of Sharia summarized his life with little affection: "Babrak Karmal committed all kinds of crimes during his illegitimate rule. God inflicted on him various kinds of hardship and pain. Eventually he died of cancer in a hospital belonging to his paymasters, the Russians."[32]

Violence between the rival factions continued in the fall of 1978, with revolts in rural areas by Islamist opponents of the regime. Taraki conducted mass arrests, tortured prisoners, and held secret executions on a scale Afghanistan had not seen in nearly a century. At a government rally in October 1978 in Kabul, for instance, government leaders unveiled a new Afghan flag, jettisoning the traditional design, which had combined deep black, green, and red. Demonstrating their Marxist pedigree, Afghan leaders unfurled a red flag with a wreath of wheat and a yellow star at the top. Revolts broke out across the country. Pashtun tribesmen in the eastern mountains grabbed their rifles to fight the government, and several areas of the east—such as Kunar

Province, the Hindu Kush, and Badakshan Province—became anti-
government strongholds. The People's Democratic Party of Afghanistan responded with widespread oppression and even more arrests
and executions, but soldiers deserted by the thousands and the Afghan
Army began to melt away. Concerned by the rising violence, Soviet
leaders sent additional KGB agents into Afghanistan.[33]

In 1979, the situation grew worse. In February, U.S. Ambassador
Adolph Dubs was kidnapped by armed Islamists posing as police. His
captors barricaded themselves in a room in the Kabul Hotel and tried to
bargain with the Afghan government. After two hours, Afghan security
forces stormed the room, and Dubs was killed in the melee. Zbigniew
Brzezinski, President Jimmy Carter's national security adviser, lamented
that Dubs's death was "a tragic event which involved either Soviet inepti-
tude or collusion."[34] The next month, violent demonstrations erupted in
Herat. The Afghan Army's 17th Division, which was ordered to quell the
riots, mutinied en masse. As a Top Secret Soviet assessment concluded,
the 17th Division "has essentially collapsed. An artillery regiment and
one infantry regiment comprising that division have gone over to the
side of the insurgents." The assessment also reported that insurgent leaders were "religious fanatics" motivated by ideology, and it was "under the
banner of Islam that the soldiers are turning against the government."[35]
Prime Minister Taraki begged the Soviets for emergency military assistance, and Soviet Premier Alexei Kosygin promised to send weapons,
ammunition, and military advisers.[36]

But the Soviets were hesitant to send troops. Kosygin told Taraki:
"If our troops were introduced, the situation in your country would
not only not improve, but would worsen." Somewhat ironically, Kosygin noted that the local Afghan population would probably rise up
against Soviet forces, as might Afghanistan's neighbors, such as Pakistan and China, who would receive help from the United States.[37]
The Central Committee (CC) of the Communist Party of the Soviet
Union (CPSU) sent a Top Secret memo to Alexander Puzanov, the
Soviet ambassador in Afghanistan, contending that while the deployment of Soviet troops "was considered in much detail," it "would be

used by hostile forces first of all to the detriment of the interests of the [Democratic Republic of Afghanistan]."[38] Politburo member and future Soviet leader Konstantin Chernenko noted that if the Soviets deployed troops and "beat down the Afghan people then we will be accused of aggression for sure. There's no getting around it here."[39]

For three days the rebels held Herat, plundering weapons stockpiles and hunting down government officials. Taraki ordered Afghan forces from Kandahar to cordon off the city while he dispatched two armored brigades from Kabul. He then struck parts of Herat and 17th Division headquarters with IL-28 bombers from Shindand Air Base. By the time the rebellion was finally crushed, as many as 5,000 people had died, including one hundred Soviet advisers and their families, whose heads were mounted on poles and paraded around the city by the insurgents. News of the events in Herat accelerated desertions and mutinies in the Afghan military. In May, for example, a motorized column from the 7th Division went over to the rebels in Paktia Province, located along the Pakistan border in eastern Afghanistan.[40]

Governance was collapsing in Afghanistan. In June 1979, fearful of an all-out civil war, the Soviet leadership deployed a special detachment of KGB paramilitary officers disguised as service personnel to defend the Soviet Embassy in Kabul.[41] Revolts continued, and in September Taraki was summoned to Moscow for consultations. On his return to Kabul, he was arrested by his deputy, Hafizullah Amin, and executed.

Amin, a Pashtun from the town of Paghman, not far from Kabul, had a master's degree in education from Columbia University in New York. According to his Soviet intelligence dossier, Amin was "marked by great energy, a businesslike nature, a desire to get to the heart of the issue, and firmness in his views and actions. He also has the talent of attracting people to him who have subordinated themselves to his influence."[42] Soviet leaders felt that Amin was too close to the United States, and they believed that Amin wanted a more "balanced policy" with the West. A Top Secret analysis warned Soviet leader Leonid Brezhnev: "It is known, in particular, that representatives of the USA, on the basis of their contacts with the Afghans, are coming to a con-clusion about the possibility of a change in the political line of Afghan-istan in a direction which is pleasing to Washington."[43] A series of KGB reports to the Politburo expressed concern that Amin would likely turn to the Americans for help.[44] But CIA officials strongly denied having any such contacts. "It was total nonsense," said the CIA's Graham Fuller. "I would have been thrilled to have those kinds of contacts with Amin, but they didn't exist."[45]

On December 8, 1979, Brezhnev held a meeting in his private office with a narrow circle of senior Politburo members: ideologue Mikhail Suslov, KGB chief Yuri Andropov, Defense Minister Dmitriy Ustinov, and Foreign Minister Andrei Gromyko. Andropov and Usti-nov expressed grave concerns that the United States was trying to increase its role in Afghanistan and that Pakistan would try to annex Pashtun areas of Afghanistan. By the end of the meeting, the group had tentatively decided to move on two fronts. The first was to have the KGB remove Amin and replace him with Babrak Karmal; the sec-ond was to seriously consider sending Soviet troops to Afghanistan to stabilize the country.[46]

On December 10, 1979, Ustinov gave an oral order to the Gen-eral Staff to start preparations for deployment of one division of para-troopers and five divisions of military-transport aviation. He also ordered increased readiness of two motorized rifle divisions in the Turkestan Military District and an increase in the staff of a pontoon regiment.[47] Nikolai Ogarkov, chief of the General Staff, was out-raged by the decision, responding that the troops would not be able to stabilize the situation and calling the decision "reckless."

Ustinov cut him off harshly: "Are you going to teach the Politburo? Your only duty is to carry out the orders."

Ogarkov replied that the Afghan problem should be decided by polit-ical means, instead of through military force, and pointed out that the Afghan people had never reacted favorably to foreign occupation.[48]

The final decision to send Soviet troops into Afghanistan appears to have been made on the afternoon of December 12 by a small group of

Soviet officials, including Brezhnev, Suslov, Andropov, Ustinov, and Gromyko. They issued a directive to "send several contingents of Soviet troops . . . into the territory of the Democratic Republic of Afghanistan for the purposes of rendering internationalist assistance to the friendly Afghan people" and to "create favorable conditions to prevent possible anti-Afghan actions on the part of the bordering states."[49] The group agreed that the situation in Afghanistan seriously threatened the security of the Soviet Union's southern borders, and the United States, China, and Iran could take advantage of this through support to the Afghan regime. In particular, Afghanistan could become a future U.S. forward operating base against the Soviet Union, lying right against their "soft underbelly" in Central Asia. Ideology also played an important role.[50] Suslov and Boris Ponomarev, head of the Communist Party's international department, argued that the Soviet Union needed to counter the challenge of Islamic fundamentalism. Ustinov was convinced that military operations could be accomplished quickly, perhaps in a few weeks or months. So was Brezhnev.[51]

"It'll be over in three to four weeks," Brezhnev told Anatoly Dobrynin, Soviet ambassador to the United States.[52]

There was some opposition to the invasion, especially in the Soviet General Staff. Generals Nikolai Ogarkov, Sergei Akhromeyev, and Valentin Varennikov, who were charged with preparing the invasion plan, filed a dissenting report to Ustinov. They warned him of the strong possibility of a protracted insurgency, especially in a country blessed with mountainous terrain and inhabited by warring tribes.[53]

The Soviet Invasion

Ronald Neumann monitored the Soviet invasion from afar. In 1970, he followed in his father's footsteps and joined the U.S. Department of State as a foreign service officer. After an initial posting in Senegal, he began to specialize in the Middle East. In 1973, he served as principal officer in Tabriz, Iran. He subsequently became desk officer for Jordan, deputy chief of mission in Yemen, deputy director of the

Office of Arabian Peninsula Affairs, and deputy chief of mission in the United Arab Emirates.

"I talked about Afghanistan on and off with my father until he died," he told me. The elder Neumann was a longtime member of the Dartmouth Conference, which was established as a high-level forum for discussing Soviet-American relations. It was cochaired by Yevgeny Primakov, who went on to become the Russian prime minister, and Harold Saunders, a CIA analyst who later served on the National Security Council. From 1960 until 1981, the conference met thirteen times—alternately in the Soviet Union and the United States—and involved a number of other influential experts. It became even more active during the Soviet War in Afghanistan, meeting nearly every six months. "The Dartmouth Conference kept my father informed about developments in Afghanistan, which he passed on to me during our conversations," Ronald Neumann recalled.[54]

On Christmas Eve 1979, elite Soviet forces began flying into Kabul Airport and the military air base at Bagram. The 357th and 66th Motorized Rifle Divisions of the Soviet Army entered Afghanistan from Kushka in Turkmenistan and began advancing south along the main highway. The 360th and 201st Motorized Rifle Divisions crossed the Amu Darya River on pontoon bridges from Termez in Uzbekistan. Dividing Afghanistan from the Soviet Union, the river flows more than 1,500 miles through Central Asia. Because Afghanistan has almost no railways, the Amu Darya played a critical transport role for the Soviet invasion, since it could be used for barge traffic.

The 360th Motorized Rifle Division reached Kabul on Christmas Day, securing the crucial Salang Pass and its tunnel en route, while the 201st moved toward Kunduz and east to Badakshan and Baghlan Provinces.[55] By December 27, 1979, there were 50,000 Soviet forces in Afghanistan, with 5,000 troops and Spetsnaz, the Soviet Union's elite special forces, in positions around Kabul. The Soviets destroyed Kabul's main telephone exchanges and took over the radio station and the Ministry of Interior. Soviet paratroopers also took control of the post office, ammunition depots, and other government buildings.

KGB special forces disguised in Afghan uniforms assaulted the presidential palace. Hafizullah Amin's guards fought back for several hours, but they were ultimately overcome, and KGB forces assassinated Amin.[56] Babrak Karmal arrived from the airport to take over the government and addressed the country on Radio Kabul:

> Today the torture machine of Amin and his henchmen, savage butchers, usurpers and murderers of tens of thousands of our compatriots . . . has been broken. . . . The great April revolution, accomplished through the indestructible will of the heroic Afghan people . . . has entered a new stage. The bastions of the despotism of the bloody dynasty of Amin and his supporters—those watchdogs of the sirdars of Nadir Shah, Zahir Shah, and Daoud Shah, the hirelings of world imperialism, headed by American imperialism—have been destroyed. Not one stone of these bastions remains.[57]

The Soviets were right to worry about possible U.S. involvement. In early 1979, the Carter administration began looking at the possibility of covert assistance to Afghanistan. By the spring, Zbigniew Brzezinski had come up with ways to undermine the Soviets in their own backyard. He convinced President Carter to sanction some initial aid to the Afghan rebels. The shipment consisted of old British .303 Lee-Enfield rifles.[58] On March 30, 1979, Deputy National Security Adviser David Aaron chaired a mini-session of the Special Coordination Committee on Afghanistan at the White House. At the meeting, Under Secretary of State for Political Affairs David Newsom argued that the United States should counter the growing Soviet presence in Afghanistan, and Pentagon official Walter Slocombe asked whether there might be a benefit in "sucking the Soviets into a Vietnamese quagmire."

Aaron concluded by asking the group: "Is there interest in maintaining and assisting the [Afghan] insurgency, or is the risk that we will provoke the Soviets too great?"[59]

Over the next few weeks, senior government officials continued discussions on possible action in Afghanistan. At the CIA, National Intelligence Officer Arnold Horelick sent Director Stansfield Turner a paper examining possible Soviet reactions to U.S. assistance. Horelick argued that covert action to help Afghan opposition leaders would hurt the Soviets. On April 6, the Special Coordination Committee, chaired by Brzezinski, met to discuss several U.S. options. The scenarios ranged from weapons and training to more benign nonlethal assistance.

After much debate, the group recommended that the CIA provide nonlethal assistance to opposition groups, and on July 3, 1979, President Carter signed the first finding to help support the mujahideen in Afghanistan. It authorized covert support for insurgent propaganda, the establishment of radio access to the Afghan population through third-country facilities, and the provision of cash and nonmilitary supplies to opposition groups.[60] Brzezinski, who was particularly concerned about Soviet designs on the region, told Carter that the Soviets might not stop at Afghanistan: "I warned the President that the Soviets would be in a position, if they came to dominate Afghanistan, to promote a separate Baluchistan, which would give them access to the Indian Ocean while dismembering Pakistan and Iran."[61]

But there were substantial disagreements about Soviet intentions. The CIA sent an Eyes Only memo to President Carter and other members of the National Security Council, concluding that it was "unlikely that the Soviet occupation is a preplanned first step in the implementation of a highly articulated grand design for the rapid establishment of hegemonic control over all of southwest Asia." Rather, it explained that the Soviets were mainly concerned about the collapse of a state in its sphere of influence. Arnold Horelick tried to split the difference. In a paper for Brzezinski, he wrote that the Soviet incursion into Afghanistan represented a "qualitative turn in Soviet foreign policy in the region and toward the third world." Stansfield Turner included a personal cover note to Brzezinski when he forwarded the memo:

> I would only add a personal comment that I would be a bit more categoric than the paper in stating that the Soviets' behavior in Afghanistan was not an aberration. I agree we do not have the evi-

dence that the Soviets are firmly committed to continuing as aggressive a policy in the third world. . . . Yet, I do believe that the Soviet track record over the past five or six years indicates a definitely greater willingness to probe the limits of our tolerance. "Détente" was not a bar to this greater assertiveness in Angola, Ethiopia, Kampuchea and Yemen. It need not be so again, even if we return to détente. As the paper concludes, how assertive the Soviets will be in the future will very likely depend upon how "successful" the Soviet leadership views their intervention in Afghanistan to have been.[62]

Despite the conflicting assessments, there is little credible evidence that Soviet leaders wanted to expand their reach into Pakistan and Iran and to the Indian Ocean. Rather, they were concerned by the collapse of governance in Afghanistan and suspicious that the United States and Afghanistan's neighbors would try to move into the vacuum.

It seems unlikely that the Soviets would have gotten involved had the Afghan state not collapsed in the first place. As Afghanistan scholar Barnett Rubin argues in his book *The Fragmentation of Afghanistan*, "In the end, the persistence of revolt and the concomitant breakdown of the state resulted from its own internal weaknesses." He continues: "The main reason the revolt spread so widely was that the army disintegrated in a series of insurrections, from unrecorded defections of small posts to mutinies in nearly all the major garrisons."[63] The uprising engulfed Afghan cities, including Herat in the west, Jalalabad in the east, and eventually Kabul itself. Some of the Afghan leaders who mutinied—such as Ismail Khan and Abdul Rauf—escaped and joined the resistance. Indeed, the dissolution of the Afghan Army in the late 1970s, rather than the strength of the insurgents, allowed the resistance to spread.[64] The Afghan state had failed to establish basic law and order and to deliver basic services. The Soviet Union stepped in to help fill this void.

CHAPTER TWO

The Mujahideen Era

IN 1979, the year the Soviets invaded Afghanistan, Zalmay Khalilzad, who would play a key role in U.S. efforts in Afghanistan after the September 2001 attacks, finished his doctoral dissertation at the University of Chicago. In 1974, he had arrived in Hyde Park, a racially diverse community situated along Lake Michigan on Chicago's South Side. The university was founded there in 1890 by the American Baptist Education Society and oil magnate John D. Rockefeller, who described his role as "the best investment I ever made." "Zal," as Khalilzad was known to his colleagues, was a resident floor adviser at the International House, an oversize Gothic building where many of the university's foreign students lived. A contemporary photograph of Khalilzad—which International House sent to him when he became U.S. ambassador to the United Nations—shows a young man in his early twenties with shoulder-length hair, a neatly trimmed mustache, and a flowery Hawaiian shirt. Already one can see the relaxed, almost unassuming aura that would become his trademark during his years as a diplomat.

Khalilzad was born in the northern city of Mazar-e-Sharif, where his father worked in the Ministry of Finance for King Zahir Shah's government. The setting for his childhood was appropriately grand. Mazar-e-Sharif means "noble shrine," a reference to the magnificent blue-tiled mosque that dominates the city's skyline and is said by some Muslims to house the tomb of the caliph Ali ibn Abu Talib, son-in-law of the Prophet Muhammad. Khalilzad's mother, he told *The New Yorker* in an interview, "did not have a formal education yet she was very modern, always very informed. She could not read or write herself, but she would have the kids read the newspapers to her. I think if she had been born at a different time she would have been quite an established political figure." He studied at the private Ghazi Lycée school in Kabul and spent a year in the United States as an exchange student, near Modesto, California. The year in California had a profound impact on him. "I had different values, greater interest in sports, a more pragmatic way of looking at things, and a broader horizon," he recalled after finishing his time there. "I had a sense of how backward Afghanistan was. And I became more interested in how Afghanistan needed to change."[1]

Khalilzad went on to get bachelor's and master's degrees from the American University of Beirut before going to Chicago to pursue a doctorate in political science. There he studied with strategic thinker Albert Wohlstetter, a prominent international relations scholar who led groundbreaking work on nuclear deterrence. Wohlstetter influenced the design and deployment of U.S. strategic forces through his research, developed the "second-strike" theory for deterring nuclear war, and originated "fail safe" and other methods for reducing the probability of accidental nuclear war.[2] Wohlstetter served as a senior policy analyst at the RAND Corporation, as an adviser to President John F. Kennedy during the Cuban missile crisis, and, beginning in 1964, as a professor at the University of Chicago. He had a significant influence on Khalilzad and helped him make contacts in Washington. After leaving Chicago in 1979, Khalilzad moved to New York to become a professor at Columbia University's School of International and Public Affairs.[3]

The Brutal-Hearted Mountain Tribes

During his studies with Wohlstetter, Khalilzad continued to monitor events in Afghanistan and, with his academic training completed, he began writing articles on the invasion using a pseudonym to protect members of his family who were still there. Khalilzad observed a military operation that proved more costly in terms of blood or money than the Soviets had bargained for. Over the three previous decades, the Soviets had tried to prop up a range of Afghan governments, providing a total of $1.3 billion in economic aid and $1.3 billion in military aid between 1955 and 1978.[4] But these costs skyrocketed in the 1980s, and the CIA estimated that the Soviet Union spent an annual average of $7 billion between 1980 and 1986.[5] When the Soviets finally withdrew in February 1989, after ten harrowing years, the country was devastated. An estimated one million Afghans had been killed, more than five million had fled abroad, and as many as three million were internally displaced. Nearly 15,000 Soviet soldiers were dead and 35,000 wounded.[6] The Russian poet Joseph Brodsky, who won the Nobel Prize for Literature in 1987, expressed the anger of the Soviet loss, as well as the vaunted defiance of the Afghan warriors, in a poem titled "On the Talks in Kabul" ("Kperegovoram v Kabule"). He referred to the "brutal-hearted" mountain tribes defined by their "long beards," "handcrafted rugs," and "loud guttural names."[7] But he was most scathing in a 1982 interview with the *Paris Review*, seven years after he was expelled from the Soviet Union. "When I saw the first footage from Afghanistan on the TV screen a year ago, it was very short. It was tanks rolling on the plateau," he remarked. "What I saw was basically a violation of the elements—because that plateau never saw a plough before, let alone a tank. So, it was a kind of existential nightmare. . . . This is absolutely meaningless, like subtracting from zero. And it is vile in a primordial sense, partly because of tanks' resemblance to dinosaurs. It simply shouldn't be."[8]

After the Soviet invasion, Babrak Karmal's Soviet-backed government tried desperately to increase its power and legitimacy. It released thousands of prisoners, declared its allegiance to Islam, restored the Islamic green stripe to Afghanistan's flag, proclaimed an amnesty for refugees and those misguided citizens it termed "deceived compatriots," and appointed several non-Party individuals to posts as advisers. Moscow and Kabul began to devise a state-building strategy based on a long-term Soviet commitment to the country, even if they envisioned a limited stay for Soviet troops.[9]

But neither Karmal nor the Kremlin could create a strong Afghan state. In 1980, the CIA found that "a vast gulf" separated the Karmal regime from the Afghan population.[10] Karmal depended on Soviet forces and aid for survival. A Soviet security detail helped protect him in the Presidential Palace, and most major policies were approved by Soviet advisers, who even helped write some of Karmal's speeches. The Soviet invasion also triggered a significant decline in the gross national product. "The effect of the Soviet occupation of Afghanistan," a Defense Intelligence Agency analysis concluded, "has been catastrophic for the development of the Afghan economy."[11] The migration of displaced Afghans to major cities resulted in substantial farm-labor losses in many rural areas. The disruption of health-care and sanitary facilities caused infant mortality and serious illnesses to rise. And skilled and educated workers left the country en masse.

Intent on increasing the Afghan state's capacity to establish law and order, the Soviets concentrated their efforts in two institutions: the military and the secret police. The secret police, officially known as the Khadamat-e Etela'at-e Dawlati (KhAD), relied on KGB advisers, while the Afghan military relied on the direct participation of Soviet troops.[12] Throughout the war, the Afghan Army was weak, divided, and frequently unreliable. It failed to conscript a sufficient number of soldiers and retain their allegiance. Factionalism within the Afghan government hindered the development of military cohesion and smothered the emergence of competent, dependable commanders. Morale was low. The army lost an average of 20,000 soldiers a year to desertion, and there were chronic shortages of equipment. What gear they did have was often unfit for serious combat.[13] Brigadier Mohammad Yousaf, who headed the Afghan Bureau of Pakistan's Inter-Services Intelligence Directorate (ISI) from 1983 to 1987 and was responsible for working with the Afghan mujahideen, argued: "This was the force that the Soviets had expected to go out and fight the guerrillas; more often it had to be locked in to prevent its men joining [the muja-hideen]."[14] The Afghan Army that the Soviets supported was ambiva-lent in its loyalties, and the bulk of it quickly melted away. By the mid-1980s, it had shrunk from 90,000 to about 30,000 men.[15]

To help establish law and order throughout the country, the Soviet invasion plan called for troops to secure the country's major cities, airfields, and roads. Motorized troops poured into Afghanistan from Kushka and Termez, secured the main highway that circled the Hindu Kush, and took control of urban centers. Soviet forces in the west targeted the strategic cities of Herat, Farah, and Kandahar, and the Soviet air force secured bases at Bagram, Jalalabad, Kandahar, Shin-dand, and Herat. In rural Afghanistan, the Soviets attempted to clear and hold a few strategic areas of the countryside and tried without success to seal the borders with Pakistan and Iran.[16] Above all, they did not want to occupy large tracts of territory, which suggests they were adopting a fairly static and defensive posture.[17]

Instead of stabilizing the situation, however, the Soviets triggered

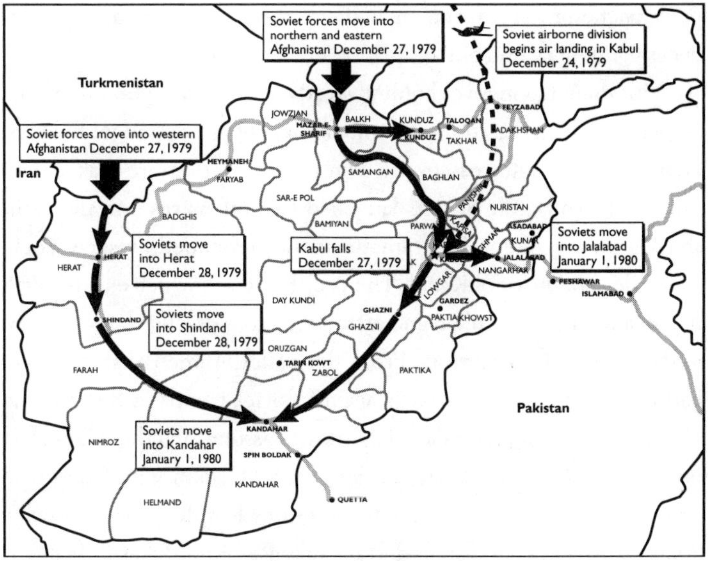

FIGURE 2.1 Soviet Invasion of Afghanistan, 1979[18]

one of the most successful insurgencies in modern times. In February 1980, an anti-Soviet demonstration in the capital turned into a riot in which 300 people were killed. Kabul's shops closed down for a week. The Soviets finally restored order with a massive display of force, which included Soviet fighters and helicopter gunships. During 1980 and 1981, the Soviets focused on securing the essential road network and setting up base camps adjacent to airfields. They also built fortified outposts along their communication lines, often manned by Afghan government troops. The Soviets' biggest challenge was establishing control in the rural areas. Reports to the Soviet Politburo in late 1981 indicated that the Afghan government controlled less than 15 percent of all villages in the country, even after two years of war.

"The rural areas," admitted one Soviet report, were "controlled by the rebels." Even if Soviet and Afghan forces could clear territory, they would "as a rule return to their bases and the regions fall back under the control of the rebels."[19] The rural nature of the insurgency foreshadowed the U.S. experience after the overthrow of the Taliban regime. A Soviet report to Defense Minister Ustinov in 1981 concluded: "The poor functioning of government bodies in the provinces negatively influences the stabilization of the situation in the country."[20]

With their troop level holding steady at around 85,000 men, the Soviets vastly increased their numbers of helicopters and jet fighters. Helicopter strength rose from 60 in mid-1980 to more than 300 in 1981.[21] In 1981, the Soviets launched two offensives into the Panjshir Valley, a geologically dramatic area, surrounded by sheer rock, 100 miles northeast of Kabul. The Panjshir River, which cuts through it, has a fertile flood plain and attracts visitors during the mulberry, grape, and apricot harvests. From this valley, Ahmed Shah Massoud had been orchestrating attacks against Soviet troops in Bagram and Charikar and along the Salang Highway. Massoud, an ethnic Tajik, had undergone guerrilla training in Egypt and Lebanon with Palestinian groups. He became known as the "Lion of Panjshir" for his brazen attacks against Soviet forces and his defense of the Panjshir Valley.[22] In 2001, journalist Sebastian Junger embedded with Massoud in the

Panjshir, shortly before the military commander's death, and described him as "a genius guerrilla leader, last hope of the shattered Afghan government."[23]

Twice the Soviets attacked Massoud's forces in the Panjshir, but they withdrew after two weeks, leaving behind the wreckage of scores of armored vehicles and newly devastated villages along the valley floor. To the extent that the Soviets penetrated into rural areas, it was with airpower, and the Afghans particularly loathed the Mi-24 Hind attack helicopter. Designed for battlefield assault and equipped with four pods for rockets or bombs under its auxiliary wings, the Mi-24 could carry 128 rockets with a full load, as well as four napalm or high-explosive bombs. Its machine guns could fire 1,000 rounds per minute, and its thick armor made it largely immune to medium or heavy machine guns. It could strafe the ground with impunity and, by staying above 5,000 feet, remain out of reach of the mujahideen's SA-7 surface-to-air missiles.[24]

In 1984, Soviet leader Konstantin Chernenko escalated the high-altitude carpet bombing and ordered more helicopter gunship attacks to accelerate the process of depopulating some rural regions that remained outside Soviet control. Hundreds of thousands of "butterfly" mines—equipped with fins to float down gently—poured out of Soviet aircraft. Once on the ground, they maimed insurgents by blowing off their legs or feet. By mid-1984, 3.5 million Afghans had fled to Pakistan and more than a million others had fled to Iran. Hundreds of thousands more were displaced internally. Kabul's population swelled from a prewar 750,000 to two million as frightened Afghans streamed in from the countryside.[25] Insurgents responded by increasing attacks on airfields, garrisons, and other military targets, and they harassed Soviet ground convoys, making road travel perilous.[26]

The ISI's War

The Soviet invasion had an enormous impact on Pakistan. Deeply troubled by the incursion of Soviet troops, President Muhammad

Zia-ul-Haq asked for an intelligence assessment from Lieutenant-General Akhtar Abdul Rehman Khan, the director-general of the ISI. Major General William Cawthorne, a British Army officer who served as army deputy chief of staff for the new state of Pakistan, had formed the ISI in 1948.[27] Cawthorne had created the ISI within the Pakistan Army to help address the lack of intelligence and military cooperation, which had proven disastrous for Pakistan in the 1947 India-Pakistan War.

Akhtar argued that the Soviet invasion threatened Pakistani security: if the Soviet army conquered Afghanistan, it would only be a short step to Pakistan. Akhtar recommended backing the Afghan resistance and turning Afghanistan into the Soviet Union's Vietnam. Zia agreed, but only up to a point. He did not want to goad the Soviets into a direct confrontation with Pakistan. This meant keeping Pakistani support covert and prohibiting Pakistani forces from engaging in direct combat in Afghanistan. Over the course of the war, however, Pakistani soldiers did accompany mujahideen during special operations. They acted as advisers and helped the mujahideen blow up pipelines and mount rocket attacks on airfields. Akhtar selected ISI Brigadier Mohammad Yousaf to coordinate training, strategy, and operational planning for the mujahideen inside Afghanistan—and later inside the Soviet Union.[28]

The ISI had been a relatively small organization throughout the previous three decades. But the Soviet invasion of Afghanistan transformed the ISI into a powerful intelligence organization.[29] Led by key individuals, including Akhtar and Mohammad Yousaf, the ISI was involved in all aspects of the anti-Soviet conflict. Virtually all foreign assistance—including that from the CIA—went through the ISI. The Soviets were well aware of the ISI's role, and one Soviet military-intelligence assessment indicates that they also knew of Western involvement: "A working group has been created in Islamabad which includes officials of the General Staff and military intelligence of Pakistan and representatives of the U.S., British, and Egyptian embassies. At a meeting of the group they discuss specific operations to conduct subversive operations and the participation of individual countries in organizing the rebel movement on [Afghan] territory."[30]

In early 1984, Zia, Akhtar, Yousaf, and other key ISI figures called a meeting with seven of the most powerful Afghan mujahideen leaders to better coordinate the insurgency. One of the great challenges for the Pakistan government, including the ISI, was the haphazard nature of the Afghan resistance, which consisted of a disorganized network of mujahideen constantly roiled by personal rivalries and grievances. In 1984, Zia's patience finally snapped, and he issued a directive that the insurgents were to form a seven-party alliance, what some CIA operatives called the "Peshawar Seven." He did not say what he would do if they failed to follow his order, but they seemed to understand that support from Pakistan was hanging in the balance. "Every Commander must belong to one of the seven Parties, otherwise he got nothing from us at ISI," recalled Yousaf, "no arms, no ammunition and no training."[31]

Just as Americans know it today, Soviet leaders were aware how important a motivation Islamic fundamentalism was for insurgent leaders.[32] Indeed, four of the seven parties were composed of Muslim fundamentalists: Gulbuddin Hekmatyar's Hezb-i-Islami; Burhanuddin Rabbani's Islamic Society of Afghanistan; Abdul Rasul Sayyaf's Islamic Union for the Freedom of Afghanistan; and Yunus Khalis's breakaway wing of Hezb-i-Islami. The moderate parties included Mawlawi Muhammad Nabi Muhammadi's Movement of the Islamic Revolution; Pir Sayyid Ahmad Gailani's National Islamic Front of Afghanistan; and Sibghatullah Mujadiddi's Afghanistan National Liberation Front. Cooperation was not easy, but the ISI tried to minimize infighting. Between 1983 and 1987, the ISI trained roughly 80,000 mujahideen in Pakistan. Their distinctive battle cry became "*Allah o Akbar. Mordabad Shuravi*" (God is Great. Death to the Soviets).[33]

One of the most ruthless of these leaders was Gulbuddin Hekmatyar. The youngest of seven children, he had a thick black beard and penetrating eyes. Hekmatyar, who spoke excellent English, was renowned for his staunch Islamic views and a disdain for the United States that was surpassed only by his hatred of the Soviets. In 1985, on a visit to the United States, he had refused to meet with President Ronald Reagan—despite repeated requests from Pakistan's leaders—out of concern that he would be viewed as a U.S. puppet. During the Afghan War, the KGB established a special disinformation team to split apart the seven mujahideen leaders, and Hekmatyar was one of its prime targets.

Milton Bearden, who served as the CIA's station chief in Pakistan from 1986 to 1989 and worked with the mujahideen, described Hekmatyar as "the darkest of the Afghan leaders, the most Stalinist of the Peshawar Seven, insofar as he thought nothing of ordering an execution for a slight breach of party discipline." Reflecting on his visits with Hekmatyar, Bearden acknowledged that "it would only be Gulbuddin Hekmatyar whom I would have to count as an enemy, and a dangerous one. And, ironically, I would never be able to shake the allegations that the CIA had chosen this paranoid radical as its favorite, that we were providing this man who had directly insulted the President of the United States with more than his share of the means to fight the Soviets."[34] William Piekney, the CIA's station chief in Pakistan before Bearden, similarly recalled: "I would put my arms around Gulbuddin and we'd hug, you know, like brothers in combat and stuff, and his coal black eyes would look back at you, and you just knew that there was only one thing holding this team together and that was the Soviet Union."[35]

Hekmatyar's Hezb-i-Islami was built on the Ikhwan model of Islamic revolution. Hekmatyar, a Ghilzai Pashtun, entered the College of Engineering at Kabul University but failed to complete his studies, instead spending the majority of his time on political activism and Islam. He became a disciple of Sayyid Qutb and the Muslim Brotherhood movement, and advocated a pure Islamic State. He was radicalized during his studies at the university, where, according to legend, his zealousness began to show its face: one story claims he sprayed acid on several female students for refusing to wear the veil. Others, however, have chalked up this story to black KGB propaganda.[36] After a brief period of involvement with Afghan Communists, Hekmatyar became a disciple of Sayyid Qutb, the Islamic scholar and leading intellectual of Egypt's Muslim Brotherhood in the 1950s and 1960s who inspired Ayman al-Zawahiri and Osama bin Laden.[37] Hekmatyar's followers addressed him as "Engineer Hekmatyar," even though he failed to complete his degree because he was imprisoned in 1972 for criticizing the monarchy.

In 1973, when Zahir Shah's government was overthrown by Daoud Khan, Hekmatyar was freed from prison and took refuge in Pakistan's border city of Peshawar with Rabbani, Qazi Muhammad Amin Waqad, and other budding jihadi leaders.[38] During that period, he developed a close relationship with Pakistan. "We had good information that he was being directly funded by Pakistan," acknowledged Graham Fuller, the CIA station chief. "This was critical because the Soviets had provided a range of assistance to individuals such as Daoud. Hekmatyar was Pakistan's answer to Daoud."[39]

According to ISI agent Mohammad Yousaf, Hekmatyar's organization was dependable and merciless: "One could rely on them blindly. By giving them the weapons you were sure that weapons will not be sold in Pakistan because he was strict to the extent of being ruthless. . . . Once you join his party it was difficult to leave."[40] From the 1980s to the early 1990s, Hezb-i-Islami received more funds than any other mujahideen faction from Pakistan intelligence. The power base of Hezb-i-Islami did not extend much beyond the network of the Islamists, but its approach to politics was that of a true political party.

Hezb-i-Islami had suffered a major split in 1979. Yunus Khalis broke away from Hekmatyar and ostensibly accused him of avoiding combat, though he kept the title of Hezb-i-Islami for his section of the organization.[41] The accusation was ironic, since Hekmatyar would eventually become the most cold-blooded of the mujahideen leaders and would go on to fight the United States after its invasion of Afghanistan in 2001. Khalis was born in 1919 in the Khogyani district of Nangarhar Province. Although he never acquired a university theological education, he became the mullah of a mosque in Kabul and was a member of the Muslim Brotherhood organization in Afghanistan. At the beginning, Khalis's organization was little more than a regional schism comprising the Khogyani of Nangarhar Province and the Pashtun from Paktia Province and south of Kabul. But he later developed a somewhat broader following.

War of a Thousand Cuts

The mujahideen, with ISI assistance, relied on two of the oldest tactics of warfare: the raid and the ambush. Soviet conscripts referred to the Afghan mujahideen as *dukhi*, or ghosts.[42] Since the Soviets were vulnerable to guerrilla warfare, the local troops slowly picked them apart in rural areas through a campaign of sabotage, assassinations, targeted raids, and stand-off rocket attacks. As Mohammad Yousaf acknowledged, "Death by a thousand cuts—this is the time-honoured tactic of the guerrilla army against a large conventional force. In Afghanistan it was the only way to bring the Soviet bear to its knees; the only way to defeat a superpower on the battlefield with ill-trained, ill-disciplined and ill-equipped tribesmen, whose only asset was an unconquerable fighting spirit welded to a warrior tradition."[43]

In rural areas, the situation worsened over time for the Soviets as mujahideen forces gained popular support and control.[44] The Soviets never committed the forces needed for a purely military conquest of the mujahideen, and, according to one assessment, they would have needed more than 300,000 troops to attain even a small chance of controlling the mujahideen.[45] The Red Army managed to occupy some areas temporarily, such as Panjshir in April 1984, and they pulverized other areas. But they were never able to clear and hold territory. More important, the Soviet troops alienated local

Afghans, failing to win their support or respect. A CIA assessment concluded: "The Soviets have had little success in reducing the insurgency or winning acceptance by the Afghan people, and the Afghan resistance continues to grow stronger and to command widespread popular support. Fighting has gradually spread to all parts of Afghanistan."[46]

Initial Soviet assessments of the war were optimistic, but by 1985, Soviet leaders had become increasingly concerned.[47] At a Politburo session on October 17, 1985, Soviet leader Mikhail Gorbachev read letters from Soviet citizens expressing growing dissatisfaction with the war in Afghanistan. At that same session, Gorbachev also described his meeting with Babrak Karmal in which he said the Soviet Union would pull its troops from Afghanistan.

"Karmal was dumbfounded," Gorbachev noted. "He had expected anything but this from us, he was sure we needed Afghanistan even more than he did, he's been counting on us to stay there for a long time—if not forever."

This is why Gorbachev believed it was essential to repeat his message. "By the summer of 1986 you'll have to have figured out how to defend your cause on your own," Gorbachev continued to Karmal, who was beside himself with shock. "We'll help you, but with arms only, not troops. And if you want to survive you'll have to broaden the base of the regime, forget socialism, make a deal with truly influential forces, including the Mujahideen commanders and leaders of now-hostile organizations."[48]

Gorbachev's ultimatum was grounded in good intelligence, and Soviet military assessments were bleak. Sergei Akhromeyev, the Soviet deputy minister of defense, told the Politburo: "At the center there is authority; in the provinces there is not. We control Kabul and provincial centers, but on occupied territory we cannot establish authority. We have lost the battle for the Afghan people."[49] At the Party Congress in February 1986, Gorbachev referred to the war as a bleeding wound. The Soviet military, he said, "should be told that they are learning badly from this war" and that "we need to finish this process as soon as possible."[50] Criticism of the Afghan War also increased from within the Soviet Union's military establishment. Colonel Kim Tsagolov, for example, sent an open letter to Defense Minister Dmitry Yazov complaining that the Soviet military had failed to stabilize Afghanistan and the Soviet Union had paid too heavy a price in blood and treasure.[51]

There was some resistance to withdrawal. Several Soviet politicians believed that withdrawal would be a serious blow to Soviet legitimacy and pride both domestically and internationally, but it was too late.[52] In 1986, Gorbachev announced a partial withdrawal of 6,000 troops from a force that had risen to 115,000.[53] In November of that year, Soviet officials finally lost faith in Babrak Karmal as leader of Afghanistan and replaced him with Muhammad Najibullah, a Ghilzai Pashtun born in Kabul who was known for his cold brutality and intimidation of political opponents. The KGB had appointed him head of KhAD, the secret police, in 1980, and had given him the code name POTOMOK. Najibullah, apparently embarrassed about the reference to Allah in his last name, asked to be called "Comrade Najib." Under Najibullah's control, KhAD arrested, tortured, and executed thousands of Afghans, and Amnesty International assembled evidence of "widespread and systematic torture of men, women and children."[54]

In December 1986, Najibullah was summoned to Moscow and told to strengthen his position at home because Soviet troops would be withdrawn within two years. He attempted to introduce a national reconciliation program, but with little success. On April 14, 1988, the Soviet Union signed the Geneva Accords, along with the United States, Afghanistan, and Pakistan. Designed to "promote good-neighborliness and co-operation as well as to strengthen international peace and security in the region," the accords covered issues ranging from refugee return to the normalization of relations between Afghanistan and Pakistan. As part of the accords, the Soviets agreed to withdraw their forces within nine months, beginning in May.[55] On February 15, 1989, the last Red Army units rolled across the Termez Bridge toward the USSR. General Boris Gromov, who commanded the Soviet 40th Army, was the last soldier in his column to cross the Amu Darya River.[56]

A Flamboyant Congressman from Texas

Outside support was critical in undermining Afghan governance and defeating the Red Army. We have already seen the role of Pakistan's ISI in providing tactical and strategic support. The CIA had known for years that the Red Army did "not have enough troops to maintain control in much of the countryside as long as the insurgents have access to strong external support and open borders."[57] The Soviets saw the support flowing across the border from Pakistan, and the United States encouraged it. As it became clear that the Afghan War was hurting the Soviets, the United States began to covertly support the Afghan insurgents. U.S. aid to the mujahideen began at a relatively low level but then increased as the prospect of a Soviet defeat appeared more likely, totaling between $4 billion and $5 billion between 1980 and 1992.[58] The CIA had provided about $60 million per year to the Afghan mujahideen between 1981 and 1983, which was matched by assistance from the Saudi government. But everything changed in 1984.

The major catalyst was Charlie Wilson, a flamboyant congressman from Texas, who saw the war as a chance to punish the Soviet Union for Vietnam. His congressional district lay in the heart of the Bible Belt in Trinity, Texas, about eighty miles north of Houston. Like many in his district, Wilson did not see much of a distinction between hellfire and Communism; the Soviet Union had nearly replaced Lucifer himself as the epitome of evil in Wilson's mind. As a senior Democrat on the Defense Appropriations Committee, he was well placed to increase U.S. assistance, and he pushed for an additional $40 million in aid to the mujahideen. "By this time I had everyone in Congress convinced that the mujahideen were a cause only slightly below Christianity," Wilson boasted. "Everyone on the subcommittee was enthusiastic. I gave them the sense they could lead the way on a just cause."

"The U.S. had nothing whatsoever to do with these people's decision to fight," he continued. "The Afghans made this decision on Christmas and they're going to fight to the last, even if they have to fight with stones. But we'll be damned by history if we let them fight with stones."[59]

Beginning in 1985, the United States increased its support to the Afghans to $250 million per year, thanks to Wilson, CIA Director William Casey, and growing public support. This shift culminated in National Security Directive 166, which was signed by President Ronald Reagan and set a clear U.S. objective in Afghanistan: to push out the Soviets.[60] The CIA was deeply involved in the distribution of wealth, providing money, arms (including heavy machine guns, SA-7s, and Oerlikon antiaircraft cannons), technical advice on weapons and explosives, strategic advice, intelligence, and sophisticated technology such as wireless interception equipment. Most of this assistance went through the ISI, rather than directly from the CIA to the mujahideen.[61]

One of the most useful U.S. weapons was the shoulder-fired Stinger missile. The Stinger fired an infrared, heat-seeking missile capable of engaging low-altitude, high-speed aircraft. Its combat debut had occurred in May 1982 during the Falklands War, fought between Great Britain and Argentina, and British Special Forces had been clandestinely equipped with several missiles. The CIA had initially opposed providing U.S.-manufactured weapons—especially the Stingers—to the mujahideen because they risked starting a major confrontation with the Soviets. The Pentagon had also opposed the deployment of Stingers out of concern that the Soviets would capture one and steal the technology. By 1986, however, U.S. policymakers saw the destruction caused by the Soviet Mi-24 Hind gunships and decided that introducing Stingers would make such a difference on the battlefield that it was worth the risks. At a meeting in January 1986, Pakistan's President Zia told CIA Director Casey: "This is the time to increase the pressure." In mid-February, the United States ordered the Defense Department to provide the CIA with 400 Stingers for use by the mujahideen.[62]

In September 1986, a force of roughly thirty-five mujahideen led by a commander named Engineer Ghaffar fired the first Stingers in Afghanistan. They crept through the underbrush and reached a small hill a mile northeast of Jalalabad airfield in eastern Afghanistan. Their targets were eight Mi-24 gunships scheduled to land that day. Ghaffar could make out the soldiers in the airfield's perimeter observation posts, and he and his men waited patiently for three hours until the helicopters arrived. They fired five missiles and downed three helicopters, as one mujahideen, shaking nervously with excitement, videotaped the attack. This first Stinger attack marked a major turning point in the war. Over the next ten months, 187 Stingers were used in Afghanistan, and roughly 75 percent hit aircraft.[63]

In addition to Wilson and Casey, a growing coterie of U.S. government officials played a role in turning Afghanistan into the USSR's Vietnam. One was Zalmay Khalilzad. In 1984, he had accepted a one-year fellowship from the Council on Foreign Relations and joined the State Department, where he worked for Paul Wolfowitz, then the director of policy planning. From 1985 to 1989, Khalilzad served in the Reagan administration as a senior State Department official advising on the Soviet War in Afghanistan. "The Stingers sent a big message," Khalilzad later remarked. "It was an open secret that we were involved, but the intelligence channel gave us deniability. The Stingers removed that. American power and prestige had become engaged, we had crossed a threshold. But, at the same time, there was a lot of soul-searching as to whether or not this was going to make it harder for the Soviets to back down."[64]

Other countries also played roles. Saudi Arabia gave nearly $4 billion in official aid to the mujahideen between 1980 and 1990, while millions of dollars also flowed from unofficial sources: Islamic charities, foundations, the private funds of Saudi princes, and mosque collections.[65] The Soviets were, of course, well aware of the U.S., Pakistani, Chinese, and Saudi activities. A report by Gromyko, Andropov, Ustinov, and Ponomarev in 1980 concluded that the United States and China were working closely with Pakistan, where "the most important bases of the Afghan bandit formations" were located.[66] A separate report by Ustinov to the CPSU Central Committee noted that the "USA and its allies are training, equipping, and sending into [Afghan] territory armed formations of the Afghan counterrevolution, the activity of which, thanks to help from outside, has become the main factor destabilizing the situation in Afghanistan."[67]

Soviet intelligence agents monitored U.S. assistance at training camps in Pakistan, as well as U.S. and other arms shipments through Pakistani ports, especially Karachi.[68] The KGB had orders to hunt for Afghan mujahideen with connections to U.S. intelligence and "undertake appropriate work with them" to extract information.[69] In the end, Soviet leaders reached the conclusion that if they pulled out of Afghanistan, the United States would not go in with military forces.[70] They were correct—at least for another decade. Instead, Afghanistan deteriorated into a bitter civil war as various militia groups fought over control of the country.

CHAPTER THREE

Uncivil War

IN LATE 1986, Deputy Director of Central Intelligence Robert Gates placed a twenty-five-dollar bet with Under Secretary of State for Political Affairs Michael Armacost that the Soviet Union would not pull out of Afghanistan before the end of the Reagan administration. Gates, a rising star in the administration, would go on to become director of the Central Intelligence Agency under President George H. W. Bush and then secretary of defense under his son, President George W. Bush.

It was a win-win bet, Gates told his colleagues. "I would get twenty-five dollars or have the pleasure of paying twenty-five dollars on the occasion of an early Soviet withdrawal. A small price to pay for a large victory."

Gates was fond of quoting an old Chinese proverb: "What the bear has eaten, he never spits out." But he lost the bet. Mikhail Gorbachev announced in February 1988, before a nationwide audience, that Soviet withdrawals from Afghanistan would begin that May, and they were completed by December 1989.

"I paid Mike Armacost the twenty-five dollars—the best money I ever spent," Gates said. "I also told myself it would be the last time I'd make an intelligence forecast based on fortune cookie wisdom."[1]

A Patchwork of Competing Groups

The initial U.S. reaction to the Soviet withdrawal was referred to as "positive symmetry." According to Robert Oakley, the U.S. ambassador to Pakistan, this meant that "the United States would keep funding the mujahideen as long as the Soviets provided assistance to the Najibullah government."[2] The Soviet withdrawal had raised hopes that an end to the conflict might be near, but the situation grew worse as Afghanistan disintegrated into a patchwork of competing groups, with Washington and Moscow backing competing sides.

"Ultimately, the insurgent forces will cause the demise of the Communist government," reported a U.S. Defense Intelligence Agency assessment of the Soviet withdrawal. "The successor government will probably be an uneasy coalition of traditionalist and fundamentalist groups, and its control will not extend far beyond Kabul."[3] The CIA had reached a similar conclusion and predicted the imminent collapse of the Najibullah government: "We judge that Mohammed Najibullah's regime will not long survive the completion of Soviet withdrawal even with continued Soviet assistance. . . . The regime may fall before withdrawal is complete."[4] Other U.S. experts on Afghanistan, such as Zalmay Khalilzad, predicted "the quick overthrow of the Najibullah government by the mujaheddin. Without the Soviets," he wrote, "the Kabul government's morale would plummet, the regime would disintegrate and the mujaheddin would sweep victoriously forward."[5]

Even Soviet assessments were bleak. According to a Top Secret report to the Politburo, political and economic conditions in Afghanistan were spiraling out of control: "The chief question on which depends the continuing evolution of the situation boils down to this: will the government be able to maintain Kabul and other large cities in the country, though above all the capital?"[6]

Unfortunately, the answer was no. Since Afghan state authority was too weak to provide order and deliver services, the objectives of opposition groups came to resemble those of competitive state-builders.

Each mujahideen leader aspired to build an army and a financial apparatus capable of supporting it. The relative success of each group depended upon its access to resources and skills in organization and leadership.[7] Rival ethnic and political interests splintered the anti-Soviet mujahideen coalition into competing factions, and fighting soon broke out. As a result, President Najibullah was able to cling to power for a further three years after the Soviet withdrawal. Though it held Kabul, the Najibullah government was unable to overcome its most significant challenge: to expand its reach into rural areas without the support of Soviet troops. Afghanistan scholar Barnett Rubin wrote, "The loss of Soviet military support, along with increased availability of arms for the resistance, led the state to lose autonomy from society in one area after another. Society, however, proved unable to organize itself to provide an alternative form of state."[8] The Soviets continued to provide assistance, and in the six months following the Soviet withdrawal, they flew nearly 4,000 planeloads of weapons and supplies into Afghanistan.[9]

Khalilzad, who began working at RAND in 1989, wrote a provocative paper titled *Prospects for the Afghan Interim Government*. The U.S. State Department had initiated and supported the report, for which Khalilzad interviewed such key Afghan figures as Sibghatullah Mujadiddi, Yunus Khalis, Gulbuddin Hekmatyar, Burhanuddin Rabbani, Jalaluddin Haqqani, and Muhammad Zahir Shah. His conclusions were bleak. Despite the creation of an Afghan interim government (AIG), he argued, "its prospects are not good. It has failed to achieve its objective, and its relative importance, never great, has declined." In addition, Khalilzad pointed out that the personal rivalries among these commanders created an untenable situation: "Instead of developing greater cohesion among the mujahedin, the AIG has intensified the political power struggle among noncommunist Afghans and therefore has had a negative effect on the struggle between the mujahedin and the regime."[10]

In January 1992, Abdul Rashid Dostum turned against the disintegrating Afghan government, which had previously supplied him with

arms. Born to a poor Uzbek family in Khvajeh Do Kuh in the northern Afghan province of Jowzjan, Dostum had a distinctive look, with
short-cropped hair, bushy eyebrows, and a thick mustache. In 1970,
he began to work in a state-owned gas refinery. When the Soviets
invaded in 1979, he supported the Soviet-backed Najibullah government and led the Afghan Army's 53rd Infantry Division against mujahideen forces. By the mid-1980s, Dostum commanded a 20,000-strong
militia controlling the northern provinces of Afghanistan. His followers gave him the title of pasha, an honor given to the region's ancient
kings. Some thought he had ambitions to emerge as the new ruler of
Afghanistan, and one Western diplomat mused, "He regarded himself
as a new Tamerlane."[11]

In April 1992, Dostum and his forces, who had deserted the Afghan
Communists, took the city of Mazar-e-Sharif with assistance from
Ahmed Shah Massoud. When Democratic Republic of Afghanistan
troops in Herat and Kandahar began to falter, the mujahideen closed
in on Kabul. Massoud and Dostum (from the north) and Hekmatyar
(from the south) converged on the capital. The Soviet Union and the
United States had cut off all assistance several months earlier, and
Najibullah resigned in April 1992. Sibghatullah Mujadiddi, leader of
the Afghanistan National Liberation Front, reached an agreement
with the mujahideen forces in Pakistan and took power. After a two-
month term, Mujadiddi transferred power to Burhanuddin Rabbani.

Son of the Water Carrier

There had been only two recent periods in Afghan history when the
Pashtuns, Afghanistan's largest ethnic group, did not rule. The first
was in 1929, when a Tajik, Habibullah Kalakani, seized power for several months. Some Pashtuns derisively referred to him as *Bacha-ye
Saqqow*, which means "Son of the Water Carrier," since his father supposedly had carried water in the Afghan Army.

The second began in 1992, when Burhanuddin Rabbani, also a
Tajik, became president of Afghanistan. A wiry man with a flowing

white beard, turban, and a soft impassive voice, Rabbani was more of
a religious figure than a politician. He was born in 1940 in Badakhshan Province in northern Afghanistan, home to the mammoth Marco
Polo sheep that Ronald Neumann tracked in 1967. After finishing
school, he went to Darul-uloom-e-Sharia, a religious school in Kabul,
then to Kabul University to study Islamic law and theology. In 1966,
he moved to Cairo to attend Al-Azhar University, where Abdullah
Azzam, the jihadi leader and onetime mentor of Osama bin Laden,
had attended. In 1968, when Rabbani returned to Afghanistan, the
high council of Jamiat-e-Islami (Islamic Society) asked him to organize university students. Considering his training, then, it was no
surprise that Rabbani's government imposed severe restrictions on
women and sought to exclude them from public life.

When Rabbani took over, pandemonium ensued. Disputes erupted
over the division of government posts, and fighting flared. Pashtun
leaders resented the handover of power to other ethnic groups, especially Tajiks and Uzbeks.[12] The United Nations tried—and eventually
failed—to broker a political settlement.[13] Afghan commanders controlled fiefdoms, and each was supported by a neighboring country,
such as Pakistan, Iran, Russia, and India.

Rabbani's presidency symbolized northern control of the capital,
since he was a Tajik. And it prompted Hekmatyar, a Ghilzai Pashtun,
to unleash vicious bombardments on Kabul from the south. According to one of his commanders, "We know that non-military people
will be killed today; if they are good Muslims, God will reward them
as martyred and send them to heaven. . . . if they are bad Muslims,
God is punishing them at the hands of his true believers."[14] Human
Rights Watch reported that Hekmatyar's bombardment "killed at
least 2,000, most of them civilians." Hundreds of thousands fled the
city and remained in makeshift camps along roads leading to Pakistan.[15] Street battles broke out in Kabul between the forces of Hekmatyar, who had Pakistani backing, and those allied with Ahmed Shah
Massoud. But Hekmatyar was ultimately too weak to seize and hold
Kabul. In 1995, the State Department issued an important cable on

the deteriorating security situation, "Discussing Afghan Policy with the Pakistanis." The document explained, "The past year has seen several dramatic reversals of fortune for the armed factions in Afghanistan as well as concurrent changes or hardening of the Afghan policies of Russia, India and, not least, Pakistan." The effect of this meddling was to lessen the prospects for success of the United Nations mediation process, increase the likelihood of internecine fighting, and continue the agony of the Afghan people.[16]

Interference from Neighbors

There were clear battle lines among neighboring countries. Iran, India, and Russia supported the Rabbani government and northern commanders such as Massoud. Pakistan and Saudi Arabia supported Pashtun opposition groups such as Hekmatyar's Hezb-i-Islami. Iran, which regarded Pashtun commanders as Sunni fundamentalist and anti-Iranian, favored the northern commanders and the Rabbani government.[17] A State Department cable found that "the withdrawal of Soviet forces from Afghanistan in February 1989 and fall of the communist regime in Kabul in April 1992, set the stage for a more or less open competition for influence in Afghanistan between Pakistan and Iran."[18]

Other U.S. government reports explicitly described Iranian funding for northern groups such as Ahmed Shah Massoud's Jamiat-e-Islami. One said, "Jamiat was receiving large amounts of cash and military supplies, mostly from Iranian government sources. The funds and supplies reportedly come from Iran to points in Tajikistan (Kulyab Airbase, for example), where they are picked up by Jamiat helicopters and ferried to the Panjshir Valley and other points."[19] The report revealed that officials from Iran's Ministry of Intelligence and Security (MOIS), as well as the Iranian Revolutionary Guards Corps (IRGC), were stationed with Massoud in the Panjshir Valley, where they helped unload and distribute the supplies.

With the collapse of the Soviet Union, fourteen of the fifteen Soviet republics had become independent states. The newly formed

Russian Federation provided what little assistance it could to Rabbani and Massoud.[20] U.S. intelligence thought Russia was concerned about the "spillover of Islamic militancy into Central Asia."[21] Consequently, Russia backed northern commanders in an effort to protect its southern flank. Following conversations with Russian government officials, U.S. Assistant Secretary of State Robin Raphel reported that while Moscow was publicly committed to the UN mediation process, it was more interested in keeping Rabbani in power. "From Washington's perspective," the 1995 cable said, "Moscow appears more committed to keeping Rabbani in Kabul and, necessarily, less committed to a UN brokered transfer of power."[22]

Indian support for Rabbani and Massoud was primarily motivated by a desire for balance against Pakistan. The 1995 cable was blunt: as "has been the case since Indian independence, New Delhi's primary foreign policy objective in Afghanistan is to counter Pakistan." U.S. intelligence understood that India's assistance to northern commanders would likely trigger an increase in Pakistani aid to the rival Pashtun groups.[23]

In the face of such entrenched resistance, Pakistan adopted an increasingly anti-Rabbani, anti-Indian, anti-Russian, and anti-Iranian stance. Even during the Clinton years, the United States understood that the Pakistan government "ha[d] contacts with all the major opponents of Rabbani and Massood and has encouraged cooperation among them."[24] The main Pakistani message, it concluded, was to unite opposition against the Kabul regime. Another State Department memo characterized the Pakistan government as "following a 'Rabbani must go at any price' policy." A major motivation, it continued, was "Pakistan's fear of an emerging 'Tehran-Moscow-New Delhi axis' supporting Kabul."[25] In his 1991 RAND paper, Zalmay Khalilzad had interviewed senior Pakistan officials, including Lieutenant General (retired) Shamsur Rehman Kallue, head of the ISI, and General Assad Durrani, head of Army Intelligence. They told him that the ISI continued to subcontract directly with key commanders, such as Hekmatyar, "for specific military operations, allowing Pakistan to increase its direct control over military operations. . . . This control remained within ISI."[26]

Saudi Arabia also provided assistance to the Pashtun groups. "The Saudis supported the Sunnis against the Shia," recalled Robert Oakley, the U.S. ambassador to Pakistan. "They continued to push the Wahhabi version of Islam into Afghanistan and Pakistan, and built *madrassas* [religious schools] and mosques in places like Pakistan's Federally Administered Tribal Areas and North West Frontier Province. As Prince Turki al-Faisal, the head of Saudi intelligence, used to tell me, 'We are simply doing Allah's work.' "[27]

Waning U.S. Interest

The official U.S. position was to back UN mediation efforts, but the Clinton administration had generally lost interest in Afghanistan. The Cold War had ended, and U.S. officials saw little geostrategic value in Afghanistan; it had become a backwater of U.S. foreign policy. U.S. Secretary of State James Baker and Soviet Foreign Minister Boris Pankin had agreed to end arms shipments to the Afghan government and rebel groups by January 1, 1992, and the CIA's legal authority to conduct covert action in Afghanistan had effectively been terminated.

Some U.S. policymakers, such as Peter Tomsen, the U.S. special envoy to Afghanistan, frantically tried to keep U.S. assistance alive. In a classified cable, he wrote that "U.S. perseverance in maintaining our already established position in Afghanistan—at little cost—could significantly contribute to the favorable moderate outcome, which would: sideline the extremists, maintain a friendship with a strategically located friendly country, help us accomplish our other objectives in Afghanistan and the broader Central Asian region." And he prophetically warned: "We are in danger of throwing away the assets we have built up in Afghanistan over the last 10 years, at great expense."[28] But Tomsen's effort failed. The U.S. Embassy in Kabul, which had been officially closed since January 1989, would not be reopened until December 2001.

The U.S. interest in neighboring Pakistan also waned with the withdrawal of Soviet forces from Afghanistan and the collapse of the Soviet Union. To make matters worse, growing Pakistani efforts to build a nuclear weapon—a process monitored by the CIA—triggered an American law known as the Pressler Amendment. Named after Larry Pressler, a deft Republican senator from South Dakota, it banned the sale or transfer of military equipment and technology to Pakistan unless the U.S. president could annually certify that Pakistan did not possess a nuclear explosive device. In October 1990, President George H. W. Bush was unable to issue this certification. As Robert Oakley recalled, "I had the unfortunate pleasure of handing President Bush's letter to the Pakistanis." The result, Oakley believed, was devastating: "The Pakistan military accused us of betraying them and leaving them defenseless against the Indians. And we lost any possibility of working with Pakistan in Afghanistan, even if we wanted to."[29] The United States declined to be a major player in the region.

Through the mid-1990s, Afghanistan remained under the control of various warlord commanders. In the north, the militias of Sayyid Mansur Nadiri and Abdul Rashid Dostum controlled vital roads and economic facilities. The Afghan government in Kabul did not have enough loyal troops or party members to defeat them. Nadiri's forces dominated the area north of the Salang Tunnel, and Dostum's forces guarded the natural-gas fields and the roads along the Uzbek steppe around Mazar-e-Sharif. Ismail Khan controlled the western provinces around Herat, and the areas to the south and east of Kabul were in the hands of mujahideen leaders such as Hekmatyar. The eastern border with Pakistan was held by a council of mujahideen, and the south was split among scores of mujahideen and bandits who used their control of the roads to extort money from the cross-border trade with Pakistan.

In 1992, a collection of mujahideen groups led by Burhanuddin Rabbani overthrew Afghan President Muhammad Najibullah. Shortly afterward, Beirut-style street fighting erupted in the city, especially between the Pashtun Hezb-i-Islami and the Tajik Jamiat-e-Islami.

Kabul, which was left virtually untouched under Soviet occupation, was savagely bombarded with rockets, mortars, and artillery by Hekmatyar. Entire neighborhoods, including mosques and government buildings, were destroyed, reducing Kabul to shambles. In Kandahar, fighting among mujahideen groups resulted in the destruction of much of the traditional power structures. In the rural areas, competition among warlords, drug lords, and criminal groups triggered a state of emerging anarchy as the tribal leadership system began to unravel.

In 1993 and 1994, the fighting continued around Kabul and throughout the rest of Afghanistan, and a vagabond government in Kabul shifted among surviving buildings. At one point during the heaviest fighting, the government operated from Charikar, the capital of Parwan Province in northern Afghanistan, roughly forty miles from Kabul. On January 1, 1994, Hekmatyar, Dostum, and Abdul Ali Mazari launched one of the most devastating assaults against Kabul to date. Their attack took several thousand lives and reduced Kabul's population—which had numbered more than two million late in the Soviet War—to under 500,000.[30] During the first week, government units lost ground in both southwestern and southeastern Kabul, but they soon regained most of their positions. In June, Massoud led an offensive that drove Hekmatyar's rocket units off two strategic hills.

As the fighting settled into a stalemate, several peace initiatives were attempted. The United Nations renewed its peacemaking role in April 1994. Ismail Khan hosted a conference in July 1994 that pushed for a transition to a new government, but Hekmatyar, Dostum, Mazari, and other commanders blocked the move. Iran and the Organization of the Islamic Conference (OIC) hosted a poorly attended peace conference in Tehran in November. On December 28, 1994, Rabbani's presidential term lapsed. But with no resolution of conflict and no consensus reached on a mechanism for transferring authority, he kept the office by default, pending a new political settlement engineered by the United Nations.[31]

The View from Afar

By the mid-1990s, Afghanistan was in tatters. Viewed from afar, the reports were troubling. In 1994, Ronald Neumann watched the civil war unfold from Algeria, where he had just been named U.S. ambassador. "The city of Kabul, which I had visited and where my father had been ambassador, was reduced to rubble," he told me. The city no longer had the splendor of the "compact and handsome" city described in the nineteenth century by Mountstuart Elphinstone, a Scottish statesman and historian:

> The abundance and arrangement of its bazaars have been already a theme of praise to a European traveller. The city is divided by the stream which bears its name, and is surrounded, particularly on the north and west, by numerous gardens and groves of fruit trees. . . . The charms of the climate and scenery of Caubul have been celebrated by many Persian and Indian writers. The beauty and abundance of its flowers are proverbial, and its fruits are transported to the remotest parts of India.[32]

As Kabul crumbled during the fighting, Zalmay Khalilzad, a senior analyst at the RAND Corporation, became perturbed at the waning U.S. interest in the region. "America has not helped Afghans and our friends in the region make the right decisions," Khalilzad wrote in a scathing 1996 opinion piece in the *Washington Post*. "After the fall of the Soviet Union we stopped paying attention. This was a bad decision. Instability and war in Afghanistan provided fertile ground for terrorist groups to train and hide," he noted cryptically. And he concluded by arguing that, "given the sacrifices made by the Afghans in the Cold War's final struggle, we had a moral obligation to assist them in achieving peace. We did not."[33] The sheer chaos in Afghanistan provided a window of opportunity for a new force to emerge, and a group of young religious zealots from southern Afghanistan seized the moment.

CHAPTER FOUR

The Rise of the Taliban

IN APRIL 1996, Mullah Muhammad Omar orchestrated a propaganda coup that rippled across the mujahideen community in Afghanistan. Omar was the leader of the Taliban, an upstart band of Islamic students who began to conquer territory in the mid-1990s from their base in southern Afghanistan. By April, they had captured Kandahar and its surrounding provinces and were preparing their siege of Kabul. In order to establish his ideological credentials and attract new recruits, Mullah Omar turned to the legend of the Prophet Muhammad's cloak. The cloak was supposedly in Kandahar, housed in a shrine with ornate walls inlaid with intricately crafted tiles of bright blue, yellow, and green. Referred to as the *Khirka Sharif*, the shrine was considered one of the holiest places in Afghanistan. Behind the shrine stood the mausoleum of Ahmed Shah Durrani, founder of the Durrani dynasty and, for many Afghans, father of the modern Afghan state.

For generations, Afghans in Kandahar had passed down legends about the cloak and Ahmed Shah. According to one version, Ahmed Shah traveled to Bokhara, a major center of Islamic scholarship and culture, and now a modern city in Central Asian Uzbekistan. He saw the sacred cloak of the Prophet Muhammad and wanted to bring it home. Ahmed Shah asked to "borrow" the cloak from its keepers, who politely refused, suspecting that he might not return it. After pondering for a few minutes, he pointed to a boulder in the ground

and made a promise to the keepers. He said: "I will never take the
cloak far from this boulder." Relieved, the keepers let him take the
cloak. Ahmed Shah kept his word, in a sense. He had the boulder
taken out of the ground and carried back to Kandahar, along with the
cloak, which he never returned. And he built a pedestal for the boulder next to the shrine. While the cloak has normally been hidden
from public view, it has been worn on rare occasions. For instance,
King Dost Muhammad Khan wore it when he declared jihad against
the Sikh kingdom in Peshawar in 1834.

In April 1996, Mullah Omar, who had limited religious education
but had fought with the Harakat-i Inqilab-i Islam during the Soviet
War, attempted to legitimize his role as a religious leader.[1] He
removed the cloak from the shrine and perched himself atop one of
the buildings in the center of Kandahar City. As a large crowd gathered and the cloak flapped in the breeze, he wrapped and unwrapped
the cloak from around his body. An Afghan legend decreed that who-
ever retrieved the cloak from the chest would be *Amir al-Mu'minin*
(Commander of the Faithful). Others in the Muslim world, however,
had adopted this title even without the cloak. Hassan II, for example,
who ascended the throne in Morocco in 1961, claimed direct descent
from the Prophet and adopted the title Commander of the Faithful.[2]
For Mullah Omar, claiming the authority of the cloak gave him influence among some Afghans who would now support the Taliban as a
legitimate Muslim entity. The cloak ceremony ended with a declaration of jihad against Burhanuddin Rabbani's government, and those
present swore *bayat* (allegiance) to Mullah Omar. For many Afghans
and Muslims, however, it was an outrageous insult. Omar was a poor
village mullah with no scholarly learning, no prestigious tribal lin-
eage, and no connections to the Prophet's family.[3]

Mullah Omar's self-appointment as Commander of the Faithful was
supported by a few other organizations, including al Qa'ida. In his
book *Knights Under the Prophet's Banner*, al Qa'ida leader Ayman al-
Zawahiri warmly referred to Mullah Omar as the Commander of the
Faithful.[4] Zawahiri later wrote: "May Allah grant long life to the peo-

ple of Jihad and Ribat in Afghanistan, and may Allah grant long life to
the Commander of the Faithful, Mullah Muhammad Omar, who didn't
sell his religion for worldly gain."[5] When Mustafa Ahmed Muhammad
Uthman Abu al-Yazid was announced as al Qa'ida's new leader for the
Afghan front, he began by pledging his personal allegiance to Mullah
Omar as the Commander of the Faithful. Even Osama bin Laden
swore allegiance, stating that the Taliban "are fighting America and its
agents under the leadership of the Commander of the Believers, Mullah Omar, may Allah protect him."[6] This was perhaps done to ensure
that the insular and xenophobic Afghans saw the insurgency as being
led by Afghan mujahideen, and not by foreign Arabs.

Roots of the Taliban

The Taliban's roots go back to Deobandism, a school of thought
emanating from the Dar ul-Ulum *madrassa* in 1867 in Deoband,
India, just north of Delhi. In some ways, the Deobandi approach was
similar to that of the Wahhabis in Saudi Arabia. Deobandism followed a Salafist egalitarian model, seeking to emulate the life and
times of the Prophet Muhammad. It held that a Muslim's primary
obligation and loyalty were to his religion, and loyalty to country
was always secondary. Some Deobandis also believed they had a
sacred right and obligation to wage jihad to protect the Muslims of
any country. The Deobandi *madrassas* were prominent and well established throughout northwest India, notably in the territories that
would later become Pakistan.[7] The Deobandis trained a corps of
ulema (Islamic scholars) capable of issuing *fatwas* (legal rulings) on
all aspects of daily life. The *ulema* would monitor society's conformity with the prescriptions of Islam and rigorously and conserva-
tively interpret religious doctrine.

Following Pakistan's independence in 1947, a variety of religious
factions campaigned for full Islamization of the new nation. One faction was rooted in the works of Sayyid Abul Ala Maududi, whose first
book, *Jihad in Islam*, was published in the 1920s. His family had a

longstanding tradition of spiritual leadership, and a number of his ancestors were leaders of Sufi orders. Maududi, born in India in 1903, was homeschooled and became a journalist, writing for Indian newspapers such as *Muslim* and *al-Jam'iyat*. Maududi favored what he called "Islamization from above," in which sovereignty would be exercised in the name of Allah, and *sharia* law would be implemented in society. He declared that politics was "an integral, inseparable part of the Islamic faith, and that the Islamic state that Muslim political action seeks to build is a panacea for all their problems."[8] For Maududi, the five traditional pillars of Islam—*shahada* (profession of faith), *salat* (prayer), *sawm* (fasting during Ramadan), *hajj* (pilgrimage to Mecca), and *zakat* (almsgiving)—were merely phases of preparation for jihad. To carry out jihad, Maududi founded Jamiat-e-Islami in 1941, which he saw as the vanguard of an Islamic revolution. The party envisioned the establishment of an Islamic state governed by Islamic law and opposed such Western practices as capitalism and socialism.

In addition to Jamiat-e-Islami, there were several political parties that gave expression to the special interests of their own professional groups and networks of pupils. One of the main groups was Jamiat Ulema-e-Islam, a Deobandi offshoot. Established in 1945, it was the largest Deobandi-based party. Its two principal factions were led for a long time by Maulana Fazlur Rehman and Maulana Sami ul-Haq. The radicalization of the Deobandi movements was later nurtured by Pakistan to support militant Islamic groups in Kashmir and Afghanistan, as well as to counter Shi'ites in Pakistan.[9] The Deobandis also benefited from Saudi bankrolling since the Saudis were keenly interested in helping build *madrassas*. Prominent Deobandis embraced an impoverished younger generation with little hope of climbing the social ladder, and violence became their main form of expression.[10]

Deobandi *madrassas* flourished across South Asia during this period, but they were not officially supported or sanctioned until Pakistan President Muhammad Zia-ul-Haq, a fervent admirer of Maududi, assumed control of the Pakistan government in 1977. He remained president until August 1988, when he died in a mysterious plane crash that also killed U.S. Ambassador Arnold Raphel and General Herbert Wassom, the senior Pentagon official in Pakistan.

Zia made implementation of *sharia* law the ideological cornerstone of his eleven-year dictatorship. One of his most significant steps was the creation of the International Islamic University in 1980 in Islamabad, where the leading Wahhabis and the Muslim Brotherhood gathered. Zia promoted Islamism to the status of an official state ideology, and Jamiat-e-Islami was rewarded with ministerial responsibilities and significant aid. Zia adopted several Islamization measures, including an examination of all existing laws to verify their conformity with *sharia*, the introduction of an Islamic penal code that included corporal punishment, and the Islamization of education.[11] In addition, Zia's government levied a 2.5 percent tax on bank accounts each year during Ramadan for *zakat*. This "legalized" almsgiving had previously been treated as a private matter in most Muslim countries. The funds raised by *zakat* served to finance the *madrassas*, which were controlled by the *ulemas*, many of whom were linked to the Deobandi movement.[12] Indeed, Zia encouraged the financing and construction of hundreds of *madrassas* along the Afghan frontier to educate young Afghans and Pakistanis in Islam's precepts and to prepare some of them for anti-Soviet jihad.

The 1979 Soviet invasion of Afghanistan, and the subsequent jihad against Soviet forces, was critical to the further radicalization of Deobandi and other militant groups. First, the jihad provided a training ground for young militants. Second, Pakistan's ISI supervised and assisted in the development of these movements to pursue its regional policies. From the hundreds of resistance groups that sprang up, the ISI recognized approximately half a dozen and established offices for them to channel covert support. Although most had a strong religious ethos, the groups were organized primarily along ethnic and tribal lines. Significantly, three of the seven were led by Ghilzai Pashtuns and none by their rivals, the Durrani Pashtuns, who were deliberately marginalized by the ISI. Third, following the 1979 Iranian revolution, Pakistani government officials had became concerned that the Iranian government was using the Shi'ites in Pakistan and Afghanistan as a "fifth column" to pursue its interests.[13] Consequently, Shi'ites were targeted. In 1985, for example, a Deobandi militant group sprang up called Sipah-e Sahaba-e Pakistan (Soldiers of the Companion of the Prophet in Pakistan), which pronounced all Shi'ites infidels and conducted a range of attacks against them. Several years later, another group called Lashkar-e-Jhangvi (Army of Jhangvi) was established and waged jihad against Shi'ites.

After the Soviet withdrawal from Afghanistan, Saudi Arabia invested heavily in the region. It funded *madrassas* in Pakistan that sought to spread the conservative Wahhabi version of Islam practiced in Saudi Arabia, and Saudi money flowed to Saudi-trained Wahhabi leaders among the Pashtuns, producing a small following. Abdul Rasul Sayyaf, who had temporarily settled in Saudi Arabia, moved to Peshawar and set up a Wahhabi party. Pakistan's Jamiat Ulema-e-Islam also helped build a network of Deobandi *madrassas* to extend their influence. These *madrassas* would eventually serve as an important educational alternative for the refugees from the anti-Soviet jihad and the subsequent civil war, as well as for poor families along the Afghanistan-Pakistan frontier who could not afford the secular schools.

The Knowledge Seekers

In late 1994, a new movement emerged in southern Afghanistan. Many of its members were drawn from *madrassas* that had been established in Afghan refugee camps in Pakistan during the 1980s. Their primary objectives were to restore peace, enforce *sharia* law, and defend the integrity and Islamic character of Afghanistan. Since most were part-time or full-time students at *madrassas,* they chose a name for themselves that reflected their status. A *talib* is an Islamic student who *seeks* knowledge, which is different from a mullah, or member of the Islamic clergy, who *gives* knowledge. The new movement, called the Taliban, began by seizing control of Kandahar before expanding to the surrounding provinces.

The Taliban leaders who emerged in the mid-1990s were an odd lot. As Pakistani journalist Ahmed Rashid pointed out, the organization's leadership could "boast to be the most disabled in the world today and visitors do not know how to react, whether to laugh or to cry. Mullah Omar lost his right eye in 1989 when a rocket exploded close by."[14] In addition, Nuruddin Turabi, who became justice minister, and Muhammad Ghaus, who became foreign minister, also had lost eyes. Abdul Majid, who became the mayor of Kabul, had lost a leg and two fingers. Mullah Dadullah Lang, a Taliban military commander (who was killed by U.S. forces in May 2007), lost a leg when fighting Soviet forces in Afghanistan in the 1980s.

The early Taliban were deeply disillusioned with the factionalism and criminal activities of the Afghan mujahideen leadership. They saw themselves as the cleansers of a war gone astray and a social and political system that had become derailed. Taliban leaders also sought to overturn an Islamic way of life that had been compromised by corruption and infidelity to the Prophet Muhammad.[15] Indeed, Mullah Omar's act of wrapping himself in the Prophet's cloak symbolized the return to a purer Islam. The Taliban recruited primarily from Deobandi *madrassas* between Ghazni and Kandahar, as well as in Pakistan. These *madrassas* had become politicized and militarized during the war, but many were linked to the centrist conservative parties of the Afghan resistance, such as Hekmatyar's Hezb-i-Islami. The Afghanistan-Pakistan border became ever more porous as Afghan Taliban studied in Pakistan, Afghan refugees enrolled in Pakistani *madrassas*, and Pakistani volunteers eventually joined the Taliban.[16]

Beginning in late 1994, Taliban forces advanced rapidly through southern and eastern Afghanistan, capturing nine out of thirty provinces by February 1995. In September 1995, the Taliban seized Herat, causing great concern in nearby Iran.[17] The Taliban then cut off Hekmatyar's supply route to Jalalabad before zeroing in on his fortress base at Charasyab, south of Kabul. After a last-ditch attempt to rally his forces, Hekmatyar was forced to flee. In 1996, the Taliban captured Kabul and, despite temporary setbacks, conquered the northern cities

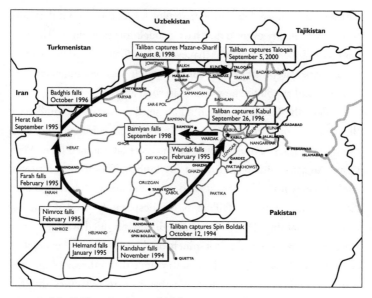

FIGURE 4.1 Taliban Conquest of Afghanistan

of Kunduz and Taloqan in 1998. As the Taliban closed in on the gem of the north, Mazar-e-Sharif, Iran helped Hekmatyar travel there to negotiate with the Taliban. But this effort failed and the city fell.[18]

The Taliban's strategy was innovative and ruthlessly effective. Unlike the Soviets, they focused their initial efforts on bottom-up efforts in *rural* Afghanistan, especially the Pashtun south. They approached tribal leaders and militia commanders, as well as their rank-and-file supporters, and attempted to co-opt them with several messages. Taliban leaders claimed to provide moral and religious clarity, since they advocated the return to a purer form of Islam; they offered to restore Pashtun control of Kabul, which was run by the Tajik Rabbani; and they tried to capitalize on their momentum by convincing locals that resistance was futile. They used their knowledge of tribal dynamics to appeal to Pashtuns and, when they didn't succeed in co-opting locals, they often resorted to targeted assassination to coerce the rest. It was a strategy accomplished on a very personal level: Taliban leaders who spoke the local dialect traveled to the Pashtun villages and district centers. In

addition, the Taliban didn't need to deploy forces throughout the countryside, and in any event didn't have enough forces to do so. The bril-
liant part of their strategy was that even while they focused on securing
urban areas, they successfully cut deals with local commanders—or
removed and appointed new ones—in rural areas.[19]

At first, the Taliban represented a rise to power of the mullahs at
the expense of tribal leaders and mujahideen commanders, even
though a number of mujahideen commanders later joined them. War-
weary Afghans initially welcomed the Taliban. The group promoted
itself as a new force for honesty and unity and many Afghans, particularly Pashtuns, saw the Taliban as the desperately needed balm of
peace and stability. The Taliban immediately targeted warlords who
were deemed responsible for much of the destruction, instability,
and chaos that had plagued the country since the outbreak of the civil
war. The Taliban, however, took Deobandism to extremes that the
school's founders would not have recognized. They instituted a brutal
religious police force, the Ministry of the Promotion of Virtue and
the Suppression of Vice (*Amr Bil Maroof Wa Nahi An al-Munkar*), to
uphold its extreme and often unorthodox interpretations of Islam.
"Throw reason to the dogs," read a sign posted on the wall of the
office of the police. "It stinks of corruption."[20]

Girls were not permitted to attend schools, most women were prohibited from working, and women were rarely permitted to venture
out of their homes—and even then could not do so without wearing a
burqa, an outer garment that cloaks the entire body. The Taliban decreed:
"Women you should not step outside your residence. If you go outside
the house you should not be like women who used to go with fashion-
able clothes wearing much cosmetics and appearing in front of every
man before the coming of Islam." It concluded: "Islam as a rescuing religion has determined specific dignity for women" and women "should
not create such opportunity to attract the attention of useless people
who will not look at them with a good eye."[21]

The U.S. State Department characterized the Taliban as "harsh and
oppressive. We continue to receive reports that the Taliban detain

Tajiks, Panjshiris, and others indiscriminately, shipping at least some to a prison in Kandahar. Women are not seen as frequently on the streets" out of "fear of being accosted."[22] Zalmay Khalilzad wrote in an essay with fellow RAND analyst Daniel Byman that "Afghan women face a horrifying array of restrictions, among the most repressive in the world." These problems, they argued, would only worsen. "'Talibanism'—a radical, backward, and repressive version of Islam similar to the Saudi 'Wahhabi' credo but rejected by the vast majority of Muslims worldwide—is gaining adherents outside Afghanistan and spreading to other countries in the region."[23]

The Taliban enforced a stringent interpretation of the Islamic dress code for men as well. They were forced to grow beards and avoid Western haircuts or dress. The Taliban closed cinemas and banned music. Another Taliban decree ordered: "In shops, hotels, vehicles and rickshaws, cassettes and music are prohibited." If music or a cassette was found in a shop, "the shopkeeper should be imprisoned and the shop locked." The same was true if a cassette was found in a vehicle.[24] The Taliban also banned many forms of entertainment, such as television, videos, cards, kite-flying, and most sports. They punished theft by amputating a hand and often punished murder by public execution. Adulterers were stoned to death. In Kabul, punishments were carried out in front of crowds in the city's former soccer stadium. And yet there was no revolt. A Canadian intelligence assessment surmised that while the Taliban imposed a harsh form of *sharia* law, "residents of Taliban-administered areas have accepted these harsh policies as the price to be paid for peace and social stability."[25]

The Taliban also destroyed hundreds of cultural artifacts that were deemed polytheistic, including the holdings of major museums and countless private art collections. Perhaps the most appalling was the Taliban's destruction of the great statues of Buddha in the city of Bamiyan, roughly eighty miles west of Kabul. Bamiyan was once the center of Buddhism and an important resting place on the ancient Silk Road, which linked the Roman Empire with Central Asia, China, and India. Two magnificent statues, carved into a sandstone cliff face and surrounded by frescoes, dominated the approach to the town. One statue stood 165 feet high, the other 114 feet. In March 2001, Taliban fighters dynamited and fired rockets at the statues, which had stood for nearly 2,000 years and had withstood waves of invading armies. In one callous act, the Taliban destroyed one of Afghanistan's greatest archaeological treasures. Mullah Muhammad Omar defended these and other actions by saying they were carried out to protect the purity of Islam.[26] While in power, the Taliban massacred thousands of ethnic Hazaras, who are predominantly Shi'ite.

The Taliban's religious ideology was particularly apparent in Kabul, a city that most Taliban viewed as modern, implacably corrupt, and bubbling with apostasy. The Taliban banned women from work there, even though women ran one-fourth of Kabul's civil service, the entire elementary-education system, and much of the health system. Girls' schools and colleges in Kabul were closed down, affecting more than 70,000 students. On September 28, 1996, Radio Kabul announced: "Thieves will have their hands and feet amputated, adulterers will be stoned to death and those taking liquor will be lashed."[27] The Taliban appropriately gave Radio Kabul a new name, Radio Shariat, to reinforce the importance of *sharia* law.

Despite their religious zealotry, however, the drug trade flourished during the Taliban years. In 1997, approximately 96 percent of Afghan poppy had come from areas under the Taliban control. The Taliban expanded the area available for opium poppy production and increased trade and transport routes through neighboring countries, especially Pakistan.[28] "Opium is permissible," acknowledged Abdul Rashid, head of the Taliban's counter-narcotics force, "because it is consumed by *kafirs* [infidels] in the West and not by Afghans."[29] But the growing levels of poppy production caused some, including in the United States government, to protest. In 1998, a Taliban representative told U.S. officials that the drug trade was a "manageable problem" and that the Taliban would consider banning it once they "gained [international] recognition and a way was found to compensate poppy growers for their losses."[30]

In July 2000, Taliban leader Mullah Omar finally banned the cultivation of opium poppy, though not the trafficking from existing
stocks. The ban caused a temporary decrease in the cultivation of
opium poppy in 2001 and a significant rise in prices, but much of the
damage had already been done. During the Taliban rule, Afghanistan
had become the world's largest producer of poppy, the source of 70
percent of all illicit poppy.

ISI Support

Much like during the anti-Soviet jihad, Pakistani support to the Taliban was critical, especially that from the ISI. Throughout the 1990s,
Islamabad pursued a pro-Taliban policy. A 1997 cable from the U.S.
Embassy in Pakistan explained that, "for Pakistan, a Taliban-based
government in Kabul would be as good as it can get in Afghanistan,"
adding that worries that the "Taliban brand of Islam . . . might infect
Pakistan" was "apparently a problem for another day."[31] Another State
Department cable concluded: "Pakistan has followed a policy of supporting the Taliban."[32] Two staple Pakistani exports to the Taliban
were wheat and fuel, which the Taliban used to help feed their troops
and run their vehicles.[33] In 1998, the Pakistan government provided
more than $6 million in direct support to the Taliban in addition to
the regular trade with their neighbors.[34]

Pakistan's ISI also played a key role. U.S. State Department officials understood that "ISI is deeply involved in the Taleban take over
in Kandahar and Qalat."[35] ISI officers were deployed to such Afghan
cities as Herat, Kandahar, and Jalalabad—and stationed in Pakistani
consulates—to provide assistance and advice.[36] Another U.S. intelligence assessment contended that the ISI was "supplying the Taliban
forces with munitions, fuel, and food," and "using a private sector
transportation company to funnel supplies into Afghanistan and to
the Taliban forces."[37] Though the CIA knew about its involvement,
the ISI was often effective in masking its activity. For example, its
operatives utilized private-sector transportation companies to funnel

supplies in convoys to Taliban forces, including ammunition, petroleum, oil, lubricants, and food. These companies departed Pakistan late in the evening and, especially if they had weapons and ammunition aboard, they concealed the supplies beneath other goods loaded onto the trucks. There were several major supply routes. One began in Peshawar, Pakistan, and passed through Jalalabad in eastern Afghanistan on its way to Kabul. Another left Quetta and passed through Kandahar before ending in Kabul. Yet another began in Miramshah, Pakistan, and continued through Khowst and Gardez before entering the Afghan capital.[38]

Sultan Amir, Pakistan's consul general in Herat (better known by his nom de guerre of Colonel Imam), helped the Taliban take that city in 1995. "I had an emotional attachment with the Taliban," he later recalled. "They brought peace, they eradicated poppies, gave free education, medical treatment and speedy justice. They were the most respected people in Afghanistan."[39]

Thus, a pro-Taliban lobby came into being in Pakistan, run by retired officers (such as Aslam Beg) and current officers (such as Colonel Imam, Fazlur Rehman, Sami ul-Haq, and General Hamid Gul). General Gul, who was defense attaché at the Pakistan Embassy in Kabul, supervised the training of Taliban militants. A number of senior ISI officers, such as General Said Safar and General Irshad, worked closely with the Taliban in the field.[40] Pakistan's army and air force also cooperated with the Taliban. As one U.S. State Department cable concluded: "Pak Air Force officials are readying Kandahar airport for support of still larger military operations to include heavier fighting in Helmand and Kandahar." ISI leaders appeared to support the Taliban partly because they believed that mujahideen forces, such as Hekmatyar's Hezb-i-Islami, could not conquer and hold Kabul, while the Taliban apparently could.[41] In September 2000, barely a year before the September 11, 2001, attacks, Assistant Secretary of State Karl Inderfurth sent a particularly troubling "action cable" to the U.S. Embassy in Islamabad:

Pakistan is stepping up support to the Taliban's military campaign in Afghanistan. Department is particularly concerned by reports that Islamabad may allow the Taliban to use Pakistani territory to out-flank Northern Alliance positions in Afghanistan. While Pakistani support for the Taliban has been long standing, the magnitude of recent support is unprecedented. . . . We have seen reports that Pakistan is providing the Taliban with materiel, fuel, funding, techni-cal assistance, and military advisors. We also understand that large numbers of Pakistani nationals have recently moved into Afghanistan to fight for the Taliban, apparently with the tacit acquiescence of the Pakistani government. Our reports further suggest that direct Paki-stani involvement in Taliban military operations has increased in the past few months.[42]

Some U.S. government documents also contend that there was direct participation by the Pakistan government's Frontier Corps, whose members were mostly Pashtun and could blend in more easily with the Taliban. The Frontier Corps, a federal paramilitary force, is stationed in the North West Frontier Province and Baluchistan Prov-ince of Pakistan. Unlike the ISI, which is run through the Army, the Frontier Corps operates under Pakistan's Ministry of Interior, acting as the primary security force in these areas. "These Frontier Corps elements are utilized in command and control; training; and when necessary—combat," concluded one U.S. intelligence report. "Ele-ments of Pakistan's regular army force are not used because the army is predominantly Punjabi, who have different features as compared to the Pashtun and other Afghan tribes."[43]

A number of Pakistani citizens, as well as prominent journalists, told senior American officials that Pakistan was supporting the Tali-ban. In a June 30, 1998, meeting with U.S. Embassy staff and Arnold Schifferdecker, a political adviser at the UN Special Mission for Afghanistan, one journalist acknowledged that "he had recently can-vassed Pakistani government officials, including Ministry of Foreign Affairs and Inter-Services Intelligence Directorate sources, about the state of Pakistan's Afghan policy." According to a U.S. State Department cable that summarized the meeting, "what he heard surprised him: To a man the [Government of Pakistan] officials were strongly supportive of the Taliban." The journalist added that the Pakistan government's Coordination Committee for Afghan Policy "had decided to provide the Taliban 300 million rupees in the next six months at a rate of 50 million rupees a month," and that "the money was earmarked to pay for the salaries of Taliban officials and commanders."[44]

Despite the overwhelming evidence compiled by United States intelligence services, Pakistan officials repeatedly denied that the government provided support to the Taliban, as they would continue to do a decade later following the U.S. invasion and the rise of Afghanistan's insurgency. Even in private meetings with U.S. and UN officials, Pakistan officials denied their involvement.[45] In one meeting, for example, Pakistan Foreign Secretary Najamuddin Shaikh called in U.S. Ambassador to Pakistan Thomas Simons to "dispel any notion that Pakistan is throwing its chips in with the Taliban." Shaikh stressed that Pakistan's only focus was to help establish a peace settlement with Afghanistan's warring parties.[46] This duplicity had serious consequences for the U.S.-Pakistan relationship, since Washington's trust in Islamabad gradually waned. U.S. government documents also indicated that Pakistan's ISI had long supported Islamic terrorist organizations, which were used as proxies to target Indian forces in Kashmir. According to a CIA assessment, some of these groups, such as Harakat ul-Ansar, also used "terrorist tactics against Westerners and random attacks on civilians that could involve Westerners to promote its pan-Islamic agenda."[47]

A Fateful Bargain

By 2001, the Taliban controlled virtually all of Afghanistan. The only exception was a small sliver of land northeast of Kabul in the Panjshir Valley, where Ahmed Shah Massoud and his Northern Alliance forces had retreated. During the Taliban era, the Afghan Army was an assortment of armed groups with varying degrees of loyalties and professional skills.[48] Mullah Muhammad Omar, as head of the armed forces, ultimately decided on military strategies, key appointments, and military budgets. The military *shura* sat below Omar, helped plan strategy, and implemented tactical decisions. *Shura* in Arabic means "consultation," and it includes the ruler's duty according to *sharia*, to consult his followers in making decisions. It also refers to the assembly that meets for this purpose. Individual Taliban commanders were responsible for recruiting men, paying them, and looking after their needs in the field. They acquired much of the money, fuel, food, transport, and weapons from the military *shura*.

While it was a detestable regime that committed gross human-rights violations, the Taliban was successful in establishing law and order throughout most of Afghanistan. "On the plus side," acknowledged a U.S. State Department report, "the Taliban have restored security and a rough form of law and order in their areas of control."[49] It was a brutal form of justice, but it was governance nonetheless. In his book *Taliban*, Ahmed Rashid explained that opposition tribal groups "had been crushed and their leaders hanged, the heavily armed population had been disarmed and the roads were open to facilitate . . . trade between Pakistan, Afghanistan, Iran, and Central Asia."[50] By the end of the century, the Taliban controlled most of Afghanistan. A CIA assessment concluded: "There was no Pashtun opposition." Opposition groups "were totally disorganized, fragmented, disarmed by the Taliban."[51] A White House document composed in January 2001 remarked that "the Northern Alliance may be effectively taken out this Spring when fighting resumes after the winter thaw."[52] Massoud's forces were so weak that foreign governments—including the United States—were unwilling to back them in any meaningful way.[53]

But the Taliban had struck a dangerous bargain with Osama bin Laden and his international jihadist network. As a Taliban official explained to a U.S. State Department representative, the Taliban considered bin Laden a "great mujahid" and supported his residence in

Afghanistan.[54] It was a fateful mistake. Bin Laden used his money and influence to support the Taliban regime and, in return, trained jihadists and planned operations on Afghan soil.[55] If Mullah Omar had been willing to shy away from a relationship with bin Laden, the United States might have left the Taliban alone. Instead, Afghanistan became a nexus for the Taliban's radical Deobandism and al Qa'ida's global jihad.

CHAPTER FIVE

Al Qa'ida's Strategic Alliance

OSAMA BIN LADEN was fond of telling his students a parable, comparing the anti-Soviet War with the Christian assault against Mecca in 570 AD. The much-better-equipped Christian army employed war elephants, and their attack was fearsome enough to warrant mention in the Qur'an, appropriately enough in the chapter *Al-Fil* ("The Elephant"). The Christians tried to destroy the Ka'aba shrine in Mecca and divert pilgrims to a new cathedral in San'a, located in modern-day Yemen. But birds showered the invading Christian army with pellets of hard-baked clay, and the Arabs eventually defeated the invaders. To bin Laden and other al Qa'ida leaders, the episode exemplified that God would be on their side when they united against a common enemy.[1]

"In the training camps and on the battlefronts against the Russians," Ayman al-Zawahiri wrote in *Knights Under the Prophet's Banner*, "the Muslim youths developed a broad awareness and a fuller realization of the conspiracy that is being weaved" by Christians and Jews. They "developed an understanding based on shari'ah of the enemies of Islam, the renegades, and their collaborators."[2] The Afghan-Soviet War triggered an epiphany among these fighters, who had trekked to Afghanistan from Egypt, Saudi Arabia, the Palestinian territories, and other parts of the Arab world. Inspired by the defeat of the Soviet Union, they began to dream about internationalizing the jihad. The defeat had emboldened them, and many believed they were invincible.

"The USSR, a superpower with the largest land army in the world," Zawahiri wrote, "was destroyed and the remnants of its troops fled Afghanistan before the eyes of the Muslim youths and as a result of their actions."[3] Saudi Arabia was crucial to the jihad, as significant amounts of money from Saudi government officials and private donors poured into Pakistan and Afghanistan. But, no matter who funded the movement, no country in the Middle East was more important to the birth of al Qa'ida than Afghanistan.

Ideological Origins

In 1745, in Saudi Arabia, Muhammad ibn Saud allied with Muhammad ibn Abd al-Wahhab (1703–1792). Inspired by a number of scholars, such as Ibn Taymiyya (1263–1328), Wahhab criticized the virulent "superstitions" that had adulterated Islam's original purity. According to Wahhab's reading of the Qur'an, the Ottoman pilgrims who traveled across Saudi Arabia each year to pray at Mecca were not true Muslims. Rather, they were blasphemous polytheists who worshipped false idols. They were Allah's enemy, he said, and should be converted or eliminated. In its simplest form, Wahhab preached that the original grandeur of Islam could be regained only if the Islamic community would return to what he believed were the principles enunciated by the Prophet Muhammad.

The Saudis began to export Wahhabi philosophy by distributing money to build mosques. In the aftermath of the 1973 Arab-Israeli War, when the Arab oil-exporting nations declared an embargo on oil destined for Israel's Western allies, Saudi Arabia found itself in an enviable economic position. Its growing oil wealth could finance a wide-ranging proselytizing campaign among the Sunnis in the Middle East and in the broader Muslim world.[4]

The Soviet invasion of Afghanistan in 1979 came at an opportune time for the Saudis. Under the stewardship of Prince Turki al-Faisal, the head of Saudi intelligence, Saudi Arabia began active campaigns in

Pakistan and Afghanistan, working closely with the CIA and the ISI to fund the Afghan mujahideen.

One of Saudi Arabia's key facilitators in Afghanistan was Abdullah Azzam, a Palestinian from Jenin. Azzam was born in 1941 and studied *sharia* between 1959 and 1966, in Damascus, where he joined the Muslim Brotherhood. Over time, he became an inspiring organizer, leading one writer to call him the "Lenin of international jihad."[5] After completing his studies at Al-Azhar University in Cairo in 1973, Azzam became a professor of *sharia* at the University of Jordan, while supervising the university's youth sector for the Muslim Brotherhood. He was later evicted from his university post and moved to Jeddah in Saudi Arabia, where he taught at King Abdulaziz University. Osama bin Laden was one of his pupils.

In 1984, Azzam moved to Peshawar, a Pashtun city in Pakistan thirty miles from the Afghanistan border. A longtime stop on the ancient Silk Road, its bazaars have attracted visitors for centuries with their gold, silver, carpets, pottery, arms, and artwork in wood, brass, and semiprecious stones. It was here, at the age of forty-three, that Azzam founded the Maktab ul-Khadamat (Services Office), which coordinated support for the mujahideen with a range of nongovernmental organizations under the guise of the Red Crescent of Kuwait and Saudi Arabia. He said the cause he "had sought for so long was the cause of the Afghan people," and acted as the primary connection between the Arabs and Wahhabi interests in Saudi Arabia.[6]

Unlike some other radicals, Azzam was opposed to targeting Muslims and pro-Western regimes such as Egypt and Saudi Arabia. But he wrote that jihad in Afghanistan was a requirement for all good Muslims, an argument he made in his book *Defending the Land of the Muslims Is Each Man's Most Important Duty*. The novelty of Azzam's work lies not in its content, since other writers had called for jihad before. Rather, his success was in his skill as an agitator, able to convince Muslims from abroad to come to Afghanistan and fight. Saudi Arabia donated millions of dollars to Azzam's Services Office and provided a 75 percent discount on airline tickets for young Muslims who wished to join the jihad. In addition, Saudi Arabia became a ferrying port and station for Arab veterans and jihadis, such as Zawahiri, who were journeying to Peshawar on their way to Afghanistan.[7] Other countries, including the United States, also played a critical role. U.S. President Jimmy Carter was in favor of the mujahideen insurgency, arguing that the Soviet invasion of Afghanistan posed one of the most serious threats to peace since World War II.[8] Zbigniew Brzezinski, Carter's national security adviser, likewise noted that the "invasion of Afghanistan made it more important to mobilize Islamic resistance against the Soviets."[9]

The Afghan jihad became the great inspiration that brought Islamic radicals together. Muslim *ulemas* issued *fatwas* interpreting the Soviet intervention as an invasion of the territory of Islam by sinners. This made it possible to proclaim a "defensive" jihad, which, according to *sharia*, obliged every Muslim to participate.[10] These first-generation volunteers were mainly Arabs from various parts of the Middle East who had come to Afghanistan to fight the Soviet Union. Once they reached Afghanistan, the Services Office generally divided them into small groups that formed entire operational units in eastern Afghanistan, along the Pakistan border.[11] A report compiled for Osama bin Laden indicated that more than 2,300 foreign fighters "from eight Arab countries have died in the course of jihad in Afghanistan. Among these martyrs 433 were from Saudi Arabia, 526 from Egypt, 184 from Iraq, 284 from Libya, 180 from Syria, 540 from Algeria, 111 from Sudan and 100 from Tunisia."[12]

In the late 1980s, elite foreign fighters began to congregate in a camp near Khowst, Afghanistan, called Al-Maasada (The Lion's Den). Osama bin Laden was the leader of this group; he said he had been inspired to call the place Al-Maasada by lines from one of the Prophet's favorite poets, Hassan Ibn Thabit, who wrote:

> *Whoever wishes to hear the clash of swords,*
> *let him come to Maasada,*
> *where he will find courageous men ready to die*
> *for the sake of God.*[13]

The Russians attacked the Lion's Den in 1987, and bin Laden fled, along with a group that included Hassan Abdel Rab al-Saray, a Saudi who later carried out the November 1995 attack on a U.S. training center in Riyadh; Abu Zubayr Madani, who was killed in Bosnia in 1992; Ibn al-Khattab, who emerged later in Chechnya; and Sheikh Tamim Adnani, who lost a son when Abdullah Azzam was killed in November 1989.

Al Qa'ida emerged shortly thereafter. In August 1988, a group gathered in bin Laden's house in Peshawar to form a new organization, which they referred to as al-Qa'ida al-Askariya (The Military Base). They created an advisory council and membership requirements.[14] According to notes taken during the meeting by one of the participants, "al-Qa'ida is basically an organized Islamic faction, its goal is to live the word of God, to make His religion victorious." Al Qa'ida leaders separated their recruits into two components: those identified for "limited duration" would fight with Afghan mujahideen for the remainder of the war; those identified for "open duration" would be sent to a separate training camp and "the best brothers of them" would be chosen to join al Qa'ida. Members were expected to pledge loyalty to the leadership: "The pledge of God and His covenant is upon me, to listen and obey the superiors, who are doing this work, in energy, early-rising, difficulty, and easiness, and for His superiority upon us, so that the word of God will be the highest, and His religion victorious." They agreed that their goal would be "to lift the word of God, to make His religion victorious" across the Arab world through armed jihad. But members were urged to be patient, pious, and obedient, since the struggle would be long and challenging.[15]

In 1990, bin Laden responded to Iraq's invasion of Kuwait by offering Saudi Arabia his band of jihadists to protect the kingdom and turn back Saddam Hussein's army, which threatened Saudi Arabia. "I am ready to prepare one hundred thousand fighters with good combat capability within three months," bin Laden promised Prince Sultan, the Saudi minister of defense. "You don't need Americans. You don't need any other non-Muslim troops. We will be enough."[16] But the Saudi government instead turned to the United States, which led a coalition of roughly 700,000 soldiers that defeated the Iraqi military in just over a month. The deployment of U.S. soldiers to Saudi Arabia was a shock to bin Laden and a clarion call for his movement. The land of Mecca and the birthplace of the Prophet, Saudi Arabia was a symbolic and political oasis for Islamic radicals everywhere. To have non-Arabs on Saudi soil was an affront, but for the Americans to lead the military assault was a grievous transgression.

The Arabs Disperse

For bin Laden, Saudi Arabia's reputation was now severely compromised by its agreement with the Americans. A U.S. State Department intelligence report later reported: "Bin Laden's terrorism represents an extreme rejection of the increased U.S. strategic and military domination of the Middle East—especially Saudi Arabia and the Gulf—that resulted from the Gulf war."[17] In May 1991, a group of Saudi preachers and university professors, including Salman al-Auda and Safar al-Hawali, signed a petition (or *khitab al-matalib*) to King Fahd. They condemned the Saudi family for its pact with the infidel Americans and triggered a movement among some Islamic radicals to target the Saudi government.[18]

By this time, many of the Arabs had dispersed from Afghanistan to other countries, such as Bosnia, Algeria, and Egypt. In each location, they attempted to transform domestic conflict into jihad. But in Bosnia, for instance, they failed to make their radical interpretation of Islam a relevant component of the civil war. In other countries, such as Algeria, they were more successful for a limited period. Most Arab states viewed the veterans of Afghanistan as a serious threat—a kind of decentralized army of several thousand warriors in search of a place to fight and hide. Egypt, Saudi Arabia, Jordan, and others established border controls against al Qa'ida.[19] According to a CIA report, bin Laden also financed the travel of several hundred veterans of the

Afghan War to Sudan, "after Islamabad launched a crackdown against extremists lingering in Pakistan. In addition to savehaven [sic] in Sudan, Bin Ladin has provided financial support to militants actively opposed to moderate Islamic governments and the West."[20]

Those who remained in Afghanistan and Pakistan were initially scattered among a variety of groups. Some fought on the side of Gulbuddin Hekmatyar against Ahmed Shah Massoud, but the majority joined with local commanders, who were nearly all Pashtuns. In the Pashtun pocket around Kunduz in northern Afghanistan, there was a strong Arab presence in the Saudi-based International Islamic Relief Organization. In the midnineties, as the Taliban came to power, Pakistani organizations, such as the Harakat ul-Mujahidin, took control of a number of training camps for Pakistani militants in Afghanistan's Paktia Province. Other camps were run by Harakat ul-Ansar (HUA) and Lashkar-e-Jhangvi. The CIA believed that Harakat ul-Ansar—an Islamic extremist group used by Pakistan in its war against India in Kashmir—posed a particular threat to the United States: "Against the backdrop of possible declining support from Islamabad," one CIA analysis concluded, "the HUA is discussing financing with sponsors of international terrorism who are virulently anti-U.S. and may encourage attacks on U.S. targets. The HUA may be seeking this assistance from such sources—including terrorist financier Usama Bin Ladin and Libyan leader Mu'ammar Qadhafi—in an attempt to offset losses resulting from the drop in Pakistani support."[21]

Meanwhile, the Taliban entrusted to Osama bin Laden control of most non-Pakistani and non-Afghan militant groups. Bin Laden installed many of the senior Arab fighters in residential complexes near Jalalabad and Kandahar, including at the old USAID agriculture complex at Tarnak Farms, while the ordinary fighters were grouped together in cantonments in Kabul and Kunduz. The leaders were drawn almost entirely from the first generation of militants who had come to Afghanistan to fight the Russians.[22] Disputes sometimes emerged between the Afghans and Pakistanis on one side and the Arabs on the other. For example, they held different opinions about praying over the body of a fallen comrade, or visiting cemeteries and honoring the dead. Foreign fighters, particularly the Arabs, considered some of the Afghan religious practices sacrilegious and tried to show them "the correct Salafi way."[23]

In 1998, bin Laden formally announced the creation of a World Islamic Front for jihad against the "Crusaders"—meaning the West and specifically the Americans—and the Jews. Most of those who signed on were leaders of peripheral factions who were beholden to bin Laden for financial support. They included Ayman al-Zawahiri of Egyptian Islamic Jihad; Rifa'i Ahmad Taha (also known as Abu Yasir) of the Egyptian Islamic Group; Sheikh Mir Hamzah of the Jamiat Ulema-e-Pakistan; and Fazlur Rahman of the Jihad Movement in Bangladesh. The largest of these fringe movements was the Egyptian Islamic Group, but Taha did not speak for the jailed senior leadership of his group and was later forced to rescind his group's participation. Zawahiri also caused a split within his own Egyptian Islamic Jihad, some of whose members preferred to focus on Egypt rather than the United States.[24] Bin Laden even began to talk about using weapons of mass destruction against the United States. In 1998, the U.S. State Department had "reliable intelligence that the bin Laden network has been actively seeking to acquire weapons of mass destruction—including chemical weapons—for use against U.S. interests."[25]

Fighting on Multiple Fronts

Ayman al-Zawahiri and the rest of the al Qa'ida leadership were prepared for sustained struggle. In *Knights Under the Prophet's Banner*, Zawahiri called for a multifaceted battle to pursue three major goals. One was to overthrow "corrupt regimes" in the Muslim world. Another was to establish *sharia* in these lands. And a third was to inflict significant casualties on "the western crusader" and to "get crusaders out of the lands of Islam especially from Iraq, Afghanistan and Palestine."[26]

As with any movement, there were differences among al Qa'ida leaders and jihadists across the globe. For some, the United States should be a secondary, not a primary, target of military escalation. There had been some entropy in the jihadist movement by the end of the 1990s, as the regimes in Egypt, Algeria, and other Arab countries crushed their jihadist opponents.[27] There were also conflicts among al Qa'ida's national contingents. According to one of bin Laden's former bodyguards, "there were rivalries among Al-Qa'idah members depending on their countries of origin. The Egyptians used to boast about being Egyptian. The Saudis, Yemenis, Sudanese, and Arab Maghreb citizens used to do the same thing sometimes." This rivalry angered bin Laden, who argued that it sowed divisions and disagreements among al Qa'ida members.[28] Lastly, there were disagreements about money. Zawahiri himself acknowledged the shortage of funds in a note to al Qa'ida colleagues: "Conflicts take place between us for trivial reasons, due to scarcity of resources."[29]

Many of al Qa'ida's leaders were inspired by such influential individuals as Islamic scholar Sayyid Qutb, who was hanged in Egypt on August 29, 1966. Qutb argued that anything non-Islamic was evil, that only the strict following of *sharia* as a complete system of morality, justice, and governance would bring significant benefits to humanity.[30] Modern-day Islam, he wrote in his book *Milestones*, had also become corrupt, and he compared the modern Muslim states with *jahiliyya*. As used in the Qur'an, the term describes the state of ignorance in which Arabs were supposed to have lived before the revelation of Islam to the Prophet Muhammad at the beginning of the seventh century.[31] In two of his key works, *In the Shadow of the Qur'an* and *Signposts on the Road*, Qutb pleaded for contemporary Muslims to build a new Islamic community, much as the Prophet had done a thousand years earlier.[32] This meant that most Muslims could not be viewed as true Muslims.

In Islamic doctrine, denying a Muslim his faith is a serious accusation, referred to as *takfir*. The term derives from *kufr* (impiety) and means that one is impure and should therefore be excommunicated. For those who interpret Islamic law literally and rigorously, *takfir* is punishable by death. Qutb's philosophy allowed for no gray areas. The difference between true Muslims and non-Muslims was the same as between good vs. evil and just vs. unjust. According to his interpretation, the only just ruler is one who administers according to the Qur'an. There is no such thing as a defensive and limited war, he argued, there is only an offensive, total war.[33] Qutb's work found an eager readership among some of the younger generation in the 1970s because of its stunning and drastic break with the status quo. One problem, however, is that he never clearly specified what the Prophet's experience had been and how it should be replicated in the modern era.[34] After his execution, Qutb's fiery ideology gradually emerged as the blueprint for Islamic radicals from Morocco to Indonesia. It was later taught at King Abdulaziz University in Jeddah and Cairo's Al-Azhar University.[35]

According to Qutb, most leaders from Islamic governments were not true Muslims. "The Muslim community has long ago vanished from existence," he wrote. It was "crushed under the weight of those false laws and teachings which are not even remotely related to the Islamic teachings."[36] Like Qutb, Abdullah Azzam had argued that Islam's main challenge was against *jahiliyya*.[37]

In the minds of Qutb and the al Qa'ida leadership, any regime that did not impose *sharia* on the country and collaborated with Western governments such as the United States was guilty of apostasy. The Prophet argued that the blood of Muslims cannot be shed except in three instances: as punishment for murder, for marital infidelity, or for turning away from Islam. Zawahiri took this line of argument to its extreme, concluding that because regimes had departed from Islam and failed to establish *sharia* law, they were not truly Muslim countries and therefore subject to attack.[38] Indeed, even Muslims could be punished if they did not obey conservative Islamic law. Abdel Aziz bin Adel Salam (also known as al-Sayyid Imam), an Egyptian militant who was one of Zawahiri's oldest associates, argued that Muslims who did not join the fight against apostate rulers were themselves impious and must be fought.[39]

What constitutes sufficient justification for *takfir* has long been disputed among different schools of Islamic thought. The orthodox

Sunni position is that sins do not prove that someone is un-Islamic, but, rather, denials of fundamental religious principles do. Consequently, a murderer may still be a Muslim, but someone who denies that murder is a sin must be a *kafir*, as long as he or she is aware that murder is a sin in Islam. The irony, of course, is that while Islamists argued that Allah's law and rule must be made supreme, translating this into concrete political terms required human interpretation. There have long been deep and even violent differences among Islamists about how to do this.[40]

This internal confusion explains the motivations of al Qa'ida leaders to overthrow successive regimes in the Middle East (the "near" enemy, or *al-Adou al-Qareeb*) to establish a pan-Islamic caliphate, as well as to fight the United States and its allies (the "far" enemy, or *al-Adou al-Baeed*) who supported them.[41] As Zawahiri wrote, the "establishment of a Muslim state in the heart of the Islamic world is not an easy or close target. However, it is the hope of the Muslim nation to restore its fallen caliphate and regain its lost glory."[42] Zawahiri argued that "the issue of unification in Islam is important and that the battle between Islam and its enemies is primarily an ideological one over the issue of unification. . . . [it] is also a battle over to whom authority and power should belong—to God's course and shari'ah, to man-made laws and material principles, or to those who claim to be intermediaries between the Creator and mankind."[43]

Like many Islamists, Zawahiri drew heavily on the Salafist teachings of Ibn Taymiyya, the thirteenth-century reformer who had sought to impose a literal interpretation of the Qur'an, which serves as the basis of *sharia* and lays out the commandments of God. Al Qa'ida leaders raised the status of militant jihad and put it on a par with the five pillars of Islam. For instance, bin Laden argued that "fighting is part of our religion and our *sharia*. Those who love God and the Prophet and this religion may not deny a part of that religion. This is a very serious matter."[44] Bin Laden considered jihad an individual duty (*fard 'ayn*) and a critical pillar of Islam. In addition, many Islamists argued that *sharia* law cannot be improved upon, despite fifteen centuries of social change, because it came directly from God. They wanted to bypass the long tradition of judicial opinion from Muslim scholars and forge a legal system that was untainted by Western influence or modernity.[45] As al Qa'ida members chanted at one training camp in Afghanistan:

> We challenge with our Qur'an,
> We challenge with our Qur'an.
> Our men are in revolt, our men are in revolt.
> We will not regain our homeland,
> Nor will our shame be erased except through blood and fire.
> On and on and on it goes.
> On and on and on it goes.
> We defend our religion with blood, with blood.
> We defend our religion with blood, with blood.
> Our Qur'an is in our hands.[46]

Suicide operations could also be advantageous, even though the Qur'an prohibits suicide.[47] For some disillusioned bombers, martyrdom offered several attractions: honor and fame; the joys of seventy-two virgins; and paradise in "gardens of bliss" for seventy members of the suicide bomber's household, who might be spared the fires of hell.[48] Yet many Muslims, including in Afghanistan, believed that suicide attacks were never justified.[49] Zawahiri had to overcome this taboo. Suicide bombers, he claimed, represented "a generation of mujahideen that has decided to sacrifice itself and its property in the cause of God. That is because the way of death and martyrdom is a weapon that tyrants and their helpers, who worship their salaries instead of God, do not have."[50] In addition, Zawahiri regarded suicide bombing as effective: "Suicide operations are the most successful in inflicting damage on the opponent and the least costly in terms of casualties among the fundamentalists."[51]

The United States was the most significant "far" enemy. "The white man" in America is the primary enemy, Qutb wrote. "The white man crushes us underfoot while we teach our children about his civilization, his universal principles and noble objectives. . . . We are endowing our children with amazement and respect for the master who tramples our honor and enslaves us." The response to this enslavement, Qutb argued, had to be anger and violence. "Let us instead plant the seeds of hatred, disgust, and revenge in the souls of these children. Let us teach these children from the time their nails are soft that the white man is the enemy of humanity, and that they should destroy him at the first opportunity."[52]

Most jihadist leaders had long advocated attacking Arab regimes, not the United States or other Western regimes. Zawahiri had made this point in his 1995 essay "The Road to Jerusalem Goes through Cairo," published in *al-Mujahidin*.[53] But after their defeat in Egypt, Algeria, and other Arab countries in the 1990s, jihadists began to focus on the West. For such leaders as Zawahiri, then, the United States only knew "the language of interests backed by brute military force. Therefore, if we wish to have a dialogue with them and make them aware of our rights, we must talk to them in the language they understand." This language was violence and force.[54] Osama bin Laden repeated this message regularly. On the eve of the sixth anniversary of the September 11 attacks, for example, he released a video clip in which he said that the goal of the United States was to wipe out Islam across the globe, and that he was left with no other recourse than to "continue to escalate the killing and fighting against you."[55]

The United States, and the West more broadly, was a corrupting influence on Islam. For Abdullah Azzam, this meant "expelling the Kuffar [infidels] from our land, and it is Fard Ayn, a compulsory duty upon all."[56] In an article in *Jihad* magazine, Azzam wrote that "jihad in God's will means killing the infidels in the name of God and raising the banner of His name."[57] This was especially true when Western or other non-Muslim armies invaded Islamic lands such as Afghanistan.

Al Qa'ida leaders also accused the United States of propping up apostate Arab countries. Consequently, in order to reestablish the Caliphate, al Qa'ida had to target these countries' primary backers.[58] The conflict with the United States, then, was a "battle of ideologies, a struggle for survival, and a war with no truce."[59] This language was remarkably similar to Harvard University Professor Samuel Hunting-ton's argument in *The Clash of Civilizations and the Remaking of World Order*. Of particular concern, Huntington argued, was a growing rift between the Judeo-Christian West and Islamic countries, which was becoming pronounced and violent.[60] In an early publication, *Loyalty to Islam and Disavowal to its Enemies*, Zawahiri argued that Muslims must make a choice between Islam and its enemies, including the West.[61] In *Knights Under the Prophet's Banner*, Zawahiri similarly wrote that the overthrow of governments in such countries as Egypt would become a rallying point for the rest of the Islamic world, leading it in a jihad against the West. "Then history would make a new turn, God willing," he noted, "in the opposite direction against the empire of the United States and the world's Jewish government."[62] In his mind, and in the minds of several of his followers, the United States was pri-marily interested in "removing Islam from power."[63]

In the early 1990s, the Saudi government's decision to allow U.S. military forces on its soil following Iraq's invasion of Kuwait had been a major blow to the jihadists. In the late 1990s, Osama bin Laden's statements began to legitimize violence against the United States. In August 1996, bin Laden issued the *Declaration of Jihad against the Amer-icans Occupying the Land of the Two Holy Places*. This long-winded eleven-page tract was crammed with quotations from the Qur'an, *hadiths* of the Prophet, and references to Ibn Taymiyya. Then, in February 1998, bin Laden, Zawahiri, and others published a *fatwa* to kill Americans: "The ruling to kill the Americans and their allies—civilians and military—is an individual duty for every Muslim who can do it in any country in which it is possible to do it, in order to liberate the al-Aqsa Mosque and the holy mosque [Mecca] from their grip, and in order for their armies to move out of all the lands of Islam, defeated and unable to threaten any Muslim."[64] The *fatwa* cited three main grievances against the United States. One was the presence of Ameri-can troops in the Arabian Peninsula, the second was America's inten-tion to destroy the Muslim people of Iraq through sanctions, and the third was the U.S. goal of incapacitating the Arab states and propping up Israel. Bin Laden accused the United States of plundering Muslim riches, dictating to its rulers, humiliating its people, terrorizing its neighbors, and turning U.S. bases into a spearhead through which to fight the neighboring Muslim peoples.

A Dangerous Alliance

Of particular concern to U.S. policymakers in the late 1990s was the growing collaboration between al Qa'ida and the Taliban. In response to bin Laden's involvement in the August 1998 attacks against the U.S. embassies in Tanzania and Kenya, the Clinton administration launched a series of cruise-missile strikes against al Qa'ida bases in eastern Afghanistan. But some classified U.S. assessments suggest that the attacks brought al Qa'ida and the Taliban closer together.[65] One State Department cable reported: "Taliban leader Mullah Omar lashed out at the U.S., asserting that the Taliban will continue to provide a safe haven to bin Laden."[66] After all, bin Laden sometimes stayed at Mullah Omar's residence in Kandahar.[67]

In July 1999, U.S. President Bill Clinton issued Executive Order 13129, which found that "the actions and policies of the Taliban in Afghanistan, in allowing territory under its control in Afghanistan to be used as a safe haven and base of operations for Usama bin Ladin and the Al-Qa'ida organization . . . constitute an unusual and extraordinary threat to the national security and foreign policy of the United States."[68] The Taliban's military structure included al Qa'ida members such as the elite Brigade 055, which consisted of foreign fighters.[69] The Taliban's alliance with al Qa'ida took a toll on its relations with several countries, especially Saudi Arabia, which had initially provided support to the Taliban through its intelligence service.[70]

Now that the United States had formally denounced al Qa'ida and, by extension, the Taliban, Saudi officials felt compelled to act. Bin Laden's involvement in the August 1998 embassy attacks, as well as his derisive statements against Saudi officials, required an urgent response. On September 19, 1998, Saudi intelligence chief Prince

Turki al-Faisal met with with Taliban leader Mullah Muhammad
Omar. The meeting began with a brief discussion about the strain
between the Taliban and Iran. Turki argued that the Taliban should
take steps to defuse the tensions, then he turned to the main topic of
the meeting: to ask the Taliban to surrender Osama bin Laden. Mullah Omar replied that the Taliban had no intention of surrendering
bin Laden or any other Arabs to the Saudi government. Omar then
questioned the legitimacy of a Saudi government that would allow
U.S. troops to be stationed in the Persian Gulf. According to U.S.
State Department accounts of the meeting, he then argued that "the
Saudi government had no business interfering in Afghan matters since
the whole Muslim 'ummah' (international community) was in the
process of rising against [the Saudi government] because of its failed
stewardship of the two holy sites."[71]

Turki's response was swift and forceful. He returned to Riyadh and
cut off all Saudi ties with the Taliban. As a State Department cable
explained, the Saudi government was even successful "in preventing
private Saudi sources, including foundations, from dispersing money
to the Taliban as they did in the past."[72] The Taliban-Saudi break angered
a number of Taliban leaders, such as deputy leader Mullah Rabbani,
who had pro-Saudi views. But neither the Saudis nor the Americans
could derail al Qa'ida. In January 2001, eight months before the September 11 attacks, counterterrorism coordinator Richard Clarke
wrote a classified memo to National Security Adviser Condoleezza
Rice: "We urgently need . . . a Principals level review of the al Qida
network." He continued by pleading, "As we noted in our briefings for
you, al Qida is not some narrow little terrorist issue that needs to be
included in broader regional policy." What was required, Clarke
argued, was "a comprehensive multi-regional policy on al Qida."[73]

Al Qa'ida had evolved from a myth to a reality. Indeed, its reputation had grown out of a fabrication that its early disciples had fever-
ishly propagated across the Arab world. Arab jihadists, they claimed,
played a critical role in defeating the Soviets in Afghanistan. "The
USSR, a superpower with the largest land army in the world," Zawa-

hiri alleged, "was destroyed and the remnants of its troops fled Afghanistan before the eyes of the Muslim youths and as a result of their actions . . . Osama bin Laden has apprised me of the size of the popular Arab support for the Afghan mujahideen that amounted, according to his sources, to $200 million in the form of military aid alone in 10 years."[74]

But this self-aggrandizement was unwarranted. Though it is a common theme in al Qa'ida lore, the contributions of Osama bin Laden, Ayman al-Zawahiri, and other Arabs were negligible to the Soviet defeat. Mohammad Yousaf, head of the ISI's Afghanistan bureau that trained the mujahideen against the Soviets, doesn't even discuss the Arab jihadists in his account of the Soviet defeat.[75] As Lawrence Wright explained in his book *The Looming Tower*, "the presence of several thousand Arabs—and rarely more than a few hundred of them actually on the field of battle—made no real difference in the tide of affairs."[76] The Afghan mujahideen would have won with or without their help, thanks in large part to the astronomical amount of arms, money, and other assistance provided by the governments of Pakistan, the United States, and Saudi Arabia.[77]

In some respects, this al Qa'ida myth was probably irrelevant. What mattered was that some people—especially its own members—believed it. By 2001, al Qa'ida had evolved into a competent international terrorist organization that had conducted bold attacks against the United States in Tanzania, Kenya, and Yemen. Its goals were compatible with the Taliban's ideology. Richard Clarke's January 2001 memo to Condoleezza Rice asserted that al Qa'ida's objective was to "replace moderate, modern, Western regimes in Muslim countries with theocracies modeled along the lines of the Taliban."[78] From its base in Afghanistan, al Qa'ida also planned the September 11, 2001, attacks in the United States.

CHAPTER SIX

Operation Enduring Freedom

THE MORNING OF September 11, 2001, began like many others for Zalmay Khalilzad, who was serving as a special assistant to President George W. Bush at the National Security Council. He was sitting in a meeting run by National Security Adviser Condoleezza Rice in the White House Situation Room when the first hijacked plane flew into the north tower of the World Trade Center, tearing a gaping hole in the building and setting it afire. "There was a TV screen hanging in a corner of the room," he told *The New Yorker*. "When the first plane hit, we had a sense that, oh, maybe it had lost its way. As soon as the second plane hit, the meeting was called to an end and she rushed away. We went outside the White House to Pennsylvania Avenue and waited awhile till we got the all-clear sign. While we were out, there had been all sorts of rumors and reports, that Capitol Hill had been hit, and the Pentagon, obviously, had been hit. Then we started to look at the intelligence. I started looking at Afghanistan, tracing al Qa'ida."[1]

The September 11 attacks opened another chapter in Afghanistan's age of insurgency. Unbeknownst to most Americans, however, the struggle for Afghanistan had already begun. On September 9, 2001, two al Qa'ida terrorists, Dahmane Abd al-Sattar and Bouraoui el-Ouaer, had assassinated Northern Alliance military commander Ahmed Shah Massoud in Afghanistan. Posing as Belgian journalists, they had been granted an interview with Massoud in his bungalow near the Tajikistan border. After setting up their equipment, Bouraoui detonated explosives concealed in his camera, riddling Massoud with shrapnel. Massoud died shortly thereafter, along with one of his assistants, Muhammad Asim Suhail, weakening the already frail Northern Alliance.

U.S. policymakers planning the response to the September 11 attacks a few days later, which they named Operation Enduring Freedom, realized the gravity of this action: the charismatic military commander they most needed to overthrow the Taliban was dead. The situation required an unconventional approach, and the CIA and the Pentagon scrambled to make plans.[2]

History Begins Today

One of the first challenges, however, was securing Pakistan's cooperation. Pakistan's strategic location next to Afghanistan and its government's involvement there since the Soviet invasion made it a key player. But the newly appointed U.S. ambassador to Pakistan, Wendy Chamberlin, had arrived in Pakistan "expecting to spend most of [her] time dealing with a humanitarian crisis unfolding in the region." A severe drought and famine in Afghanistan had caused refugees to flee to Pakistan, which was perhaps the most important domestic issue that summer.[3] But the September 11 attacks changed everything.

A few weeks before the attacks, Chamberlin had a private dinner with President Pervez Musharraf at the house of Mahmud Ali Durrani, who would later become the Pakistani ambassador to the United States. "My vision of the country hinges on increasing foreign investment in Pakistan and economic growth," Musharraf told Chamberlin. "But," he continued, "the level of domestic terrorism is currently too high," making it difficult to bring in outside capital. Musharraf also told her: "Pakistan needs strategic depth in Afghanistan to ensure that there is a friendly regime on Pakistan's western border."[4] The timing was ironic. In less than a month, the United States would ask Musharraf to overthrow the very Taliban government that the ISI had painstakingly supported for nearly a decade, which meant putting his "strategic depth" in jeopardy.

On September 11, just hours after the attacks, Deputy Secretary of State Richard Armitage met with the head of the ISI, Lieutenant General Mahmoud Ahmed, who was visiting Washington. Armitage delivered a stern message: Pakistan's leaders had to choose between the United States or the terrorists; there was no middle ground. "No American will want to have anything to do with Pakistan in our moment of peril if you're not with us," Armitage told him. "It's black or white." When Ahmed began to waver, pleading that Armitage had to understand history, Armitage cut him off. "No," he replied, "the history begins today."[5] Armitage is an imposing figure. Barrel-chested, with broad shoulders and a thick neck, he had recently told President Bush he was still bench-pressing "330/6," which meant six repetitions of 330 pounds each. It was down from a few years earlier, he remarked, when he had been bench-pressing 440 pounds.[6]

On September 12, Ambassador Chamberlin received State Department instructions to see President Musharraf in Islamabad and ask him a simple question: "Are you with us or against us?" The meeting, which took place the next day in one of Musharraf's Islamabad offices, was tense. America was reeling from the terrorist attacks, and President Bush wanted a quick answer from Musharraf. After an hour, there had been little progress. Musharraf was waffling in his commitment to the United States, so Chamberlin resorted to a bit of drama. Sitting close to him, she half turned away and looked down at the floor in a display of exasperation. "What's wrong, Wendy?" he asked. "Frankly, General Musharraf," she responded, "you are not giving me the answer I need to give my president." Almost without hesitation, Musharraf then replied, "We'll support you unstintingly."[7]

They agreed to discuss further details on September 15. Chamberlin presented a series of discussion points, such as stopping al Qa'ida operatives at the Pakistan border; providing blanket U.S. overflight and landing rights in Pakistan; ensuring U.S. access to Pakistani military bases; providing intelligence and immigration information; and cutting off all fuel shipments to the Taliban. A final request was bound to be controversial, as Secretary of State Colin Powell professed to Armitage: "Should the evidence strongly implicate Osama bin Laden and the al Qa'ida network in Afghanistan and should Afghanistan and the Taliban continue to harbor him and his network, Pakistan will break diplomatic relations with the Taliban government, end support for the Taliban and assist us in the aforementioned ways to destroy Osama bin Laden and his al Qa'ida network."[8]

Musharraf had his own negotiating points. "He wanted us to pressure the Indians to resolve the Kashmir dispute in favor of Pakistan," noted Chamberlin. "Even without instructions from Washington, I said no immediately, explaining to Musharraf that this was about the terrorists who attacked America on our soil and not about Kashmir."[9] He also asked that U.S. aircraft not use bases in India for their operations in Afghanistan, to which Chamberlin agreed. Musharraf clearly was interested in using his bargaining position to gain leverage over India. In the end, Musharraf agreed to most of America's requests, though he refused to allow blanket U.S. overflight and landing rights, or access to many of Pakistan's naval ports and air bases. And the United States agreed to many of Musharraf's requests. U.S. aircraft could not fly over Pakistani nuclear facilities, the United States could not launch attacks in Afghanistan from Pakistani soil, and the United States would provide economic assistance to Pakistan.

Musharraf's support was pivotal for America's initial success in Afghanistan. "Pakistan was very cooperative," Chamberlin stated. "Their support was critical."[10]

Jawbreaker

With Pakistan's collaboration ensured, the United States could now turn more assuredly to planning combat operations in Afghanistan. On September 13, CIA Director George Tenet had briefed President George W. Bush on the agency's plan for conducting operations in

Afghanistan. He and his counterterrorism chief, Cofer Black, out-lined for Bush a strategy that merged CIA paramilitary teams, U.S. Special Operations Forces, and airpower into an elaborate and lethal package to bring down the Taliban regime.

"Mr. President," Black noted at the briefing, staring intently at Bush, "we can do this. No doubt in my mind. We do this the way that we've outlined it, we'll set this thing up so it's an unfair fight for the U.S. military."

"But you've got to understand," he continued, choosing his words carefully, "people are going to die."[11]

Two days later, at Camp David, Tenet explained that the plan "stressed one thing: we would be the insurgents. Working closely with military Special Forces, CIA teams would be the ones using speed and agility to dislodge an emplaced foe."[12]

General Tommy Franks, head of U.S. Central Command, also began working on war plans. On September 20, 2001, Franks arrived at the Pentagon from Tampa, Florida, to brief Secretary of Defense Donald Rumsfeld, Deputy Secretary of Defense Paul Wolfowitz, and the Joint Chiefs of Staff on his plan for invading Afghanistan. Wolfo-witz outlined his views in a classified September 23 paper for Rums-feld entitled "Using Special Forces on 'Our Side' of the Line." He argued that U.S. Army Special Forces should be used on the ground with Northern Alliance forces to help direct U.S. air attacks, gather intelligence, and help deliver humanitarian aid where needed. Wol-fowitz, well aware of the Soviet experience in Afghanistan in the 1980s, was concerned that the United States would fall into the same trap.[13] The thinking was that the blending of U.S. and Afghan forces would limit American exposure in Afghanistan.

A CIA team led by Gary Schroen, appropriately code-named Jaw-breaker, landed in the Panjshir Valley in northeastern Afghanistan on September 26, 2001, only two weeks after the attacks on the United States. The team was part of the agency's Special Activities Division, the paramilitary arm of the CIA. At the time, it had no more than a few hundred officers with both classic intelligence and special operations backgrounds. Schroen and his team were soon joined on the ground by several U.S. Special Operations Forces A-teams, including operational detachment alpha (ODA) 555, known as "Triple Nickel." These forces worked with local Afghan commanders and provided arms, equipment, and military advice, as well as coordinated U.S. airstrikes.

They also provided money to buy—or at least rent—the loyalty of local commanders and their militia forces. Schroen once frankly acknowledged, "Money is the lubricant that makes things happen in Afghanistan."[14]

Overthrow of the Taliban Regime

The U.S. bombing campaign began the night of October 7, 2001. The initial objective was to destroy the Taliban's limited air-defense and communications infrastructure. American and British Special Operations teams had been conducting scouting missions in Afghanistan. Some of the first major combat actions of the war occurred in the mountains near Mazar-e-Sharif, as the teams working with Northern Alliance Generals Abdul Rashid Dostum and Atta Muhammad fought their way north up the Dar-ye Suf and Balkh River Valleys toward the northern city.[15]

The terrain and conditions were unlike anything the Americans had ever seen. They found themselves traversing steep mountain paths next to thousand-foot precipices. Since even four-wheel-drive vehicles couldn't effectively maneuver on the winding mountain trails, military and intelligence forces used Afghan horses to haul their equipment. Many of the Americans had never been on a horse before. Because of the sheer drop-offs, they were told to keep one foot out of the stirrups so that if the horse stumbled, they would fall onto the trail as the horse slid off the cliff. In especially steep areas, U.S. forces were prepared to shoot any stumbling horse before it could drag its rider to his death.[16] Mike DeLong, deputy commander of U.S. Central Command, captured the novelty of the situation appropriately, if a bit sarcastically:

> After a day or two of riding, our troops were terribly saddle sore, to the point of serious disability. To ease the friction, we sent in a hundred jars of Vaseline. But in Afghanistan the dirt is a fine dust and it's everywhere; it lingers in the air and covers you from head to foot. This fine dust collected on the Vaseline; instead of helping, it converted the Vaseline into sandpaper. Now their legs were being cut up. What they really needed were chaps, like cowboys wear. But there wasn't time to measure them for chaps. So we decided on pantyhose. We sent over two hundred pairs. If it worked for Joe Namath in Super Bowl '69, why not for our troops? Lo and behold, it worked like a charm. The pantyhose saved the day.[17]

The first forays against the Taliban were in northern Afghanistan because Tajik and Uzbek opposition to the Pashtun regime was strongest there. Dostum's forces took the village of Bishqab on October 21. Engagements followed at Cobaki on October 22, Chapchal on October 23, and Oimetan on October 25. On November 5, Dostum's cavalry overran Taliban forces occupying old Soviet-built defensive posts in the hamlet of Bai Beche. Atta Muhammad's forces then captured Ac'capruk on the Balkh River, finally opening the door for a rapid advance to Mazar-e-Sharif, which fell to Atta Muhammad's and Dostum's forces on November 10, 2001.[18]

The fall of Mazar-e-Sharif unhinged the Taliban position in northern Afghanistan. Taliban defenders near Bamiyan in central Afghanistan briefly resisted before surrendering on November 11, and Kabul fell without a fight on November 13. The Taliban collapse was remarkable. Only two months after the September 11 attacks, the most strategically important city in Afghanistan—Kabul—had been conquered.

American and Afghan forces then encircled a force of some 5,000 Taliban and al Qa'ida survivors in the city of Kunduz; following a twelve-day siege, they surrendered on November 26.[19] With the fall of Kabul and Kunduz, attention shifted to the Taliban's stronghold of

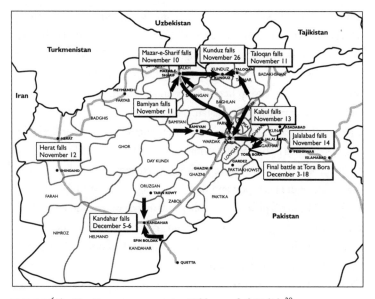

FIGURE 6.1   Key Engagements against Taliban and al Qa'ida[20]

Kandahar in the south. Special Operations Forces in support of
Hamid Karzai advanced on Kandahar City from the north. Born in
Kandahar in 1957, Karzai was the fourth of eight children. His
father, Abdul Ahad Karzai, served as chief of the Popalzai tribe until
he was assassinated in 1999 by "agents of the Taliban." Karzai's childhood was rather unremarkable. He went to high school in Kabul and
attended graduate school in India before joining the mujahideen
during the Soviet War. He spent the Taliban years in Pakistan, but
several weeks before the September 11 attacks he had received an
ultimatum from the ISI to leave the country by September 30. As
chief of the Popalzai tribe, centered on Kandahar Province, Karzai
brought with him the support of one of Afghanistan's most powerful
southern tribes. And he was catapulted to prominence for his actions
in the U.S.-led Coalition.[21]

In addition to Karzai's troops, Special Operations Forces in support
of Gul Agha Shirzai—nicknamed "Bulldozer" for his coercive tactics—

advanced from the south. The first clashes occurred in late November at Tarin Kowt and Sayed Slim Kalay, just north of the city. There were also several skirmishes along Highway 4 south of Kandahar from December 2 to 6. On the night of December 6, Mullah Omar and the senior Taliban leadership fled the city and went into hiding, effectively ending Taliban rule in Afghanistan.[22] Allied forces subsequently tracked a group of al Qa'ida survivors, thought to include Osama bin Laden, to a series of caves in the White Mountains near Tora Bora. The caves were taken in a sixteen-day battle ending on December 17, but many al Qa'ida defenders escaped and fled across the border into Pakistan.[23]

As the Taliban's power base collapsed, international and local attention turned to nation-building and reconstruction. The United Nations had helped organize a meeting of Afghan political leaders in Bonn, Germany, in late November 2001. On December 5, with Coalition troops about to overtake Kandahar, Afghan leaders signed an agreement that established a timetable for the creation of a representative and freely elected government. The following day, the UN Security Council endorsed the outcome in Resolution 1383.[24] Under the Bonn Agreement, the parties agreed to establish an interim authority comprising three main bodies: a thirty-member acting administration headed by Hamid Karzai, a Pashtun, which took power on December 22; a supreme court; and the Special Independent Commission for the Convening of the Emergency Loya Jirga (a traditional meeting of Afghan tribal, political, and religious leaders).

The capture of Kabul and other cities by U.S. and Afghan forces pushed surviving fighters east toward the Pakistan border. In January and February 2002, the U.S. military and the CIA began to collect intelligence about a concentration of a thousand or so holdouts from al Qa'ida, the Islamic Movement of Uzbekistan, the Taliban, and other groups in the Shah-i-kot Valley and surrounding mountains east of Gardez. A combined offensive by Afghan, U.S., and other Western forces, code-named Operation Anaconda, aimed to take out this threat. The operation began on March 2, 2002, and continued through March 16. The group, truly reflecting the U.S.-led Coalition, com-

prised U.S. forces from the 101st Airborne Division and 10th Mountain Division. Special Operations Forces from the United States,
Australia, Canada, Denmark, Germany, France, and Norway were
also involved in the operation.[25]

The fighting was intense. Insurgent fighters were equipped with
sniper rifles, machine guns, recoilless rifles, rocket-propelled grenades, and man-portable air defenses (MANPADS). The rugged,
mountainous terrain offered excellent concealment for enemy fighters, who scattered in small teams and hid in caves and along steep
ridgelines. It was virtually impossible for Coalition forces to sur-
round and seal off the area, or even to target insurgents from the
B-52s and AC-130 Spectre gunships circling overhead. An al Qa'ida
manual recovered during the operation, titled *The Black Book of Mountainous Operations and Training*, outlined the utility of rugged terrain
for defeating larger forces.

U.S. and allied forces eventually cleared the valley of al Qa'ida and
other fighters, but not without a price. The insurgents shot down two
Chinook helicopters using rocket-propelled grenades, eight U.S. soldiers were killed, and approximately eighty were wounded. Coalition
forces killed a number of fighters, though few bodies were ever found.
Hundreds more fled to Pakistan.

Escape to Pakistan

Pakistan's help in overthrowing the Taliban regime had catapulted
Pervez Musharraf to stardom. "Musharraf became an international
hero," remarked Ambassador Chamberlin. "Money was flowing into
Pakistan. And Pakistan was no longer a pariah state. The situation was
euphoric. Musharraf was on the cover of every magazine and newspaper."[26] But despite these promising developments, peace and stability were fleeting. There was a worrisome exodus of fighters from
Afghanistan to Pakistan, as well as disturbing new wrinkles in the
complex web of alliances among the Taliban, al Qa'ida fighters, and
the Pakistani military.

"The movement of Taliban and al Qa'ida fighters into Pakistan came in waves," recalled Robert Grenier, the CIA's station chief in Islamabad following the September 2001 attacks.[27] A polished operator, always impeccably dressed, Grenier was also a passionate Boston Red Sox fan who had received a bachelor's degree in philosophy from Dartmouth College. He served a distinguished twenty-seven-year career in the CIA, including a stint as chief of "The Farm," the CIA's basic-training facility, where he was responsible for guiding and preparing all officers entering the CIA's clandestine service. From his perch in Islamabad, he monitored the exodus of insurgents from Afghanistan into Pakistan.

In December 2001, after the fall of Kabul and Kandahar, a large contingent of Taliban leaders escaped into Pakistan's Baluchistan Province, among them Mullah Omar. According to the chief of targeting operations for U.S. Central Command at the time, "we conducted several strikes against Mullah Omar in late 2001, none of which were successful."[28] In November, for example, U.S. forces targeted a qanat (underground tunnel) in Kandahar where they had intelligence that he was hiding. In Afghanistan, water is often drawn from springs and rivers and distributed through these qanats, which are excavated and maintained via a series of vertical shafts. U.S. Navy planes initially missed the target with several 2,000-pound general-purpose guided bomb unit-10s (GBU-10). But a subsequent U.S. Air Force strike hit the qanat with a guided bomb unit-28 (GBU-28), a 5,000-pound laser-guided conventional weapon often called a "bunker buster," with a 4,400-pound penetrating warhead. The GBU-28 collapsed the tunnel, but it did not kill Mullah Omar.

Mullah Omar eventually arrived in Pakistan, and some speculated that he did so on a Honda motorcycle. As President Musharraf quipped to Japanese Prime Minister Junichiro Koizumi, "the best advertisement for Honda would be an advertising campaign showing Mullah Omar fleeing on one of its motorcycles with his robes and beard flowing in the wind."[29]

Al Qa'ida fighters, including Osama bin Laden, escaped across the

Pakistani border en masse. In November 2001, in one of his last public appearances, bin Laden gave a stirring homily to a gathering of local tribal leaders at the Islamic Studies Center in Jalalabad. He promised that they could teach the Americans "a lesson, the same one we taught the Russians." He was dressed in a gray *shalwar kameez*, the long shirt and loose trousers worn by most Afghans, and a camouflage jacket. According to some accounts, he distributed cash to the tribal leaders to ensure their support, while many in the crowd shouted "*Zindibad* [Long live] Osama."[30] American intelligence officials believe that over the next few weeks nearly 1,000 al Qa'ida fighters escaped through Tora Bora and other areas along the Afghanistan-Pakistan border.

"You've got to give him credit," noted the CIA's Gary Schroen. "He stayed in Tora Bora until the bitter end."[31]

In mid-December 2001, according to some American intelligence estimates, bin Laden left Tora Bora for the last time, accompanied by a handful of bodyguards and aides. CIA forces on the ground repeatedly requested an additional battalion of U.S. Army Rangers to block bin Laden's escape, but the U.S. military relied on local Afghan forces. Some reports indicate that bin Laden paid Afghans to let him through.[32] According to one Pakistani military assessment, the fighters "hid in urban areas and mingled with the local populace by maintaining a relatively low profile."[33] While al Qa'ida leaders dispersed via a number of different routes, bin Laden journeyed on horseback south toward Pakistan, crossing through the same mountain passes through which the CIA's convoys passed during the mujahideen years. Along the route, in the dozens of villages and towns on both sides of the frontier, Pashtun tribes allied with the Taliban helped guide the horsemen as they trekked through the hard-packed snow and on toward the old Pakistani military outpost of Parachinar. The CIA later learned that a "group of two hundred Saudis and Yemenis . . . was guided by members of the Pushtun Ghilzai tribe, who were paid handsomely in money and rifles."[34]

Pakistan's Frontier Corps, the paramilitary force in the border regions, picked up some of the fighters streaming across the border.

Al Qa'ida and foreign fighters were turned over to the ISI, and many were handed over to the U.S. government, which housed them temporarily in secret prisons in Kandahar, Bagram, and other locations. Al Qa'ida operatives relied on links with Pakistani militant groups, such as Lashkar-e-Taiba (Army of the Pure), in cities such as Lahore and Faisalabad, to hide from Pakistan and U.S. intelligence services. They didn't want to remain in Pakistan, however, because the government was cooperating with the United States. According to CIA assessments, most of the al Qa'ida and foreign fighters were trying to get to Iran, where they could temporarily settle or transit to other areas, such as the Persian Gulf.

By 2002 and 2003, though, the CIA began to gather intelligence indicating that al Qa'ida operatives were increasingly infiltrating back into Pakistan's tribal areas. Many went to remote locations, such as the Shakai Valley in South Waziristan, hoping the Pakistani government would leave them alone to resettle among some of the local tribes. Sporadic Pakistani military operations in South Waziristan triggered an exodus of militants to North Waziristan. "It was harder for Pakistan government forces to get to them there," said Grenier. "The social structure was more hospitable, and there was a heavier influence of mullahs and religious clerics."[35]

An Ideal Sanctuary

Over the next several years, these extremists used Pakistan's northern Baluchistan Province, the Federally Administered Tribal Areas, and the North West Frontier Province as sanctuaries to rest and rearm. Sanctuary was critical for all major groups that targeted NATO forces and the Afghan government. "The Taliban was a flourishing dynamic network," according to a joint European Union and United Nations document, "which relied on a strong and unchallenged support and recruitment base in Pakistan."[36] In past insurgencies, border areas and neighboring countries have often been exploited by militants. Groups can plot, recruit, proselytize, contact supporters around the world, raise money, and enjoy a respite from the government's efforts, enabling operatives to escape from the constant stress that characterizes life underground.[37] Pakistan's border region was an ideal sanctuary for several reasons.

First, it was close to the Taliban and al Qa'ida strongholds in eastern and southern Afghanistan, which would be convenient once they decided to launch efforts to overthrow the Karzai regime. And virtually all major insurgent leaders had spent time in Pakistan, often at one of the Deobandi *madrassas*. Second, Pakistan included roughly twenty-five million Pashtuns, double the number in Afghanistan, many of whom were sympathetic to the Taliban.[38] Third, some insurgent groups also had close ties to individuals within the Pakistan government. The Taliban, as discussed earlier, had received significant support and legitimacy from Pakistan's ISI back in the 1990s. Fourth, Pakistan's mountainous terrain near the Afghan border offered superb protection.

"The role of geography, a large one in an ordinary war, may be overriding in a revolutionary war," wrote David Galula in his classic book *Counterinsurgency Warfare*. Galula served in the French Army in North Africa and Italy during World War II, and later in the insurgencies in China, Greece, Indochina, and Algeria. "It helps the insurgent insofar as it is rugged and difficult."[39] As Galula and others have pointed out, mountainous terrain can be useful for insurgent groups because it is difficult for indigenous and external forces to navigate and easier for insurgents to hide.[40]

The border region was also deeply disputed. No modern government of Afghanistan had ever formally recognized the British-drawn border that divided the Pashtun territories. On November 12, 1893, Sir Henry Mortimer Durand, the British foreign secretary of India, signed an agreement with the Afghan ruler, Amir Abdur Rehman Khan, separating Afghanistan from what was then British India. The Durand Line, as it became known, divided the Pashtun tribes in order to weaken them, making it easier for the British to pacify the area. On their side of the frontier, the British created autonomous tribal agencies controlled by British political officers with the help of tribal chieftains whose loyalty was ensured through regular subsidies. The British used force to put down sporadic uprisings, but they generally left the tribes alone in return for stability along the frontier.[41] In 1949, Afghanistan's *loya jirga* declared the Durand Line invalid and viewed Pashtun areas as part of their country, especially since British India ceased to exist with the independence of Pakistan in 1947.

The 1,519-mile border has continued to be a source of tension. In the June 2006 issue of *Armed Forces Journal*, retired U.S. Army Lieutenant Colonel Ralph Peters suggested a radical realignment of the boundaries of the greater Middle East. Peters generously gave part of western Afghanistan to Iran, but he balanced this by giving Afghanistan the Pashtun areas of Pakistan. Peters argued: "What Afghanistan would lose to Persia in the west, it would gain in the east, as Pakistan's Northwest Frontier tribes would be reunited with their Afghan brethren. . . . Pakistan, another unnatural state, would also lose its Baluch territory to Free Baluchistan. The remaining 'natural' Pakistan would lie entirely east of the Indus, except for a westward spur near Karachi."[42] Though considerable blood might have to be spilled to move the borders, several senior Afghan officials praised Peters and expressed their support for redrawing the colonial boundaries. Shortly after the article was published, one senior Afghan official told me, "At least one American understands Afghanistan."[43] Not surprisingly, Pakistani officials have been less than enthusiastic about the idea.

U.S. Limitations

The U.S. invasion of Afghanistan had aimed to overthrow the Taliban regime and destroy al Qa'ida's organizational infrastructure. It achieved the former but not the latter. Key al Qa'ida training camps, such as Tarnak Farms outside of the city of Kandahar, were destroyed. But the Taliban, al Qa'ida, and other militants simply slipped across the border into Pakistan, where they established new camps. Over the next several years, these groups recruited, rearmed, and plotted their return. The Pakistani military conducted combat operations against foreign fighters—especially Central Asians and Arabs—in the Federally Administered Tribal Areas, but the government refrained from conducting operations against most high-ranking Taliban leaders.[44] On September 15, 2001, President Musharraf told Ambassador Chamberlin: "We will hand over captured al Qa'ida operatives to you. But we will handle the Pakistanis and other locals ourselves."[45]

The Pakistan government's desire to protect some of its assets was not lost on U.S. policymakers. Deputy Secretary of State Armitage argued, for example, that "Musharraf did not push hard against the Taliban" and was "only cooperative in targeting some key al Qa'ida militants."[46] The CIA's Grenier similarly acknowledged: "The ISI worked closely with us to capture key al Qa'ida leaders such as Khalid Sheikh Muhammad, Ramzi Binalshibh, Abu Faraj al-Libbi, and Abu Zubeida. But they made it clear that they didn't care about targeting the Taliban." Neither did the CIA or the U.S. government more broadly. "The U.S. government was focused on al Qa'ida," Grenier continued, "not on capturing or killing Taliban leaders. The U.S. considered the Taliban a spent force."[47]

Neglecting the Taliban, who had invited al Qa'ida into Afghanistan in the first place, was a dangerous gamble. A joint paper by the government of Afghanistan, the United Nations, Canada, the Netherlands, Britain, and the United States later warned that insurgents were directing "their campaign against Afghan and international forces from Pakistan," and most fighters were "trained in Pakistan in combat, communications, IEDs and suicide ops."[48]

Militant Groups Resettle

Among the groups that settled in Pakistan was Gulbuddin Hekmatyar's Hezb-i-Islami. After the September 2001 attacks, Hekmatyar openly pledged to cooperate with al Qa'ida and Taliban forces to fight the "Crusader forces" in Afghanistan.[49] Hekmatyar's organization, which included several hundred fighters, sought to overthrow the

Afghan government and install him as leader. The group's area of operations included Pakistan's North West Frontier Province and the northern part of the Federally Administered Tribal Areas, as well as the Afghan provinces of Nuristan, Kunar, Laghman, and Nangarhar.[50] Despite occasional overtures to the Afghan government, one joint European Union and United Nations assessment revealed that Hekmatyar was periodically "offered funds to fill his empty coffers" by the Taliban and "agreed not to negotiate further with the Afghan government."[51]

In addition to Hekmatyar's fighters, Yunus Khalis's branch of Hezb-i-Islami also began to rearm in Pakistan. One of Khalis's sons, Anwar al-Haq Mojahed, began to gather a group of Hezb-i-Islami fighters, disgruntled tribesmen, and some ex-Taliban. So did a group called Tehreek-e-Nafaz-e-Shariat-e-Mohammadi (TNSM), which was led by Sufi Mohammad, whose objective was to impose *sharia* law in Afghanistan and Pakistan by force if necessary. He encouraged and organized thousands of people to fight against the United States and the Northern Alliance in Afghanistan as the Taliban regime began to crumble in 2001, but the group was banned by Pervez Musharraf, and Sufi Mohammad was jailed in 2002. The group continued to rebuild, however, thanks to the untiring work of his son-in-law, Mullah Fazlullah, an influential firebrand known for his long, flowing hair. He was dubbed "Mullah Radio" because of his pirate FM radio broadcasts.

There were also a number of groups that rested and rearmed in Pakistan's tribal areas. As Figure 6.2 illustrates, there are seven agencies (Khyber, Kurram, Orakzai, Mohmand, Bajaur, North Waziristan, and South Waziristan). There are also six frontier regions: Peshawar, Kohat, Bannu, Dera Ismail Khan, Tank, and Lakki Marwat. The Pashtun tribes that controlled this region had resisted colonial rule with a determination virtually unparalleled in the subcontinent. The tribes were granted maximum autonomy and allowed to run their affairs in accordance with their Islamic faith, customs, and traditions. Tribal elders, known as *maliks*, were given special favors by the British in return for maintaining peace, keeping open important roads such as

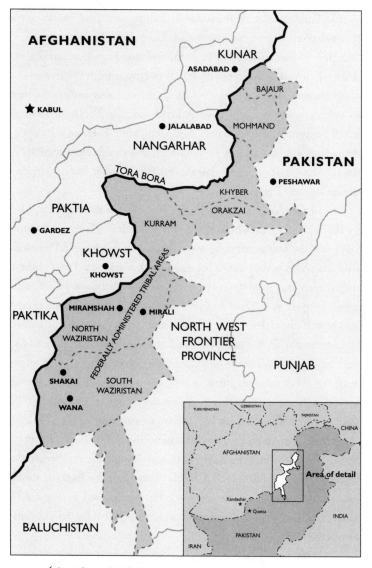

FIGURE 6.2 Pakistan's Tribal Agencies *Courtesy of RAND Corporation*

the Khyber Pass, and apprehending criminals. After partition in 1947, Pakistan continued this system of local autonomy and special favors.

Pakistan's founder, Muhammad Ali Jinnah, laid the foundation for this independence in remarks to a tribal *jirga* in Peshawar in 1948: "Keeping in view your loyalty, help, assurance and declarations we ordered, as you know, the withdrawal of troops from Waziristan as a concrete and definite gesture on our part. . . . Pakistan has no desire to unduly interfere with your internal freedom."[52] The system of administration remained fairly consistent after Pakistan's independence, despite demands by the educated and enlightened sections of the tribal population, and Pakistani courts and police had no jurisdiction in the tribal areas.

One of the most significant groups harbored in this region was led by the legendary mujahideen warrior Jalaluddin Haqqani. Born in 1935 into the Jadran tribe, he was educated at a *madrassa* in Peshawar, Pakistan. With penetrating eyes and a thick black beard that became tinged with gray over time, Haqqani was described by a Soviet intelligence report as a "cruel and uncompromising person." The report said he had close ties to Saudi Arabia and was a committed Islamist. "Jelaluddin regularly visits Saudi Arabia, where he holds direct talks with representatives of the government of that country. . . . He wages armed combat on a platform of establishing an Islamic republic on orthodox Islamic principles."[53] Upon returning to Afghanistan, he opened his own *madrassa* in Afghanistan's eastern province of Paktia, along the Pakistani border, and became active in the Muslim Brotherhood during the rule of Zahir Shah and Daoud Khan. During the Soviet War, Haqqani operated south of the Parrot's Beak in Paktia Province, near bin Laden's territory. He was viewed by some CIA officers in Islamabad as perhaps the most impressive battlefield commander in the war.

As a prominent jihadi leader, Haqqani sponsored some of the first Arab fighters who faced Soviet forces in 1987, and he was in frequent contact with bin Laden and ISI. Pakistan intelligence and the CIA relied on Haqqani to experiment with new weapons systems and tactics. The CIA officers working from Islamabad regarded him as a proven commander who could put a lot of men under arms on short notice.[54] It was with Haqqani's militia that U.S. Congressman Charlie Wilson traveled in Afghanistan in May 1987; Wilson was one of the few American government officials to step foot in the country during the Soviet War. He had wanted to fire a Stinger missile at a Soviet aircraft during the trip, but Haqqani's men couldn't pull it off. Milton Bearden, then the CIA's station chief in Pakistan, recalled, "Though he never got to fire his Stinger—Haqqani's people had actually dragged chains and tires on the dirt roads in a futile attempt to attract enemy fighter aircraft to the clouds of dust—he did manage to have a memorable combat tour at the front."[55]

After the overthrow of the Taliban, Haqqani's network regrouped in towns such as Miramshah and Mir Ali in Pakistan's tribal areas, as well as in a swath of territory in the Afghan provinces of Khowst, Paktia, Ghazni, and Paktika.[56] Haqqani was loosely allied with the Taliban leadership at this time, but he separately commanded several hundred fighters. Moreover, he had close relations with the Pakistani government, including the ISI.[57] Given the risks of traveling to Afghanistan, Haqqani spent this period expanding his base in Pakistan's tribal areas.[58] His most ambitious son, Sirajuddin, known as "Siraj," also became involved as the group prepared to fight the Americans in Afghanistan and overthrow the Karzai government. Siraj, the oldest of Haqqani's sons, had a strong resemblance to his father, with a jet-black beard and similar facial expressions. He bragged that "we are waging jihad against the U.S. forces and our objective is to tire them out."[59]

Several of al Qa'ida's key leaders also began to regroup in this area, along with a variety of other foreign groups, such as the Islamic Movement of Uzbekistan. The foreign jihadist contingent included two major types: those from the Caucasus and Central Asia (such as Chechens, Uzbeks, and Tajiks) and Arabs (such as Saudis, Egyptians, Somalis, and Yemenis). Many had settled in North and South Waziristan during the mujahideen wars against the Soviets; others streamed over after the collapse of the Taliban. A number of these foreigners were directly or indirectly affiliated with al Qa'ida, though some were simply inspired by the broader jihadist goal of pushing U.S. and other Western forces out of Afghanistan.[60]

Much of al Qa'ida's fighting force was located in an area that began around the Bajaur tribal agency in Pakistan. The leaders were mostly Arabs. Ayman al-Zawahiri was an Egyptian. Mustafa Abu al-Yazid, bin Laden's former treasurer, who headed al Qa'ida's operations in Afghanistan, was also an Egyptian.[61] Abd al-Hadi al-Iraqi, a senior al Qa'ida operative who was captured in 2006 in Turkey, was born in the northern Iraqi city of Mosul. He served in Iraq's army under Saddam Hussein and rose to the rank of major. He then joined the Afghan muhajideen and fought the Red Army in the 1980s. Finally, Abu Ubaydah al-Masri, who headed al Qa'ida's external operations from Waziristan and died in 2007 of hepatitis, was yet another Egyptian.

There was some support from local tribes in the region. Academic Mariam Abou Zahab reported that "after the American intervention, foreign militants, Taliban, and others who fled Afghanistan entered the tribal areas and a sizeable number of foreigners settled in Waziristan where they developed deep links with Ahmedzai Wazirs." Most disturbingly, she wrote, "almost every tribe supported al Qa'ida, actively or passively, as guests."[62] Nek Muhammad, a Taliban leader who was killed in June 2004 by a CIA Predator strike, was from the Ahmadzai Wazir tribe. So was Maulana Noor Muhammad, who joined the Jamiat Ulema-e-Islam and received Arab money and weapons in the 1980s. He was elected to the Pakistani Parliament in 1997 and became a prominent supporter of the Taliban in Waziristan.

Several individuals from the Ahmadzai Wazir tribe based in Wana, Pakistan, helped raise funds and recruited militants to fight in Afghanistan.[63] After the March 2003 capture of Khalid Sheikh Muhammad, al Qa'ida's head of external operations, the group received protection and support from local clerics and tribal members of the Mehsud and Wazir tribes. The Ahmadzai Wazirs and local Taliban members of the clans living in the Shakai Valley were the main hosts of the Arabs, while the Yargulkhel subclan of the Ahmadzai Wazirs became the main host of the Uzbeks in South Waziristan.[64]

Finally, the Taliban resettled in Pakistan and began to reestablish political, military, and religious committees in the vicinity of Quetta. This city was critical because it allowed easy access to Afghanistan's southern provinces, including Kandahar, a key front in the insurgency. The State Department realized the Taliban were attacking on two fronts, and one report said, "Quetta is the hinge, enabling communication between fronts and providing safe haven for Taliban leadership, logistics and information operations (IO). Dislocating this hinge would severely disrupt Taliban strategy, but would require a much greater degree of commitment and activity from Pakistan than we have seen to date."[65]

The Taliban sited propaganda and media committees in various locations, but most prominently in Peshawar, as well as in North and South Waziristan. They created a variety of Websites, such as www .alemarah.org (now defunct), and they used al Qa'ida's production company, Al-Sahab Media, to make videos. They also established a radio outlet, Voice of Sharia, with mobile transmitters in several provinces. Some Taliban fighters even took video cameras onto the battlefield to videotape improvised-explosive-device (IED) attacks and offensive operations, which were useful for propaganda.[66] Indeed, the Taliban's strategic information campaign significantly improved after September 11, 2001, thanks in part to al Qa'ida. After the U.S. invasion of Afghanistan, the Taliban's videos became notably better in quality and clarity of message, and its use of the Internet dramatically increased to spread propaganda and recruit potential fighters. The Taliban also published several newspapers and magazines, such as *Zamir*, *Tora Bora*, and *Sirak*. Finally, the Taliban began to relocate much of their financial base to Karachi, Pakistan's financial and commercial center on the Arabian Sea.

Over time, the Taliban began to link up with a number of Pashtun tribes, especially Ghilzais. Special arrangements allowed border

tribes freedom of movement between Afghanistan and Pakistan—
they were not subjected to any scrutiny and were allowed to cross the
border merely on visual recognition or identification. A number of
these tribes had lands that had been divided by the Durand Line, such
as the Mashwani, Mohmands, Shinwaris, Afridis, Mangals, Wazirs,
and Gulbaz. Pashtun military prowess has been renowned since Alexander the Great's invasion of Pashtun territory in the fourth century
BC. When asked about his identity, Abdul Wali Khan, a Pakistani politician, confidently responded: "[I am] a six thousand year old Pashtun, a thousand year old Muslim and a 27 year old Pakistani."[67]

The southern front also boasted a number of criminal groups, especially drug-trafficking organizations, which operated on both sides of
the border. Farther north, there were Russian, Tajik, Uzbek, and Turk-
men drug-trafficking organizations. Tajikistan served as a primary trans-
shipment locale for opiates destined for Russia. Drug traffickers in
Afghanistan used produce-laden trucks as a cover for drugs sent north
toward Tajikistan, where the goods were handed off to other criminal
organizations. Tajik criminal organizations were the primary movers of
this contraband. Approximately half of the heroin that passed through
Tajikistan was consumed in Russia. The rest transited Russia to other
consumer markets in Western and Eastern Europe.[68]

In light of this regrouping, it seems the overthrow of the Taliban
regime was Janus-faced. The sheer alacrity with which United States
and Northern Alliance forces overthrew the Taliban regime was awe-
inspiring. It took less than three months and cost America only twelve
lives—surely one of the most successful unconventional operations
in modern history. But many senior Taliban and al Qa'ida leaders had
not been killed or captured—they had escaped across the border into
Pakistan. This haunting reality was not lost on many U.S. military and
CIA officials on the ground at the time. Hunting them down, especially the Taliban, would be shelved for another day as U.S. policymakers turned to stabilizing Afghanistan.

CHAPTER SEVEN

Light Footprint

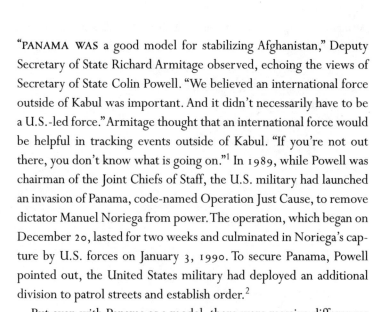

"PANAMA WAS a good model for stabilizing Afghanistan," Deputy Secretary of State Richard Armitage observed, echoing the views of Secretary of State Colin Powell. "We believed an international force outside of Kabul was important. And it didn't necessarily have to be a U.S.-led force." Armitage thought that an international force would be helpful in tracking events outside of Kabul. "If you're not out there, you don't know what is going on."[1] In 1989, while Powell was chairman of the Joint Chiefs of Staff, the U.S. military had launched an invasion of Panama, code-named Operation Just Cause, to remove dictator Manuel Noriega from power. The operation, which began on December 20, lasted for two weeks and culminated in Noriega's capture by U.S. forces on January 3, 1990. To secure Panama, Powell pointed out, the United States military had deployed an additional division to patrol streets and establish order.[2]

But even with Panama as a model, there were massive differences in 2001 within the U.S. government—and among key allies—about how to stabilize Afghanistan. Perhaps the most acrimonious debate was between senior State Department officials, who favored a peacekeeping force in Afghanistan that could stabilize key urban areas, and Pentagon officials, who vehemently opposed any pretense of nationbuilding.

Naïve and Irresponsible

There were two main camps. The first included those who believed that a peacekeeping force was necessary to ensure security across the country over the long run. One proponent was Powell, who argued that the U.S. strategy needed to involve taking "charge of the whole country by military force, police or other means."[3] Another proponent was James Dobbins, the Bush administration's special envoy to the Afghan opposition. According to Dobbins, it was "naïve and irresponsible" to believe that "Afghanistan could be adequately secured by Afghans in the immediate aftermath of a twenty-three-year civil war."[4] A small NATO presence in Kabul, Dobbins believed, would be helpful for establishing security and luring Afghan leaders back to their national capital. Kabul was peaceful, and there was no large-scale looting, as would occur in April 2003 in Baghdad after the overthrow of Saddam Hussein's government. However, Dobbins argued that international forces were necessary in key Afghan cities to ensure security across the country. He was supported by Zalmay Khalilzad, then serving on President Bush's National Security Council (NSC) staff.[5]

Other proponents included Hamid Karzai, the interim Afghan leader, as well as such Afghan officials as Muhammad Qasim Fahim and Abdul Rashid Dostum. Fahim, the defense minister of the Northern Alliance, worked with the CIA and U.S. Special Operations Forces to liberate the Afghan capital from the Taliban. Dostum had returned from exile in Turkey in April 2001 and had worked with CIA and U.S. Special Operations Forces to overthrow the Taliban from Mazar-e-Sharif.

Lakhdar Brahimi, former Algerian foreign minister and longtime confidant of UN Secretary-General Kofi Annan, also supported an international peacekeeping force outside of the capital. Brahimi served as the special representative of the UN Secretary-General for Afghanistan and played a leading role during the Bonn negotiations in 2001. The Bonn Agreement called for an international security force in Kabul with the explicit possibility of expansion:

Conscious that some time may be required for the new Afghan security and armed forces to be fully constituted and functioning, the participants in the UN talks on Afghanistan request the United Nations Security Council to consider authorizing the early deployment to Afghanistan of a United Nations mandated force. This force will assist in the maintenance of security for Kabul and its surrounding areas. Such a force could, as appropriate, be progressively expanded to other urban centers and other areas.[6]

On February 6, 2002, when briefing the UN Security Council on factional clashes in the countryside and the relative safety of the capital, Brahimi appealed for extending the force beyond Kabul: "This has led to increasingly vocal demands by ordinary Afghans, as well as by members of the Interim Administration and even warlords, for the expansion of ISAF [International Security Assistance Force] to the rest of the country," he argued. "We tend to agree with these demands, and we hope that these will receive favorable and urgent consideration by the Security Council."[7]

There were also supporters in the United Kingdom, such as Robert Cooper, the British representative at the Bonn negotiations who was assigned to Prime Minister Tony Blair's staff in the Cabinet Office. Cooper argued that a NATO peacekeeping presence outside of Kabul was critical for establishing security. One possibility he suggested was a British-led force. Other than the United States, Great Britain was the only country able to deploy the needed force quickly enough. British troops were already operating in Afghanistan in small numbers, and the United Kingdom had begun to establish the logistics network necessary to sustain them. How many international troops were necessary? U.S., British, and Afghan officials had discussed the possibility of perhaps 25,000 peacekeeping forces deployed to Kabul and key Afghan cities. In December 2001, for example, Dobbins met with Secretary of Defense Donald Rumsfeld at Bagram Air Base in Afghanistan. Rumsfeld asked what to expect in his upcoming meetings with Afghan officials.

"They will ask that ISAF be deployed beyond Kabul to cover the country's other major population centers," Dobbins noted.

"How many men would that take?" Rumsfeld asked.

"The British believe a force of five thousand adequate to secure Kabul. Given that the next four or five cities are all considerably smaller, perhaps another 20,000 men might suffice," Dobbins responded.[8]

The second camp included those who supported a peacekeeping force in Kabul but generally opposed extending its reach outside of the capital. They included many in the U.S. and British militaries, as well as key individuals in their political establishments. Pentagon officials, such as Secretary Rumsfeld and General Tommy Franks, head of U.S. Central Command, were particularly adamant that there should be no international peacekeeping force outside of Kabul, especially one involving U.S. forces. Some, like Under Secretary of Defense for Policy Douglas Feith, were not necessarily averse to sending peacekeeping forces outside of Kabul, but they were strongly opposed to having U.S. forces involved in peacekeeping. "We couldn't put U.S. forces in ISAF," said Feith, "because other countries might conclude that the United States would bail them out if they got into trouble. The State Department answer to stabilizing Afghanistan was to expand ISAF. We wanted to allow the Afghans to establish their own security." In a series of NSC meetings, for example, Rumsfeld made it clear that he wanted U.S. forces out of Afghanistan as quickly as possible.[9] The logic, one senior U.S. official told me, was that "the U.S. military was already thinking about moving on to Iraq." He added that the military was primarily intent on "targeting bad guys and cleaning up after the overthrow of the Taliban regime. Ultimately, they believed that cleaning up Afghanistan was not the U.S.'s responsibility—it was Afghanistan's responsibility."[10]

"Nation-building is not our key strategic goal," Feith told Rumsfeld in a classified memo in late 2001. "The term 'nation-building' had baggage," he noted, since the Clinton administration's policies "in Bosnia in 1996 and in Kosovo in 1999" had "effectively turned those areas into long-term wards of the international community. Large numbers of U.S. and other outside forces were involved for many years in both places." The implication was clear, Feith felt: "We did not want the Afghans to think we intended to take the same approach to their country."[11]

In fact, during the 2000 presidential campaign, George W. Bush had repeatedly made the bold statement that nation-building and peacekeeping were not roles for American troops.[12] Key U.S. officials, starting with the president, did not want American troops involved in nation-building in Afghanistan, and they did not want to bail out other countries if they ran into trouble. As President Bush put it: "Better yet than peacekeepers . . . let's have Afghanistan have her own military."[13] White House spokesman Ari Fleischer reiterated this view several weeks later: "The President's position is unchanged about the use of the United States combat forces. The President continues to believe the purpose of the military is to be used to fight and win wars, and not to engage in peacekeeping of that nature."[14] U.S. policymakers argued that what the Bonn Agreement had called an "international security force" for Afghanistan should be renamed the "International Security Assistance Force"—ISAF. The word *assistance* was inserted to eliminate any suggestion that international soldiers might provide security for the Afghan population. As far as Washington was concerned, public safety was an Afghan responsibility.

Within the U.S. government, the most notable fissure existed between the State and Defense Departments. The national media picked up on this almost immediately. Michael Gordon of the *New York Times* asked Rumsfeld whether there was any truth to reports that peacekeepers might be dispatched to other cities in Afghanistan. Rumsfeld argued that deploying a peacekeeping force outside of Kabul would be unnecessary and would divert resources from the broader American campaign against terrorism. He preferred to spend the money on training an Afghan national army.

"The question is, do you want to put your time and effort and money into the International Security Assistance Force—take it from, say, 5,000 to 20,000 people? . . . Why put all the time and money and effort in that? Why not put it into helping them develop a national army so that they can look out for themselves over time?"

Gordon then called James Dobbins, who said: "What the State Department is suggesting is that there are a few other places outside of Kabul where the international force could assist the Afghans in providing security. As a result the Afghans would do a better job and would be less likely to fall into conflict with each other in doing so."[15] Dobbins would later be chastised by National Security Adviser Condoleezza Rice for going public with his comments and for exposing divisions between the State and Defense Departments. She had one of her deputies, General Wayne Downey, call Dobbins to complain.

Eventually the issue came to a head. In February 2002, a meeting of National Security Council principals was called to decide whether or not to expand the NATO mission outside of Kabul. In preparation for the meeting, NSC staffer Elliott Abrams had circulated a paper arguing that peacekeeping was a concept that never worked in practice, as demonstrated by the Clinton administration's forays into Somalia, Haiti, Bosnia, and Kosovo. The principals met in the White House Situation Room. Powell and Dobbins attended for State. Rice chaired. Others present included Rumsfeld, CIA Director George Tenet, and Lewis "Scooter" Libby, Vice President Dick Cheney's chief of staff. Powell and Rumsfeld were at loggerheads. Tenet argued that there had been some skirmishing among commanders who were theoretically under Karzai's authority, and there was some possibility that this fighting could escalate. A peacekeeping force might not be a bad idea. In theory, the CIA was supposed to provide intelligence and analysis, not policy advice. But it had played such an unusually direct role in overthrowing the Taliban regime that Tenet sometimes offered advice rather than just intelligence.

After several inconclusive exchanges between Powell and Rumsfeld, Rice asked all the backbenchers to leave the room. This allowed the principals to discuss the matter in private, which they did for another fifteen minutes. In the end, everyone agreed that Afghanistan's warlords were likely to resume fighting if left to their own devices. But Rumsfeld was adamantly opposed to the deployment of peacekeepers. Rather, he proposed that U.S. military teams working with Afghan commanders should use their influence to ensure peace among them. Powell relented and Rice agreed. So there would be no call for more international troops or peacekeepers, no additional forces, and no public-security duties for American soldiers. But an effort would be made to discourage fighting among Afghan commanders. Powell told Dobbins after the meeting: "It's the best I could do. Rumsfeld said he would take care of the problem. What more could I say?"[16] Armitage summarized it more bluntly: "Rumsfeld simply steamrolled the decision through."[17] In the end, the United States deployed 8,000 troops to Afghanistan in 2002, with orders to hunt Taliban and al Qa'ida members, and did not engage in peace-keeping. The 4,000-member international peacekeeping force in Kabul did not venture outside the capital.

Out of this debate emerged the watchword of American and international involvement in Afghanistan: a "light footprint." In hindsight, this would prove to be a serious misstep that contributed to the collapse of governance in Afghanistan. Low troop levels made it extremely difficult to establish law and order throughout the country. And there was almost no chance to revisit the decision. Once the United States began planning the war in Iraq, the light-footprint plan was virtually impossible to alter; the United States could not deploy additional forces to Afghanistan because they were committed elsewhere. Under the light footprint, U.S. and other NATO forces could clear territory occupied by Taliban or other insurgent groups but could not hold it. This was especially true in the south, the traditional heartland of the Taliban. In addition, the U.S. and other countries could not provide sufficient development assistance in rural areas of Afghanistan, where the bulk of the fighting occurred.[18]

A Marshall Plan for Afghanistan?

Despite the limited troop commitment, there were initial indications that the Bush administration might provide significant financial assistance to Afghanistan. In a speech on April 17, 2002, at Virginia Military Institute (VMI), President Bush invoked the Marshall Plan. The setting was highly symbolic. George C. Marshall graduated from VMI in 1901 as senior first captain of the Corps of Cadets. He served as secretary of state under President Truman and formulated an unprecedented program of economic and military aid to postwar Germany and other nations recovering from World War II. On June 5, 1947, Marshall addressed the graduating class of Harvard University, promising American aid to promote European recovery and reconstruction. While the speech itself contained virtually no details and no numbers, the United States under the Marshall Plan would go on to provide billions of dollars in aid to Western European countries between 1947 and 1951.[19]

Bush's 2002 speech at VMI had similar overtones. He remarked, for example: "We know that true peace will only be achieved when we give the Afghan people the means to achieve their own aspirations." He then invoked Marshall in describing the road ahead in Afghanistan:

> By helping to build an Afghanistan that is free from this evil and is a better place in which to live, we are working in the best traditions of George Marshall. Marshall knew that our military victory against enemies in World War II had to be followed by a moral victory that resulted in better lives for individual human beings. After 1945, the United States of America was the only nation in the world strong enough to help rebuild a Europe and a Japan that had been decimated by World War II. Today, our former enemies are our friends. And Europe and Japan are strong partners in the rebuilding of Afghanistan.[20]

As with Marshall's address at Harvard, Bush's speech was vague on details, and the president did not specifically say that the United States would provide comparable levels of aid to Afghanistan. But the repeated references to the Marshall Plan certainly gave that impression. In any case, that's how senior Afghan officials saw it; they interpreted the speech as a commitment to significant assistance.[21] But the State Department, the Office of Management and Budget (OMB), and the NSC initiated no major efforts to assess the requirements for a successful reconstruction effort or to generate the funding that would be necessary. Not until the fall of 2002 was Congress asked for additional money for Afghanistan, and most of that went to the Defense Department.

Despite the hope engendered by Bush's speech, U.S. military officials had several reasons for adopting a light footprint. They wanted to prevent large-scale popular resistance similar to what the Soviet Union had encountered in the 1980s; they did not want the U.S. military engaged in peacekeeping or nation-building operations; and they ultimately believed that small numbers of ground troops and airpower, working with Afghan forces, would be sufficient to establish security.[22]

General Tommy Franks, who remained head of U.S. Central Command until 2003, argued that "our footprint had to be small," after major combat ended, "for both military and geopolitical reasons. I envisioned a total of about 10,000 American soldiers, airmen, special operators, and helicopter assault crews, along with robust in-country close air support."[23] Several of his key advisers agreed, including General Victor "Gene" Renuart, the director of operations, and Lieutenant General Paul T. Mikolashek, the ground component commander. In several video teleconference calls, Franks and Secretary Rumsfeld agreed that the United States should not flood Afghanistan with large formations of conventional troops. "We don't want to repeat the Soviets' mistakes," he told Rumsfeld during one meeting. "There's nothing to be gained by blundering around those mountains and gorges with armor battalions chasing a lightly armed enemy."[24] Instead, they sent in three brigades from the 10th Mountain and 101st Airborne (Air Assault) Divisions, as well as the Marine Expeditionary Unit already at Camp Rhino in Kandahar. As mentioned earlier, most senior U.S. officials—especially in the Defense Department and the White

House—did not support deploying a peacekeeping force outside of Kabul, preferring to spend the money on training an Afghan army.

U.S. military officials were also primarily interested in countering al Qa'ida, not in nation-building. One senior U.S. official explained to Afghanistan National Security Council staffer Daoud Yaqub: "Our objective in Afghanistan is to combat al Qa'ida. Everything else is incidental."[25]

The UN's Lakhdar Brahimi also agreed on a light footprint. While he had advocated expanding NATO's peacekeeping presence outside of Kabul, his vision of the international community's role in Afghanistan was different. Brahimi felt that the guiding principle of international efforts in Afghanistan should be to bolster Afghan capacity—both official and nongovernmental—and to rely on as limited an international presence and as many Afghan staff as possible. This marked a significant departure from the expansive UN missions in Kosovo and East Timor. Both missions, which began in 1999, included a large international military and police presence per capita, and the United Nations temporarily took over governance in both cases. Afghanistan needed to be different, Brahimi argued, and a heavy international footprint was "not necessary and not possible." Bolstering Afghanistan's capacity to govern itself, he thought, required Afghans taking charge of their situation wherever possible, an end that could be compromised by throwing international staff into the mix.[26]

In practice, the light footprint translated into one of the lowest levels of troops, police, and financial assistance in any stabilization operation since the end of World War II.

International troops and police are critical to establish security after a major war. Often, in the immediate aftermath of civil or interstate conflict, states will undergo a period of anarchy in which groups and factions seek to arm themselves for protection.[27] These groups and factions may have offensive intentions and want to impose their ideology on others, seize the property of rival factions, or exploit public resources for private gain. Large numbers of troops and police

are critical for defeating and deterring these groups, patrolling borders, securing roads, combating organized crime, and policing the
streets. Many of these general law-enforcement functions are best
performed by police and units specially trained for urban patrols and
crowd control.[28]

There is no simple metric for determining how many troops are
necessary to secure a population.[29] As Figure 7.1 illustrates, 89.3
U.S. troops per thousand inhabitants were necessary to establish
security in the American sector of Germany after World War II, 17.5
troops per thousand were used in Bosnia, 35.3 per thousand were
used in Eastern Slavonia, 19.3 per thousand were used in Kosovo,
and 9.8 per thousand were used in East Timor. None of those conflicts were resolved easily, even at those levels of troop involvement.
But the U.S. and other international forces had only about 1.6 soldiers per thousand Afghans. In terms of historical troop levels, the
Afghan mission ranks with some of the international community's
most notable failures: the UN mission to the Belgian Congo (1.3
troops per thousand); the American and international intervention in

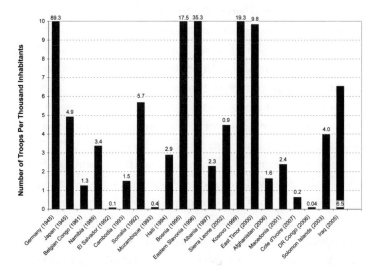

FIGURE 7.1   Peak International Military Presence Per Capita[30]

Somalia (5.7); the U.S. rescue of Haiti (2.9); and the French operation in Cote d'Ivoire (0.2).

There were also no international civilian police deployed to Afghanistan to conduct law-enforcement operations.[31] As Figure 7.2 shows, this was in marked contrast to such operations as Bosnia and Kosovo, where international paramilitary police had been used effectively to help establish law and order. In Bosnia, Italy deployed a small battalion of its *carabinieri* as part of the Multinational Specialized Unit to assist with refugee return, help with crowd and riot control, and promote public security by acting as a strategic reserve force.[32] In Kosovo, the *carabinieri* joined the French paramilitary *gendarmerie* as part of the Multinational Specialized Unit to engage in patrolling, riot control, criminal investigation, and other public-order tasks.[33] These paramilitary police forces interacted with the UN's International Police and Training Force, who worked with civilian police. In both Bosnia and Kosovo, international police were pivotal in establishing security.

The United States has traditionally lacked a national police force like the *carabinieri* and the *gendarmerie* that it could deploy abroad. Rather, it has approximately 20,000 state and local police forces in jurisdictions scattered across the United States.[34] Policing and law-enforcement services have historically been under the jurisdiction of local government. The Federal Bureau of Investigation (FBI) is involved in high-level investigations but has little experience in such policing tasks as patrols and riot control. International police training has been handled by two federal agencies: the State Department's Bureau of International Narcotics and Law Enforcement Affairs and the Justice Department's International Criminal Investigative Training Assistance Program. Neither, however, has a cadre of civilian police ready to be deployed abroad. Both have instead relied on private firms such as DynCorp International to recruit and deploy civilian police abroad. The Central Intelligence Agency and the Department of Defense have also been involved in police training, but policing is not a core mission of either of those organizations.[35]

At $60 per Afghan, foreign assistance over the first two years of a

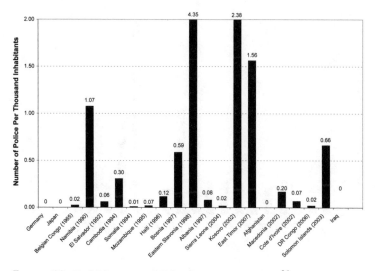

FIGURE 7.2   Peak International Police Presence Per Capita[36]

nation-building operation was lower than most operations since World War II (see Fig. 7.3). States emerging from interstate or civil war have generally suffered significant damage.[37] High levels of funding are necessary to cover the costs of deploying military forces and police, train indigenous police and army officers, provide lethal and nonlethal equipment, and build infrastructure.[38] Assistance generally comes from an amalgam of donor states and international organizations such as the IMF, the World Bank, and the European Union. Despite the fact that Afghanistan was a safe haven for al Qa'ida terrorists and that it was the first front in what the administration referred to as a "global war on terrorism," a wide array of U.S. government officials from the beginning of the conflict strongly opposed providing more resources for reconstruction efforts.[39]

Despite promises of aid, many countries never delivered. In 2002, Rumsfeld appointed Dov Zakheim—who was already serving as the under secretary of defense (comptroller) and chief financial officer for the Department of Defense—as the Pentagon's coordinator of civilian programs in Afghanistan. Zakheim had played a pivotal role as

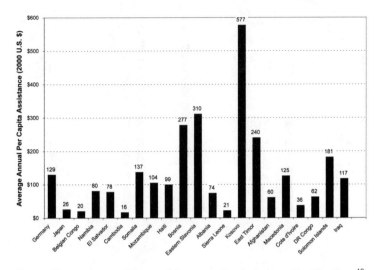

FIGURE 7.3   International Financial Assistance Per Capita over First Two Years[40]

Rumsfeld's principal financial adviser, overseeing all aspects of the department's accounting and auditing systems, and negotiating major defense agreements with U.S. allies and partners. Rumsfeld asked Zakheim to take the lead in getting nonmilitary equipment to Afghanistan, including trucks and potable water. Zakheim then began a tour of allied capitals with Under Secretary of the Treasury for International Affairs John Taylor, asking for contributions from U.S. allies.

"It was like pulling teeth," Zakheim said. "In general, the levels of assistance were too low. We got some help from Gulf states, including some logistical support and petroleum, oil, and lubricants. But most of this was for support to forces moving through their countries. We didn't get a lot of material support in theater. Allies simply weren't providing a lot of support." Zakheim and Taylor heard the same message during their meetings: "We have limited resources. We'll see what we can do." And then, Zakheim complained, "we just wouldn't hear back."[41]

U.S. assistance was also low. A major hurdle for U.S. policymakers in the Departments of State, Defense, and Treasury was the Office of

Management and Budget. "The biggest scandal was OMB," said Zakheim. "It was beyond our comprehension at the Pentagon that OMB refused to provide more support to Afghanistan than it did." Zakheim and his staff found this baffling, because Afghanistan was largely peaceful. "There was no major insurgency in 2002 and 2003, yet we couldn't get funding. The levels of poppy cultivation were low, and we lobbied to get assistance for alternative crops. But we couldn't get it from OMB. Neither could State or USAID."[42]

According to several senior officials at the White House and in the Departments of State, Defense, and Treasury, one of the biggest obstacles at OMB was Robin Cleveland, associate director for national security programs. "We repeatedly hit a brick wall with her," one senior White House official told me. "Robin was the single biggest problem because reconstruction is partly a function of money. And we had major troubles getting it."[43]

During this early period (2002 and 2003), the funding would have been especially useful for implementing reconstruction projects, because several competent Afghan government officials were overseeing finances. One was Ashraf Ghani, Afghanistan's finance minister, recognized in 2003 as the best finance minister in Asia by *Emerging Markets* magazine. He was seriously considered for the post of UN Secretary-General, which he didn't get, but Afghan Foreign Minister Rangin Dadfar Spanta described him in a private letter to UN officials as combining an unusual blend of "vision, management skills and a deep understanding of regional and global issues."[44] Ghani had earned master's and doctoral degrees in anthropology from Columbia University and later served on the faculties of Kabul University, the University of California (Berkeley), and Johns Hopkins University. He joined the World Bank in 1991, working on projects in East and South Asia. Despite Ghani's best efforts, however, he was unable to obtain adequate assistance from the United States and its allies.

That Colin Powell had been opposed to the light-footprint approach was not surprising. After all, he had espoused a doctrine of military engagement that came to be known as the "Powell Doctrine": Military force, when used, should be overwhelming and disproportionate to the force used by the enemy during stability operations.[45] When the United States deploys troops, he said, "we should win and win decisively."[46] But Rumsfeld's position ran contrary to the Powell Doctrine as well as to former Secretary of Defense Caspar Weinberger's theory that "in those cases where our national interests require us to commit combat force we must never let there be doubt of our resolution. When it is necessary for our troops to be committed to combat, we *must* commit them, in sufficient numbers and we *must* support them, as effectively and resolutely as our strength permits. When we commit our troops to combat we must do so with the sole object of winning."[47]

Without significant numbers of military personnel, ensuring security in an insurgency historically has been more difficult. Dissidents may be emboldened to use force. Borders may become porous and facilitate the movement of insurgents, drug traffickers, and other criminal organizations. Security along roads and highways may deteriorate, allowing criminals and insurgents easier transport.

It soon became clear that the light footprint allowed for too few U.S. and Afghan government troops to stabilize the country.[48] Small numbers of CIA and Special Forces were sufficient to overthrow the Taliban regime in 2001, but they were not strong enough to establish basic security. The small number of military forces, coupled with low numbers of trained Afghan military and police, failed to establish security in rural areas of Afghanistan. Because the Coalition did not venture into Pakistan, where significant numbers of Taliban and al Qa'ida militants had fled, they were not able to defeat Taliban, Hezb-i-Islami, and al Qa'ida insurgent forces.[49]

A Fait Accompli

In the end, the result of the Powell-Rumsfeld showdown was moot; the war in Iraq obliterated America's ability to contain the gradually deteriorating situation in Afghanistan. "From day one it was Iraq,

Iraq, Iraq," remarked Deputy Secretary of State Richard Armitage. "Afghanistan was really an accidental war for much of the Administration. No one wanted to do it. And once it became clear the Taliban was likely to fall, senior Pentagon officials wanted to turn to Iraq as quickly as possible." Most senior Bush administration officials supported an invasion of Iraq in principle. They differed, however, on such issues as how and when it would be done. Secretary of State Powell, for example, wanted to go in with much larger numbers and with overwhelming force. "My objection was timing," said Armitage. "I wanted to turn to Iraq perhaps in November 2004, after the elections and after Afghanistan was somewhat under control."[50]

The prospect of invading Iraq surfaced immediately after the September 11 attacks. In a National Security Council meeting on September 13, President Bush asked CIA Director George Tenet whether he was looking into the possiblity of Iraqi involvement. "It's a worldwide effort, yes," Tenet responded. Rumsfeld went even further, contending that Saddam Hussein was a threat to the region and to the United States. "Iraq," he noted, "was a state that supported terrorism, and that might someday offer terrorists weapons of mass destruction to use against us." He added that, in Iraq, "we could inflict the kind of costly damage that could cause terrorist-supporting regimes around the world to rethink their policies."[51]

Tension over Iraq surfaced again among senior U.S. policymakers at Camp David on September 15 and 16, 2001. Before the meeting, the staff of National Security Adviser Condoleezza Rice had prepared three options for review. The first option was to attack only al Qa'ida targets, the second was to attack the Taliban and al Qa'ida, and the third added Iraq to the list. In a classified memo to Rumsfeld, Douglas Feith and Assistant Secretary of Defense for International Security Affairs Peter Rodman supplemented Rice's three options. They argued that "the immediate priority targets for action" should be al Qa'ida, the Taliban, and Iraq. Iraq was critical because Saddam Hussein's regime posed a "threat of WMD terrorism." The purpose of invading Iraq, their memo argued to Rumsfeld, would be "to destabilize a regime that engages in and supports terrorism, that has weapons of mass destruction and is developing new ones, that attacks U.S. forces almost daily and otherwise threatens vital U.S. interests."[52]

At Camp David, some of the most intense disagreements were between Colin Powell and Paul Wolfowitz. Powell told Wolfowitz "that Afghanistan was the main issue, not Iraq. The Taliban regime was a terrible regime, which the U.S. needed to get rid of. And al Qa'ida leaders planned and trained for the September 11 attacks from Afghan soil." He maintained that the United States had significant multilateral support for the mission in Afghanistan and once the Taliban was overthrown, "the United States then needed to stabilize Afghanistan."[53] Most of the officials at Camp David supported this logic. But Wolfowitz pushed particularly hard for an Iraq invasion. He was concerned that large numbers of American troops would get bogged down in Afghanistan, as the Red Army had done. But Iraq was doable, he said; Iraq was a brittle regime, and there was a 10 to 50 percent probability that Saddam Hussein was involved in the September 11 attacks. At this particular meeting, President Bush ultimately decided to focus on Afghanistan, but Iraq would resurface again soon.[54]

In November 2001, before the fall of the Taliban, Tommy Franks asked General Gene Renuart to put together a special planning group for Iraq based out of U.S. Central Command at MacDill Air Force Base, near Tampa, Florida. Rumsfeld had flown to MacDill to meet with Franks and ask him to produce a rough concept, not a finished plan for execution, for overthrowing Saddam Hussein's government.[55] In order to meet this demand, a number of individuals had to reassign critical staff working on the war in Afghanistan. For instance, Lieutenant Colonel Edward O'Connell, the chief of targeting at Central Command, had to release several of his key staff, such as Lieutenant Commander J. D. Dullum, to the Iraq effort.

"I didn't have a choice," said O'Connell. "I had to give up several of my Afghan targeters to support this new secret Iraq planning. It was still 2001. And we hadn't finished the Afghan war yet."[56]

As the Afghan insurgency worsened, the U.S. faced a fait accompli almost entirely of its own making. Before the year was out, and even before the United States attacked bin Laden at Tora Bora, the U.S. government began downsizing its commitment of resources to Afghanistan. While U.S. policymakers had been hesitant to provide assistance to Afghanistan from the beginning, the invasion of Iraq ensured that Afghanistan would take a backseat in money, policy attention, and military and nonmilitary aid. It became more difficult to include discussions of Afghanistan in the schedule of the National Security Council. Assistance was cut significantly, and any suggestions for new initiatives received short shrift from policymakers, who were focusing their attention on diplomatic and military preparations for Iraq. After the overthrow of Saddam's government, this attention shifted to stabilizing an increasingly violent Iraq torn apart by Sunni/Shi'ite fissures.

"The war in Iraq drained resources from Afghanistan before things were under control," noted Armitage. "And we never recovered. We never looked back."[57] According to Gary Schroen, leader of the first CIA team in Afghanistan in 2001, the war in Iraq drained key CIA personnel and resources from Afghanistan, "making it increasingly difficult to staff the CIA teams in Afghanistan with experienced paramilitary officers."[58] Several intelligence operations directed at al Qa'ida and other terrorist groups were redirected to the Persian Gulf. Linguists and Special Operations Forces were reassigned, and several ongoing antiterrorism intelligence programs were curtailed.[59] The CIA's Robert Grenier acknowledged that "the best experienced, most qualified people who we had been using in Afghanistan shifted over to Iraq," including the agency's most skilled counterterrorism specialists and Middle East and paramilitary operatives. This shift reduced America's influence over powerful Afghan warlords who were refusing to give to the central government tens of millions of dollars they had collected as customs payments at border crossings. While the CIA replaced its officers shifted to Iraq, it did so with younger agents, who lacked the knowledge and influence of the veterans. "I think we could have done a lot more on the Afghan side if we had more experienced folks," Grenier told me.[60]

The pattern continued at the very highest levels of military personnel and hardware. Covert Special Mission Units, such as Delta Force and Navy SEAL Team Six, shifted from Afghanistan to Iraq. Sophisticated Predator spy planes rolled off assembly lines in the United States, but most were shipped to Iraq, undercutting the search for Taliban and other terrorist leaders in Afghanistan and Pakistan. U.S. forces in Afghanistan never had sufficient intelligence, surveillance, and reconnaissance (ISR) assets, such as Predators and Rivet Joints. Rivet Joint reconnaissance aircraft are extensively modified C-135s that support battlefield commanders with real time on-scene intelligence collection, analysis, and dissemination capabilities. The ratio of key ISR assets divided between Iraq and Afghanistan was typically 4:1 or 5:2. That is, for every four Predators that were shipped to Iraq, one went to Afghanistan. Or for every five Predators shipped to Iraq, two went to Afghanistan. Special Operations Forces were also reallocated from Afghanistan and Pakistan to Iraq. And the U.S. military focus on Iraq meant that Afghanistan had to use National Guard forces, rather than active-duty soldiers, to train Afghan National Army soldiers. These were not the "A team" of trainers. Lieutenant General Karl Eikenberry repeatedly requested active-duty trainers to work with Afghan security forces, but he was told there simply were none available.[61]

U.S. financial support was also low. "Iraq definitely affected funding levels for Afghanistan in two respects," explained Dov Zakheim. "The first was that we had only so much money and attention. We couldn't keep going back to the same well. The second was probably unhappiness among some allies at the war in Iraq. It likely spilled over into other areas, including an unwillingness to help in Afghanistan in 2003 and beyond."[62] Sarah Chayes, who ran a nongovernmental organization in Kandahar Province, contended that a significant reason "why the great [American] machine that was supposed to deploy on all fronts churning out reconstruction for Afghanistan failed to gear up" was "the war in Iraq."[63]

Low levels of money, energy, and troops made it nearly impossible to secure Afghanistan after the overthrow of the Taliban regime and almost certainly increased the probability of an insurgency. Ahmed Rashid, author of *Taliban*, concluded: "The main factor in preventing a stronger international commitment was the United States' diversion of its effort and interest from 2002 onwards to Iraq. Within three months of the overthrow of the Taliban regime, the United States was pulling out from Afghanistan."[64] By 2003, the U.S. government had become convinced that Iraq, not Afghanistan, was the central hub in the war on terrorism. In a phone conversation in August 2003 with L. Paul Bremer, head of the Coalition Provisional Authority in Iraq, Condoleezza Rice said: "Colin [Powell] and I are convinced that Iraq has become the decisive theater in the war on terrorism and that if we win in Iraq, Islamic terrorism can be defeated."[65]

Examination of internal U.S. government memos supports this argument. In a 2003 letter to Bremer, Jeb Mason, associate director of the White House's Office of Strategic Initiatives, requested the adoption of "talking points" on progress in the "war on terror." He wrote: "Iraq is now the central front in the War on Terror. As Vice President Cheney said on Sunday: 'If we're successful in Iraq . . . so that it's not a safe haven for terrorists, now we will have struck a major blow right at the heart of the base, if you will, the geographic base of the terrorists who have had us under assault now for many years, but most especially on 9/11."[66] Afghanistan and Pakistan had been relegated to secondary fronts. The United States lacked the military, financial, and political resources and attention to secure Afghanistan because they were diverted to Iraq. The result was too few soldiers, too little assistance, and too little awareness of what was happening.

Warlords

The light-footprint approach had another unforeseen repercussion. With too few international forces and too few competent indigenous forces, local militia commanders, or warlords, filled the vacuum.

Some were aided by the U.S. military.[67] Since it was not politically feasible to increase the number of U.S. forces in Afghanistan, the U.S. military decided that the need to fight al Qa'ida was urgent enough that the United States simply couldn't wait to develop Afghan government forces. Lieutenant General John R. Vines, commander of Combined Joint Task Force 180 in Afghanistan, acknowledged that "militia are part of the existing reality."[68]

Local-warlord militia forces "led every mounted patrol and most major operations," partly because, according to one U.S. military assessment, "they knew the ground better and could more easily spot something that was out of place or suspicious."[69] Such forces were often used for the outer perimeter of cordon-and-search operations. In several operations, such as the Battle of Deh Chopan, militia forces were critical in providing intelligence and the bulk of the maneuver force.[70]

In the east, the United States gave money, arms, and other equipment to Pacha Khan Zadran, whose forces were based in Paktia Province. In the west, U.S. forces provided assistance to Ismail Khan, allowing him to establish significant political and fiscal autonomy in Herat Province. He controlled military and civil administration there, supported by large amounts of customs revenues from trade with Iran, Turkmenistan, and other Afghan provinces.[71] In the south, U.S. forces provided money and arms to Gul Agha Shirzai and others to help target al Qa'ida operatives.[72]

The U.S. assistance to warlords weakened the central government. President Karzai made a halfhearted attempt to reduce the power of warlords who also served as provincial governors by reassigning them away from their geographic power base. But Karzai's tendency was to *move* warlords, not to *remove* them. Consequently, their networks continued to influence provincial- and district-level administration.[73] Public-opinion polls showed that the warlords' increasing power alarmed many Afghans. One poll conducted for the U.S. military concluded: "A high percentage of respondents identified local commanders as bringers of insecurity to their district."[74] According to the Afghanistan

National Security Council's *National Threat Assessment*: "Non-statutory armed forces and their commanders pose a direct threat to the national security of Afghanistan. They are the principal obstacle to the expansion of the rule of law into the provinces and thus the achievement of the social and economic goals that the people of Afghanistan expect their Government, supported by the International Community, to deliver."[75] An Afghan provincial governor reinforced this conclusion, observing that "keeping warlords in power is weakening the government. The more the government pays them off, the stronger they will become and the weaker the government will be."[76]

This brings up an important dilemma. In past counterinsurgencies, the local country has usually needed to take the lead over the long run for successful operations. A large foreign presence—especially foreign military forces—has often undermined local power and legitimacy. But what if there is no competent government force in the early stages of an insurgency? In the Afghan case, there were no Afghan Army forces and no trained police. While there are no ideal options in these situations, the most effective strategy may be to: (a) work with legitimate indigenous forces (especially police); (b) effectively train and mentor them as quickly as possible; and (c) backfill with sufficient numbers of U.S. and other international forces to accomplish key security tasks such as patrolling streets and villages, monitoring borders, and protecting critical infrastructure. Higher per-capita levels of U.S. and Coalition military and police might have been useful in the immediate aftermath of the Taliban's overthrow. Preparations for the war in Iraq made this impossible.

Learning the Right Lessons?

The light-footprint plan was based on the assumption that a heavy footprint would lead to a Soviet- or British-style quagmire. A key lesson from the past was that a large foreign army would elicit large-scale popular resistance. U.S. officials also believed that small numbers of ground troops and airpower, working with Afghan forces, would be sufficient to establish security. "The history of British and Soviet military failures in Afghanistan," said Douglas Feith, "argued against a large U.S. invasion force."[77]

But this was a misreading of the Soviet experience. The key lesson was not the number of Soviet forces deployed but rather how they were used. One of the most comprehensive studies of Soviet combat tactics in Afghanistan, Lester Grau's book *The Bear Went Over the Mountain*, concludes: "The Soviet Army that marched into Afghanistan was trained to fight within the context of a theater war against a modern enemy who would obligingly occupy defensive positions stretching across the northern European plain." The Soviets used artillery, tanks, and ground forces to destroy Afghan positions, and "Soviet tactics and equipment were designed solely to operate within the context of this massive strategic operation."[78]

The Soviets used conventional tactics to fight an unconventional war. They terrorized the population rather than trying to win support for the Afghan regime. This allowed the United States, Pakistan, Saudi Arabia, and other governments to exploit the resentment by providing military and financial assistance to the mujahideen.[79] In short, the problem with the Soviet approach was not a heavy footprint. Rather, the Soviets were unprepared to fight a counterinsurgency that required them to focus on garnering the support of the local population. The Soviet footprint was, in reality, light. In January 1984, for instance, CIA Director William Casey informed President Ronald Reagan that the Afghan mujahideen, with backing from the U.S., Pakistan, and Saudi intelligence services, controlled two-thirds of the countryside. He argued that the Soviets would have to triple or quadruple their deployments in Afghanistan to put down the rebellion. Rather than being overcommitted, they were underresourced.[80]

Was the light-footprint approach a wise one? In one of his final reports before leaving Kabul as the European Union's special representative to Afghanistan, Francesc Vendrell poignantly remarked in 2008 that the "UN decision to adopt a 'light' footprint deprived the organization of the tools to undertake the kind of reforms the Afghans desired." In addition, he contended that the "U.S. obsession with Iraq diverted energies from Afghanistan, while the decision to limit the deployment of the International Security Assistance Force (ISAF) to Kabul . . . limited its effectiveness."[81] The rest of this book argues that while the light footprint may not have been the direct cause of the Afghanistan insurgency, it certainly played an important role. The low levels of international assistance—including troops, police, and financial aid—made it difficult to stabilize Afghanistan as the insurgency began to worsen. And it strengthened the role of local warlords. Despite these challenges, however, the initial engagement in Afghanistan had some early successes.

CHAPTER EIGHT

Early Successes

IN SEPTEMBER 2004, Zalmay Khalilzad flew to the western Afghan city of Herat to meet with the Tajik warlord Ismail Khan. With his bushy white beard, Khan had a reputation for running the best fiefdom in Afghanistan. At the request of President Bush, Khalilzad had left Washington in November 2003 to become the U.S. ambassador to Afghanistan. He was going to see Ismail Khan on a sensitive mission, and he had the support of Washington and President Karzai.

"We had been encouraging the removal of several governors who were weakening the power of the central government," Khalilzad told me. So he flew to Herat, met with Ismail Khan, and, standing next to him, announced that Ismail Khan had agreed to move to Kabul.[1]

This brazen act—putting Ismail Khan on the spot by offering him a position in Karzai's cabinet, which he reluctantly accepted—was vintage Khalilzad. He was the only senior White House official in the Bush administration who had lived in Afghanistan, and he had a visceral feel for the country's social, cultural, and political intricacies. As an Afghan, he understood the people of Afghanistan and their warrior spirit, and his familiarity with Pashtun culture, including his fluency in both national Afghan languages, Dari and Pashto, made him a tremendous asset. His influence among Afghan officials was unparalleled among U.S. diplomats in the country. Behind his thick, six-foot frame was a charming, almost unassuming, personality. But Khalilzad could also be an imposing figure. He exuded an extraordinary sense of confidence and authority when he walked into a room, but his true métier was the face-to-face meeting.

Herat, in the fertile Hari River Valley, lies seventy miles from the Iranian border, along the ancient trade routes that linked Europe with the Middle East, India, and China. The city was later used by the British, Soviet, and Taliban armies, each of whom conquered the city and constructed key military installations. Ismail Khan had been a staple figure in Herat for several decades, participating in the Soviet War in the 1980s and the Afghan civil war in the early 1990s, until he was captured by the Taliban later in the decade. He escaped from a Taliban prison in 2000 and assisted United States forces during the 2001 invasion.

As U.S. forces withdrew to Iraq and international support withered, Ismail Khan became the de facto ruler of Herat. A decade earlier, the city's western suburbs had been a sea of ruins littered with burned-out tanks and land mines, a far cry from the city that Mountstuart Elphinstone had described two centuries earlier as the most stunning city in Afghanistan, with its "beauty and variety from the mosques, tombs, and other edifices, intermixed with numerous trees and gardens, with which it is embellished, and from the lofty mountains by which it is surrounded."[2] After coming to power, Ismail Khan began a major architectural refurbishing of this once-beautiful city. He orchestrated a flurry of new construction projects, including modern apartment blocks and tree-filled parks, and ensured a regular supply of electricity. Streetlights with energy-efficient bulbs gave the city an eerie, almost modern glow.[3]

But there was a problem. Ismail Khan had established security with his own militia forces and had retained most of the customs revenue from the trade that flourished between Herat and Iran and Central Asia. Other Afghan warlords were doing the same, but Ismail Khan posed one of the greatest challenges to Hamid Karzai and U.S. officials, including Khalilzad, who were trying to establish a strong, viable central government. Fighting involving tanks and mortars had erupted in March 2004 between Khan's forces and Afghan National Army units under General Abdul Zahir Nayebzadeh. Gunmen killed Ismail Khan's son, Mirwai Sadeq, the minister of civil aviation and tourism in Karzai's cabinet. On March 22, the Afghan government dispatched a force of 1,500 soldiers, headed by Defense Minister Muhammad Fahim, to restore order in Herat. But tensions continued, so Khalilzad made his trek to the city.

This period was, in many ways, a high-water mark of the U.S. experience in Afghanistan. Within the first two years of U.S. engagement, Afghanistan made significant gains on the political front. It held presidential and parliamentary elections, and the levels of insurgent violence stayed relatively low. But this hopeful opportunity for peace would eventually be squandered, as Khalilzad—ironically because of his success—was later moved to become U.S. ambassador to Iraq, and the United States increasingly shifted its attention and resources away from Kabul and the war in Afghanistan.

Important Strides

Even before Khalilzad's trip to Herat, the Afghan government had made extraordinary progress. In late 2001, James Dobbins had been appointed the U.S. envoy to the Afghan opposition; he was tasked with leading U.S. efforts to establish an Afghan government. Dobbins had no experience in Afghanistan, but he had performed admirably as U.S. special envoy to four major hotspots in the 1990s: Somalia, Haiti, Bosnia, and Kosovo. He was, he told me, "the State Department's handyman of choice in the increasingly busy craft of nation-building." Dobbins's goal was to broker an interim government among Afghan political leaders. While the United States would be deeply involved in this process, Dobbins admitted that the United States wanted to avoid "any appearance of occupying Afghanistan or selecting its new government." Consequently, the United States asked the

United Nations to take the lead. UN Secretary-General Kofi Annan assigned the job to Lakhdar Brahimi.[4]

In late November 2001, Brahimi, Dobbins, Khalilzad, and senior officials from India, Pakistan, Iran, Russia, and a number of European countries hammered out an agreement with Afghan leaders. The negotiations were fraught with difficulties. One delegate, Haji Qadir, abandoned the conference in a well-publicized huff, claiming that his ethnic group, the Pashtuns, was underrepresented. His tense departure raised the specter of further defections, which threatened to undermine the credibility of the whole process. Perhaps the most rancorous debates occurred during the choices of a leader and key cabinet ministers. Hamid Karzai was the leading candidate of the Iranians, Indians, Russians, and many of the European delegates. Pakistan's ISI also suggested Karzai as a candidate, something they undoubtedly regretted several years later. But the Afghans could not agree. Many wanted Abdul Sattar Sirat, a respected scholar of Islamic law who had been teaching in Saudi Arabia for several years. Finally, after intense pressure from Brahimi, Dobbins, and ultimately the Russians, the delegates agreed to an interim constitution and cabinet.

As Dobbins recalled: "The critical moment came when the Russian Ambassador in Kabul interrupted a meeting of the Northern Alliance top leadership to deliver a message from Moscow. The Russian government wanted the Northern Alliance leadership to understand that if they did not accept the package which was on the table in Bonn, they should expect no further Russian aid."[5]

On December 5, 2001, Afghan leaders officially signed the Bonn Agreement, and the UN Security Council endorsed it the following day.[6] The parties at Bonn had also asked the United Nations to "monitor and assist in the implementation of all aspects" of the agreement. UN Security Council Resolution 1401, passed on March 28, 2002, established the UN Assistance Mission in Afghanistan (UNAMA).[7]

In January 2002 in Tokyo, international donors pledged more than $4.5 billion to reconstruction efforts. Additional roles were assigned:

Britain agreed to be the lead nation for counternarcotics, Italy for justice, the United States for the army, Germany for police, and Japan for the disarmament, demobilization, and reintegration of former combatants. The emergency *loya jirga*, which was attended by about 2,000 people, took place between June 12 and June 19, 2002, following extensive preparations and countrywide consultations. At the conclusion, Afghan delegates chose Hamid Karzai as president of the transitional administration and head of state, and approved his nominees for key posts in the administration. Karzai gave the defense and foreign-affairs portfolios to the mainly Tajik Northern Alliance, and the Ministry of Interior portfolio to a Pashtun regional governor.

Following this breakthrough, media outlets thrived in the more permissive environment. Within three years, the government had registered 350 publications, 42 radio stations, and 8 television channels. Tolo TV, the most popular television station in Afghanistan, introduced a mixture of drama and satire to those Afghans who could afford televisions.[8]

Afghanistan also established the National Security Council (NSC) to provide advice and analysis to Karzai. "It was modeled after the United States NSC system," explained Daoud Yaqub, director for security-sector reform on the Afghan NSC. "But the British played the critical role of funding it and ensuring that it got off the ground."[9] Yaqub, an erudite, bespectacled Afghan-American with olive skin and carefully combed hair, had received his law degree from the University of Pittsburgh. In addition to Yaqub, Karzai appointed Zalmai Rassoul, a physician who had served at the Paris Cardiology Research Institute, as the first national security adviser. By 2003, the National Security Council had expanded to twenty members, meeting twice a week and coordinating among Afghan ministries.

Like Yaqub, Rassoul and Finance Minister Ashraf Ghani, many of Afghanistan's key policymakers were Western educated and had extensive experience living abroad. Ali Jalali, the minister of interior in charge of Afghanistan's vast police apparatus, was an American citizen who had served as the director of the Afghanistan National Radio

Network Initiative and chief of the Pashto Service at the Voice of America in Washington, DC. Muhammad Hanif Atmar, the minister of rural rehabilitation and development who later became minister of education, received his bachelor's degree in international relations and postwar development from York University in England. The fact that so many prominent senior Afghan government officials had lived abroad, however, naturally caused resentment among Afghan officials who had never left.

"Accelerating Success"

When Khalilzad took over as U.S. ambassador in 2003 from Robert Finn, America's first ambassador after the Taliban collapse, one of his most important contributions was bringing roughly $2 billion in additional assistance to Afghanistan—nearly twice the amount of the previous year—as well as a new political-military strategy and private experts to intensify rebuilding.[10] Relations were close between Khalilzad and Lieutenant General David Barno, the commander of U.S. forces in Afghanistan. A native of Endicott, New York, seventy miles south of Syracuse, Barno was congenial, almost unassuming, and was well liked by his staff. He was also extremely smart and surprisingly easy to get along with.

Barno moved into a half-trailer on the U.S. Embassy compound and established an office next to Khalilzad's. Each day, Barno attended country-team and security-group meetings with Khalilzad, and the two developed a common view of counterinsurgency operations. Barno also seconded five military staff officers to Khalilzad to make up an interagency planning group. This small core of talented planners—referred to as "the piglets"—applied structured military staff planning to the requirements Khalilzad faced in shaping the interagency response in Afghanistan.[11] Together, they developed a broad strategy in Afghanistan, though the planning had been underway for several months.

In early 2003, Marin Strmecki at the Department of Defense had helped develop an acceleration package for Afghanistan, which he had presented to Secretary Rumsfeld. The plan outlined a process for building Afghan institutions and defeating a low-level insurgency. Strmecki was a bright, somewhat reserved intellectual who had a law degree from Yale and a PhD from Georgetown University. He had served for sixteen years as a foreign-policy assistant to Richard Nixon, helping him with the research and writing of seven books on foreign policy and politics. At the time, Strmecki was the U.S. Department of Defense's Afghanistan policy coordinator and also served as the vice president and director of programs at the Smith Richardson Foundation.

Khalilzad, then at the National Security Council and a close confidant of Strmecki, took the acceleration package for Afghanistan to the White House and helped push it forward. It evolved into a Power Point presentation of roughly thirty slides that set U.S. goals for Afghanistan. The document assumed that Afghanistan was a central front in America's war against terrorism and, as Khalilzad prophetically warned, that a "lack of success—a renewed civil war, a narcostate, a successful Taliban insurgency, or a failed state—would undermine the Coalition's efforts in the global war on terrorism and could stimulate an increase in Islamist militancy and terrorism."[12] The "accelerating success" concept was approved by the Deputies Committee of the National Security Council on June 18, by the Principals Committee on June 19, and by President Bush on June 20, 2003. Khalilzad then began to work on obtaining additional funding even before he became ambassador to Afghanistan.

"There were several components of the strategy," noted Khalilzad. "The first was getting Afghan institutions built."[13] His goal was to enable the Afghan people to elect their government and build a national government with viable ministries that could deliver services to the population. "A key point of emphasis in our program," Khalilzad asserted, would be "on rural development and the private sector in Afghanistan. Economic development—the establishment of a thriving private sector—is as important as rebuilding infrastructure, schools, and clinics."[14] This was an important lesson from

Afghanistan's history, since Afghan wars have typically been won—and lost—in rural areas, not in the cities. One of the first orders of business would be jump-starting reconstruction. Khalilzad vowed to finish the road from Kandahar to Kabul, and he started a new one from Kandahar to Herat.

"A second component," Khalilzad continued, "was changing the balance in the Afghan government by removing some members and adding others in order to broaden support for the government and increase its competence."[15] When Ali Jalali, a Pashtun, was appointed minister of interior, some thought his appointment was political, a way of balancing ethnicities in Karzai's cabinet. But he had his own talents. The author of several books, Jalali had been a former colonel in the Afghan Army and was a top military planner with the Afghan resistance against the Soviets. His book *The Other Side of the Mountain* included more than 100 firsthand reports from mujahideen veterans and provided riveting accounts of the mujahideen experience in ambushes, raids, shelling attacks, and urban warfare.[16] In 2002, he had written an influential critique of reconstruction efforts in Afghanistan, arguing that they had enhanced the power of warlords. "Ethnic warlords with questionable track records claim to represent different ethnic groups and geographic regions in the country," Jalali wrote. "Despite their nominal support of the interim administration in Kabul, provincial strongmen and warlords maintain their private armies, sources of income, foreign linkages, and autonomous administrations."[17]

A final concern was "on the disarmament, demobilization, and reintegration of militia and weakening warlords, as well as reaching out to the Taliban through a reconciliation process"[18]—in other words, undermining Ismail Khan and the other warlords.

This strategy shifted the U.S. focus from counterterrorism to nation-building and counterinsurgency. Up to that point, the U.S.-led Coalition comprised more than 12,000 troops representing nineteen nations. It was led by Combined Joint Task Force-180, based at the old Soviet air base at Bagram, a twenty-minute helicopter flight north of Kabul. The United States had downsized the original Combined Joint Task Force in the spring of 2003, replacing a powerful and well-resourced three-star-led headquarters (XVIII Airborne Corps) and a subordinate division headquarters (Task Force 82) with a single division-level headquarters (10th Mountain Division). At the time, the declared aim of the military was to hunt down the remnants of al Qa'ida and Taliban leaders across the rugged landscape of southern and eastern Afghanistan, and to build the Afghan National Army. "Nation-building" was explicitly not part of the formula.[19]

In 2002 and 2003, U.S. soldiers could not use the word *counterinsurgency* to describe their efforts. Lieutenant General John R. Vines refused to countenance it. He was the commander of Coalition Task Force 82 in Afghanistan from September 2002 until May 2003, and then commander of Combined Joint Task Force 180 until October 2003. U.S. soldiers were told they were fighting terrorists.

Toward Counterinsurgency

Khalilzad and Barno's strategy ushered in a number of changes. Beginning in 2003, Barno established two ground brigade-level headquarters, one assigned to the hazardous south and the other to the east. As Figure 8.1 shows, the northern half of the country remained largely free from any enemy threat, which meant few international forces were necessary to stabilize the area. The brigade headquarters in the south and east became regional command centers, and each brigade was assigned an area of operations spanning its entire region. All organizations operating in this battle space worked directly for, or in support of, the brigade commander. These numbers eventually increased to 20,000 American and 10,000 NATO soldiers—which still left a ratio of only one soldier per 1,000 Afghans.[20] Barno recast United States and other Coalition units to fight a counterinsurgency rather than a counterterrorism mission, and he assigned forces specific territory where they were to secure the population.[21] He focused on putting a military and civilian presence in the south and east to create a "security halo" that would ensure protection for the local population.

FIGURE 8.1   U.S. and Coalition Battlefield Geometry, May 2004[22]

The early results were laudable. Following a visit to Afghanistan in October 2003, Secretary of Commerce Donald Evans wrote a memorandum for President Bush stating that Afghanistan was experiencing significant improvement. He visited an Afghan school, had lunch with U.S. troops, held meetings with key Afghan-American business leaders, and talked with senior Afghan government officials, such as Commerce Minister Sayed Mustafa Kazemi. Evans was buoyant, telling President Bush: "I witnessed a people who are enjoying freedom from the repressive Taliban regime. Four years ago there were 800,000 students (all boys) in the Afghan school system. Today, there are 4.5 million students—1.5 million who are girls—embracing their ability to pursue an education and to live in a country of hope and equality."[23]

The Afghan National Army (ANA) also made some progress against insurgents. In July 2003, for example, the ANA launched Operation Warrior Sweep with U.S. forces in Paktia Province against Taliban and al Qa'ida forces. This was followed in November 2003 by Operation Mountain Resolve in Nuristan and Kunar Provinces. The ANA deployed outside of Kabul to stem interfactional fighting in such areas as Herat and Meymaneh. During the constitutional *loya jirga* in December 2003, the ANA was deployed in the capital region to enhance security for the delegates. In 2004, the ANA conducted combat operations with such names as Operation Princess and Operation Ticonderoga in a number of provinces in the east and south. In March 2004, the government deployed some of its newly trained ANA soldiers to Herat to patrol roads, secure government and UN buildings, and institute a curfew following the removal of Ismail Khan. At first their efforts were marred by tensions and frustration. Afghan Army forces clashed with Ismail Khan's militia, and more than a hundred people were killed. But the ANA eventually succeeded in establishing law and order.

"Perhaps the best example of the competence of the Afghan National Army was their performance in Herat in 2004," Barno told me. "They didn't fire into the crowd and they established order. It was a good marker for their capability."[24]

One of the greatest achievements for both U.S. and Afghan forces was the return of democracy after a thirty-year hiatus, harkening back to Zahir Shah's "blueprint for democracy" period in the 1960s and early 1970s. Afghanistan, U.S. policymakers crowed, was establishing a viable and democratic government. In his 2004 State of the Union speech, President Bush announced: "As of this month, that country has a new constitution, guaranteeing free elections and full participation by women." He continued that the "men and women of Afghanistan are building a nation that is free and proud and fighting terror—and America is honored to be their friend."[25] In January 2004, Afghans had adopted a new constitution, and in October 2004 they elected Hamid Karzai as president. The United States and other Coalition forces had made securing the elections its strategic priority, and it had paid off handsomely.

"It was our main effort," noted Barno. "Successful elections took a tremendous amount of air out of the Taliban."[26]

In September 2005, Afghans elected a new parliament, which included a number of ex-Taliban ministers. One was Abdul Salam Rocketi, a fiery speaker who had earned the alias "Rocketi" for his exceptional skills in targeting Soviet tanks with RPG-7 rockets during the 1980s. Another was Mawlawi Arsallah Rahmani, who was elected to the upper house (*Meshrano Jirga*). The Hezb-i-Islami party was registered after pledging it had cut ties with Gulbuddin Hekmatyar. Its leader, Khalid Farooqi, was elected to the lower house (*Wolesi Jirga*).[27] Opinion polls showed high levels of support for Karzai. According to one poll in 2005, for example, 83 percent of Afghans rated President Karzai's work as either excellent or good.[28] This was a greater level of support than most Western leaders enjoyed, including George W. Bush, whose approval rating was only 45.7 percent in 2005 as the war in Iraq began to heat up.[29]

War in Iraq

The gains made by Khalilzad, Barno, and their Afghan allies looked especially promising compared to Iraq, which had quickly deteriorated into a bloody insurgency. Ronald Neumann had gone to Iraq in 2004 as part of the Coalition Provisional Authority (CPA). He went on to serve as the U.S. Embassy's principal interlocutor with the Multi-National Command in Baghdad, where he was deeply involved in coordinating the political part of military operations in Fallujah, Najaf, and other areas. With great dismay, Neumann watched the situation deteriorate in Iraq. In an informational memo to CPA Administrator Paul Bremer, he described the growth of coordinated "attacks across the country, primarily aimed at police forces in various locations." Neumann explained that "enemy cells, associated with the Zarqawi group, were moving out of Syria that possibly had the Green Zone on their target list," referring to the location in central Baghdad that housed the CPA and much of the international personnel.[30]

In fact, security in Iraq had been deteriorating since the summer of 2003. While senior U.S. government officials publicly assured

Americans that the situation was not as bad as press reports indicated, internal CPA documents showed growing alarm. In a June memo to Defense Secretary Rumsfeld, as they prepared to brief President Bush, Bremer noted that the threat to U.S. forces had become multifaceted.

First, elements of the former regime, such as Ba'athists, Fedayeen Saddam, and intelligence agencies had focused their attacks on three targets: Coalition forces, infrastructure, and Iraqi employees of the Coalition. "To date," Bremer wrote, "these elements do not appear to be subject to central command and control. But there are signs of coordination among them."[31] Former officers of the Mukhabarat, Iraq's intelligence service, were active in a number of ways, including making radio-detonated bombs. They used money channeled through radical Islamic clerics, who had been funded by wealthy donors in the United Arab Emirates and other Gulf countries.[32] Second was Iranian subversion: "Elements of the Tehran government are actively arming, training and directing militia in Iraq. To date, these armed forces have not been directly involved in attacks on the Coalition. But they pose a longer term threat to law and order in Iraq." Third, international terrorists—especially jihadists from Saudi Arabia, Syria, and Yemen—had arrived in Iraq to target the United States.[33]

In a briefing to President Bush at a July 1, 2003, National Security Council meeting, Bremer stated bluntly that "security is not acceptable." The threat, he continued, was from a conglomeration of Ba'athists, terrorists, Iranians, and criminals. The Iranian focus "is on Shias using several political parties."[34] U.S. security assessments also suggested an increasing tempo of attacks against Coalition forces using small arms, mortars, rocket grenades, and improvised explosive devices (IEDs). According to a CPA analysis, the "attack patterns show emerging regional coordination in: Baghdad, Karbala, Fallujah, Mosul, and Tikrit." In response, the Coalition conducted a series of offensive operations to pressure insurgent groups and disrupt their activities.[35]

Reports of the deteriorating security environment began to resonate with the Iraqi public. One of the first public-opinion polls in Iraq after the fall of Saddam Hussein confirmed that Iraqis were "unhappy" with their country.[36] A Gallup poll shared among CPA staff indicated that 94 percent of Iraqis in Baghdad believed the city was a more dangerous place to live after the U.S.-led invasion. Majorities also said they were afraid to go outside of their homes during the day (70 percent) and night (80 percent). And anti-American sentiments in much of Iraq were extremely high.[37]

By 2004, the security situation had become even worse in Iraq. Insurgents mounted attacks on the oil pipelines, denying the government petroleum revenues. A CPA assessment of critical infrastructure declared that "the Former Regime Elements demonstrate some agility in switching their attacks between Oil, Power and Rail—but greater ruthlessness should be anticipated. Damage to pylons, oil pipes and rail track is unacceptable but relatively easily repaired; sabotage of a power plant or refinery (Critical Infrastructure) is catastrophic." At one point there was an average of two attacks per day on infrastructure.[38] With more than 12,000 miles of infrastructure to protect, the Coalition and Iraqi security forces stood no chance of securing the entire system. Instead, they focused on critical infrastructure, developed intelligence-directed patrolling and air-surveillance capabilities, and invested in rapid repair techniques.[39]

Most alarmingly, reports from the CPA's regional offices suggested a spreading insurgency. "A number of incidents have occurred which have served to reinforce that this is a dangerous place," wrote Regional Security Coordinator Bill Miller in March. "We have had numerous attacks, bombings, rocket attacks, and improvised explosive devices."[40] After the assassination of CPA members Fern Holland, Salwa Oumashi, and Bob Zangas, staffers began wearing more protective equipment, varying times and routes of travel, increasing the presence of Gurkhas to provide security at camps, and taking State Department counterthreat classes. Bremer became sufficiently concerned about the security situation that he postponed U.S. congressional visits to Iraq, though not all members of Congress complied. Military convoys were being attacked so regularly that on April 17 Bremer seriously considered ordering food rationing at the CPA.[41]

Warning Signs

The levels of violence and sheer brutality continued to increase in Iraq, with the introduction of grisly suicide bombings and a string of beheadings in 2004. Afghanistan, by comparison, was relatively quiet. The Taliban and other insurgent groups, bolstered by the American preoccupation in Iraq and America's unwillingness to target them in Pakistan, began to conduct small-scale offensive operations to overthrow the Afghan government and coerce the withdrawal of U.S. and Coalition forces.[42] In April 2002, insurgents orchestrated a series of offensive attacks in Kandahar, Khowst, and Nangarhar Provinces. In 2003 and 2004, the Taliban continued a low-level insurgency from bases in Pakistan. Perhaps the most significant event was the September 2004 rocket attack against President Hamid Karzai in the eastern Afghan city of Gardez.

Insurgents also began to target international aid workers. Afghans organizing or otherwise involved in election work were attacked or killed. So were nongovernmental organization (NGO) workers and Afghan citizens believed to be cooperating with Coalition forces or the Afghan government. In October 2004, three UN staff members were abducted in Kabul. Attacks occurred throughout the country, though most were in the south and east, in such provinces as Nangarhar, Paktia, Paktika, and Khowst.[43]

The result was a decrease in security for Afghans and foreigners, especially those living in the east and south, but "the level of criminal activity—characterized by increasing numbers of armed robberies, abductions, and murders even in areas controlled by the ANA and police patrols—[was] still high."[44] Interfactional fighting continued among regional commanders in Herat, Nangarhar, Nuristan, Lowgar, Laghman, and Badghis Provinces.[45] The withdrawal in July 2004 of the NGO Médecins sans Frontières (Doctors without Borders), which had been in Afghanistan for nearly three decades, was a sobering testament to the deteriorating security environment. A month earlier, five Médecins sans Frontières workers had been ambushed and shot in the head in the northwestern province of Badghis.

"We began to get concerned about the insurgency in late 2003 with the shift in tactics," noted Afghan National Security Council official Daoud Yaqub. "There was an increase in the number of improvised explosive devices, and soft targets were increasingly attacked." But the U.S. position was different, he contended. "U.S. officials in Afghanistan didn't see the Taliban as a strategic threat then."[46]

Indeed, Lieutenant General Barno believed that "the Taliban were a fairly amateurish organization. There were only a few Arabs from al'Qaida present in Afghanistan, and we killed most of them. In 2004, we killed insurgents video-taping helicopter take-offs near Jalalabad. Most of the insurgent deployments we were seeing were in the 10s and 20s, not in the 100s of fighters. It was a ragtag group."[47] Nonetheless, there was thinning patience with the slow pace of killing or capturing insurgents in Afghanistan and Pakistan. Secretary Rumsfeld wrote a memo in October 2003 to the chairman of the Joint Chiefs of Staff and several top-level officials expressing frustration that "we are having mixed results with Al Qa'ida, although we have put considerable pressure on them—nonetheless, a great many remain at large." The United States had made some progress in capturing top Iraqi insurgents, but it "has made somewhat slower progress tracking down the Taliban—Omar, Hekmatyar, etc."[48]

Bitter Irony

Despite these concerns, the levels of violence in Afghanistan were relatively low. Fewer than 300 Afghans died in 2004 because of the insurgency, which paled in comparison with the tens of thousands who died in Iraq in 2004.[49] Most Afghans believed the security situation was somewhat better than under Taliban rule. An opinion poll conducted by the Asia Foundation indicated that 35 percent often or sometimes feared for their personal safety, a decline from 41 percent during the Taliban period.[50] And another poll showed that 84 percent of Afghans believed that their living standard had improved since the end of the Taliban government.[51]

Yet fate took a strange twist. In 2005, Zalmay Khalilzad replaced John Negroponte as U.S. ambassador in Iraq. It was a move symptomatic of the U.S. government's tunnel vision on Iraq. The State Department had taken one of its most seasoned and effective ambassadors, who spoke Afghanistan's two main languages and had a special rapport with its political leaders, and moved him to Baghdad during an extraordinarily fragile period in Afghanistan's history. Lieutenant General David Barno was replaced by Lieutenant General Karl Eikenberry, effectively shattering the military-civilian coordination Khalilzad and Barno had painstakingly fashioned during their tenure together. Perhaps it shouldn't have come as a surprise. Iraq had taken center stage as America's most important foreign-policy concern. Proven staff were in great demand and Khalilzad and Barno had thus far been among the best. Still, it was a dangerous gamble.

The rise of an insurgency in Afghanistan was a serious and unfortunate development. Insurgencies frequently lead to the death of thousands—and sometimes millions—of civilians. To paraphrase Princeton history professor Arno Mayer, if war is hell, then insurgency belongs to hell's darkest and most infernal region.[52]

CHAPTER NINE

The Logic of Insurgency

ONE OF THE twentieth century's most successful insurgents, the Chinese leader Mao Zedong, wrote that there is an inextricable link in insurgencies "between the people and the troops. The former may be likened to water and the latter to the fish who inhabit it."[1] Insurgencies require a motivated leadership but, more important, they can only form amid a disillusioned population. Mao had both. He led China's beleaguered peasants, who had been harshly oppressed by the feudal landowners, in a violent insurgency that toppled the government and Chiang Kai-shek's National Revolutionary Army in 1949.

Mao's experience was comparable to that of countless other insurgencies, virtually all featuring poorly trained and badly equipped guerrillas overwhelming a much more powerful opponent. In the American Revolutionary War, Francis Marion, better known as the "Swamp Fox," organized a disheveled band of fighters in South Carolina against the British. Operating with great speed and elusiveness from inaccessible bases, and taking advantage of local hatred against the British, Marion's troops struck isolated garrisons, convoys, and other targets in rapid succession. The British, unable to effectively counter Marion, complained that he fought neither "like a gentleman" nor "like a Christian." His actions inspired the "Song of Marion's Men," by the American poet William Cullen Bryant, which hailed the geographical advantage held by the Americans:

Our fortress is the good greenwood,
Our tent the cypress-tree;
We know the forest round us,
As seamen know the sea.[2]

Bryant's poem highlights a practice that Afghan insurgents would mimic several centuries later: the use of guerrilla tactics against a better-equipped conventional military. This chapter seeks to understand insurgencies at a systematic level in order to explain the situation in Afghanistan. Why do insurgencies begin? The first question to ask is: What exactly is an insurgency?

Understanding Insurgencies

An insurgency is a political-military campaign by nonstate actors who seek to overthrow a government or secede from a country through the use of unconventional—and sometimes conventional—military strategies.[3] Insurgent actions also cover a range of unconventional tactics, from small-scale ambushes and raids to large-scale, lethal violence.[4] They usually involve four principal actors.

The first are *insurgents*, those hoping to overthrow the established national government or secede from it.[5] In Afghanistan after the 2001 fall of the Taliban, key insurgent forces included the remnants of the Taliban, Gulbuddin Hekmatyar's Hezb-i-Islami, the Haqqani network, al Qa'ida and other foreign fighters, criminal groups, and a host of Afghan and Pakistani tribal militias. The second is the *local government*, which includes the government's security forces, the army and police, as well as key national and local political institutions. In states with weak central governments, such as Afghanistan, tribal militias may also serve these purposes. The third group consists of *outside actors*: external states and other nonstate entities, which might support either side. Outside actors can tip the balance of a war in favor of either insurgents or the government, but they can rarely win it for either side. There were two sets of external actors in Afghanistan. The United States, NATO forces, and the United Nations supported the Afghan government; the international jihadi network and some individuals from neighboring states—such as Pakistan and Iran—supported the insurgents.

Finally, the *local population* is the most important group; it is for their hearts and minds that the war is being fought in the first place. The support of the population is the *sine qua non* of victory in counterinsurgency warfare.[6] As one study of the insurgency in El Salvador concluded: "The only territory you want to hold is the six inches between the ears of the *campesino*."[7] Each side needs money, logistics, recruits, intelligence, and other aid to achieve its objectives.[8] Support is especially critical for insurgents, who must fight asymmetrically. Political scientist Daniel Byman writes,

> Pity the would-be insurgent. He and his comrades are unknown to the population at large, and their true agenda has little popularity. Indeed, most countries around the world oppose their agenda. Many of the fighters are not experienced in warfare or clandestine operations, making them easy prey for the police and intelligence services. Their families are at the mercy of government security forces. The government they oppose, in contrast, is relatively rich, has thousands or even millions of administrators, policemen, and soldiers, and enjoys considerable legitimacy.[9]

If insurgents manage to separate the population from the government and external forces, however, and acquire its active or passive support, they are more likely to win the war. In the end, the exercise of political power depends on the tacit or explicit agreement of the population—or, at worst, on its submissiveness.[10]

While outside actors often play an important role, they rarely stay for the duration of the conflict, and the result of the war is almost always a function of the struggle between the local government and insurgents.[11] My analysis of insurgencies since 1945 shows that successful counterinsurgency campaigns last for an average of fourteen years, and unsuccessful ones last for an average of eleven years. Many also end in a draw, with neither side winning. Insurgencies can also be brutal, drawn-out affairs: more than a third of all insurgencies last more than twenty years, with the incumbent governments winning slightly more than twice as often as the insurgents.[12] Again, only a few of these conflicts are fought—and won or lost—by foreign armies. Most countries quickly tire of having their troops deployed abroad, as the Soviets did during their Afghan campaign. Moreover, most local populations view foreign armies as occupiers, which impedes success.[13] A lead indigenous role, on the other hand, can provide a focus for national aspirations and show the population that they—and not foreign forces—control their destiny.

Research on past cases suggests that two factors correlate strongly with the beginning of an insurgency: weak governance and a well-articulated cause from insurgent leaders. Competent governments that can provide services to their population in a timely manner are rarely beset with insurgencies. But there are also uncontrollable factors: countries with low per-capita incomes are at a greater risk of insurgency. Geographical factors are important too. Mountainous terrain can have a compounding effect on the grievances of a restive population.[14] David Galula, a French military officer and counterinsurgency expert, wrote that the ideal location for insurgents is a landlocked country with mountains along the borders, a dispersed rural population, and a primitive economy.[15] If ever a country matched this description, it surely would be Afghanistan.

Governance Collapse

Weak and ineffective governance—the ability to establish law and order, effectively manage resources, and implement sound policies— is a necessary precondition for the rise of insurgencies.[16] It creates a supply of disgruntled locals eager to find other ways of governing themselves. Political scientist Stathis Kalyvas explains:

> Insurgency can best be understood as a process of competitive state building rather than simply an instance of collective action or social contention. . . . State building is the insurgent's central goal and renders organized and sustained rebellion of the kind that takes places in

civil wars fundamentally distinct from phenomena such as banditry, mafias, or social movements.[17]

If insurgents take advantage of weak governance and assume state-like functions, they can raise tax money, set up administrative structures, and begin to perform government functions.

In the Canipaco Valley of central Peru, for example, the Shining Path (*Sendero Luminoso*) guerrillas "assumed control and organized every aspect of the inhabitants' daily life. Sendero undertook the administration of justice and played the role of a moralizing force. Shining Path settled marital conflicts, supervised the work of teachers, mediated the relationships between the *comuneros* and those authorities and state functionaries who were not obliged to quit, executed thieves who robbed livestock from the herders and even organized recreation."[18]

In Vietnam, the Vietcong were able to establish a highly sophisticated five-level "shadow" administrative infrastructure run by close to 40,000 full-time employees by the end of 1968. "One of the striking conclusions from interviewing [Vietcong] defectors," wrote Jeffrey Race in *War Comes to Long An*, "is the total absence of government movement in revolutionary areas for years at a time, except on occasional large-scale sweep operations which had little impact on the Party's local apparatus."[19] According to another account, "peasants conscripted into the revolutionary organization became more than soldiers in a temporary fighting force; they potentially became subjects integrated into a new institution founding the basis for a nation-state."[20] Even before Vietnam, in the Philippines during the 1950s, "one government was legal, but in these areas had little or no physical control. The insurgent government was illegal, but had partial or complete control and enforcement capability."[21]

A key essence of weak governance, then, is enforcement. Following Max Weber, any government that cannot control a monopoly on physical force will be unable to force people to comply with the state's laws.[22] Since the Enlightenment, philosophers in the tradition of Hobbes and Kant have seen a link between strong and responsible governments with peace and order. Even Adam Smith, the English economist and philosopher famous for advocating a minimal government role and the invisible hand of the market, supported a strong and competent security force to establish domestic order.

So how does weak governance contribute to the outbreak of an insurgency? By definition, weak states cannot meet the basic needs of their population.[23] They cannot consolidate authority over all their territory and they often do not succeed in maintaining order within the territory they do control.[24] They fail to use state resources to promote security or serve the public interest.[25] Weak states lack sufficient bureaucratic and institutional structures to ensure the functioning of government. They often lack trained civil servants and thus can barely operate school systems, courts, welfare systems, and other essentials for social functioning.[26] It is not just that law and political institutions in these states are ineffective. It is that the faith in law and political institutions that underpins policing and order does not exist.[27] Without confidence in the rules of society, including the quality of contract enforcement, the police, and the courts, the general public will look to other organizations to provide structure and order.

Political scientists David Laitin and James Fearon, who examined all civil wars and insurgencies between 1945 and 1999, found that "financially, organizationally, and politically weak central governments render insurgency more feasible and attractive due to weak local policing or inept and corrupt counterinsurgency practices."[28] Another study found that between 1816 and 1997, "effective bureaucratic and political systems reduced the rate of civil war activity."[29]

In many cases, weak governments have stemmed from the legacy of colonization, since most colonies of the post–World War II era were unprepared for independence when it arrived. The imperial powers put little thought or effort into establishing in their colonies domestic governance structures that could function on their own.[30] A few colonies, such as India and Sri Lanka, had been allowed a degree of self-government. But others, such as Somaliland, were little more than outposts. Somalia struggled with a weak state after its independence in 1960 and experienced several major insurgencies. The structural fragmentation of the Somali state was a relic of the circumstances of its independence, which required the unification of two separate colonial administrative structures. Each half of Somalia had its own judicial system, currency, administrative rules, taxation rates, accounting systems, and legal histories, which had to be unified into a single system.[31] Somalia also faced a severe lack of resources. Scholar Patrick Brogan has written that Somalia confronted "a depressing future as a perpetually impoverished Third World country with very few natural resources, constantly burdened by drought and the refugees from Ethiopia."[32] Somalia's security forces also lacked the capacity to contain conflict. Without a strong central state, the country reverted to its nineteenth-century condition—with no internationally recognized polity, no national administration exercising real authority, no formal legal system, no banking and insurance system, no police and public-security service, no electricity or piped-water system, and weak officials serving on a voluntary basis surrounded by violent bands of armed youths.[33]

In the Philippines, the weak state under Ferdinand Marcos contributed to the insurgency beginning in 1972. The army was "rotten to the core" and rampantly corrupt.[34] Marcos himself was notorious for his graft. He dismantled the democratic structures bequeathed to the country by the United States and reduced an already-poor country to near-insolvency.[35] In Lebanon, a delicate sectarian balance led to the emergence of a weak state in the 1970s, which fueled competition among the three leading religious communities—the Maronites, Sunnis, and Shi'ites—triggering an insurgency that lasted from 1975 to 1991.[36]

There are dozens of examples—from Bosnia and Georgia in Europe to Mozambique in Africa. In many cases, the states were so weak that they could not establish order in peripheral geographic areas. In each case, these gaps were filled by insurgents. In Cuba, Fidel Castro and his guerrillas used the Sierra Maestra Mountains as a base of support to train new recruits, rearm and regroup, and prepare for forays into the countryside.[37] Again, in Peru, Shining Path units formed in Ayacucho, a rural area that had historically received little government attention and control. In Ayacucho, a Peruvian newspaper editor said, "There are no liberated areas, only abandoned areas."[38]

In Congo, the insurgency that began in 1960 in Katanga Province was based on fundamental structural weaknesses inherited from Congo's Belgian colonial legacy. To the degree that any state structure existed, it was "virtually improvis[ed] from scratch" and essentially a replica of the Belgian constitution that had been revised for the Congo only five months earlier.[39] The constitutional framework of the government collapsed less than three months after independence. When Angola became independent in 1975, it inherited a weak state structure that suffered from a lack of adequate governmental capacity, bureaucratic structures, and governmental experience. Nearly all of the skilled labor in the country was Portuguese, and 90 percent of the Portuguese fled the country before independence. This loss of skilled labor led to plummeting agricultural exports and the collapse of the service sector.[40] These structural weaknesses directly contributed to the rise of an insurgency.

The reverse is also true: strong governance can prevent insurgencies. There was a good possibility of an insurgency in Kenya in the 1980s because of intense ethnic antagonisms, electoral violence, and a coup attempt in August 1982. But the relative strength of the state helped avert major violence.[41] Despite deep concerns about insurgencies arising in Kazakhstan and Uzbekistan after the collapse of the Soviet Union, there were none. One factor was the rise of strong, though undemocratic, governments that were able to control their minority (and majority) populations.

Insurgent Motivations

If weak and ineffective governance served as a precondition, what motivated insurgent groups to fight? Some have argued that the ethnic grievances averted in some former Soviet republics were responsible for insurgent motivations. Ethnic ties, it is claimed, are stronger, more rigid, and more durable than the social ties in ordinary social or political groups.[42] Consequently, ethnic combatants are more committed than other groups and less likely to make negotiated concessions. The Afghan insurgency seems to sustain the theory that ethnic violence is U-shaped. In other words, it is less likely to occur in highly homogeneous and highly heterogeneous countries and more likely in countries (such as Afghanistan) with an ethnic majority and numerous small ethnic minorities.[43] In addition, hypernationalist rhetoric and real atrocities can harden identities to the point that cross-ethnic political appeals are unlikely to be made and even less likely to be heard. As a result, restoring civil politics in multiethnic states shattered by war is difficult because the war itself destroys the possibilities for cooperation.[44]

Following the overthrow of the Taliban government in 2001, Afghanistan's ethnic mix was approximately 50 percent Pashtun, with smaller percentages of Tajiks, Uzbeks, Hazaras, and other ethnic groups.[45] Such diversity, this argument assumes, created competing ethnic power centers, even among Northern Alliance forces.[46] As early as 2001, the CIA had "detected serious rifts and competition between the Tajiks, Hazaras and Uzbeks." One assessment reported: "Afghanistan truly is a zero sum game. Anytime anyone advances all others consider this to be at their expense."[47] Consequently, many have assumed that the insurgency was caused by interethnic grievances, especially among Afghanistan's Pashtuns, who believed they were being marginalized by northern ethnic groups.[48] The United States and Afghan governments, according to Afghanistan expert Thomas H. Johnson, inevitably faced "an extremely difficult challenge of unifying a fragmented society and fostering the development of a national identity because each ethnic group [attempted] to gain a foothold in government often at the expense of other groups." Since the "attempt at entering government is taken from an ethnic approach, rather than a national one, the fragmentation of society will continue until either one dominant ethnic group controls all of the governmental power or ethnic politics makes way for increased internal conflict."[49]

But there is little evidence to support this argument. The Taliban and its network were not motivated to fight because of ethnic concerns. Nor did the population support the Taliban and other groups because of ethnic ties. In fact, there were deep divisions among the Pashtun ethnic majority about the Taliban. The Taliban had support from a number of Pashtun Ghilzai tribes, as well as such Durrani tribes as the Nurzai and Ishaqzai in southern Afghanistan. But most Durrani Pashtuns did not support the Taliban, nor did a number of other eastern and southern Pashtun groups. Nor was ethnicity a major factor in how Afghans voted. Hamid Karzai won the 2004 presidential elections with support in Pashtun provinces as well as in non-Pashtun northern provinces such as Balkh and Kunduz.[50] In a 2004 Election Day survey during the presidential elections, only 2 percent of Afghans said they voted for a candidate based on ethnicity.[51] In addition, public-opinion polls conducted in Afghanistan suggested that ethnic grievances were not a major concern of the Afghan population. An opinion poll conducted by the U.S. State Department, for example, found that most Hazaras, Pashtuns, Tajiks, and Uzbeks did not view ethnicity as a dividing factor. Instead, a large majority (85 percent) thought it was essential for Afghanistan to remain one nation. The data show that most Afghans did not see "their country headed toward an irresolvable ethnic clash" but rather endorsed a "unified, multi-ethnic state."[52] Other opinion polls found that most people identified themselves as Muslims and then Afghans, but rarely by ethnicity.[53]

Even among disaffected Afghans most likely to support the Taliban, ethnicity does not seem to have been a major concern. In a 2004 public-opinion poll conducted by the Asia Foundation, for example, Afghans reported being most concerned about governance failures.[54] This finding was supported in later Asia Foundation polls.[55]

Rather than exacerbating tensions, the Afghan government successfully balanced the country's ethnic groups through representation in the national government. Even though Tajik and Uzbek military forces were the leaders in the victory over the Taliban in 2001, Afghan representatives at the December 2001 Bonn Conference chose Karzai, a Pashtun, as their interim leader. James Dobbins, the U.S. envoy at the Bonn Conference, recalled that negotiators made a concerted effort to compose "a balanced cabinet, balanced among political factions, ethnicities, and gender."[56] Over the next several years, the U.S. government and President Karzai consciously worked to establish ethnic balance at the level of ministers and deputy ministers, who were ordered in turn to consider ethnic diversity when appointing governors and police chiefs.[57]

Insurgent leaders were primarily motivated by religious ideology, rather than by ethnic grievances or profits from drugs or other commodities. An ideology is an organized collection of ideas—or, as the French Enlightenment philosopher Count Antoine Destutt de Tracy once noted, it is the "science of ideas." For insurgents, an ideology provides a normative vision of how society should be structured, including its political system.[58]

As has been noted, the Taliban were motivated by a radical interpretation of Sunni Islam derived from Deobandism. The leaders of most other insurgent groups—from the Haqqani network to Gulbuddin Hekmatyar's Hezb-i-Islami, al Qa'ida, and Tehreek-e-Nafaz-e-Shariat-e-Mohammad—had strong religious motivations to fight. A Taliban field manual titled *Military Teachings: For the Preparation of Mujahideen* lucidly argued that "in a situation where infidels and their crooks are ruling the world, it is the prime duty of all the Muslims to take arms and crush those who are bent upon crushing the Muslims throughout the world. . . . This is the best time to take on the usurpers and occupants of our holy land.[59] Together, the leaders of these and other groups wanted to overthrow Hamid Karzai's government and replace it with a regime that adopted their own extreme version of Sunni Islam.

In short, there was a supply of disgruntled locals because of the collapse of Afghan governance, and a demand for recruits by ideologically motivated insurgent leaders. This combination proved deadly for the beginning of Afghanistan's insurgency. Over time, too little support to the government from the United States and its allies, and too much support to insurgents from outside states and the international jihadi community, contributed to these problems.

The Need for Effective Police

Each of these insurgencies, from the Philippines to Afghanistan, necessarily begs the question of who should have kept order in these countries in the first place. While military and paramilitary forces play a key role in maintaining safety and security for society, the police are perhaps the most critical component for ensuring the safety of the people. They are the government's primary arm focused on internal-security matters. Unlike the military, the police usually have a permanent presence in cities, towns, and villages; a better understanding of the threat environment in these areas; and better intelligence. This, of course, makes them a direct target of insurgent forces, who often try to kill or infiltrate them.[60] Nevertheless, an effective police force is critical to establishing law and order. Government military forces may be able to penetrate and garrison an insurgent area and, if well sustained, may reduce guerrilla activity. But once the situation in an area becomes untenable for insurgents, they will simply transfer their activity to another area and the problem will remain unresolved.[61] A viable indigenous police force with a permanent presence in urban and rural areas is a critical component of counterinsurgency.

Without a strong local police force, warlords and political entrepreneurs often flourish and finance their private militias through criminal activity, including trafficking in arms and drugs. Simple banditry—fueled by military desertion, the breakdown of social structures, and demobilization of government forces—may be endemic and crime will increase.[62] In Afghanistan, too little outside support for the Afghan government and too much support for insurgents further undermined Afghan governance. This combination proved deadly for the onset—and continuation—of the insurgency. Among the first Afghan institutions to teeter, much like during the Soviet period, were the police and the other security services.

CHAPTER TEN

Collapse of Law and Order

BEGINNING IN 2005, Afghanistan's fragile national-security architecture began to crumble. The Taliban and other insurgent groups
began to mount more aggressive offensive operations, and Afghan
forces proved incapable of counterattacking and protecting the population. To better understand this development, Amrullah Saleh, the
head of Afghanistan's intelligence agency, the National Directorate of
Security (NDS), commissioned a study on the state of the insurgency.
Saleh was a Panjshiri Tajik who had been a trusted protégé of Ahmed
Shah Massoud and had worked closely with the CIA before the September 11 attacks. He spoke excellent English and wore neatly pressed
Western suits. Barely thirty years old in 2004, when Karzai appointed
him to run Afghanistan's spy agency, Saleh was a reformer with a reputation for great efficiency. He "had a real impact" on NDS, recalled the
CIA's Gary Schroen, "moving it forward with reorganization and
restructuring, instituting training at all levels, establishing a recruitment program based on talent rather than ethnic or family background, and dramatically improving morale and performance."[1]

Saleh based the study, titled *Strategy of Insurgents and Terrorists in
Afghanistan,* on intelligence reports from NDS stations across Afghanistan, reports from informants in Afghanistan and Pakistan, detainee
interrogations, meetings with Taliban leaders, open-source information, and interviews with Afghan National Army commanders and a

variety of national and local officials. It was designed to be the most comprehensive study of the current situation yet assembled. The study found that the Afghan police and army forces were failing in their primary mission on a monumental level. "When villagers and rural communities seek protection from the police, either it arrives late or arrives in a wrong way." U.S. forces, still operating at "light-footprint" levels, could not fill the vacuum. The lack of security began to undermine local support, and many who had cooperated with the government were killed, intimidated into silence, or fled. "Those who are collaborating with the government or coalition forces are now forced to move their families to the cities fearing attacks from the Taliban. This exodus of government informants and collaborators from the villages is a welcome development for the Taliban, insurgents and terrorists."

The result was that increasing amounts of territory fell into the hands of the Taliban or allied groups. Saleh's report continued: "The villages are gradually emptied of pro-government political forces and individuals. These rural areas become sanctuaries for the Taliban and the population is left with no choice but to become sympathizers of the insurgents." In these pockets, he found exactly what we might expect: The Taliban had begun to establish a shadow government, including an administrative structure and courts. Lamenting these disturbing results, Saleh wrote:

> I wish to be contradicted in my analysis of the situation and our perspective of what is going on and what is going to happen. Unfortunately, everybody I have so far talked to agrees with this picture in general terms. It is unfortunate because it is no longer only terrorism. It is insurgency. It is not about which individual is hiding where but about a trend which is undermining us in the rural areas. I still hope that I am wrong.[2]

A Monopoly of Force?

It was no surprise that the police weren't living up to expectations. Afghan police had not received formal training for at least two decades.[3] Germany, which had sent special forces to Afghanistan in late 2001 and had hosted the Bonn Conference, had volunteered to assess and rebuild the police. The initial German fact-finding mission in January 2002 discovered that "the police force is in a deplorable state just a few months after the dissolution of the Taliban regime" and that "there is a total lack of equipment and supplies. No systematic training has been provided for around 20 years. At least one entire generation of trained police officers is missing."[4] The first team of German police advisers arrived in March 2002 to train police instructors at their academy in Kabul. Officers, mostly inspectors and lieutenants, started a three-year course, taking classes in human rights, tactical operations, narcotics investigations, traffic, criminal investigations, computer skills, and Islamic law.[5]

By 2003, however, officials at the U.S. State and Defense Departments and the White House became increasingly agitated about the German approach. Many argued that it was far too slow, trained too few police officers, and was seriously underfunded. As one high-level U.S. official told me: "When it became clear that they were not going to provide training to lower-level police officers, and were moving too slowly with too few resources, we decided to intervene to prevent the program from failing."[6] German assessments of progress in rebuilding the police noted that a paltry "17 German police officers—men and women from both our federal and state police forces—are advising the Afghan Transitional Authority on this challenging task of crucial importance for the country's democratic future."[7] One can hardly blame U.S. government officials for thinking the Germans were not serious about training. In 2003, Donald Rumsfeld wrote to CPA Administrator Paul Bremer and General John Abizaid, commander of U.S. Central Command, scoffing, "Colin Powell told me this morning that the Germans have offered to help train police in Iraq. I mentioned that I thought they had a done a pretty slow job in Afghanistan."[8]

After supplementing German efforts, the United States reorganized the program to train recruits at a central facility in Kabul, as well as at regional centers in Kandahar, Mazar-e-Sharif, Gardez, and Jalalabad. The State Department's Bureau of International Narcotics and Law Enforcement Affairs (INL) oversaw the entire program. Since the end of the Cold War, INL had played an increasingly prominent role in civilian police efforts abroad. It had some administrative, budgetary, and managerial capacity to organize and run a policing program, but it had no police to deploy and no significant operational capabilities. Consequently, it contracted the private security firm DynCorp International, headquartered in the leafy Washington suburb of Falls Church, Virginia, to build facilities and help train the police in Afghanistan.[9]

DynCorp emerged out of two companies formed in 1946: California Eastern Airways and Land-Air, Inc. In 1951, California Eastern acquired Land-Air, and over the next several decades the company changed its name several times, settling on DynCorp in 1987. They were largely involved in providing mission support and repair to U.S. military aircraft. But after the collapse of the Soviet Union and the increase in U.S. stability operations in Haiti, Bosnia, and Kosovo, DynCorp broadened its scope to police training and security protection. DynCorp was not alone. With military costs rising and an increased number of operations abroad, the U.S. government began to rely on a growing list of companies—including Military Professional Resources Incorporated (MPRI) and Blackwater—to provide such security functions as police training, protective security, convoy protection, border enforcement, and even drug eradication in failing states.

For their mission in Afghanistan, DynCorp recruited retired U.S. police officers, as well as some active members of state and local police forces, to serve as the U.S. contingents of civilian police teams. From the beginning, senior U.S. military officials had worried that the INL program was not doing a good job of creating more competent Afghan police, and others were concerned that many of the Dyn-Corp advisers had had little experience training police from a Third World tribal society such as Afghanistan. This led to growing tension between the Defense and State Departments in Washington and Afghanistan. The relationship became so bad at times that key INL personnel were not allowed without an escort onto Camp Eggers in Kabul, the headquarters of U.S. police training efforts.

Afghan government officials also began to grow increasingly concerned about the shoddy state of the police and the unwillingness of the international community to make police training a priority. For example, Minister of Interior Jalali met with National Security Adviser Rice in Washington to push for police reform. He pleaded with her, arguing that the police "should be the front line in protecting highways, borders, and villages." In September 2003, during Donald Rumsfeld's five-day swing through Afghanistan and Iraq, Jalali lobbied the secretary to focus on the police. In a 2004 meeting in Berlin with Zalmay Khalilzad and German Interior Minister Otto Schily, Jalali suggested that the international community "should adopt the Balkans model of policing," which would require the use of competent, high-level police such as the *carabinieri* and the *gendarmerie* to train and mentor Afghan police, as they had done in Bosnia and Kosovo.[10] But U.S. policymakers were more interested in building the Afghan National Army than in training police. And German policymakers were reluctant to increase their commitment to police training.

By 2004, there was growing impatience in the White House and the Department of Defense that the State Department effort was failing in the police effort. Rumsfeld wrote a series of "snowflakes"—short, pithy memos that he frequently sent to senior Pentagon officials—expressing concern that the police program was undermining U.S. and broader NATO counterinsurgency efforts. His letters expressed a profound lack of confidence in the State Department's police-training capability.

In 2004, Lieutenant General David Barno held a series of video teleconferences (VTCs) with Secretary Rumsfeld, telling him that "police training needed to be done more systematically. They needed a strategy, he said, for what the end state needed to look like, and what kind of resources were needed to get there."[11] According to Barno, Secretary Rumsfeld and Condoleezza Rice, by then the secretary of state, finally agreed to get the Defense Department more directly involved in police training, but only in the spring of 2005. This process had taken at least a year. Barno, Khalilzad, Rumsfeld, and other U.S. officials, including Under Secretary Douglas Feith, were supportive of this shift. But Robert Charles, assistant secretary at INL, who had developed a reputation as hardheaded and abrasive among those who worked with him inside and outside the State Department, blocked the shift. Turf concerns between State and Defense may have partly caused the resistance, since INL was the lead U.S. agency for training foreign police. Whatever the cause, the Department of Defense only became involved after Charles departed.[12]

Lieutenant General Karl Eikenberry, who succeeded Barno in May 2005 as commander of Combined Forces Command—Afghanistan, is a strikingly intelligent career soldier who earned master's degrees from Harvard University in East Asian Studies and Stanford University in political science. He also served as a National Security Fellow at Harvard's Kennedy School of Government. Nora Bensahel, who later went on to Harvard University's John M. Olin Institute for Strategic Studies and the RAND Corporation, was in the same PhD class at Stanford University before Eikenberry was called back to the Pentagon in 1994. "He was very smart," Bensahel recalled, "and brought a tremendous amount to the program. Not only could he talk international relations theory, he was a practitioner as well."[13] But some of his staff also found him confrontational. In a meeting with Afghan Minister of Defense Abdul Rahim Wardak in 2005, for example, he capped a testy conversation by saying: "Minister Wardak, I know your army better than you do."

Eikenberry appointed Major General Robert Durbin in late 2005 to head the office in charge of training the Afghan police and army, which was saddled with an unwieldy name: Combined Security Transition Command—Afghanistan. Durbin had a reputation as a tough soldier who could also be thoughtful and reflective. Arriving in Kabul in January 2006, he found the police in terrible shape; the United States had people with the wrong skill sets in key positions, and their tours were only four to six months. "I honestly believed I could change the police force in a few months," noted Durbin. "After a number of months, however, I began to realize that it would take over a decade. The amount of institutional change needed was immense."[14] It took Durbin until March 2006 to put together a plan to staff, equip, and train the Afghan National Police. By then, he had concluded that the United States needed to implement a program for the police similar to the one they had put in place for the Afghan National Army.

Durbin continued to develop the police plan until June 2006, when he was asked to put a price tag on this effort. After going back and forth with Eikenberry, the two agreed to request a total of $8.6 billion for the Afghan National Army and Afghan National Police: $5.9 billion for fiscal year 2007 and $2.7 billion for fiscal year 2008. Roughly two-thirds of the money they requested was for new equipment for the police. The amount was astounding, more than the gross domestic product of about fifty countries.[15] Through dogged efforts over several months, Durbin finally managed to get the budget approved, despite the initial displeasure of Secretary Rumsfeld.

Durbin also ramped up efforts to build an effective Ministry of Interior. He secured the assistance of the private contractor MPRI, which helped build personnel and logistics systems. MPRI helped the ministry formulate the budget, pay the soldiers, and perform other basic functions, but they also made sure the system was "Afghanized" by working with key Afghans in the ministry. Durbin's plan envisioned three years to build what he called "base functionality" in the Ministry of Interior, since it was starting from scratch. In August 2006, he identified fifteen key systems and focused on the top five: personnel, finance, logistics, training management, and communications. Durbin told me, "We started at the top of the ministry and worked our way down." His goal was to create full operating capacity within a year.[16]

For Durbin, one of the most challenging aspects of the police program was the number of countries involved. The United Kingdom, Canada, Netherlands, Germany, and other nations working with Afghan police all wanted a say in how their money and resources were spent. This was understandable, but it also made coordination problematic and made it difficult to assign police resources in the places where Durbin assessed gaps. Most countries tended to have parochial visions of the program. After Afghan police graduated from the regional training centers, NATO countries had different—and sometimes entirely incompatible—programs for developing police in the field. One senior Pentagon official told me:

> Coalition efforts to build Afghan police and army forces were, to put it diplomatically, deeply challenging. The South Koreans pulled their forces out of Afghanistan in 2007, and then volunteered a few slots in their defense college for Afghan soldiers. How was this going to help us? Do three or four Afghans really need to go to South Korea for training? The Germans also wanted us to build a military logistics school for Afghans in the north, but not for all of Afghanistan. Our response was: we need to develop a program for all of Afghanistan, not just in specific sectors.[17]

Policing Woes

The painfully slow progress in refashioning Afghanistan's police force created a slew of challenges. General Durbin told Condoleezza Rice in June 2006 that there was no office in the United States government that could effectively build a foreign government's police force; INL did not have experience in rebuilding a large country's police force, nor did the Departments of Defense and Justice.[18]

Consequently, government analysts began to express increasing alarm at the state of the Afghan police. The Offices of Inspector General of the Departments of State and Defense reported that the readiness of the Afghan police force "to carry out its internal security and conventional police responsibilities is far from adequate. The obstacles to establish a fully professional [Afghan National Police] are formidable." It found major obstacles: "no effective field training officer (FTO) program, illiterate recruits, a history of low pay and pervasive corruption, and an insecure environment."[19] Another assessment led by U.S. Colonel Rick Adams lambasted the Ministry of Interior as "ineffective," "poorly led," and "corrupt," and the police forces as "poorly equipped."[20]

A number of Afghan government officials agreed, at least in theory.[21] But the Afghan government was sometimes its own worst enemy. In 2003, Interior Minister Jalali had pushed for the implementation of what became known as the Afghan Stabilization Program. As envisioned by President Karzai's cabinet, the program was intended to spread the central government's authority to all provinces and districts. Working on the assumption that all politics in Afghanistan are local, the Afghan Stabilization Program included the construction of key infrastructure in each district, such as police barracks, a prison, a post office, and a mosque. Ideally, well-trained and well-paid Afghan police thus could be sent to a functioning district center. But the program became bogged down in interministerial turf battles, with several key ministers—from the Ministries of Finance, Rural Rehabilitation and Development, and Communications—fighting over a share of the money. There was also significant disagreement about which areas of the country the program should target. Some pushed for Balkh, a relatively quiet province in the north that was home to such strongmen as Abdul Rashid Dostum. But others argued that it should focus on the east and the south, where the Afghan government and NATO forces were fighting insurgents.[22] In the end, the Afghanistan Stabilization Program floundered. In a moment of polite understatement, a private consulting firm reported that the plan fell "short of requirements."[23]

The police were sorely needed to help establish order in urban and rural areas, but, as we've seen, they were poorly equipped, corrupt, and badly trained. Worst of all, they lacked any semblance of a national police infrastructure. This was especially true in southern Afghanistan. In 2006, the U.S. military concluded that in the south, the Afghan National Police had only "87 percent of weapons with 71% of ammunition; 60% of vehicles; 24% of communications; and 0% of individual equipment such as body armor, batons, handcuffs, binoculars, jackets and first aid equipment."[24] They also lacked uniforms, police stations and jails, national command and control, and investigative training.[25] The Ministry of Interior was in particularly bad shape. Another U.S. military report found that the "MoI Finance is broken at every level." There was "no actual disbursement capability" to pay police officers, "no formal lines of accountability" which "perpetuates corruption at every level."[26]

Afghan, U.S., and European officials involved in police training reported pervasive corruption throughout the force. An Afghan trucker put it succinctly: "Forget about the Taliban, our biggest problems are with the police."[27] Police regularly demanded bribes to allow drugs and other licit and illicit goods to pass along routes they controlled. Police chiefs were frequently involved in skimming money they received to pay their police officers.[28] Some district- and provincial-level police chiefs were also involved in "ghost police" schemes. Since the international community paid law-enforcement salaries, some chiefs inflated the number of officers on their payrolls and pocketed the extra money.[29] Colonel Rick Adams, who headed the Police Reform Directorate for the U.S.-led Combined Security Transition Command—Afghanistan, said the first challenge in reforming the police was "overcoming a culture of corruption."[30] An Afghan government report was even more frank, claiming that "allegations of nepotism and unethical recruitment practices are commonplace," and "financial improprieties have been one of the most visible problems afflicting the Ministry and the police reform process."[31] These findings led to a flurry of efforts within the U.S. military and the State Department to curb corruption in the police. Durbin and his staff began vetting top-level police officials, trying to audit cash flows for paying police officers. They also increased the number of police paid through electronic funds transfers at local banks, rather than giving the money to police commanders, who inevitably would pocket some of it.

Nevertheless, U.S. State and Defense Department officials acknowledged that it was extremely difficult to vet Afghan police officers or units.[32] There was little systematic information on the background of individuals or units, and documents frequently were destroyed by the Afghan Ministry of Interior—or never existed in the first place. The office in charge of training the Afghan police and army, Combined Security Transition Command—Afghanistan, focused largely on vetting top-level Ministry of Interior officials. There was comparatively little focus on mid- and lower-level police.[33] As discouraging as it was, corruption appeared to be more pervasive in the police than in the other security forces.[34]

The result was that Afghan National Police were often overmatched in conducting counterinsurgency and counternarcotics operations, as well as curbing cross-border infiltration. In some cases, including in southern Afghanistan, Afghan police actively collaborated with Taliban. A German assessment of the border police reported: "Neither the Afghan border police nor the customs authorities are currently in a position to meet the challenges presented by this long border."[35] Interior Minister Jalali argued that "because of the late start in comprehensive police development, the [Afghan National Police] continues to be ill-trained, poorly paid, under-equipped, and inadequately armed."[36] Afghan forces had a difficult time even against criminal organizations. In one incident in Balkh Province, police forces were attacked, captured, and disarmed by a drug cartel after an armed clash.[37] And again, in the days following a police-led operation to capture Taliban fighters in Sangsar village in the southern province of Kandahar, an after-action report found that there was "no joint plan," "no unity of command," and "no intel sharing" between the police and Afghanistan's intelligence service. The result was seven casualties and one friendly-fire incident. All Taliban escaped.[38]

In many ways, however, the police were an afterthought; the international training for law enforcement was simply not as good as it was for the Afghan National Army. In the course of four years, control over the police was shifted among three agencies—from the German lead in 2002, to the U.S. State Department in 2003, and finally to the U.S. Defense Department in 2005. DynCorp International set the tone for this sorry state of affairs early on, and some of the blame can be assigned to them. The State Department and DynCorp focused largely on "outputs," such as the number of police trained, rather than "outcome" measures such as police performance against insurgents or drug traffickers. They had too few people and too few resources.[39] The quality of DynCorp police trainers varied widely. Some had significant international police training experience and were competent in dealing with police in a tribal society in the middle of an insurgency. But many other DynCorp trainers had little experience in such an environment.[40]

Senior Bush administration officials had more scathing criticism of DynCorp. Ambassador Ronald Neumann told me: "What DynCorp did was take a police officer out of a cesspool, train him for a few weeks, and throw him back into a cesspool. This," he said pointedly, "did not result in a lot of cleanliness over the long run."[41] Yet Neumann was quick to acknowledge that building competent and legitimate police has been a major problem in past counterinsurgency operations. "The early focus on low-level training was inadequate," said Neumann. "DynCorp was executing the contract they were given and I do not think one can entirely hold them reponsible for how the contract was structured."[42] Deputy Secretary of State Richard Armitage similarly told me that "DynCorp simply didn't do a good job in training the police."[43] Afghan officials repeated this charge. Minister of Interior Jalali said, "The DynCorp police trainers were a mixed bag. I personally rejected a number of DynCorp contractors because they had little or no useful background for training police in Afghanistan." He noted that DynCorp "checked boxes"—they were more interested in completing a contract, not in creating a competent, viable police force.[44]

To help alleviate the police concerns, the Afghan government and the Combined Security Transition Command—Afghanistan came up with a plan to build what became known as the Afghan National Auxiliary Police. "There were not enough guns and people to protect local villagers," remarked Ambassador Neumann. "This is counterinsurgency 101: to protect the local population."[45]

In February 2006, Ambassador Neumann and General Durbin were approached by senior officials from the Afghan Ministries of Interior and Finance while General Eikenberry was out of town. The Afghans wanted to hire an additional 200 to 400 police per district. The idea was to create a new force, to be called the Afghan National Auxiliary Police. Durbin and his deputy, Canadian Brigadier General Gary O'Brien, briefed Neumann on the initial concept in the spring of 2006, and Durbin then briefed President Karzai in May 2006. The plan was to establish a police force designed to fill the local gaps in Afghan security forces.[46] The auxiliary-police program meant training a local force for ten days and equipping its members with guns. They were then sent to secure static checkpoints and to conduct operations with Coalition forces against insurgents in six unstable provinces: Helmand, Zabol, Kandahar, Farah, Oruzgan, and Ghazni.[47] At the same time, Durbin moved to dissolve the Highway Police, who were interminably corrupt, regularly took bribes at checkpoints along major highways, and harassed local Afghans.

U.S. officials pointedly tried to avoid turning the auxiliary police into a village militia by recruiting them individually and paying and supervising them through the Ministry of Interior. "There were numerous efforts on the provincial level by local officials to recruit on a militia basis," said Neumann. "We tried to fix those problems by sending out mixed teams from the U.S. Embassy, CSTC—A [Combined Security Transition Command—Afghanistan], and DynCorp to see what was happening on the local level. We fixed some of those problems." But the auxiliary-police program still ran into additional snags. Ministry of Interior officials began recruiting without supervision in other provinces and then went to U.S. officials for reimbursement. "I refused to concur with this request and blocked it," remarked Neumann, "on the grounds that the recruits had not been vetted."[48]

Still, the auxiliary police were never well integrated into Pashtun tribes, subtribes, clans, and qawms in the south and east—and, consequently, were never accepted at the social level.

The program was opposed by some senior U.S. military leaders, such as General Eikenberry, who argued that it was only a stopgap measure—a tactical solution to a systemic problem with the police. But Eikenberry, who wanted to avoid a major fight with the State Department and the White House, ultimately did not pull out a "red card" and kill the program.[49] In retrospect, he didn't have to. The auxiliary-police program eventually lost steam. When I visited Kandahar and Helmand Provinces in September 2007, for example, most auxiliary police were being used intermittently. By 2008, when I went back again, they were essentially gone.

Afghan National Army

The Afghan National Army was better. The United States led rebuilding efforts for the ANA, although French, British, and Turkish instructors, as well as instructors from other Coalition countries, were also involved.[50] Training commenced in May 2002, when the Afghan Army's first regular army battalion began ten weeks of infantry and combat training at the Kabul Military Training Center. The United States then assigned some of its best soldiers, from 1st Battalion, 3rd Special Forces Group, to organize the initial effort.[51] Unlike the police program, the effort to build a viable army began immediately after the overthrow of the Taliban.

In the fall of 2002, Secretary Donald Rumsfeld asked General Eikenberry to help coordinate security-sector efforts in Afghanistan. Eikenberry then headed the Office of Military Cooperation—Afghanistan, which was charged with building the Afghan National Army. He developed a comprehensive approach, so one of his most significant contributions was to reform the Ministry of Defense. "There was an existing ministry and a General Staff that had been taken over by members of the Northern Alliance in 2002," Eikenberry noted, "but it was dysfunctional and not inclusive of all ethnic groups." Eikenberry and his team, with assistance from MPRI, built an organizational diagram of the Ministry of Defense that included key offices and positions. "My next step was to begin compiling a list of candidates for the top 35 positions in the General Staff with an eye toward creating an ethnically-balanced, merit-based ministry," he continued. The process for choosing candidates was fairly transparent and done with Afghan partnership.

"In the late spring and early summer of 2003, my team and I briefed President Karzai and other key Afghan leaders, who provided additional candidates for the 35 positions," he recalled. "I wanted to create sustainable institutions that were well-vetted with and trusted by the Afghans."[52]

Eikenberry's efforts had a significant impact on the training of Ministry of Defense officials and soldiers.[53] New Afghan recruits received training in basic rifle marksmanship, platoon- and company-level tactics, use of heavy weapons, and engineering and other skills. Desertion rates were initially high—Afghanistan's 1st Battalion had a desertion rate of approximately 50 percent per month—but the rate eventually dropped to 10 percent per month by the summer of 2003, between 2 percent and 3 percent per month by 2004, and 1.25 percent per month by 2006.[54]

Afghan Army efforts ran into trouble after Eikenberry left Afghanistan in 2003, though he returned in 2005 as head of Combined Forces Command—Afghanistan. He was followed by two U.S. Air Force generals with little experience in building foreign armies: U.S. Air Force Major General Craig P. Weston and U.S. Air Force Major General John T. Brennan. "Putting Air Force personnel in charge of army training was like putting an Army general in charge of building an Afghan Air Force. He wouldn't know what to do," one senior U.S. Army official told me.[55]

In December 2005, Secretary Rumsfeld visited Kabul and met with Minister of Defense Wardak, National Security Adviser Zalmai Rassoul, and Minister of Finance Anwar ul-Haq Ahadi. Wardak is a burly, overbearing figure who became an officer in the Afghan Army in the 1980s but later defected to the mujahideen and joined the National Islamic Front of Afghanistan of Pir Sayyid Ahmad Gailani. He was involved in one of the most lethal attacks against the Soviet Union, code-named Operation Avalanche, a 1987 ambush against a Soviet convoy that inflicted one of the highest levels of Soviet casualties in one day since World War II.[56] Wardak had an affinity for the United States, testifying several times before the U.S. Congress during the Soviet War, and received medical treatment in the United States after being wounded by a Scud missile in 1989. Ahadi also had close connections with the United States, having received his PhD in political science from Northwestern University. He had taught at Carleton and Providence Colleges.

"Rumsfeld read us the riot act," recalled Daoud Yaqub, who was present at the December meeting. An Afghan army of 70,000, which Minister of Defense Wardak had supported, was simply unsustainable. Rumsfeld said an army with between 45,000 and 52,000 soldiers was "a bit more reasonable." If the Afghans wanted to have a 70,000-man army, he warned, they would have to take money from somewhere else. This triggered major budget discussions within the Afghan government, although the funds were eventually found to support the larger number.[57] With Durbin at the helm of Combined Security Transition Command—Afghanistan in 2006, performance steadily improved. Several units of the ANA were deployed throughout Afghanistan to conduct combat operations and establish law and order.

In 2005, Afghan National Army forces had notable success in Kunar Province with Operation Catania, which targeted insurgent hideouts prior to the September parliamentary elections.[58] In 2006, ANA soldiers played a key role in two major counterinsurgency offensives— Operation Mountain Thrust in southern Afghanistan and Operation Mountain Lion in Kunar—among several others.[59] Soldiers from the 3rd Brigade of the Afghan National Army's 203rd Corps fought alongside members of U.S. Task Force Spartan, made up of soldiers from the 3rd Brigade Combat Team of the 10th Mountain Division and Marines from the 1st Battalion, 3rd Marine Regiment. More than 2,500 Afghan National Army and Coalition forces were involved in the operation.[60] In 2007, ANA units, backed by a small contingent of U.S. military forces, played the leading role in Operation Maiwand in Ghazni Province against the Taliban. They also played critical roles in fighting Taliban forces during Operation Achilles in Helmand Province.

Sometimes members of the ANA were helpful in more lighthearted ways. In 2006, for example, U.S. Special Operations Forces and Afghan Army forces were involved in heavy fighting near Tarin Kowt, a small, dusty town of 10,000 in central Afghanistan's Oruzgan Province. The town's only airstrip was on the military base of the NATO provincial reconstruction team, which was locally called "Kamp Holland" since it housed a sizable contingent of Dutch soldiers. One Special Operations soldier watched, somewhat perplexed, as an Afghan Army soldier put down his Kalashnikov during the fighting, looked toward Mecca, and prayed to Allah. He repeated the action far more than the five obligatory daily prayer times for Muslims.

At the end of the battle, the U.S. soldier asked him what he was doing. "I was praying to Allah to deliver U.S. Apache helicopters," the Afghan responded. "And you know what? Allah listened. The Apaches showed up and saved the day." Just as the Russians had relied heavily on helicopter support, the Apache attack helicopter was deployed fairly often by the United States against insurgents operating in rural areas. It could lay down a dizzying display of fire from 30-millimeter automatic cannons that could shoot 625 rounds per minute, Hellfire antitank missiles, and rockets. The Hellfire thermobaric missiles carried by some Apaches were particularly ruthless. "The effect of the explosion within confined spaces is immense," one CIA report noted. "Those near the ignition point are obliterated. Those at the fringe are likely to suffer many internal and thus invisible injuries."[61]

Afghan National Army soldiers began to earn a reputation as tenacious fighters in battle. By all accounts, they were more proficient in tactics, techniques, and procedures for fighting counterinsurgency warfare after their U.S. training. When asked to perform crowd control, deliver humanitarian assistance, gather intelligence about insurgents and their support network, and assist in other civil-action projects, the ANA impressed many observers.[62] They were also effective in gathering intelligence about insurgents, their support network, and weapons caches. Some argued, however, that the emphasis on quality had had too high a price tag. A World Bank study found that the "ANA salary structure, determined apparently without reference to fiscal constraints or pay elsewhere in the civil service, has set a precedent which the police and other sectors aspire to and which will be fiscally costly."[63]

Despite increasing levels of competence, however, Afghan Army forces still suffered from a lack of indigenous air support and the absence of a self-sustaining operational budget. They relied on embedded international forces and U.S. air support during combat, and their weapons were shoddy. As with the police, many soldiers had little ammunition and few magazines. Afghan Army units had few mortars, machine guns, MK-19 grenade machine guns, and artillery. They had almost no helicopter or fixed-wing transport, and no attack aviation. They had little or no body armor or blast glasses, Kevlar helmets, up-armored Humvees, or light-armor tracked vehicles with machine-gun cupolas and slat armor.[64] This impacted their ability to conduct sustained operations on their own against well-equipped Taliban raiding forces, who possessed rocket-propelled grenades, recoilless rifles, and antiaircraft artillery such as the Russian-made DShK 12.7-millimeter machine gun.[65]

Protecting the Local Population

The inability to establish law and order in rural areas of Afghanistan pushed local communities into the hands of the Taliban. Afghan intelligence admitted, "We have not been able to provide policing and protection for the villages against the insurgents or the negative elements in general."[66] Other internal Afghan documents reiterated this problem. There "is a perception amongst the population that not enough is being done to improve their security and that widespread criminality and corruption contribute to a situation not dissimilar from that which led to the rise of the Taliban [in the early 1990s]."[67] This was a striking conclusion. As one senior Afghan official told me: "The Afghan National Army goes into a town, clears it of insurgents, stays for a few days, and then leaves. But it doesn't provide long-term security. This causes significant unhappiness among the local population." He continued: "Much of the local 'support' for the Taliban is passive. People fear for their lives if they oppose the Taliban."[68]

A public-opinion poll conducted for Combined Forces Command—Afghanistan acknowledged that approximately 50 percent or more of most respondents in the east and south had *no weekly contact* with the Afghan National Police. The same poll found that less than 20 percent of local respondents in most eastern and southern provinces trusted the police.[69] This had a ripple effect on rural villagers. Afghans who cooperated with the government, or even openly supported it, often faced grave danger from Taliban and other insurgent forces across the south and east of the country.

By late 2005, a growing number of villages in these rural areas were emptied of pro-government political forces and supporters, and they gradually fell into the hands of the Taliban and other insurgent groups. This process was not entirely different from the approach that Afghan mujahideen took during the Soviet War, focusing most of their efforts on rural areas. The population was left with little choice but to become active or tacit supporters of the insurgents. A study for NATO forces in Afghanistan discovered that support for the Taliban was positively correlated with rural areas, partly because they had little or no government security presence. "The capacity of the government to protect people is more limited outside the centre of the province," it acknowledged. "A majority of people in provincial centres believe that the government can protect them from insecurity, compared to a minority outside the centres."[70]

While the United States had committed sufficient attention and resources to building the Afghan National Army, it took a pass on the police. It handed over the police program to Germany, which failed to seriously fund or manage the program. Initial U.S. efforts to salvage the police floundered, as the State Department relied on DynCorp International, which lacked the capacity to rebuild a broken police force from scratch in a tribal society. By the time the U.S. military tried to bail out the police program in 2006, incalculable damage had already been done. These challenges might have been mitigated had the Afghan government not begun to come apart at the seams in other areas.

CHAPTER ELEVEN

A Growing Cancer

A FEW YEARS after the fall of the Taliban regime, a joke began to work its way through Afghan intellectual circles. An Afghan goes in to see the minister of interior. "Minister," he pleads, "you need to fix the growing corruption problem in our government. The people are becoming increasingly frustrated with government officials who are corrupt and self-serving." After listening carefully, the minister responds: "You have convinced me there is a problem. Now how much money will you give me to fix it?"

Afghan faith in their government waned as they became concerned about skyrocketing corruption and incompetence. Senior U.S. officials were acutely aware of these problems. Lieutenant General David Barno argued that a critical pillar in counterinsurgency efforts in Afghanistan was "good governance," which included the provision of essential services to the population.[1] International organizations such as the World Bank were equally keen to support governance. One World Bank assessment emphasized "investments in physical infrastructure (especially roads, water systems, and electricity), agriculture, securing land and property arrangements, creating a healthy business climate with access to skills and capital, good governance, health, and education."[2]

The problem was *not* that Afghan and international leaders failed to understand the importance of governance and its impact on the insurgency. Virtually everyone paid lip service to governance. Rather, it was prioritizing governance over other efforts and translating this into reality. "Most people complained about policy," explained Ronald Neumann, reflecting on his tenure as U.S. ambassador in Afghanistan over coffee one day in downtown Washington, DC. "But what we lacked was an ability to *implement* [it]."[3] The challenge, he told me, was like Aesop's fable "Belling the Cat." A group of mice called together a committee to consider how to protect themselves from a cat that was harrassing them. The best solution, one mouse proposed, was to bell the cat, which was met with general applause. But this left one key question: Who would put the bell around the cat's neck? "This was a question of implementation," argued Neumann. "Since there were no volunteers, the policy was useless."[4]

In a 2004 public-opinion poll conducted by the Asia Foundation, Afghans responded that two of the biggest problems in their local areas were the lack of jobs and the lack of electricity.[5] Over the course of the next two years, jobs and electricity would remain the most significant infrastructure problems, in addition to access to water.[6] U.S. government polls—most of which were not released publicly—showed similar results. In one survey conducted between August 30 and September 9, 2006, by the U.S. State Department, Afghans who supported the Taliban complained that they had little access to clean water and employment.[7]

There was international assistance to fix these problems, but it didn't always reach its intended targets. One study found that the primary beneficiaries of assistance were "the urban elite."[8] This triggered deep-seated frustration and resentment among the rural population. There's no doubt that the Afghan government suffered from a number of systemic problems and had difficulty attracting and retaining skilled professionals with management and administrative experience. Weak administration and lack of control in some provinces made tax policy and administration virtually impossible. In many rural areas, the government made no effort to collect taxes. In 2004, the World Bank warned of "a distant and hostile central administration that cannot provide pay or guidance to its staff in the provinces and districts in a timely manner." It concluded that Afghan government personnel "at the provincial and district levels urgently need the resources and support necessary to do their jobs. In turn, mechanisms are needed at all levels of government to ensure that real accountability . . . is built into the administrative system."[9]

Fixing the Dam Problem

By 2005, only 6 percent of the Afghan population had access to power from the electricity grid.[10] Those who did have power suffered through low voltage, intermittent supply, and blackouts. The dire situation reflected a lack of investment by the Afghan government and the international community, as well as insufficient maintenance. In addition to grossly insufficient generation capacity (which was augmented by power imported from neighboring countries), the system was plagued by inadequate transmission, poor distribution, and lack of backup equipment. Most efforts focused on bringing electricity to urban areas of the country, not to rural areas in danger of succumbing to the Taliban.

Ambitiously, the Afghan government set a goal to increase coverage of the electricity grid in urban areas to 90 percent by 2015.[11] For those rich enough to buy generators, electricity was not a problem; their needs were met by the Afghan economy's dominant informal sector. A large portion of the electricity supply, for example, was provided by small-scale generators. "The bulk of Afghans," reported the World Bank, however, "still do not have reliable electric power supply and clean water. Thus the situation that prevailed in the 1970s and during the long period of conflict—basic social services not reaching most of Afghanistan's people—has not yet been fundamentally changed, with the only partial exception being primary education, which actually improved considerably after the U.S. arrived in 2001."[12]

Numerous government efforts to increase electricity ground to a halt. In 2002, for example, President Karzai's cabinet explored the possibility of importing electricity into Kabul from Uzbekistan, which already supplied electric power to the northern area around Mazar-e-Sharif, supplementing a small local gas-fired power plant. Kabul received minimal electricity from three hydroelectric power dams: the 100-megawatt Naghlu Dam, the 66-megawatt Mahi Par Dam, and the 22-megawatt Sarobi Dam. Due to a lack of water flow on the Kabul River, however, only the Naghlu Dam was operational year-round.[13] The Uzbek government had agreed in principle to provide energy to Afghanistan, but it requested in return that the Afghan government help pay for refurbishing and constructing transmission lines on a short stretch of land in Uzbekistan near the Afghan border. Debate in the cabinet stalled, and no decision was taken until 2004. By 2007, for bureaucratic reasons, electricity had still not been exported from Uzbekistan to Kabul, and the transmission lines from Uzbekistan to the Afghan border had still not been built.[14]

Of the Afghan power projects, few were as important as the Helmand Province's Kajaki Dam, built in the 1950s with funding from the U.S. Export-Import Bank. The dam sits near the head of the Helmand River, fifty-five miles northwest of Kandahar City, surrounded by rolling hills and some of Afghanistan's most fertile land. In 1975, the U.S. Agency for International Development (USAID) commissioned the installation of two 16.5-megawatt generating units in a powerhouse constructed at the base of the dam.[15] Twenty-six years later, U.S. aircraft bombed the Kajaki Dam powerhouse during the early stages of Operation Enduring Freedom. Transmission lines were also hit by a U.S. airstrike in November 2001, but they were repaired the following year. Over the next several years, the United States led efforts to rebuild the dam, but in 2006, the Taliban began a series of attacks on transmission lines, periodically cutting off power to Kandahar. With each outage, NATO began to recognize more fully the dam's strategic importance and defended it more carefully. In reponse, the Taliban stepped up their campaign.

NATO Secretary-General Jaap de Hoop Scheffer noted that "when the turbine in that dam is [installed], it will give power to 2 million people and their businesses. It will provide irrigation for hundreds of farmers. And it will create jobs for 2,000 people. The Taliban, the spoilers, are attacking this project every day to stop it from going forward."[16]

But protecting the dam was extraordinarily difficult, and the effort nearly collapsed several times. Perhaps the closest call was in 2006. USAID had contracted refurbishment of the dam's turbines to the Louis Berger Group, a U.S.-based company that specialized in the planning, design, and construction management of highways, dams, and other infrastructure. Louis Berger subcontracted security for the dam to U.S. Protection and Investigations (USPI), a private company involved in armed escort and security protection in such countries as Nigeria, Algeria, Colombia, and Saudi Arabia. USPI, in turn, hired local Afghans to stand guard.

In the fall of 2006, the security situation at Kajaki became increasingly tenuous as the Taliban laid siege to the dam and Afghan security guards began to mutiny. The Taliban had intimidated local Afghans and threatened to kill anyone who cooperated with NATO, and the frightened police stopped showing up for work. Afghan engineers and American security contractors at the dam began to grow desperate; they had little food and other materials, since trucks couldn't get through to resupply the few workers who remained. USAID personnel asked NATO for an emergency resupply. One NATO official said, "The situation was dire. If any more Afghan security officials had departed, USAID was going to pull out. There was no security. The dam was being attacked with recoilless rifles, rockets, and mortars."[17]

Security of the dam was a frequent subject of discussion between Ambassador Neumann and General David Richards, head of the NATO International Security Assistance Force. "The basic problem was that our understanding of the situation on the ground was different, and worse, than ISAF's understanding," acknowledged Neumann. He took a trip to the dam with Brigadier General Stephen Layfield, ISAF's deputy commander for security, on August 28, 2006, to assess the situation. They discovered that "the Taliban controlled everything around the dam and security was worse than ISAF thought because of the lack of ANA and desertions from the local security force. After that trip, U.S. Embassy and ISAF understanding of the situation seemed to improve."[18]

Nevertheless, British forces operating in Helmand Province refused to provide security, since they were already bogged down elsewhere in combat operations against Taliban and other fighters. In desperation, Michelle Parker, the NATO USAID development adviser, went to General Richards and pleaded for help. Richards, who had served three tours in the British Army in Northern Ireland, was a keen student of military history. He came through. Combat resupply reached the Kajaki Dam in thirty-six hours, though the lack of security complicated the mission. A lumbering Chinook, the versatile, twin-engine heavy-lift helicopter used by the U.S. military, had to turn around on the initial trip into the dam and enlist armed Apache AH-64 helicopter escorts because of attacks from Taliban ground forces. Fully resupplied, the dam now needed security, so General Richards ordered a platoon of British troops to protect it.[19]

The struggle to rebuild the dam, to provide electricity to parts of southern Afghanistan, and to counter local frustration highlights one of the core paradoxes of reconstruction in Afghanistan. How do you build infrastructure and deliver key services in a deteriorating security environment? Two years later, in September 2008, a convoy of 4,000 Coalition troops, 100 vehicles, and helicopter and airplane escorts fought their way through Taliban-controlled areas to deliver a new turbine to the Kajaki Dam. The turbine was flown into Kandahar Airfield and escorted 110 miles to the dam site.

Several Canadian International Development Agency officials lamented the difficulties of reconstruction in a war zone. One official, based out of Kandahar Province, told me: "Our biggest challenge is security. Virtually all non-governmental organizations have left the province because of the insurgency, except for a few pockets in urban areas such as Kandahar city. . . . The Canadian government, like the U.S. and British governments, faces extraordinary challenges in convincing civilians from development agencies to come here. It is too dangerous. The result," he acknowledged, almost apologetically, "is that the military is stuck with reconstruction."[20]

Operational Primacy

Just months after the crisis at the Kajaki Dam, Lieutenant General Karl Eikenberry, as commander of Combined Forces Command—Afghanistan, commissioned a major new strategic assessment. Dubbed Operational Primacy, it identified provinces ready to assume and sustain Afghan leadership, including leadership from the Afghan National Police and the Afghan National Army. The purpose of the study was to examine whether—and when—Afghan provinces could function "either alone or with minimal international assistance" to establish security and govern the population.[21] The title of the study irked some Afghans, including Minister of Defense Abdul Rahim Wardak, who interpreted it to mean abandonment. In developing this analytic tool, the U.S. military worked closely with the U.S. Embassy in Kabul, the government of Afghanistan (especially the Ministries of Defense and Interior), the United Nations, and several nongovernmental organizations. The Operational Primacy assessment asked a series of questions: Do the people accept the government of Afghanistan? Do the people believe the government will meet their needs? How capable are the appointed and elected officials? How well can the government administer?

The results were troubling, though not surprising. Perhaps the biggest shortcoming was in reconstruction. The study found that numerous reconstruction programs "need the attention, buy-in, and assistance of the [Government of Afghanistan]," but that they were "confusing, uncoordinated, and create[d] staff redundancies."[22] According to internal memos, international involvement in providing essential services to rural areas was deeply challenging. There were also challenges with U.S. and NATO Provincial Reconstruction Teams (PRTs), which often consisted of between 60 and 100 civilians and soldiers deployed to operating bases to perform small recon-

struction projects or provide security for others involved in reconstruction. A separate Pentagon report found that the major national
reconstruction programs "were poorly coordinated with US-led
PRTs. Lack of coordination limited the ability of the US-led PRT to
align these programs to support the broader stabilization and reconstruction strategy. Additionally, nationally implemented donor programs had limited geographic reach."[23]

As the situation began to destabilize, the federal government grew
more concerned. In 2006, Secretary of Defense Donald Rumsfeld
asked Marin Strmecki to go to Afghanistan and assess the state of governance and the insurgency. Rumsfeld sent one of his "snowflakes"
arguing that part of the Taliban's success in Afghanistan was due to
poor governance in the south, so he needed an assessment of Afghan
governance and an analysis of possible solutions. Strmecki spent two
weeks in Afghanistan, where he interviewed Afghan, U.S., NATO, and
other allied government officials about the deteriorating security environment. He confirmed that one of the primary drivers was poor governance, particularly in southern Afghanistan, that created a power
vacuum into which insurgents could move. He also reported that the
region was controlled by corrupt or ineffective governors and district
administrators, and patrolled by corrupt and incompetent police. He
concluded that the Afghan government, in close cooperation with the
international community, should systematically assess the capability of
these officials province by province and district by district. It should
replace ineffective or corrupt officials and appoint individuals who
could win the support and confidence of local communities.[24]

But little of Strmecki's assessment was ever implemented. No
senior U.S. government official took decisive action, and President
Karzai did not appear to see governance as an acute concern—or, at
the very least, he was unwilling to take the risks involved with removing corrupt or incompetent officials.

These challenges not only had a debilitating impact on stabilization
efforts but also strengthened the hand of insurgents. The absence of
governance in rural areas and the lack of progress in key services—

especially employment, electricity, and water—caused growing frustration among the Afghan population. The Taliban was quick to use U.S. and Afghan failures in its recruitment propaganda, which created a band of "swing villages" in eastern, southern, and western Afghanistan, an area dominated by Pashtuns. Given sustained security and assistance, villages across this swath of territory might have sided with the Afghan government, but without that help, it moved toward the insurgents. Zabol Province was a good example. "The economy is the key solution," noted Dalbar Ayman, the governor of Zabol. "If it is good, there will be no Taliban. But now, I cannot even support my brothers in Zabol with a piece of bread."[25]

Across greater parts of the south, local groups began to support the Taliban. An internal United Nations study examined the Musa Qala area of Helmand, a Taliban stronghold: "Government capacity is virtually non-existent in most areas of Helmand. The limited level of government activity in Musa Qala reflects a similar level across the province." It added that "the population and the Shura clearly want more assistance," and that this was a significant factor fueling the insurgency.[26] Michael Semple, the deputy European Union Special Representative for Afghanistan, told me after returning from a trip to the south: "The local population in these areas are revolting against the government. The Taliban move into areas where there is already unhappiness with the government's performance, send night letters, and intimidate the population." This was, he said, a standard "bed and breakfast guide" to Taliban operations. "Often, there is no government response."[27] The Taliban strategy was straightforward. They approached local tribes and commanders at the village and district levels. Sometimes they were well received because of common tribal affinities or, especially, because locals had given up on the Afghan government. Where they weren't well received, they resorted to brutal tactics and intimidation. They also targeted weak points, such as undermanned district police stations.[28] In some cases, Afghan National Police forces directly supported Taliban operations against NATO or Afghan forces.[29]

Among the most important factors was poverty. A memo produced by the Afghan government, the United States, and other international actors concluded that widespread poverty and the lack of essential services to rural areas "make people more susceptible to indoctrination and mean that the life of a fighter may be the only attractive option available."[30] A separate United Nations study found that "government corruption and poor governance increases the attraction for the Taliban in the population." It continued that "ongoing trends point to a further attrition of the government's ability to project good governance and hint at a further isolation of the political leadership of Afghanistan and the international community from the population."[31] This concern was reiterated in internal Afghan documents, such as *The National Military Strategy*, which noted in 2005 that if key essential services were "not provided quickly, the people will be more vulnerable to extremist elements claiming to offer a better alternative."[32]

At the close of his tenure as commander of Combined Forces Command—Afghanistan in 2007, Lieutenant General Eikenberry prophetically warned: "The long-term threat to campaign success, though, is the potential irretrievable loss of legitimacy of the Government of Afghanistan. If the Afghan Government is unable to counter population frustration with the lack of progress in reform and national development, the Afghan people may lose confidence in the nature of their political system." The result, he cautioned, would be a point "at which the Government of Afghanistan becomes irrelevant to its people, and the goal of establishing a democratic, moderate, self-sustaining state could be lost forever."[33]

Corruption and Drugs

For rural villagers, suffering under crushing poverty and pressure from the Taliban, there was one significant way out. Each spring, Afghanistan is awash in a beautiful sea of white, pink, red, and magenta poppy fields. For Afghans and Westerners, poppies have long symbolized sleep and death. The Minoan poppy goddess wore poppy-seed capsules, a source of narcosis, in garlands in her hair. In ancient Roman mythology, Somnus, the god of sleep, wore a crown of poppies and was frequently depicted lying in a bed of poppies. Likewise, the twin brothers Hypnos and Thanatos, the Greek gods of sleep and death, were often depicted carrying poppies in their hands. The Roman goddess of the harvest, Ceres, grew poppy to help her sleep after the loss of her daughter to Pluto, god of the underworld.

For Afghanistan, this metaphor of sleep and death was all too apt. The cultivation, production, and trafficking of poppy skyrocketed after the U.S. invasion, which had a debilitating impact on governance and contributed to widespread corruption at all levels of the Afghan government. As Figure 11.1 illustrates, poppy cultivation increased virtually every year after the overthrow of the Taliban regime, though it decreased 19 percent between 2007 and 2008. The drug trade eroded efforts to improve governance, fostered widespread corruption throughout the government, and hampered the development of a licit economy.[34]

The implications were staggering. "The drug problem is difficult to overstate," Doug Wankel told me in late 2005 as we sipped tea in a cafeteria on the grounds of the U.S. Embassy in Kabul.[35] Wankel, the

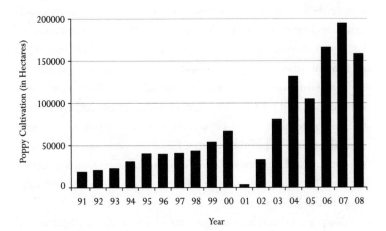

FIGURE 11.1   Opium Poppy Cultivation, 1991–2008[36]

director of the Office of Drug Control in the embassy, was a former
Drug Enforcement Administration (DEA) official who was hired in
2003 to organize the U.S. government's counternarcotics effort in
Afghanistan. He had previously served in Kabul as a young DEA official in the late 1970s. "I left on a flight to New Delhi a couple of hours
before the Soviets rolled in," he said. "People thought it was because I
knew it was coming. I didn't; I just happened to be leaving on a trip.
But the Soviets branded me a C.I.A. agent, and so I couldn't come
back—until now, that is."[37] As we talked, the drug trade was down
that year but still, he said, "it reaches into all facets of life in Afghanistan and undermines the very fabric of governance."[38]

Laboratories in Afghanistan convert opium into morphine base,
white heroin, or one of several grades of brown heroin. But they
could not do it alone. Afghanistan produces no essential or precur-
sor chemicals for the conversion of opium into morphine base. Ace-
tic anhydride—the most commonly used acetylating agent in heroin
processing—is regularly smuggled into Afghanistan from Pakistan,
India, Central Asia, China, and Europe. Some of the largest processing labs are located in Badakhshan, Nangarhar, and Helmand Provinces.[39] Most of the opiates produced in Afghanistan are smuggled
to markets in the West, although some were consumed in Afghanistan or the region as both opium and heroin. U.S. intelligence estimates indicate, for example, that "hundreds of kilograms of
high-grade heroin destined for Saudi Arabia and Kuwait transit Iraq
each month from the source countries of Afghanistan and Iran."[40]
Afghan heroin moves via many routes; traffickers adjust their routes
constantly based on law-enforcement and political actions. Afghan
traffickers travel mostly by car and truck on overland routes to move
drug shipments out of the country. Illicit drug convoys go regularly
to southern and western Pakistan, while smaller shipments of heroin
are sent through the frontier provinces to Karachi for onward shipment to the United States.[41]

"Drugs are critical for insurgent survival in southern Afghanistan,"
one 82nd Airborne intelligence officer told me at Bagram Air Base,

thirty miles north of Kabul and the hub of U.S. forces operating in eastern Afghanistan. "Insurgents further north along the Afghan-Pakistan border," he said, "get funding from a range of other sources like wealthy Arabs, *zakat* from mosques, and the trade in goods such as timber. But not a lot of drugs."[42]

Drug and other criminal groups have developed an intricate transportation network connecting Afghanistan to Pakistan and other neighboring countries. The Taliban was involved at all levels: with farmers, opium brokers, lab operators, smugglers, and major drug barons, as well as the export to international markets. Where they controlled territory, the Taliban levied a tax on poppy farmers and offered farmers protection from the government's eradication efforts. The Taliban was also paid by drug-trafficking organizations to provide security along key routes. And a number of Taliban fighters were directly involved in the poppy harvest, thus largely unavailable to fight until after the harvest ends in the spring.[43]

The Taliban had long been involved in drug trafficking. In 1997, for example, the Taliban received $75 million from drug smuggling between Afghanistan and Pakistan.[44] They had been nominally opposed to drugs, even creating an antinarcotics office. But they often turned a blind eye to the industry. The head of the Taliban's antinarcotics forces in Kandahar was quoted as saying that "opium is permissible because it is consumed by *kafirs* [unbelievers] in the West and not by Muslims or Afghans."[45]

According to Afghan intelligence estimates, roughly 30 percent of the Taliban's income came from involvement in drug trafficking.[46] But Afghan government officials were equally culpable. News reports circulated about high-level Afghan government officials involved in the drug trade. One of those most often accused was Ahmed Wali Karzai, brother of President Hamid Karzai. ABC News, for example, obtained U.S. military documents that alleged that the president's brother "receives money from drug lords as bribes to facilitate their work and movement."[47] And an investigative *New York Times* article that included interviews with senior U.S. government officials reported: "The White

House says it believes that Ahmed Wali Karzai is involved in drug trafficking, and American officials have repeatedly warned President Karzai that his brother is a political liability."[48] A number of senior U.S. intelligence officials, however, argued that the information on Ahmed Wali Karzai was based on second- and thirdhand reporting, and sometimes from people with an ax to grind against the Karzais.[49] Whatever the reality, there was certainly a strong perception among some Afghans that he was complicit in the drug trade.

There were also regular allegations that other government officials were involved in bribery and drug trafficking. An investigative report by The Times (London), for example, named several individuals, including General Azzam, chief of staff to the interior minister. The report found that the "Ministry of Interior, key to establishing security in the country, remains the worst offender." It found evidence pointing to "General Azzam, recently appointed Chief of Operations after his stint as Chief of Staff, and his deputy General Reshad as the prime recipients of bribes." The Afghan government categorized Afghanistan's thirty-four provinces using a three-tiered scale. "A" denoted those with the highest potential profits for drug running; "C" provinces were the least remunerative; and "B" provinces were in between. Counternarcotics officials estimated that one border police commander in eastern Afghanistan took home $400,000 a month from heroin smuggling.[50] At the very least, these allegations increased the perception among Afghans that their government was corrupt, including those officials who were supposed to be leading counternarcotics efforts. As an editorial in the newspaper Daily Afghanistan summarized:

> People definitely do not trust the government. Governors warn that nobody should cultivate poppies and say the poppy fields will be destroyed, but they encourage farmers to keep up poppy cultivation by any means because the government officials make most of their money from poppy cultivation. There are reports that a minister ordered farmers to cultivate only poppies. . . . The government should identify these corrupt officials and should not fail to cut off their hands; otherwise it will face further challenges.[51]

There were some occasional bright spots in the drug war. In 2005, for instance, American and Afghan officials were cheered when poppy-cultivation numbers dropped, though they soared even higher the next year. Most of the reduction appeared to have been the result of Herculean efforts by Afghan leaders with international support. One of the most significant of these counternarcotics programs was implemented by the governor of Nangarhar, Haji Din Muhammad, and the police chief, Hazrat Ali.

They were an odd couple. Haji Din Muhammad came from a distinguished Pashtun family, and his great-grandfather, Wazir Arsala Khan, served as foreign minister of Afghanistan in 1869. Six feet tall and well built, Muhammad had an imposing presence. He was well educated and had the aura of an elder statesman, with a gentle demeanor, preferring to speak in soft, measured tones and capable of pontificating for hours. Hazrat Ali couldn't have been more different. He was not a Pashtun but a Pashai, an ethnic group with a distinct language concentrated in northeastern Afghanistan. He had grown up in the isolated mountain village of Kushmoo, earning him the derogatory nickname *Shurrhi*, meaning "redneck" or "hillbilly" in Pashto. He was also illiterate, which did little to legitimize him among the Pashtun elite in Nangarhar. But Hazrat Ali was fortunate. He had been catapulted to power during the overthrow of the Taliban regime through the patronage of U.S. Special Forces. They had provided him money and weapons to target Taliban forces, and they viewed him as a reliable ally because of his close ties to Northern Alliance leaders.

Despite their differences, Haji Din Muhammad and Hazrat Ali developed a common strategy to decrease poppy in Nangarhar. Under Hazrat Ali's orders, police jailed locals who cultivated poppy until they agreed to plow under their fields.[52] The coercion was effective. According to public-opinion polling in Nangarhar, most villagers reported that they reduced or stopped poppy cultivation out of concern that they would be imprisoned or that their fields would be plowed under by Afghan authorities.[53] In addition, Haji Din Muhammad and Hazrat Ali leveraged the support for President Karzai in the region to convince villagers to buy into the counternarcotics plan. Almost three-fourths of the eradication (72 percent) in 2005 took place in Nangarhar and Helmand Provinces, where, in 2004, poppy cultivation had ranked highest in the nation.[54] Indeed, provinces where declines in cultivation were most striking (Nangarhar—96 percent, Badakshan—53 percent), and where cultivation remained relatively stable (Helmand—10 percent), were the same three provinces that received the largest contributions for alternative development. Nangarhar received $70.1 million in assistance and Badakshan and Helmand received $47.3 million and $55.7 million, respectively.[55]

Yet these successes were no match for the broader problems in the justice system. Studying Afghan perceptions of the rule of law, the World Bank found that Afghanistan's justice system was in the bottom 5 percent in the world by 2006, the exact same ranking as in 2000, the last full year of the Taliban regime.[56] Reconstruction had done nothing to improve things. In comparison with other countries in the region—such as Iran, Pakistan, Russia, Tajikistan, Turkmenistan, and Uzbekistan—Afghanistan's justice system was the least effective. A major reason for this was endemic corruption. Unqualified personnel loyal to various factions were sometimes installed as court officials, and the Supreme Court and the Attorney General's Office were accused of significant wrongdoing.[57]

An Afghanistan intelligence assessment complained that "criminals do not receive fair justice. This is another factor which has boosted the Taliban morale in southern Afghanistan. They are almost confident that they can buy justice at some stage."[58] A corrupt judiciary was a serious impediment to the success of the counternarcotics campaign. But more broadly, it further undermined governance and popular support for Karzai's government, and it crippled the legal and institutional mechanism necessary to prosecute insurgents and criminals.

Afghans were well aware of the problem. An Asia Foundation poll in 2006 found that 77 percent of respondents said corruption was a major problem in Afghanistan; 66 percent believed corruption was a major problem in the provincial government; 42 percent said corruption was a major problem in their daily lives; and 40 percent said corruption was a major problem in their neighborhoods. Moreover, most Afghans believed that the corruption problem was getting worse. Approximately 60 percent of respondents believed that corruption had increased over the past year at the national level, and 50 percent believed that it had increased at the provincial level. Many had been directly involved in bribery, such as providing cash to a government official. Thirty-six percent said they had been involved in bribery with a police officer, 35 percent with a court official, and 34 percent with officials when applying for work.[59] Things were much worse in the areas of greater Taliban presence. People in southern and western Afghanistan were most likely to say they had personally experienced corruption, and those in central and northern Afghanistan were the least likely.[60]

Much of the blame was leveled at the top echelons of the Afghan government. A 2006 State Department poll found that more than 50 percent of Afghans thought President Karzai and his administration failed to combat corruption. This tended to fuel support for the Taliban. According to the same State Department poll, 71 percent of Taliban backers said there was corruption among the police, 66 percent said there was corruption in the local government, and 68 percent said there was corruption in the courts.[61]

A number of sensitive Afghan national security documents expressed growing alarm at the link between poppy and government corruption. The Afghanistan National Security Council's annual *National Threat Assessment*, for example, argued in 2004 that the "continued growth of the heroin and opium-producing poppy remains a major threat to the security of Afghanistan. The corruption and crime association with the drug trade will proliferate in and around Afghanistan, discouraging international investment and assistance in rebuilding Afghanistan."[62] The following year's *National Threat Assessment* went even further, noting that the "corruption and crime associated with the drug trade will proliferate in Afghan society and the government administration."[63]

The cost of corruption, according to numerous Afghan and international assessments, was increased support for the Taliban and other insurgent groups. One joint European Union and United Nations assessment found that the Taliban "exploit certain sentiments that resonated within the general population," such as the "corrupt state."[64] An Afghan intelligence report concluded: "The propaganda effort of the enemy in rural areas is massive and strong. The theme is corruption in the government. . . . Their main target population is rural Afghanistan. . . . only good governance and sound leadership at the local level can counter this effectively and strongly."[65] The Taliban and other insurgent groups pointed out in their propaganda the growing Afghan corruption on the district, provincial, and national levels. A joint paper produced by the Government of Afghanistan, the U.S. government, and other key international actors more boldly concluded: "The appointment of unprofessional, corrupt and ineffective government officials has reduced the trust and confidence of the people, especially in the provinces."[66]

A Cancer in the Government

Reflecting on his term as Afghan foreign minister, Dr. Abdullah Abdullah told me in 2007 that his government had made some mistakes. "Where are the state institutions?" he asked. "There aren't any." We were sitting in his flat in Kabul, which was comfortably furnished with plush chairs and Western amenities, including a flat-screen television. Since it was Ramadan, Abdullah was fasting, but he thoughtfully offered me a glass of cold water. He said, ruefully, that "people are losing hope in their government. Villages cannot be protected. If villagers say something against the Taliban, they could be beheaded. We are losing the support of our population."[67]

Abdullah was an ophthalmologist and a protégé of Ahmed Shah Massoud, the charismatic Northern Alliance military leader. Well organized and smartly dressed, with a neatly trimmed beard, often preferring Western suit and tie to native Afghan clothes, he spoke excellent English with a slight accent. During the Bonn negotiations in late 2001, Abdullah impressed U.S. and other Western diplomats by joining them at meals during the month of Ramadan, even though he was fasting. "He always said he felt no pangs of hunger," recalled U.S. Special Envoy James Dobbins, who worked with Abdullah. Dobbins described him as someone who "would speak with controlled passion about the travails his country had experienced over the past several decades."[68] Abdullah's comments about Afghan governance were a sobering and brutally frank admission of the challenges his government faced. They were seconded by a former Afghan provincial governor who complained: "The government has essentially collapsed. It has lost its meaning in the provinces, it has lost the security situation and lost its grip on civil servants. Corruption is playing havoc with the country."[69]

After Operation Mountain Thrust in the summer of 2006, during which American, Canadian, British, and Afghan forces conducted offensive actions in southern Afghanistan, Ambassador Ronald Neumann was briefed by the U.S. military on the results of the interrogations of more than 100 Taliban and other fighters. "We found that the critical reasons why these fighters supported the Taliban had little to do with religious ideology. Rather, they had to do with bad government and economics. The government could not protect them or deliver services, and they were often simply paid better by the Taliban."[70]

This was consistent with the findings of Afghan and NATO officials. As one senior Afghan intelligence official told me, the results of detainee interviews and intelligence assessments showed that "neither Afghan police, army, or NATO can protect villages and districts from the Taliban. This forces people to support the Taliban, even if they don't like them. The other option, which was death," he noted wryly, "was not palatable for most villagers."[71] One Afghan summed up the dilemma: "In the daytime, this government is coming to us, and in the nighttime the Taliban are coming to us. We are stuck in the middle."[72]

When the Taliban was overthrown in 2001, Afghanistan was an underdeveloped country whose levels of basic services and social indicators were near the bottom of the world. Afghanistan's health indicators were among the worst on earth: it had an under-five mortality rate of 172 per 1,000 live births, infant mortality rate of 115 per 1,000 live births, maternal mortality rate of 16 per 1,000 live births, and 50 percent rate of chronic malnutrition. Life expectancy was estimated at 43 years, and only 9 percent of rural households reported a health facility in their village.[73]

But Afghanistan's underdevelopment was not the reason an insurgency began. Rather, the prevailing condition was the inability of that government to improve life in rural areas of the country. An internal memo from the UN and the European Union was deeply pessimistic: "Afghanistan's current trajectory was negative: there was burgeoning disillusionment with government. Even officials were fed up, with governors voicing scathing criticism at the lack of tangible support for their work." It went on to say that the "government was losing prestige; its image and influence were waning. Without a change in approach, Afghanistan and its international partners would lose ground: their fortunes were now linked. Civilians would be more likely to fight their 'disgusting government' both because they detested it and because they feared the consequences of not fighting."[74]

The damage was done. The government was unable to provide key services or protect the local population, especially in rural areas, and the government was widely viewed as corrupt. To make matters worse, the United States and its allies had focused almost entirely in a top-down strategy to stabilize the country by creating a strong central government. Not only was a strong Afghan state ahistorical, but U.S. policymakers spent little time trying to co-opt Pashtun tribes, subtribes, clans, and other local institutions in the south and east. There was little bottom-up strategy to complement top-down efforts. Storm clouds had been gathering for several years, waiting to burst. In 2006, they finally did.

CHAPTER TWELVE

The Perfect Storm

RONALD NEUMANN was reaching for the light switch in his hotel room at the Crowne Plaza in Amman, Jordan, when the phone rang.

"Hello?" he asked, somewhat perplexed. It was 2005, and he was on a brief layover on his way back to the United States from Iraq, where he had been serving as a senior political-military officer and the U.S. Embassy's principal interlocutor with the Multi-National Command.

It was Robert Pearson, director general of the State Department's Foreign Service: "I understand you are arriving in Washington tomorrow," he said.

"I am," Neumann replied.

"The Secretary of State would like to see you about where you're going next," Pearson noted. "But it's not where you think." That was it. He said nothing else.

Neumann could barely sleep that night, anxious about what awaited. Two days later, when he walked into the office of Secretary of State Condoleezza Rice, she asked him whether he would be interested in serving as U.S. ambassador to Afghanistan. Without hesitation, he said yes.

He later recalled: "It was the only time I was asked directly by the Secretary of State to serve as an ambassador." Neumann, who had served as U.S. ambassador to Algeria and Bahrain, didn't leave his

Baghdad position until several months later. His final recollections were poignant. "I remember driving up Route Irish in a sandstorm in a convoy," he recalled, referring to the excruciatingly dangerous road to the Baghdad Airport. "We couldn't get a helicopter out because of the sandstorm, but we were able to hitch a ride with General Casey," the commanding general of Multi-National Force—Iraq.[1] It was an ironic twist of events. Neumann was leaving Iraq during a sandstorm and entering Afghanistan during what Lieutenant General Karl Eikenberry would eventually call "the perfect storm." The Afghan insurgency was about to explode.

Eikenberry recalled, "Several things came together. The Taliban and al Qa'ida had sanctuary in Pakistan and conducted operations from bases in Pakistan. Local governance was not taking hold. Narcotrafficking and associated criminality were emerging as significant threats to security. The planning and implementation of critical economic infrastructure projects—roads, power, and water management—were lagging." As these problems became more acute, however, the United States neglected to respond with sufficient resources. "There were too few international and Afghan National Security forces. In the case of the U.S. forces," said Eikenberry, "we had one less infantry battalion in the summer of 2006 than in the summer of 2005. All these factors—a complex mix of security, governance, and economic elements—combined to make for a perfect storm as NATO began its enlargement into southern Afghanistan in June 2006."[2] Senior Afghan officials had also become increasingly alarmed. Dr. Abdullah, Afghanistan's foreign minister, worried that the United States and the broader international community mistakenly believed that the Taliban and al Qa'ida were finished. "Our intelligence estimates," he repeatedly warned U.S. officials, "show quite the reverse." In his final meeting with Secretary Rice in March 2006 before he left the Afghan government, Dr. Abdullah warned her not to let Afghanistan continue to slip into conflict. "I am deeply worried about the rising insurgency," he said. "People are beginning to lose hope in their government. We are losing the support of our population."[3]

But there was some disagreement among the U.S. policymakers about the severity of the insurgency. "My take on the situation in Afghanistan," said General James Jones, the Supreme Allied Commander, Europe, in early 2006, "is that the Taliban and al Qa'ida are not in a position where they can restart an insurgency of any size and major scope."[4] Jones was a steely Marine who would become President Barack Obama's national security adviser. He also became outspoken in his assessment of the insurgency in his 2008 *Afghanistan Study Group Report*, which concluded that the progress in Afghanistan was "under serious threat from resurgent violence, weakening international resolve, mounting regional challenges and a growing lack of confidence on the part of the Afghan people about the future direction of their country."[5] The day after General Tommy Franks, head of U.S. Central Command, had been battered by the Joint Chiefs of Staff on his war plan for Afghanistan in their conference room (known as "the Tank"), Franks had confronted Jones and Admiral Vern Clark of the U.S. Navy and told them: "Yesterday in the Tank, you guys came across like a mob of Title X mother——ers, not like the Joint Chiefs of Staff."[6] The reference was to Title X of the U.S. Code, which outlines the role of the armed forces, including the Army, Navy, Marine Corps, and Air Force. Whatever the staff disagreements may have been in the armed services, the writing in Afghanistan was on the wall by the end of 2006. Levels of violence had reached their highest levels since the overthrow of the Taliban in 2001.

Upbeat Assessments

The year 2006 did not begin so badly, at least among many policymakers in Washington. Estimates in some sectors were upbeat. According to the World Bank, for example, Afghanistan's economy grew an estimated 14 percent in 2005 and 5.3 percent in 2006.[7] Annual end-period inflation, as measured by the consumer price index for Kabul, decreased to 4.8 percent. Annual end-period "national" inflation, covering Kabul and five other cities, was 3.9 percent.[8] In addition, construction was booming in some Afghan cities, several major roads were built, markets were full of goods, small and large shops had sprouted up, and several large telecommunications companies and commercial airlines were operating and competing for business.

"Cell phones are a wonderful boon in this city," said one Afghan in Kabul to me, gripping his bright yellow phone and his Roshan calling card. "I don't know what I'd do without mine." *Roshan,* which means "light" in both Dari and Pashto, was one of Afghanistan's largest telecommunications companies. In February 2005, Roshan won the Best Marketing Award at the Mobile World Congress, the mobile-phone industry's leading annual event. In September 2006, it won the Best Brand Award at the CommsMEA Awards Ceremony in Dubai. This marked a breathtaking change.

In 2002, more than 99 percent of the Afghan population had no access to telecommunications services. Only five major cities had telephone services, and Kabul accounted for about two-thirds of the country's 57,000 functioning lines. The country had little or no access to the Internet, and postal services were still recovering from years of conflict. By 2006, the number of telephones in Afghanistan had increased to 2.16 million, and all provinces were connected to a national telecommunications network. Mobile-phone prices dropped from about $400 in 2002 to less than $50 in 2006, and calling costs fell dramatically. The telecommunications sector attracted more than $300 million in private investments—60 percent of all foreign direct investment in Afghanistan.[9]

Robert Gates, who replaced Donald Rumsfeld as U.S. secretary of defense in 2006, argued that "notwithstanding the news [the American people] hear out of Afghanistan, the efforts of the United States, our allies, and the Afghan government and people have been producing solid results." He noted that, contrary to the situation during the Taliban era, when few Afghans had access to health care, 670 clinics and hospitals were built or refurbished and nearly 11,000 doctors, nurses, and midwives were trained. Fewer than a million children were in school in 2001. "Now more than five million students—at least one and a half million of them girls—are enrolled in school." He also pointed out that the country's central bank had been rebuilt and supported with more than $2.5 billion in reserves—a remarkable feat, since there was no commercial banking under the Taliban.[10]

Reading the Tea Leaves

But all was not well, and violence in 2006 reached the highest levels since U.S. forces had invaded Afghanistan in 2001. Observers who hadn't visited Afghanistan, or who hadn't traveled outside of major urban areas, could be forgiven for thinking there was security and a viable government. The truth, however, was that governance did not extend into rural areas of the country. As former Taliban commander and Afghan Parliament member Abdul Salam Rocketi told me over lunch one day in 2006, "we have created a government that looks good on paper but is very weak in reality. Most Afghans in rural areas never see or hear anything from it."[11]

Key metrics of violence showed a disturbing increase. The number of suicide attacks increased from one in 2002 to two in 2003, six in 2004, 21 in 2005, 139 in 2006, and 140 in 2007. Between 2005 and 2006, the number of remotely detonated bombings more than doubled, from 783 to 1,677, and armed attacks nearly tripled, from 1,558 to 4,542.[12] In 2007, insurgent-initiated attacks rose another 27 percent from the 2006 levels, and Helmand Province witnessed among the highest levels of violence, rising 60 percent between 2006 and 2007.[13] The Taliban and other groups assassinated Afghan government supporters in district and provincial centers. Key targets included police, Afghan intelligence agents, judges, clerics, NGO workers, and any others believed to be collaborating with the government.[14]

Public-opinion polls showed that Afghans had noticed the trend. In 2006, just under 50 percent of Afghans said the biggest problem in their country was the lack of security, including from the Taliban and warlords. Concerns were most acute in the south and east.[15] A public-opinion poll for U.S. Central Command indicated that 41 percent of Afghans said they felt less safe in 2007 than in 2006, compared with only 28 percent who said they felt safer. Support levels for the Taliban doubled during the same time period. "The largest increases in Taliban support," the report concluded, "are among rural people, women, and in Pakistan border regions."[16] While a bare majority of Afghans continued to believe the country was moving in the right direction, the percentage had decreased from 77 percent in 2005 to 55 percent in 2006 and 54 percent in 2007.[17]

In a press conference with President Bush at Camp David in August 2007, Afghan President Hamid Karzai optimistically reported that the Taliban was "a force that's defeated."[18] But this was plainly not the case. In private, the Afghan government's own security assessments had been getting progressively more alarming.

As far back as 2004, Afghanistan's *National Threat Assessment* warned that the drug trade, among other factors, was making "Afghanistan an attractive haven for international terrorist groups, organized crime and other extremists while also funding the continued, destabilizing presence of non-statutory armed forces."[19] The 2005 *National Threat Assessment* was even less rosy, finding that the security environment was declining and that "the primary source of political subversion comes from internal actors, non-statutory armed forces and their commanders. . . . [The] window of opportunity that the Government and International Community have to deliver security and improvements to the quality of life of ordinary Afghans is limited, before people become impatient."[20] And Afghanistan's 2006 *National Security Policy* noted: "Non-statutory armed forces and their commanders pose a direct threat to the national security of Afghanistan. They are a major obstacle to the expansion of the rule of law into the provinces."[21]

U.S. intelligence assessments expressed similar alarm. In November 2006, the CIA reported that "the Taliban has built momentum this year. The level of violence associated with the insurgency has increased significantly and the group has become more aggressive than in years past." It warned that the "Taliban almost certainly refocused its attacks in an attempt to stymie NATO's efforts in southern Afghanistan."[22] Defense Intelligence Agency analysts reached a similar conclusion, deducing that levels of violence had hit an all-time high. One report, titled *The Current Situation in Iraq and Afghanistan*, was ominous: "If a substantial international military and Afghan security presence throughout the volatile Pashtun south and east is not established alongside credible civil administrations, central government control over these areas will be substantially restricted."[23]

United Nations assessments were similarly alarming: "The security situation in Afghanistan is assessed by most analysts as having deteriorated at a constant rate. . . . The Afghan National Police (ANP) has become a primary target of insurgents and intimidation of all kinds has increased against the civilian population, especially those perceived to be in support of the government, international military forces as well as the humanitarian and development community."[24]

In February 2006, Ambassador Neumann sent a cable to Secretary of State Rice offering the unfortunate news that "2006 was likely to be a bloody year in Afghanistan." He warned that the Taliban had successfully regrouped in Pakistan, and neither the United States nor Pakistan had effectively targeted them in their border sanctuaries. The United States had also largely left alone Afghanistan's lawless south, the Taliban's traditional heartland. The United States military had some Special Operations Forces in Helmand and other provinces, but most of its resources were focused on counterterrorist operations in the east.[25] Unit commanders had been told not to use the word *counterinsurgency* in describing their operations, since they were only supposed to be conducting "counterterrorist" operations, in keeping with the national strategic guidance and an operational focus on fighting al Qa'ida.[26] The same thing was true for CIA personnel.[27]

Alarmed at the violence, Neumann argued that the U.S. Congress should at least double the current aid to Afghanistan since, "if we take our hand off too early, it can still come apart on us."[28] Neumann asked for approximately $600 million for the fiscal year 2006 supplemental budget, but he received only $43 million, of which $11 million was for debt reduction for Afghanistan.[29] He was outraged. The Office of Management and Budget (OMB), which vehemently opposed increased aid levels for Afghanistan, proved a major hindrance to funding. In his outbrief with President George W. Bush, Ambassador Neumann was blunt: "I would use a JDAM on OMB if I could," referring to the joint direct attack munition, a guidance kit placed on the tail of a bomb that converted it from an unguided, or "dumb," free-fall bomb into an accurately guided "smart" weapon. President Bush reportedly chuckled.[30]

Frustrations with OMB were not limited to U.S. efforts in Afghanistan. U.S. policymakers in Iraq were also frustrated with what L. Paul Bremer, administrator of the Coalition Provisional Authority, referred to as the petty "small-change struggle" with OMB bureaucrats.[31] In a memo to Secretary Rumsfeld, for example, Bremer contended that the "assertion by OMB that it has authority over how Iraqi monies are used is an overreach of U.S. government authority." OMB, he said, is "making efforts to speed up rehabilitation of the Iraqi economy more difficult and time consuming," and he pleaded with Rumsfeld to "change this."[32] Rumsfeld had asked John Hamre, a former deputy secretary of defense under President Clinton, to go to Iraq with a team to assess the situation on the ground. In a private note to Rumsfeld, Hamre argued: "I was astounded to hear the constraints your low level folks live with to get money and contracts. It is taking up to 10 days for OMB to approve fund requests after you approve them." He urged Rumsfeld to "take this opportunity to get OMB off your back now when the White House knows that we have problems in Iraq and need to give the CPA Administrator all the flexibility he needs."[33]

Epic Battles

The years 2006 and 2007 witnessed some of the most intense battles since the Taliban was overthrown in 2001. Fighting became so fierce that British soldiers had to fix bayonets for hand-to-hand combat in Helmand Province against well-equipped Taliban militants. Beginning in January 2006, troops from NATO's International Security Assistance Force (ISAF) started to replace U.S. troops in southern Afghanistan. The British 16th Air Assault Brigade, later reinforced by Royal Marines, formed the core of the force in southern Afghanistan, along with troops and helicopters from Australia, Canada, and the Netherlands. The initial force consisted of roughly 3,300 British soldiers, 2,500 Canadians, 1,963 Dutch, and forces from Denmark, Australia, and Estonia. Air support was provided by U.S., British, Dutch, Norwegian, and French combat aircraft and helicopters.

The British recognized the Taliban threat. "We underestimate, at our peril the resilience of the Taliban and its capacity to regenerate," a British assessment acknowledged. "The Taliban gain influence and control of the population through coercion, intimidation, and their extensive tribal ties across Helmand."[34]

In early February 2006, Afghan forces, backed by U.S. warplanes, engaged in intense fighting in the Sangin district of Helmand Province. The battle began the evening of February 2, when approximately 200 Taliban fighters targeted an Afghan police convoy. American A-10 ground-attack aircraft and B-52 bombers and British Harrier jets supported Afghan ground forces over two days of fighting, which resulted in about twenty Taliban deaths and seven Afghan police and soldiers killed. On February 13, four U.S. soldiers were killed when their Humvee was hit by a remote-controlled bomb while they were patrolling with Afghan National Army forces in the southern province of Oruzgan. The patrol then came under attack from small-arms fire and rocket-propelled grenades, forcing it to call in U.S. Apache helicopter and B-52 bomber support. On March 1, one U.S. soldier was killed and two were wounded in a clash with Taliban insurgents in Oruzgan, after a roadside bomb destroyed a U.S. vehicle and U.S. forces engaged the insurgents. A week later, another roadside bomb killed four U.S. soldiers in eastern Afghanistan.

In response to Taliban penetration of the east, U.S. and ANA forces launched Operation Mountain Lion on March 25, 2006, in Kunar

Province, east of Kabul.[35] On June 15, 2006, more than 11,000 U.S., British, Canadian, and Afghan troops engaged insurgents in southern Oruzgan and northern Helmand Provinces during Operation Mountain Thrust. The mission was designed to eradicate Taliban penetration in these provinces and establish a secure environment in which reconstruction could begin. Prior to the operations, these provinces had seen little military presence. During June and July, there was heavy fighting between NATO and Taliban forces, with the Taliban exhibiting a high degree of coordination in their combat operations. Despite the reported killing of more than 1,000 Taliban insurgents and the capture of almost 400 more, the Taliban continued to exert a presence in these areas. In early August, the Taliban mounted a number of ambushes against NATO forces.

As in many other operations, the insurgent response to Operation Mountain Thrust was to flee from the area and prepare to fight another day.[36] This classic guerrilla tactic—especially against a more capable conventional adversary—was regularly used by mujahideen fighters during the Soviet War.

By the summer of 2006, the Taliban began to concentrate their efforts on southern Afghanistan—including Kandahar Province—in what would become one of the largest and most important battles of the war. "Truthfully, I was surprised by the resistance they put up," said Canadian Major Geoff Abthorpe, commander of Bravo Company. "We came at them with what I perceived to be a pretty heavy fist."[37] The southern provinces of Kandahar and Helmand represented the Taliban center of gravity. Since several key Taliban leaders came from Kandahar, they had one of their greatest support networks there. The Canadian military, which had just deployed to Kandahar, had not engaged in serious ground combat since the Korean War; their focus had been on peacekeeping operations in the Balkans and other locations. But they were eager to fight.

"I know about all this cultural sensitivity stuff," said Canadian Sergeant John May. "But I am here to fight. If those [Taliban] are going to set ambushes and IEDs, I am going to kill them. That's my job."[38]

Afghanistan's Key Players (U)

PARTIES	LEADERS	COMMENTS	ETHNICITY
Taliban The Taliban—ostensibly a movement of religious students—emerged in late 1994. The group's stated goals are to establish a proper Islamic government in Afghanistan, rid the country of oppressors, and to disarm the various factions. Inspired by its leader's alleged vision from Allah, the group has seized approximately 85% of Afghanistan's territory and is pursuing the remaining land in a civil war with the Northern Alliance.	Mullah Mohammad Omar	Leader and founder of movement...revered by followers...wants Islamic state with Sharia (Islamic law) enforced...defends Usama Bin Ladin's stay in Afghanistan.	PASHTUN
	Mullah Mohammad Rabbani	Second in command to Omar...more moderate...periodically sidelined by Omar...possibly at odds with Omar over Usama Bin Ladin.	PASHTUN
	Maulawi Wakil Mutawakil	Foreign Minister...close to Omar...relays Omar's views to outside world...well-spoken...formerly the group's spokesperson...has led delegations to other countries, including the United States.	PASHTUN
	Mullah Abdul Jalil PHOTO UNAVAILABLE	Deputy Foreign Minister...close advisor to Omar...may serve as liason with Bin Ladin.	PASHTUN
Northern Alliance Nominal alliance of different political parties, including Jamiat-i-Islami (JI), Hezbi Wahdat - Khalili (Islamic Unity Party) (HWK); Hezbi Wahdat Akbari (Islamic Unity Party) (HWA).	Ahmad Shah Masood (JI)	Dominant military figure in coalition...respected for military tactical capabilities...some ties to Iran, Russia...Panjsher Valley stronghold.	TAJIK
	Burhanuddin Rabbani (JI)	Former nominal President of Afghanistan...diminishing role and power in alliance...some ties to Iran, Russia.	TAJIK
	Abdul Karim Khalili (HWK)	Currently in Iran...wary of Taliban's Shia policies...wants Shia role in future government.	HAZARA (Shia)
	Ustad Mohaqqeq (HWA)	Major Shia commander...works nominally with Masood...well-respected by his troops.	HAZARA (Shia)
	Abdul Rashid Dostam (NIM)	Was associated with the Northern Alliance but was forced out of the country...currently moves between Iran and Turkey.	UZBEK
Other Parties Key players not necessarily aligned with either faction. Include Islamic Union for the Liberation of Afghanistan (Ittihad-i-Islami Barai Azadi Afghanistan) (IULA); Hezbi Islami-Gulbuddin (HIG); Hezbi Wahdat Akbari (Islamic Unity Party) (HWA); Jumbesh-i-Milli Islami (National Islamic Movement) (NIM).	Abdul Rasul Sayyaf (IULA)	Close to Masood...connected with terrorist training camps...ties to Saudis...anti-Shia...radical Islamist.	PASHTUN
	Gulbuddin Hekmatyar (HIG)	Former Prime Minister...radical Islamist...dislikes and mistrusts Masood...diminished militarily...ties to Pakistan...considered a turncoat...currently in Iran.	PASHTUN
	Mohammad Akbar Akbari (HWA)	Shia leader...wants guarantee of Shia rights, role in future government.	HAZARA (Shia)

This chart is Unclassified.

Central Intelligence Agency memo identifying Afghanistan's key players, circa 2001.
National Security Archive

Decades of fighting destroyed much of Kabul, leaving thousands of burnt-out buildings scarred by bullets and artillery shells. *United Kingdom Ministry of Defence*

Aerial view of Paktia Province from a U.S. Army Blackhawk helicopter. Afghanistan's mountainous terrain has long made it difficult for invading armies to conquer. *Obaid Younossi*

Top: Afghan national security forces prepare for operations against insurgents in Helmand Province in January 2008. While Afghan National Police suffered from incompetence and corruption, the Afghan National Army became increasingly competent at conducting counterinsurgent operations. *U.S. Department of Defense, Specialist David Gunn*

Right: Dr. Abdullah Abdullah, Afghanistan's minister of foreign affairs, shown here speaking at a NATO event in August 2003, repeatedly warned Washington policymakers that the security situation was getting more dangerous. *NATO*

Top, left: Lieutenant General David Barno (foreground), Major General Lloyd Austin (left), Secretary of Defense Donald H. Rumsfeld (center), and U.S. Ambassador Zalmay Khalilzad (right) meet in Kabul on December 4, 2003, to talk about stabilization efforts. *U.S. Department of Defense, Technical Sergeant Andy Dunaway*

Top, right: Zalmay Khalilzad, U.S. ambassador to Afghanistan, briefs journalists at the Pentagon on October 15, 2004. Khalilzad was instrumental in developing a strategy on "Accelerating Success" in Afghanistan. *U.S. Department of Defense, R. D. Ward*

Right: Lieutenant General David Barno, commander of U.S. forces in Afghanistan, at a press conference at the Pentagon on October 19, 2004. One of his most successful efforts was helping provide a secure environment for the presidential elections that year in Afghanistan. *U.S. Department of Defense, R. D. Ward*

Two Afghan women, wearing bright blue *burqas*, show their ink-stained fingers after voting for parliamentary elections on September 18, 2005. *U.S. Department of Defense, Staff Sergeant Jacob Caldwell*

Children peer through the damaged wall of their schoolhouse in Kabul. After the 2001 overthrow of the Taliban regime, increasing numbers of boys and girls went to school in Afghanistan. *U.S. Department of Defense, Corporal Matthew Roberson*

Afghan laborers build the perimeter wall at a NATO Forward Operating Base in
Badghis Province. NATO completed its movement to western Afghanistan in September
2005. *U.S. Department of Defense, Technical Sergeant Laura K. Smith*

U.S. Army soldiers establish a security perimeter after exiting a U.S. Army CH-47 Chinook helicopter near Bagram, Afghanistan, in 2005. Insurgent violence grew steadily throughout 2005 and hit unprecedented levels in 2006. *U.S. Department of Defense, Specialist Harold Fields*

A U.S. Marine (left) inspects a poppy plant next to an Afghan National Army soldier (right) during a patrol in Helmand Province. Poppy is most heavily cultivated in southern Afghan provinces like Helmand. *U.S. Department of Defense, Staff Sergeant Luis P. Valdespino Jr.*

Aerial view from a U.S. Army Blackhawk helicopter in Nangarhar Province near Jalalabad. Despite insurgent violence, the United States was still involved in a range of reconstruction projects in the cities and villages of Nangarhar and other provinces in eastern Afghanistan. *Obaid Younossi*

An F-15E Strike Eagle from the 391st Expeditionary Fighter Squadron at Bagram Air Base, Afghanistan, launches heat decoys during a close-air-support mission over Afghanistan. Afghans became increasingly angry as close air support caused more civilian casualties. *U.S. Department of Defense, Staff Sergeant Aaron Allmon*

U.S. Ambassador Ronald Neumann (front) in Nuristan Province with Alonzo
Fulgham (center), the U.S. Agency for International Development's mission director
in Afghanistan, and Governor Tamim Nuristani (back). Neumann's father had been
the ambassador to Afghanistan during the reign of Zahir Shah. Three decades later,
Neumann faced the challenge of working with Hamid Karzai to establish security and
eradicate corruption in the Afghan government.   *Photo by Jennifer Harris and courtesy of
Ronald Neumann*

Top: Lieutenant General Karl Eikenberry, former head of Combined Forces Command—Afghanistan, briefs journalists at the Pentagon on December 8, 2005. Eikenberry, who was instrumental in helping build the Afghan army, and who is now the U.S. ambassador in Kabul, faced a "perfect storm" that hit Afghanistan in 2006 as violence levels skyrocketed. *U.S. Department of Defense, R. D. Ward*

Left: Dutch soldiers in Uruzgan Province launch mortar rounds near Mirabad. While some NATO countries engaged in combat, U.S. government officials increasingly complained that most NATO countries shied away from fighting. *NATO*

Admiral Michael Mullen, chairman of the Joint Chiefs of Staff, greets the Pakistani chief of Army Staff, General Ashfaq Kayani, aboard the USS *Abraham Lincoln* in 2008. With the U.S. war in Iraq winding down, U.S. military leaders were finally able to give more attention to Afghanistan. At this meeting, they discussed a range of security issues, including Afghan insurgents operating from Pakistani soil. *U.S. Department of Defense, Petty Officer 1st Class William John Kipp Jr.*

An armed MQ-9 Reaper unmanned aerial vehicle (UAV) taxis down a runway in Afghanistan on its way to a wartime mission in 2008. The United States increasingly used UAVs to target insurgents across the border in Pakistan. *U.S. Department of Defense, Staff Sergeant Brian Ferguson*

U.S. Secretary of Defense Robert Gates (left) and Afghanistan President Hamid Karzai (right) meet in Kabul in June 2007. They discussed the insurgency, civilian casualties, and efforts to build Afghan national security forces. *U.S. Department of Defense, Cherie A. Thurlby*

U.S. Marines prepare for an attack against a Taliban stronghold in Now Zad, Afghanistan in 2008. Anticipating heavier fighting, the Marines increased their presence in Afghanistan's violent southern regions in 2009. *U.S. Department of Defense, Sergeant Freddy G. Cantu*

Operation Medusa

The Taliban had developed an important sanctuary in Panjwai and Zhare districts, located west of Kandahar City. The mujahideen had scored important victories there over the ill-fated Soviet 40th Army in the 1980s. Grapes and other fruit grew there, and the fields, vineyards, compounds, and ditches that dotted the landscape offered ideal defensive terrain for the Taliban, with a self-sustaining food supply.[39]

The city of Kandahar was the urban hub for Operation Medusa. The terrain was marked by Highway 1, which ran northeast to Kabul and northwest to Herat, and Highway 4, which ran south to Quetta, Pakistan. Kandahar Airfield, the headquarters of NATO operations in southern Afghanistan and a former Soviet air base, sat along Highway 4 to the south of the city. Panjwai and Zhare districts lay to the west, and the Arghandab River sliced through the area. The bulk of the activity during Operation Medusa took place in what became known as the "Pashmul pocket," situated next to the town of Pashmul.

In July 2006, Canada's Task Force Orion, with roughly 1,200 soldiers, saw a sharp increase of Taliban activity in Panjwai district. The local Taliban, who had long relied on small-unit attacks and ambushes throughout the area, were starting to control ground. The Taliban had allied themselves with local Nurzai tribes in Kandahar.[40] On August 3, four soldiers were killed and ten were wounded near Pashmul in close fighting. Mao Zedong once wrote that insurgencies can be divided into three stages: (1) political preparation, (2) limited attacks, and (3) conventional war, typified by insurgents beginning to control territory and massing in large numbers. Lieutenant Colonel Omer Lavoie, commander of the Task Force 3-06 Battle Group, told his planning staff that this was "classic stage three of an insurgency."

"Basically, they want us to become decisively engaged," he said. No one, least of all the Canadians, had expected the Taliban to conduct conventional operations. Since 2002, the Taliban had used asymmetric tactics, such as ambushes and roadside bombs, to target NATO and Afghan forces. "I have to admit that this is not where I expected to be," Lavoie explained. "For the last six months I trained my battle group to fight a counterinsurgency, and now find that we are facing something a lot more like conventional warfare."[41]

Over the last two weeks of August, Taliban forces became increasingly aggressive. They ambushed several convoys and regularly mortared Patrol Base Wilson, about twenty-five miles west of Kandahar City. They appeared to be looking for a fight, hoping to draw Canadian forces into a pitched battle. One of their most provocative moves was to take control of Highway 1 in Kandahar, setting up checkpoints and threatening the city. A legitimate government does not permit an insurgent group to administer a major roadway. The Canadian Expeditionary Force Command asserted: "The securing of these routes . . . was a vital phase in [Operation] MEDUSA."[42] NATO intelligence reports indicated that hundreds of Afghan civilians were fleeing Kandahar on a daily basis in fear of the Taliban.[43]

In an effort to roust the Taliban from one of their most important sanctuaries, the Canadian planning staff designed an effort to clear the eastern pocket of Panjwai district. The battle group they commanded consisted of three infantry companies, an artillery battery, a squadron of engineers, and an armored reconnaissance troop. Aerial reconnaissance assets monitored enemy movement when they moved in the open. By late August, a combined force of soldiers from the Canadian Task Force 3-06 Battle Group, Afghan National Army, United States, Dutch, and eventually Danish forces waited for H-hour—when the operation was set to begin. The Canadian brigade staff issued a warning to all noncombatants who lived in Panjwai to leave immediately. This left Taliban alone in the area, waiting for the fight they had surely been expecting.[44]

Air operations commenced on September 2, 2006, while ground forces positioned themselves in a pincer formation north and south of the district. Canadian artillery, made up of Echo Battery, 2nd Regiment Royal Canadian Horse Artillery, fired hundreds of 155-millimeter rounds into the area of operations. Apache helicopters from the Neth-

erlands and the United Kingdom fired rockets and 30-millimeter cannons. Harrier jets from Britain's Royal Air Force and F-16 Falcons from
the Royal Netherlands Air Force dropped 500-pound bombs, and B-1B
Lancer bombers from the U.S. Air Force dropped precision-guided
munitions. As the attack unfolded, Canada's Charles Company, under
the command of Major Matthew Sprague, positioned itself at Ma'sum
Ghar, across the Arghandab River from Pashmul. They established a firing line looking northwest toward the "white schoolhouse," a known
Taliban strongpoint.[45] Bravo Company, under the command of Major
Geoff Abthorpe, provided a screen in the north along Highway 1.

On September 3, Charles Company was ordered to cross the
Arghandab River and move into Pashmul. Enemy resistance was stiff.
The Taliban set up an ambush and destroyed several Canadian vehicles, killed four Canadian soldiers, and wounded nine in intense
fighting. Explosions echoed across grape and pomegranate fields, and
clouds of dust rose amid the greenery and mud houses. The Taliban
used layered defensive positions with trenches and fought with recoilless rifles, mortars, RPG-7s, and machine guns.[46] Under supporting
fire from artillery and with close air support directed by forward air
controllers, Charles Company made a tactical retreat back to the
original Ma'sum Ghar firing line. They left behind three damaged
vehicles: a bulldozer, a Mercedes Benz G-Wagon, and a LAV III in the
vicinity of the white schoolhouse.[47] The LAV III is an 8x8 wheeled
vehicle that carries a 25-millimeter cannon and can reach top speeds
of more than sixty miles per hour. It is vastly more rugged than the
G-Wagon, a four-wheel sport utility vehicle also used in the field.
Neither was a great loss, but the troops were unnerved by their
retreat. On the same day, a British Nimrod reconnaissance aircraft
had crashed, killing all on board. Despite these losses, aerial bombardment and artillery fire continued, along with fire from LAV IIIs
and Coyote reconnaissance vehicles.

On September 4, close air support sorties engaged Taliban targets
in the Pashmul pocket, including the white schoolhouse, which was
leveled by a 500-pound bomb. That same day, Charles Company suf-

fered another setback as a U.S. A-10A Thunderbolt mistakenly targeted Canadian forces, strafing the position of Charles Company with
30-millimeter high-explosive incendiary rounds. The attack killed
Private Mark Graham, a member of Canada's 4x400-meter relay
team at the 1992 Olympic Games in Barcelona. "He was such a strong
and sweet man," his fiancé wrote in a statement after his death. "He
had strong morals, values, ethics and they showed in everything he
did."[48] In addition, thirty Canadians were wounded that day, including several senior noncommissioned officers and the company commander, Major Sprague. A Board of Inquiry report convened by
Canadian Expeditionary Force Command found that the U.S. pilot
had lost his situational awareness. He mistook a garbage fire at the
Canadian location for his target, without verifying the target through
his targeting pod and heads-up display. The forward air controller
reacted immediately to the friendly-fire incident, screaming, "Abort!
Abort! Abort!" on his radio.[49]

"I had been off to the side and heard the A-10 sound. I hit the
ground, and when I got up I saw all the [injured] laying there," said
Corporal Jason Plumley.[50] An aerial medevac team rapidly arrived. In
less than thirty-six hours, Charles Company had lost much of its leadership at the officer and noncommissioned-officer level. All four of
its warrant officers had been either killed or wounded. Captain Steve
Brown was suddenly in charge of a company that had a corporal acting as company quartermaster and a sergeant as company sergeant
major. There was a lull in ground operations after the friendly-fire
incident, and the north, along Highway 1, then became the main theater of operation.[51]

So-called friendly fire is an unfortunate reality on the battlefield.
Two years earlier, U.S. Army Ranger Pat Tillman had been accidentally killed by his own platoon members in eastern Afghanistan. A
long-haired, hard-hitting safety with the Arizona Cardinals in the
National Football League, he held the franchise record of 224 tackles.
Tillman turned down a three-year, $3.6 million contract in the spring
of 2002 to join the U.S. Army with his brother, Kevin. As he remarked

the day after the September 11 attacks: "At times like this you stop and think about just how good we have it, what kind of system we live in, and the freedoms we are allowed. A lot of my family has gone and fought in wars and I really haven't done a damn thing."[52]

But the circumstances of his death were contentious. Initial reports stated that Tillman was killed by hostile fire, but a month later the Pentagon notified the Tillman family that he had died because of friendly fire. The family alleged that the Department of Defense delayed the disclosure out of a desire to protect the image of the U.S. military, and a subsequent Pentagon investigation concluded: "Corporal Tillman's chain of command made critical errors in reporting Corporal Tillman's death," and "Army officials failed to properly update family members when an investigation was initiated into Corporal Tillman's death."[53] A similar congressional report found "serious flaws" in the Pentagon's investigation and suggested that "the combination of a difficult battle in Fallujah, bad news about the state of the war, and emerging reports about Abu Ghraib prison" may have created a motive to obfuscate the details of Tillman's death.[54]

With Canadian forces still reeling from the friendly-fire incident, five members of Bravo Company were injured on September 5, 2006, when they were hit by mortar fire in the Pashmul pocket while they were resupplying their armored vehicles. The Taliban had almost certainly been monitoring Canadian movements, and waited for an opportune time to strike. As forces were redeployed to the north, reconnaissance patrols were sent out almost daily. Intelligence reports noted that the artillery fire and air support, which had been unceasing since operations began, were taking a toll.[55] The Taliban found it difficult to resupply and maintain control. On September 6, Bravo Company breached the treeline that divided Canadian from Taliban territory. With the forward position established, they began a systematic move southward. They engaged in firefights, seized and cleared territory, and then waited for the next forward passage of lines. Troops from the Canadian Battle Group, a U.S. company drawn from the 10th Mountain Division, and Afghan

National Army troops methodically cleared the compounds, houses, and fields of enemy forces.[56]

By September 10, Canadian, Afghan, and other NATO forces had advanced deep into Taliban territory. Air support from U.S. Navy F/A-18 Super Hornets joined the attack from the U.S.S. *Abraham Lincoln* in the Indian Ocean. Engineers blew holes in the walls of buildings allowing soldiers to enter, and bulldozers opened routes through fields and vineyards.

"I thought I had some idea of what I was going to be going through," said Canadian Corporal Jason Legros. "I figured I would be shot at a few times but I didn't expect to be ambushed."[57]

Follow-On Operations

On September 13, Coalition forces had reached the Arghandab River. By September 17, NATO forces had cleared most of Panjwai. Estimates of insurgent dead were well into the hundreds, and hundreds more had attempted to flee to Helmand Province or to other pockets of Kandahar Province.[58] NATO forces in Kandahar followed Operation Medusa with reconstruction and development efforts. They provided emergency water, food, shelter, health care, and animal feed to local Afghans in the area of operations, and they assisted the return of locals who had fled.[59]

But there were complaints from local villagers and human-rights organizations that civilians had been unnecessarily impacted. As Human Rights Watch wrote in a letter to NATO Secretary General Jaap de Hoop Scheffer, "during Operation Medusa, NATO troops killed large numbers of livestock and destroyed numerous vineyards that insurgents were using as cover . . . causing much economic damage to civilians and fostering resentment towards NATO troops."[60] Human Rights Watch pointed out that NATO lacked a compensation program for Afghan families who suffered losses because of NATO operations, and the organization strongly urged a change in policy.

In tandem with Operation Medusa, approximately 4,000 Afghan and 3,000 U.S. troops initiated Operation Mountain Fury in September 2006 to defeat Taliban resistance in Paktika, Khowst, Ghazni, Paktia, and Lowgar Provinces in east-central Afghanistan. Fighting continued throughout that autumn and into December. During the early morning hours of December 15, NATO aircraft attacked a Taliban command post in Kandahar. The same day, aircraft began dropping three sets of leaflets over the region. The first warned the population of the impending conflict, the next was a plea for locals to turn their backs on the Taliban and support NATO, and the third consisted of an image of a Taliban fighter with a large "X" through it to warn Taliban to leave the area. During the days prior to the operation, Canadian soldiers held several meetings with tribal elders to discuss reconstruction efforts and persuade them to keep the Taliban out of the area. While en route to one of these meetings, a Canadian soldier from the Royal 22ᵉ Régiment—the "Vandoos," out of Quebec— stepped on a land mine. The soldier, Private Frederic Couture, suffered severe but non–life-threatening injuries and was transported to a military hospital.[61]

On December 19, limited offensive operations began against Taliban forces. A massive barrage of Canadian artillery and tank fire rained down on their positions. The barrage lasted for forty-five minutes and was supported by heavy machine-gun fire from Canadian .50-caliber guns. Shortly after the barrage ended, Canadian armored convoys set up a perimeter around the village of Howz-e Madad. Over the next few days, NATO forces secured several towns with little resistance from Taliban fighters. Near Howz-e Madad, a ten-square-kilometer area with mud-walled fortresses provided refuge to a larger group of Taliban fighters. NATO forces gave the surrounded fighters two days to surrender. After the forty-eight hours, the Taliban fired on the Canadian forces. Two rockets flew past Charles Company just south of Howz-e Madad. The Afghan National Army responded with a burst of machine-gun fire, but no one on either side took casualties. On January 5, a forty-five-minute firefight erupted between about twenty members of the Royal 22ᵉ Régiment and a force of Taliban fighters about half that size near the village of Lacookhal, just south of Howz-e Madad, where the soldiers from the Royal 22ᵉ Régiment had been looking for arms caches and Taliban. The Taliban used automatic rifles, machine guns, rocket-propelled grenades, and mortars. By the time the firefight ceased, at least two of the Taliban fighters had been killed. There were no Canadian or Afghan National Army casualties.

The year concluded with a controversial ceasefire between British troops in Musa Qala and the Taliban. British troops agreed to move quietly out of Musa Qala, and the Taliban agreed not to conduct attacks in the area. The two sides had thus far fought to a stalemate, with casualties on both sides. In a sense, the ceasefire allowed British forces to withdraw from a tenuous and undesirable situation. It was sanctioned by Muhammad Daud, governor of Helmand Province, and most tribal elders, who felt they could now exercise control over the Taliban themselves. But neithear Daud nor the tribal elders could prevent the return of insurgent fighters. The truce only succeeded in strengthening the Taliban's penetration of northern Helmand. General David Richards, the NATO commander in Afghanistan, said at the time that the British deal turned northern Helmand into "magnets" for the Taliban.[62] Apparently he was fuming about the deal. Several months later, a UN report concluded that the ceasefire allowed the Taliban "to move freely in the area."[63]

Back to Baghdad

U.S. government officials finally had begun to acknowledge the growing violence in Afghanistan. A 2007 National Security Council assessment of the war in Afghanistan concluded that wide-ranging strategic goals that the Bush administration had set in Afghanistan had not been met, even as Coalition forces scored significant combat successes against resurgent Taliban fighters. The NSC evaluation examined progress in security, governance, and the economy, but it concluded that only "the kinetic piece"—individual battles against Taliban fighters—showed substantial progress, while improvements in the other areas continued to lag. This judgment reflected sharp differences between U.S. military and intelligence officials on where the Afghan War was headed. Some intelligence analysts acknowledged the battlefield victories, but they highlighted the Taliban's unchallenged expansion into new territory, an increase in opium-poppy cultivation, and the weakness of President Karzai's government as signs that the war effort was deteriorating. While the military found success in a virtually unbroken line of tactical achievements, U.S. intelligence officials worried about a looming strategic failure.[64]

But the war in Iraq continued to siphon off funds and attention. In an unusually frank admission in December 2007 before the House Armed Services Committee, Joint Chiefs of Staff Chairman Admiral Michael Mullen observed that an American military stretched by the war in Iraq could only do so much in Afghanistan. "Our main focus, militarily, in the region and in the world right now is rightly and firmly in Iraq," he noted. "It is simply a matter of resources, of capacity. In Afghanistan, we do what we can. In Iraq, we do what we must."[65]

In addition, Secretary of Defense Gates initially blocked a push by the U.S. Marine Corps to move into Afghanistan. In December 2007, for example, Gates met at the Pentagon with General James T. Conway, the Marine Corps commandant, to discuss a formal proposal that would shift Marine forces from Anbar Province in Iraq to Afghanistan. The proposal called for a Marine integrated "air-ground task force" of infantry, attack aircraft, and logistics to carry out the Afghanistan mission and build on counterinsurgency lessons learned by Marines in Anbar.[66] But senior Pentagon officials, including Gates, were concerned that reallocating resources to Afghanistan would jeopardize some of the fragile gains the U.S. military had made in Iraq in 2007. "The secretary understands what the commandant is trying to do, and why the commandant wishes to transition the

Marine Corps mission to Afghanistan," said Geoff Morrell, the Pentagon press secretary, "but he doesn't believe the time is now to do that. Anbar is still a volatile place."[67]

A small contingent of U.S. Marines eventually deployed to southern Afghanistan, but it was only a token force. By then, insurgent groups led by the Taliban had mounted a challenge to NATO and the Afghan government.

CHAPTER THIRTEEN

A Three-Front War

IN LATE 2006 and early 2007, Lieutenant General Karl Eikenberry conducted a series of briefings on the Afghan insurgency for senior U.S. policymakers, including National Security Adviser Stephen Hadley, Secretary of State Condoleezza Rice, CIA Director Michael V. Hayden, Secretary of Defense Robert Gates, Chairman of the Joint Chiefs of Staff General Peter Pace, and Vice President Dick Cheney. The presentation showed where the command-and-control locations for the Taliban and other insurgent groups were headquartered, especially in Pakistan's Federally Administered Tribal Areas. In one section, for example, the briefers interspersed satellite images of a major compound used by Taliban ally Jalaluddin Haqqani in Miramshah with video footage from the PBS *Frontline* documentary "The Return of the Taliban."

At one point in the documentary, producer Martin Smith asked Munir Akram, Pakistan's ambassador to the United Nations: "Let me just raise a few things they say you can do. Haqqani, Jalaluddin Haqqani—why don't you arrest him?"

Akram confidently responded: "Well, I think Jalaluddin Haqqani, if he's found, I'm sure he'll be arrested."[1]

The briefing team then presented satellite imagery of a wider area, which showed offices of the Pakistan Army next door. "Not only does Pakistan know where Haqqani is," one of the briefers noted to senior

U.S. officials, "but they are virtually co-located with him. If they wanted to get him, they could."

The Pakistani government was also shown a version of the briefing, though the *Frontline* segment was taken out. It was a disturbing reminder to those at the highest levels of the U.S. government that insurgent groups operating in Afghanistan, who were killing U.S., NATO, and Afghan forces and civilians, used Pakistan as a sanctuary, especially for their top-level commanders.

Complex Adaptive System

The perfect storm that hit Afghanistan in 2006 involved a disparate set of groups that established a sanctuary in Pakistan. There were two striking themes. One was the sheer increase in the number of insurgent groups over the course of the decade. Some groups, such as Laskhar-e-Taiba and Jaish-e-Muhammad (Army of Muhammad), migrated to the Afghanistan theater. Both were formed in the early 1990s to fight against India over control of Jammu and Kashmir. Another theme was the diffuse, highly complex nature of the insurgency, which was perhaps best described as a *complex adaptive system*. This term refers to systems that are diverse (made up of multiple interconnected elements) and adaptive (possessing the capacity to change and learn from experience). Examples of complex adaptive systems include the stock market, ant colonies, and most major social organizations.[2]

At least five different categories of groups were included in this system. The first were insurgent groups, who were motivated to overthrow the Afghan government and coerce the withdrawal of international forces. They ranged from the Taliban to smaller groups such as the Haqqani network, Gulbuddin Hekmatyar's Hezb-i-Islami, Tehreek-e-Nafaz-e-Shariat-e-Mohammadi (TNSM), and al Qa'ida. A second category included criminal groups involved in such activities as drug trafficking and illicit timber and gem trading. The third included local tribes, subtribes, and clans that allied with insurgent

groups. Most were Pashtun. The fourth category comprised the warlord militias, many of whom had become increasingly powerful after
the 2001 overthrow of the Taliban regime. A fifth category included
local or central government forces complicit in the insurgency, such
as the Afghan National Police and the Pakistani Frontier Corps.

These groups could be divided along three geographic fronts: northern, central, and southern. Figure 13.1 provides a rough illustration.

The *northern front* stretched from Pakistan's North West Frontier
Province to Afghan provinces of Nuristan, Kunar, and Nangarhar. The
largest of the groups in this region was Hekmatyar's Hezb-i-Islami,
but other groups were also operating in this front. One was an offshoot of Hezb-i-Islami led by Anwar al-Haq Mojahed, whose group
was made up of former Hezb-i-Islami fighters, disgruntled tribesmen, and some ex-Taliban. Another was TNSM, whose objective was
to enforce *sharia* law in Afghanistan and Pakistan. TNSM fractured
into three blocs based out of Pakistan: Sufi Mohammad's loyal following, a Swat-based faction started by Sufi Mohammad's son-in-law

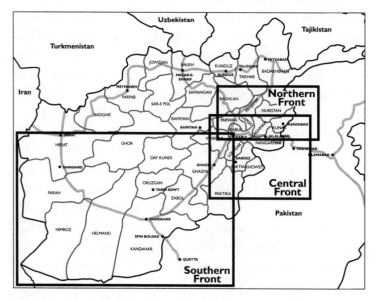

FIGURE **13.1** The Insurgent Fronts

Mullah Fazlullah, and a Bajaur-based militant group led by Mullah Faqir Muhammad. Bajaur is located at the northern tip of Pakistan's Federally Administered Tribal Areas, and Swat district is located east of Bajaur in the North West Frontier Province.

Lashkar-e-Taiba was active on this front, as was al Qa'ida, including Abu Ikhlas al-Masri, an Egyptian who had fought against the Soviets in the 1980s and had married a local woman. There was also a variety of criminal organizations, especially groups involved in the illicit timber and gem trades. Timber was smuggled across the border into Pakistan by networks run by timber barons. Some Afghan and Pakistani government officials were also involved in assisting insurgents and criminal organizations—often to take a cut of lucrative business opportunities. "Illicit timber trading was big business," noted Larry Legree, the Provincial Reconstruction Team commander from Kunar. "Everyone, from government officials to insurgent groups, had their hands in the profits."[3]

The *central front* lay farther south along the Afghanistan-Pakistan border. It stretched from Pakistan's Federally Administered Tribal Areas to eastern Afghan provinces of Paktika, Khowst, and Lowgar. One of the most significant groups was led by Jalaluddin Haqqani's son Sirajuddin ("Siraj"), who was especially elusive. U.S. military and intelligence analysts strained to get a good photograph of him. Haqqani's organization had close links with Pakistan's ISI, from which it received aid, and it became lethal at conducting attacks deep into Afghanistan. Haqqani also had close ties to an umbrella group, Tehreek-e-Taliban-Pakistan, which operated out of Waziristan and was led by Baitullah Mehsud. Both the Pakistani government and the Central Intelligence Agency publicly stated that Mehsud was involved in the assassination of former Pakistan Prime Minister Benazir Bhutto on December 27, 2007.[4] Al Qai'da also operated in this area, along with a number of other foreign groups, such as the Islamic Movement of Uzbekistan.

Finally, there was the *southern front*, in the southern Afghan provinces of Helmand and Kandahar, as well as in Pakistan's Baluchistan Province. The largest group in this front was Mullah Omar's Taliban, based near Quetta. The Taliban linked up with a number of Pashtun tribes, especially Ghilzai tribes, which provided logistical support, fighters, and local legitimacy. Its strategy involved approaching local tribes and commanders at the village and district levels. In some cases, Taliban commanders were well received because of common tribal affinities or because locals had become disillusioned with the Afghan government—fed up with the slow pace of reconstruction and the paucity of security. Where they weren't well received, they sometimes resorted to brutal tactics. "They have perfected the art of targeted assassination," one soldier noted, "to intimidate locals who support the Afghan government. A bullet in the head is all it takes."[5] The southern front also boasted criminal groups, especially drug-trafficking organizations, which operated on both sides of the Afghanistan-Pakistan border. The skyrocketing trade in poppy was a boon to insurgent organizations such as the Taliban, as well as to Afghan government officials.

There was evidence of some coordination among the major insurgent groups at the tactical, operational, and strategic levels, including through several *shuras*, or Islamic councils, located in Pakistan.[6] But there was no unified leadership.

"Learning Organizations"

These groups focused on classic guerrilla warfare. Promoting disorder among the population is a key objective of most insurgents, and disrupting the economy and decreasing security helps produce discontent with the indigenous government, undermining its legitimacy. Once insurgents establish a hold over the population, those who are hostile to the insurgents often become too fearful to oppose them. Some may be eliminated, providing an example to others. Some may escape to other areas, and still others may be cowed into hiding their true feelings. By threatening the population, insurgents keep individuals from cooperating with the indigenous government and external actors.[7]

Afghan and Pakistani insurgent groups were successful at adapting their tactics, techniques, and procedures to become "learning organizations."[8] The command-and-control structure of the insurgent groups was fragmented. Within the Taliban, for example, the inner *shura* maintained links to field commanders through a weak hierarchical structure. A district or village commander usually had a connection to one or two *shura* members, as did a more important commander who operated in a wider geographic area. One UN study found that "there is no area ownership among TB [Taliban] commanders. Several TB commanders may carry out operations in the same area of operation without recognizing a hierarchy amongst them. Regular competition between commanders seems to be the norm rather than the exception." It continued: "Once commanders grow in importance by laying claim to military success they receive special attention from al-Qaida and foreign donors. They subsequently adopt a more independent stature and start individual fundraising."[9]

Insurgent groups conducted a wide variety of attacks against U.S., Coalition, and Afghan security forces as well as Afghan and international civilians. They generally yielded the population centers to U.S. and Afghan forces, choosing instead to base operations in rural areas. They staged ambushes and raids using small arms and grenades, and they shelled U.S. and other NATO troops using 107-millimeter and 122-millimeter rockets and 60-, 82-, and 120-millimeter mortars. The weapon that received the most media attention was the improvised explosive device (IED), which was particularly effective against Coalition ground convoys. Most shelling and rocket fire was not accurate, though there was some evidence that insurgent forces considered the simple harassment of enemy forces and populations to be valuable. Insurgent groups, especially the Taliban, also succeeded in capturing government installations, villages, and occasionally district centers, though usually for brief periods. They intimidated local villagers by distributing *shabnamah*, or night letters, leaflets that warned villagers not to cooperate with foreign forces or the Karzai regime. In addition, insurgents conducted targeted assassinations, torched reconstruction and development projects, and set up illegal check-points along major roads.[10]

The Taliban and other groups also began to stage kidnappings. Taliban commander Mansour Dadullah acknowledged: "Kidnapping is a very successful policy and I order all my mujahideen to kidnap foreigners of any nationality wherever they find them and then we should do the same kind of deal."[11] Kidnappings were increasingly used to raise money. They had been profitable in Iraq, especially since a number of governments—such as France and Japan—paid ransoms for the release of hostages.[12] This practice had caused L. Paul Bremer to send out a memo to foreign embassies in Iraq condemning ransom payments. Bremer's words were just as true for Afghanistan as they were for Iraq: "There is no greater spur and no greater encouragement to hostage takers, than the payment of ransom money in return for the liberation of hostages. Such payments make hostage takings more likely; they increase the level of jeopardy for present and future hostages; and they have the potential to fund the procurement of weapons that will be used to continue the terror that is damaging this nation and killing its people."[13]

In Afghanistan, there were strong indications that foreign governments, including South Korea and Italy, paid for the release of hostages.[14] In 2007, dozens of hostages were taken, including an Italian journalist in Helmand Province, two French and three Afghan aid workers in Farah Province, two German engineers and four Afghan nationals in Wardak Province. The worst incident involved the kidnapping of twenty-three South Koreans in Ghazni Province. But the kidnappings were only the beginning. One Taliban military official said: "Our military tactic is to control a district center, kill the government soldiers there, and withdraw to our mountainous strongholds, where it would be very difficult for the government to pursue us."[15] Some, if not many, of these tactics, techniques, and procedures were similar to those used by mujahideen forces against Soviet and Democratic Republic of Afghanistan army forces during the Soviet-Afghan War.[16]

In such southern provinces as Helmand, insurgents deployed in larger numbers. In 2002, they operated in squad- and platoon-size units. In 2005, they operated in company-size units of up to a hundred or more fighters. In 2006 and 2007, there were a few cases in which they operated in battalion-size units of up to 400 fighters, though they deployed in smaller units as well.[17] This suggested that insurgents moved around with more freedom without being targeted by Afghan or Coalition forces. They also shifted from hard targets, such as U.S. and other NATO forces, to soft targets, such as Afghans involved in election work, nongovernmental organization workers, Afghan National Police, and Afghan citizens believed to be cooperating with Coalition forces or the Afghan government.

Some of the most brutal incidents were the executions by insurgents of "collaborators" who sided with the Afghan government or Coalition forces.[18] Taliban fighters killed Islamic clerics critical of their efforts, including Mawlawi Abdullah Fayyaz, head of the Ulema Council of Kandahar.[19] Schools were increasingly targeted, and as one Taliban night letter warned: "Teachers' salaries are financed by non-believers. Unless you stop getting wages from them, you will be counted among the American puppets."[20] This rationale also extended to election candidates and members of Parliament, since "the elections are a part of the American program" and those who participate in the elections "are the enemies of Islam and the homeland."[21]

The "New" Taliban

The Taliban was the largest of these groups. Its leadership's ideological vision did not change significantly after its regime's overthrow in 2001, and its senior leaders remained motivated to impose in Afghanistan a radical interpretation of Sunni Islam derived from the Deobandi school of thought.[22] The Taliban's primary means for accomplishing this objective were to overthrow the new Afghan government, break the political will of the United States and its Coalition partners, and coerce foreign forces to withdraw. They patiently prepared to outlast the international presence in Afghanistan. "We do have to bear in mind however that in an insurgency of this nature the insurgent wins if he does not lose and we lose if we do not win," noted a British government assessment. "For the insurgent this places considerable emphasis on astute information operations, management of perceptions, retaining consent of the local population (by whatever means) and being patient. The longer he endures the more likely he will just wait out the counterinsurgency effort."[23]

The Taliban included an influx of new members—sometimes referred to as the "neo-Taliban"—who were recruited at *madrassas* and other locations in Afghanistan and Pakistan.[24] The Taliban organization that emerged over the course of the insurgency involved two main tiers. The top tier included the leadership structure and key commanders. They were motivated by a radical version of Islam and saw the insurgency as a fight between Islam on one side and Western infidels and the West's "puppet government" in Kabul on the other side. The Taliban's inner *shura* was responsible for strategic decisions and for addressing the most egregious problems. Examples can be found in the Taliban Code of Conduct (*Layeha*), which included orders not to engage in separate negotiations and to report captures and wait for leadership decision.[25] Following the 2001 overthrow of the Taliban regime, the leadership moved to Pakistan. The top tier included the leadership structure and key commanders and was run by a *shura* headed by Mullah Omar.

With Mullah Omar at the top, the Taliban *shura* was divided into a series of functional committees: military, propaganda, finance, religious, political, and administrative. At various points, key members of the inner *shura* included such individuals as Mullah Omar, Mullah Berader (former Taliban governor of Herat), Akhtar Muhammad Mansour (former Taliban head of aviation), Mullah Nuruddin Turabi (former Taliban justice minister), Mullah Abdul Jalil (former Taliban minister of foreign affairs), and Noor Muhammad Saqib (former chief justice of the Supreme Court). Regional *shuras* in such locations as Peshawar and Waziristan also included political, military, finance, and other committees.

The bottom tier of Taliban guerrillas included thousands of local fighters—men from rural villages paid to set up roadside bombs, launch rockets and mortars at NATO and Afghan forces, or pick up a gun for a few weeks or months. The Taliban also organized a parallel Afghan government, which included governors for Afghan provinces and ministers for such areas as defense and justice.[26]

While the Taliban remained a puritan religious movement, it had little political vision other than the establishment of *sharia* law. As scholars Mariam Abou Zahab and Olivier Roy maintained, the Taliban had little beyond "the Shari'a, the whole Shari'a, and nothing but the Shari'a."[27] Mullah Dadullah Lang, the Taliban military commander who was killed by U.S. forces in 2007, declared: "We are not fighting here for Afghanistan, but we are fighting for all Muslims everywhere and also the Mujahideen in Iraq. The infidels attacked Muslim lands and it is a must that every Muslim should support his Muslim brothers."[28] This argument was echoed by other insurgents, such as former Taliban spokesman Mofti Latifollah Hakimi: "The issue of Afghanistan is connected with the ongoing war between Islam and blasphemy in the world. Mullah Mohammad [Omar] is representing a huge umma, and a large nation is behind him."[29] The Taliban used young Pakistan-trained mullahs to glorify their cause in mosques in Afghanistan's east and south.

There were two notable differences between the Taliban's religious ideology during the 1990s and their ideology after 2001. The Taliban eased some of their aversion to modern technology. During the 1990s, they generally discouraged the use of the Internet and television by closing down Internet cafés and banning television. After their overthrow, however, they leveraged Al-Sahab, al Qa'ida's media enterprise, to distribute video propaganda and recruit supporters. Key Taliban leaders, such as Mullah Dadullah Lang, were comfortable and relaxed in front of a camera, reciting passages of the Qur'an and outlining the Taliban's ideology.

In addition, the Taliban adopted suicide bombing as a tactic against Afghan and international forces with the assistance and encouragement of key al Qa'ida leaders, such as Ayman al-Zawahiri. During the 1990s, the Taliban conducted no suicide attacks, presumably because the Qur'an prohibits suicide. This changed by 2003 and 2004, though not all Taliban appeared to be on board with this new tactic. Signals and human intelligence picked up by NATO officials indicated that there were divisions within the Taliban about the use of suicide attacks. For some, collateral damage—especially when Afghan women and children were killed in the vicinity of a suicide attack—was unjustifiable. Infidels were fair game, but not innocent bystanders. The Taliban's ideology seemed to be somewhat flexible over time, as long as it served strategic purposes.

Gulbuddin Hekmatyar's Hezb-i-Islami was also active, based out of such areas as the Shamshattu refugee camp near Peshawar.[30] He argued that jihad was critical in order to fight Western forces and to establish *sharia* law in Afghanistan. "Believe me," he thundered in a video clip in response to questions from Agence France Presse, "we do this jihad as we pray, as we fast, or conduct hajj."[31] His daily newspapers, the *Shahaadat Daily* and *Tanweer Weekly*, were available on the streets of Pakistani cities, especially Peshawar. They denounced the Afghan government for apostasy and called Hamid Karzai a puppet of the West. Hekmatyar argued that Western forces were infidels who occupied the land of Muslims. In a video, he proclaimed the United States as "the mother of problems" and warned that Afghanistan's turmoil would not end until U.S. forces left the region. "The occupying forces . . . have only one successful way and . . . that is to pull out of Afghanistan as soon as possible."[32] In another video, Hekmatyar argued that "the Afghan mujahideen have pledged to themselves that they will force America out of their country like the Soviet Union and will not lay down their arms until they drive the occupying forces out of their country."[33] This comment was notable not only for its anti-American rhetoric but also for its reference to the jihad against the Soviet Union. Hekmatyar, of course, had participated in that war with CIA assistance.

Hekmatyar's traditional influence was strongest among Pashtun communities in Afghanistan's northeast. Hezb-i-Islami generally enrolled Pashtuns and was implacably hostile to any form of political compromise with Western countries. From its earliest days, Hezb-i-Islami defined the "good Muslim" as one who was no longer defined by his religious attitude but by his political actions. Following the writings of Ibn Taymiyya, Hekmatyar believed it was possible to define a Muslim as a *takfir* for purely political reasons.[34] This gave Hezb-i-Islami notable credentials with the Muslim Brotherhood, Sayyid Abul Ala Maududi's Jamiat-e-Islami in Pakistan, and the Saudi networks. Hekmatyar had particularly close ties with Jamiat-e-Islami and its view that the five pillars of Islam were merely phases of preparation for jihad and Islamic revolution. In a sense, their goal was to "Islamize modernity" by domesticating Western techniques and knowledge and putting them to work on behalf of an Islamic state. This differentiated them from Deobandi groups, such as the Taliban, who rejected such modernity out of hand.[35] Hekmatyar also adhered to Sayyid Qutb's views about the need to vanquish corrupt Muslim leaders in order to establish true Islamic government.

Unlike either the Taliban or al Qa'ida, Hezb-i-Islami also became involved in politics. "The influence of Hezb-i-Islami in Afghan politics, including in the Parliament," one senior Afghan official told me, "is significant."[36] A number of Hezb-i-Islami members were elected to the Afghan Parliament in the September 2005 elections, though many claimed they had broken ranks with Hekmatyar. This suggested that it was not a unified organization. But it allowed Hezb-i-Islami to play a double game: some of its adherents targeted Afghan and NATO forces in the east and some participated in Afghan politics in Kabul and its outlying provinces. Political participation was strongly shunned by al Qa'ida leaders and other Islamists, who considered the democratic political system corrupt and contrary to the establishment of God's law within a country. In addition, not all members of Hezb-i-Islami agreed on tactical, operational, or strategic decisions of other groups, especially the Taliban. One United Nations report asserted that Hekmatyar's Hezb-i-Islami faction was for the Taliban a "particularly troublesome co-opted group" because "some of its members proved entirely incompatible with the [Taliban's] ideology and campaign plan."[37]

Competing Motivations

The leaders of most major insurgent groups—especially the Taliban, Hezb-i-Islami, and al Qa'ida—were motivated by religion. There were also a number of smaller groups active in Afghanistan and Pakistan that professed somewhat similar ideologies, such as the Islamic Movement of Uzbekistan. The IMU's leaders were motivated to establish an Islamic state under *sharia* in Uzbekistan, though they also supported efforts to establish *sharia* in neighboring countries, including Afghanistan. This religious ideology helps explain why, even after the overthrow of the Taliban regime in 2001, these groups wanted to target Hamid Karzai's government.

There were, of course, some tensions and ideological differences across these groups. CIA estimates after the September 11 attacks, for example, found deep divisions between the Taliban and al Qa'ida. Al Qa'ida utilized support from the Taliban for outer-perimeter security, but many al Qa'ida fighters looked disdainfully on the masses of Taliban, and many Taliban viewed al Qa'ida members as unwelcome foreigners. The personal and ideological link between bin Laden and Mullah Omar was crucial to keeping intact an unsteady relationship.[38] Despite these and other differences, however, they shared several common characteristics.[39]

To begin with, they were *jihadist*—that is, their supporters advocated the necessity of jihad in order to recover "occupied" Muslim lands, or even to struggle against Muslim regimes regarded as traitorous. They were also loosely Salafist, demanding a return to strict Islam.[40] Many Salafist movements are opposed to armed jihad, either tactically or by conviction, and advocate the *da'wa*, or "call" to Islam, as a preferred form of action. For those who advocate both jihad and

Salafism, jihad is the way by which Muslims can be united and recalled to the true practice of Islam. The underlying idea is that when the majority of Muslims return to the strict interpretation of Islam, they will be able to reestablish the Muslim *umma* (the community of all Muslims). In addition, these groups gave the Muslim *umma* priority over ethnic or national identities and interests. Al Qa'ida leader Abu Laith al-Libi—who was intimately involved in the Afghan insurgency against U.S. forces and was killed in a missile strike in January 2008—argued that in Afghanistan, "the jihad is a story which carries in its twists and turns the just cause of the *umma*, which seeks in overall terms to establish the religion on earth."[41] Finally, the groups often overlapped geographically. Although the Taliban had no serious objectives outside the frontiers of Afghanistan, they provided space within their territory for training camps for foreign volunteers and made use of units made up of such volunteers in their military campaigns.[42]

Insurgent groups used religion as a propaganda tool in at least two respects. The Taliban regularly used arguments that "Western countries are trying to destroy Islam" in their conversations with tribal elders and in their night letters.[43] As Mullah Dadullah Lang argued: "God be praised, we now are aware of much of the U.S. plans. We know their target, which is within the general aim of wiping out Islam in this region."[44] And the Taliban and other insurgent groups used religion in their recruitment efforts for suicide bombers.

These efforts had mixed success in Afghanistan, but more success in Pakistan. Since mosques historically served as a tipping point for major political upheavals in Afghanistan, Afghan government officials focused their attention on the mosques. One Afghan intelligence report stated: "There are 107 mosques in the city of Kandahar out of which 11 are preaching anti-government themes. Our approach is to have all the pro-government mosques incorporated with the process and work on the eleven anti-government ones to change their attitude or else stop their propaganda and leave the area."[45] Another major factor was a public campaign by Afghan religious figures. For example, the Ulema Council of Afghanistan called on the Taliban to abandon violence and support the Afghan government in the name of Islam. They also called on the religious scholars of neighboring countries—including Pakistan—to help counter the activities and ideology of the Taliban and other insurgent organizations.[46] A number of Afghan Muslim clerics publicly supported the Afghan government and called the jihad un-Islamic.[47] Moreover, the Ulema Council and some Afghan *ulema* issued *fatwas* that unambiguously opposed suicide bombing. They argued that suicide bombing did not lead to an eternal life in paradise, did not permit martyrs to see the face of Allah, and did not allow martyrs to have the company of seventy-two beautiful maidens in paradise.[48]

But religious ideology was not a sufficient condition for the rise of Afghanistan's insurgency. Local Afghans were generally not motivated by religion to support insurgent groups and oppose the Afghan government. Rather, they were motivated by poor or nonexistent governance. In most cases, the Taliban and other insurgent groups were not necessarily popular; the Afghan government was simply unpopular. Support for the Taliban would undoubtedly have been greater had they not run Afghanistan with an iron fist in the 1990s. As Ambassador Ronald Neumann remarked to me, "The Taliban conquest of Afghanistan in the 1990s had a silver lining: it gave Afghans a chance to see what they were really like."[49]

Yet despite these challenges, the Taliban and other groups mounted increasingly effective operations across Afghanistan's south and east in 2006 and 2007. They were met by NATO forces that struggled mightily to keep pace.

CHAPTER FOURTEEN

National Caveats

STANDING NEXT TO Canada's command headquarters at Kandahar Airfield when I visited it in 2007 was a makeshift war memorial. The faces of fallen Canadian soldiers were etched in chiseled marble. There were no obelisks or ostentatious monuments, just faces. Corporal David Robert Braun. Private Blake Neil Williamson. Warrant Officer Richard Francis Nolan. The list went on. Each face stared back at those who paid tribute, usually fellow Canadian soldiers shuffling into and out of the command headquarters. Some of the faces smiled sheepishly from the blackened marble, while others stared intently. All had served their country and paid with their lives. Next to each face were their names, biographical data, and units. 2nd Battalion, Princess Patricia's Canadian Light Infantry (Shilo, Manitoba). 1st Battalion, The Royal Canadian Regiment (Petawawa, Ontario). 2nd Battalion, Royal 22ᵉ Régiment (Valcartier, Québec).

The inscription on the memorial read: "Dedicated to those Canadians who gave their lives in the service of peace while serving in Afghanistan." Visitors placed flowers and photographs of their fallen comrades across the nameplates. Amid the daily commotion of Canada's headquarters and the constant roar of fighter jets overhead, the memorial was strangely serene.

Unlike the war in Iraq, which was largely unilateral, the war in Afghanistan was at first fought by a true multinational coalition.

NATO eventually became engaged as a full partner in combat operations and reconstruction. But it didn't start off that way. Following the September 2001 attacks, NATO invoked for the first time Article V of the 1949 Washington Treaty, its founding document. Article V embodied the allies' collective-security commitment to one another, stating that the "Parties agree that an armed attack against one or more of them in Europe or North America shall be considered an attack against them all."[1] Since the United States had been attacked, they felt obliged to step in.

Within months of the U.S. invasion, a number of NATO countries made Special Forces and intelligence assets available. Many went to Afghanistan, but U.S. policymakers chose to use most NATO assets in the United States. NATO fighter aircraft flew combat air patrols over some thirty U.S. cities and key infrastructure, with continuous patrols over Washington, DC, and New York City. U.S. Air Force and NATO air crews flew more than 13,400 fighter, tanker, and airborne early warning sorties over the United States. There were more sorties flown in the United States than during the war in Afghanistan up to mid-April 2002, when the continuous air patrols in U.S. cities ended.[2]

By 2006 and 2007, NATO began to play a more significant role in counterinsurgency operations in Afghanistan, especially in the violent south. Despite a growing list of NATO countries that deployed forces to Afghanistan, however, many countries refused to allow their forces to engage in combat operations. One senior NATO official acknowledged, "It was like fighting with one hand tied behind our backs."[3]

"Lead Nation" Strategy

Beginning in 2002, there were few non-U.S. NATO forces in Afghanistan; Secretary Rumsfeld had opposed the deployment of a stabilization force outside of Kabul. With rare exceptions, the 4,000-member International Security Assistance Force (ISAF) did not venture beyond the capital. Its purpose was to protect the Afghan interim administration and help provide security in the capital. Rather than deploy troops for combat operations, several NATO countries volunteered to help the Afghan government rebuild its depleted security sector. The effort was referred to as the "lead nation" approach. The United States volunteered to lead the construction of the Afghan National Army; Germany was responsible for training the Afghan National Police; the United Kingdom led the counternarcotics effort; Italy was the lead for rebuilding Afghanistan's decrepit justice system; and Japan (with UN assistance) was the lead for the disarmament, demobilization, and reintegration of former combatants. In theory, each lead nation was supposed to contribute significant financial assistance, coordinate external aid, and oversee reconstruction efforts in its sector.

In practice, this approach was a disaster. Assessments from the Pentagon were scathing. "This 'lead nation' strategy produced mixed results, but overall it was a failure," acknowledged Under Secretary of Defense Douglas Feith, specifically calling attention to the "efforts of the British, Germans, and Italians."[4]

Afghans were equally critical. Daoud Yaqub, the director for security sector reform at the Afghanistan National Security Council, bemoaned the challenges of coordination. To get everything done, officials had to negotiate along four tracks: between Afghan government ministries, between international donors, between donors and the Afghan government, and within donors' own agencies. "When disagreements broke out between the donors and us, the donors would come to me and say quite matter-of-factly: 'It's our money. We'll do with it what we want.' There was little I could do."[5]

The justice system was perhaps the most significant challenge. To be fair, no formal justice system existed in Afghanistan after the U.S. invasion in 2001. The United Nations Development Program announced shortly after the overthrow of the Taliban regime that "the physical infrastructure of [the justice] institutions has been destroyed." Even more critically, it fretted that "the country's legal 'software'— the laws, legal decisions, legal studies, and texts of jurisprudence— are largely lost or scattered across the world."[6] The December 2001

Bonn Agreement called for the interim Afghan government to establish a judicial reform commission to "rebuild the domestic justice system in accordance with Islamic principles, international standards,
the rule of law, and Afghan legal traditions."[7] Consequently, Karzai's
government established the Judicial Reform Commission to oversee
and coordinate reconstruction of the justice system.[8]

As the lead nation for justice-sector reform, Italy had the job of
helping to establish a body of laws; train prosecutors, lawyers, and
Ministry of Justice officers; build physical infrastructure; and improve
detention and prison capacity. But assistance was fractured and Italian
policymakers had difficulty coordinating the disparate range of aid
pouring in from nations, the UN, the World Bank, and nongovernmental organizations. One study concluded that the "overall coordination and cooperation in the justice sector [was] lacking." The
Italian government also "maintained distance from the Afghan institutions. Rather than support Afghan-led decision-making, the Italian
effort . . . preferred to choose and implement its projects with limited consultation."[9]

Even if the Italians had done everything right, they still needed to
overcome severe divisions among the Afghan justice departments.
President Karzai had created the Judicial Reform Commission to
coordinate reforms, but by empowering the commission, Karzai also
removed authority and control of foreign assistance from the permanent institutions. The commission was meant to set policy and priori-
ties for the justice sector, and, in practice, to determine where donor
funds would be directed. From the start, the commission had no
capacity, funding, or political cover to manage this significant task.
Without intervention from the presidency, a turf war raged among
the Supreme Court, the Ministry of Justice, the Office of the Prose-
cutor General, and the commission.

Under Secretary Feith and other Pentagon officials complained
incessantly about the Italians. "Italy made the underperforming Germans look good," Feith noted sarcastically, referring to the German
effort to train the Afghan National Police. "For well over a year the

Italians failed to send to Afghanistan a team of experts; in fact, they did not send a single person. When I raised the problem with Italy's Defense Minister, Antonio Martino—as thoughtful and reliable an ally as one could hope for—he said he would try to help, but judicial matters were not handled by his ministry."[10]

Needless to say, the Italian reforms did not earn Afghanistan's justice system high marks. The World Bank ranked Afghanistan in the top 2 percent of most corrupt countries worldwide every year between 2002 and 2006, with little difference between the late Taliban years.[11] And Transparency International, a nongovernmental organization based in Berlin that monitored corruption, ranked Afghanistan almost at the bottom—172 out of 179—of its corruption index. Only a few countries, such as Haiti, Iraq, and Somalia, were more corrupt than Afghanistan.[12] In fact, the World Bank judged that Afghanistan's justice system had *worsened* over the period of Italy's tenure. By 2007, for example, Afghanistan ranked in the top 99.5 percent of most ineffective justice systems worldwide. It compared poorly even with other countries in the region, such as Iran, Pakistan, Russia, Tajikistan, Turkmenistan, and Uzbekistan.[13]

There was little improvement in other areas, including the disarmament, demobilization, and reintegration of former combatants. The United States, the UN, and the Afghan government, with Japanese funding, collected a significant number of heavy weapons. But Afghanistan was still awash in weapons and ammunition, and there was an *increase* in the number of insurgent and other illegal groups. Warlords such as Abdul Rashid Dostum and Atta Muhammad retained large militia forces. Even Ismail Khan, who was brought to Kabul by President Karzai to serve as minister of water and energy, still commanded a formidable militia force in western Afghanistan. "The disarmament program was not successful," remarked NSC staffer Daoud Yaqub; it only "went after low-hanging fruit." The more powerful leaders refused to disband their militias. Since Coalition forces offered rewards for disbanding militias, commanders frequently demobilized "ghost soldiers" who never existed. This was one of many monetary inducements that proved counterproductive. An Afghan could turn in an AK-47 and get as much as $200 from the government. Some entrepreneurial Afghans realized that this was "profitable since AK-47s could be purchased in Pakistan for less than half that price."[14]

NATO's Expansion

With the lead-nation approach stumbling, it seemed NATO would be given a second chance to play a more serious part. The United States had occasionally discussed an increased NATO role in Afghanistan in the early years after the overthrow of the Taliban regime. On a trip to Gardez in 2003, Secretary of Defense Rumsfeld had told senior U.S. military officials in Afghanistan, including General Eikenberry, that he was tired of being blamed for preventing NATO from expanding its mission in Afghanistan. Now he wondered whether it was worth putting NATO to the test.[15]

In 2003, General James Jones, who had recently become NATO's Supreme Allied Commander, Europe, was at an ambassadors' lunch at the British Embassy in Brussels. He had prepared extensively to answer questions on a range of NATO issues, especially Bosnia and Kosovo. But he was surprised to hear one question repeatedly from the group: "How do we get NATO to Afghanistan?" After the meeting, he went back to his staff and began to put together an operational plan for Afghanistan. In August 2003, NATO officially took command of the International Security Assistance Force. It was based in Kabul, with its chain of command extending directly to NATO headquarters in Brunssum, Netherlands, and Mons, Belgium. In October 2003, the UN Security Council authorized the expansion of the NATO mission beyond Kabul.[16] On October 24, 2003, the German Bundestag voted to send German troops to the quiet, northern province of Kunduz. A stronghold of the Taliban in northern Afghanistan during the late 1990s, the region was remarkably diverse. Tajiks, Uzbeks, Pashtuns, and Hazaras lived in relative peace, farming wheat, rice, and millet. About 230 additional soldiers were deployed by NATO, marking the first time that ISAF soldiers operated outside of Kabul.[17]

General Jones presented a detailed operational plan to NATO defense ministers in February 2004. The plan that was eventually developed, illustrated in Figure 14.1, called for a series of phased expansions beginning in Kabul and then working counterclockwise to the north, west, south, and the east. Over the next eight months, NATO completed Stage 1 of its expansion to the north. On June 28, 2004, NATO proclaimed the creation of four new Provincial Reconstruction Teams (PRTs) in northern Afghanistan: in Mazar-e-Sharif, Meymaneh, Feyzabad, and Baghlan. Stage 1 was completed in October 2004. NATO's takeover had begun.[18]

With the Iraq insurgency worsening, senior U.S. policymakers decided to hand off more responsibility to NATO in Afghanistan, thus freeing up U.S. forces to go to Iraq. In 2005, during a series of video teleconferences with senior U.S. military officials, including Lieutenant General David Barno, Secretary Rumsfeld argued that the

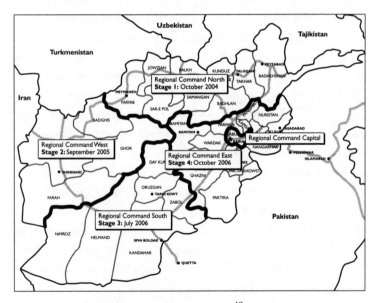

FIGURE 14.1   Stages of NATO Expansion, 2007[19]

United States needed to "reduce the amount of money it was spending in Afghanistan and the number of troops it had deployed there." With losses mounting in Iraq, Rumsfeld said these numbers were "not sustainable." At the time, the United States was spending between $600 million and $1 billion per month in Afghanistan and had roughly six battalions of infantry soldiers stationed there. NATO was a perfect organization to fill in the gaps left by redirected U.S. troops. NATO was looking for a twenty-first-century mission, and Afghanistan would suit the bill.[20] Other senior military officials supported the secretary.

One of the strongest advocates for NATO's increased involvement was John Abizaid, who had been head of U.S. Central Command since July 7, 2003. Abizaid was born in Coleville, California, to a Lebanese-American father and an American mother. He learned Arabic and earned the nickname "the mad Arab." His faculty adviser at Harvard University, where he received a master's degree in Middle Eastern Studies, praised his intellect, stating that his 100-page paper on Saudi Arabia's defense "was absolutely the best seminar paper I ever got in my 30-plus years at Harvard."[21] Abizaid had been tapped for great responsibility early in his career. In 1983, during a briefing at Fort Knox, Army Vice Chief of Staff General Max Thurman turned to his colleagues and exclaimed: "Let me tell you, there is this young captain who's going to be one of the Army's future leaders." Thurman then meticulously went through the captain's past record and said he would be a general unless he screwed up somewhere along the line. "His name is John Abizaid. Watch out for him."[22]

With support from influential Americans such as Rumsfeld and Abizaid, Stage 2 of NATO's expansion followed in September 2005, when NATO expanded to the west under the regional command of Italy.[23] It established Provincial Reconstruction Teams in Badghis, Farah, Ghor, and Herat Provinces. Abizaid remarked in late 2005: "It makes sense that as NATO forces go in . . . we could drop some of the U.S. requirements somewhat."[24] While NATO countries began to ramp up activities in Afghanistan, the United States continued to discuss downsizing. In December 2005, for example, Rumsfeld signed orders to reduce American troop levels in Afghanistan. Under the plan, the number of U.S. forces would decrease from 19,000 in December to 16,000 by the spring of 2006. The fourth brigade of the 10th Mountain Division, based at Fort Polk, Louisiana, would send a battalion task force of 1,300 soldiers instead of the entire unit of more than 4,000 troops.[25]

For some NATO countries, Afghanistan presented a chance to rejuvenate the alliance that had been torn apart by the war in Iraq. On January 22, 2003, French President Jacques Chirac and German Chancellor Gerhard Schröder had issued a joint declaration opposing the Bush administration in Iraq.[26] The date commemorated the fortieth anniversary of the Franco-German Treaty negotiated by Charles de Gaulle and Konrad Adenauer as a bulwark against American hegemony. During his 2002 reelection campaign, Schröder ran on a political platform that emphasized German opposition to the U.S. war against Iraq.[27] When the United States and Britain pushed for a second United Nations Security Council resolution in March 2003 that would effectively authorize military action, Berlin and Paris were opposed. As Chirac explained on French television, his government would oppose the resolution "*quelles que soient les circonstances*" (whatever the circumstances).[28] Both countries also refused to offer significant political and military support to the reconstruction effort after major combat ended, even as U.S. casualties began to mount.[29]

There was nearly universal consensus among member countries that this was one of the most serious schisms between Europe and the United States since the formation of NATO. "The road to Iraqi disarmament has produced the gravest crisis within the Atlantic Alliance since its creation five decades ago," concluded former Secretary of State Henry Kissinger.[30] U.S. Secretary of State Colin Powell remarked: "Who's breaking up the alliance? . . . The alliance is breaking itself up because it will not meet its responsibilities."[31] Ivo Daalder, a scholar at the Brookings Institution in Washington and former director for European affairs in the Clinton administration's National Security Council, argued that one consequence of the war in Iraq "is the effective end of Atlanticism—American and European foreign policies no longer center around the transatlantic alliance."[32] Nevertheless, there was broad consensus among NATO members that Afghanistan was a conflict worth engaging in. Some members felt they could make up for their lack of support in Baghdad by committing to Kabul.

Contrary to some arguments, most NATO governments understood that this would involve deploying some soldiers to conduct counterinsurgency operations, not just peacekeeping. Canadian Colonel S. J. Bowes, who headed a Canadian civil and military reconstruction team, went on record in 2005 saying that his country would use the same rules of engagement used by American forces. "In Canada, it's clear that this is not a peacekeeping mission," he remarked. "We understand that there is an active insurgency."[33] As 5,000 British troops were preparing to deploy to Helmand Province in 2005, British Defense Secretary John Reid stated: "The Taliban are still active in the area. So are the drug traffickers. We must be prepared to support—even defend—the provincial reconstruction team." When asked by a journalist whether British troops would be placed in danger, Reid bluntly replied: "Yes, it is going to be [dangerous] and that is why we should be so proud of our servicemen and women."[34] Several months before the official handoff of operations in Afghanistan's south from the United States to NATO, NATO Secretary-General Jaap de Hoop Scheffer argued that "people have to realize that there are spoilers, that roadside bombs and improvised explosive devices can be put along a road."[35]

In July 2006, NATO formally expanded its mission to the south, thus completing Stage 3 of its initial plan. British General David Richards assumed command of what became known as ISAF IX. The expansion involved the deployment of 12,000 NATO soldiers to six southern provinces: Helmand, Kandahar, Nimroz, Oruzgan, Zabol, and Day Kundi. The largest contingent in this force was British, which included 3,600 soldiers based in Helmand Province. Canada also deployed a fairly large contingent. By a close vote in the Canadian

Parliament in May 2006, the government designated 2,300 troops for Afghanistan, most of whom were sent to Kandahar Province. The debate in the Dutch Parliament was also contentious, but after initial opposition, the government chose to assign between 1,400 and 1,700 troops for duty in NATO's Stage 3. Most went to Oruzgan Province, in central Afghanistan. The principal town was Tarin Kowt, with a population of 10,000 on the eastern shore of the Tirinrud River.

By 2007, international forces in Afghanistan were divided into five Regional Commands (RCs): Regional Command Capital headquartered in Kabul, Regional Command North in Mazar-e-Sharif, Regional Command West in Herat, Regional Command South in Kandahar, and Regional Command East in Bagram.

NATO's Paradox

With NATO forces trying to cover most of Afghanistan, the organization soon found itself underresourced. NATO leaders had approved the operational plan for Afghanistan, but they deployed forces outside of Kabul without forcing member nations to fulfill their matériel requirements. They were short staffed, and the soldiers lacked maneuver battalions and aircraft—especially attack helicopters, dedicated fixed-wing close air support, and heavy- and medium-utility helicopters. Yet NATO pushed ahead.[36] Suddenly, NATO found itself in the position of fighting its first foreign war without the resources to win. The shortfalls became increasingly problematic as the levels of violence rose in 2006 and 2007.

In 2007, NATO was still at least 3,000 troops short of its manpower goal in Regional Command South, and its ability to sustain force levels and capabilities over the longer term was tenuous. As NATO General Richards argued in testimony before the British House of Commons, the number of troops was his most significant concern: "Simply being able to move [NATO] troops from the North to the South would not have been a solution to me at all because we have got just about the right number of troops in the North to contain the situation there, which is broadly stable. . . . What I was really after was . . . an increase in the overall number of troops."[37] There were roughly 47,000 troops in Afghanistan in mid-2007: approximately 36,000 were under NATO command and 11,000 were under U.S. command through Operation Enduring Freedom. There were also a handful of Special Operations units under U.S. command—teams from Canada, United Kingdom, Poland, United Arab Emirates, Italy, and Jordan.[38]

What made matters worse was the refusal of most NATO countries to become involved in combat operations. Indeed, the most significant split involved not whether to go into Afghanistan but what to do there. Some allies, including Germany, vehemently opposed expanding NATO's role to include riskier combat missions. Germany's defense minister, Peter Struck, had argued at NATO defense meetings in Berlin in September 2005 that merging NATO's peacekeeping mission with the American combat operation in Afghanistan would fundamentally change NATO's role and "would make the situation for our soldiers doubly dangerous and worsen the current climate in Afghanistan." Furthermore, he acknowledged that "NATO is not equipped for counterterrorism operations" and "that is not what it is supposed to do."[39]

In November 2006, at NATO's summit in Riga, Latvia, tensions over national caveats had become acute. France, Germany, Spain, and Italy remained reluctant to send their troops to southern Afghanistan. These four nations said they would send help to trouble zones outside their areas only in emergencies. But it was unclear whether and when these commanders would have to request permission from their civilian governments to do so. Countries agreeing to ease the restrictions on deployment against the Taliban insurgency included the Netherlands, Romania, and smaller nations such as Slovenia and Luxembourg.

U.S. commanders referred to the refusal to become involved in combat operations as "national caveats," which were triggered by at least two concerns. First, several NATO countries had a different philosophy about how to operate in Afghanistan and how to conduct counterinsurgency operations. They were particularly adamant that development and reconstruction efforts were the recipe for success and convinced that combat operations were likely to alienate the Afghan population, especially if they led to civilian casualties. Second, political leaders were reluctant to deploy their forces into violent areas because of low domestic support for combat operations.

A British House of Commons investigation discovered: "In Madrid, we were told by politicians and academics that while Spanish public opinion supported troops working on reconstruction projects in Afghanistan, it would not support a war-fighting role. In Berlin, we were told about the constitutional restrictions on Germany's military operating abroad."[40] In a German Marshall Fund poll in 2007, for example, 75 percent of Germans, 70 percent of Italians, and 72 percent of Spanish did not support the deployment of their troops for combat operations in Afghanistan.[41] "Our domestic political situation certainly restricts our activities," noted German General Markus Kneip in 2006, commander of NATO forces in Regional Command North.[42]

The result was that countries such as France, Germany, Italy, Spain, Greece, and Turkey held restrictive views of the NATO mission and repeatedly balked at providing troops for counterinsurgency operations in the south. Their hesitation created two tiers within NATO: those involved in ground combat (United States, Canada, United Kingdom, Netherlands) and those who were not (everyone else). To be clear, those countries involved in combat also participated in reconstruction efforts. The two were not mutually exclusive.

Defense Secretary Rumsfeld spoke for a number of Americans, frustrated by NATO's inaction, when he likened the situation to "having a basketball team, and they practice and practice and practice for six months. When it comes to game time, one or two say, 'We're not going to play.' "[43] But the Americans weren't the only ones upset; the two-tiered structure also created significant friction among other nations. Several British and Canadian military and diplomatic officials

I interviewed became increasingly frustrated. "The national caveats are a source of extraordinary tension within NATO," noted Canadian Ambassador David Sproule.[44]

Germany, which had been reluctant to commit troops in the first place, was frequently singled out as an egregious violator. The German Parliament did not allow the *Bundeswehr*—the German armed forces—to take part in combat operations against the Taliban in the south and east, except in emergencies. Indeed, German political leaders were extremely risk averse in Afghanistan. On my repeated trips to visit German troops in Kunduz and Mazar-e-Sharif, I noted several restrictions. German forces were generally prohibited from participating in offensive military operations. In addition, German forces initially were permitted to patrol in armored vehicles only during the day; some patrols were limited by the Bundeswehr regulation that military ambulances had to accompany all German patrols outside of Kunduz; and PRT commanders were usually unwilling to have their troops patrol in areas that were not secure. In response to a deteriorating security environment in the north in 2006 and 2007, the German reaction was often to establish more defensive measures, such as limiting the scope and range of patrols. This caused frustration among conventional German soldiers. It also angered some German Special Forces, who complained that they were not allowed to fight against terrorist and insurgent groups, for which they had been trained.[45]

Others questioned the German military's ability to conduct sustained counterinsurgency operations. German army units, such as mechanized infantry and airborne brigades, had extensive experience in peacekeeping. But they lacked sufficient trained personnel, combat equipment, and supporting communications and intelligence gear necessary to perform offensive attacks, raids, and reconnaissance patrols. While Germany had approximately eighty Tiger attack helicopters, none were deployed to Afghanistan during the first several years of the mission; the German government refused to authorize their use in combat. The Germans also had some Tornado multipurpose combat aircraft, but reconfiguring them for close air support would have been challenging. The German Parliament would have needed to issue a new mandate to arm the aircraft for ground-attack missions, pilots would have required more combat training, and logistics-support systems would have necessitated enhancements—none of which were possible in Germany's antiwar political climate.

Several other countries lacked adequate enabler forces—including attack and lift helicopters, smart munitions, intelligence, engineers, medical staff, logistics, and digital command and control—to fully leverage and sustain their ground-combat power.[46] But, more important, there was no unity of command. In previous nation-building missions, such as the one in Bosnia, the international community had created a team (headed by the High Representative) tasked with overseeing reconstruction and stabilization. This did not happen in Afghanistan on either the civilian or the military side. The result was several external forces operating in the same area with different missions and different rules of engagement.

Command-and-control arrangements had been challenging from the beginning. In December 2001, the commander of Task Force Dagger (essentially the 5th Special Forces Group plus supporting units) was in direct contact with General Tommy Franks, the head of U.S. Central Command. The subordinate elements of Task Force Dagger had the most current and accurate intelligence about the situation on the ground. But this changed when the 10th Mountain Division assumed operations in Afghanistan in March 2002, and again when the XVIII Airborne Corps took over control of the Afghan theater in June 2002. By late 2002, the bureaucracy had become so oppressive that a request by a Special Forces unit to conduct an operation potentially had to be processed through six levels of command before being approved. One general officer said there was simply "too much overhead" to get anything done.[47] These challenges persisted over the next several years, especially as NATO began to take a more active role in 2006 and 2007.

In testimony before the House Armed Services Committee in

December 2007, Secretary of Defense Robert Gates sharply criticized NATO countries for not supplying urgently needed soldiers and other aid as violence escalated. He stated: "NATO still has shortfalls in meeting minimum requirements in troops, equipment, and other resources," and the "Afghanistan mission has exposed constraints associated with interoperability, organization, critical equipment shortfalls, and national caveats."[48] For Gates and other senior U.S. policymakers, it was unconscionable that some NATO countries refused to deploy troops to southern Afghanistan as violence skyrocketed. In a broadside to America's partners a month later, Gates later criticized most of the allies for failing to understand and prepare for counterinsurgency warfare. "Most of the European forces, NATO forces, are not trained in counterinsurgency; they were trained for the Fulda Gap," he observed, referring to the region on the former East German–West German border where a Soviet ground invasion of Western Europe hypothetically might have occurred.[49]

Clearing, but Not Holding

The national caveats and light-footprint approach had a debilitating impact on NATO's counterinsurgency operations and put undue strain on a select group of countries that chose to pursue combat *and* development. In previous counterinsurgencies, success had been achieved by defeating insurgent forces and their political organization in a given area, holding it, and implementing reconstruction projects.[50] This has been called a "clear, hold, and build" strategy. Military forces set up secure zones and then slowly expand them outward like ink spots on blotting paper. Since only small numbers of U.S., Coalition, and Afghan forces were available, this strategy could be applied only in a few sectors of the country. Forces were assigned to contested areas to regain government presence and control, after which they conducted military and civil-military programs to expand the control and edge out insurgents. Counterinsurgency forces were supported with civil-affairs and psychological operations personnel.[51]

International forces in Afghanistan cast a wide net of operations outside their force-protection zone to disrupt and interdict insurgent operations. Units were required to live among the local population for significant amounts of time to gain their trust and support. Then they would proceed with patient intelligence work to ascertain the location of insurgents' weapons caches, safe houses, and transit support systems. Once the hostile zones had been cleared, the force was to move to outer zones, where the population was neither friendly nor hostile to the counterinsurgency unit's efforts. Occasional operations were conducted in these areas to keep the population "neutral" to the idea of supporting the insurgents. Battalion-size sweeps and clearing operations involving several hundred soldiers generally reaped far less than the effort required because of the difficulty of finding and fighting elusive insurgents.[52] U.S., British, Dutch, and Canadian forces were sometimes successful at clearing territory through armed reconnaissance and specialized raiding. Individual units patrolled suspected insurgent areas. AC-130 Spectre gunships, Predator unmanned aerial vehicles, and other remote-reconnaissance tools helped support the patrols to keep insurgents off balance and disrupt their timing.[53]

The "clear, hold, and build" strategy seemed straightforward, but low levels of troops made it virtually impossible to hold territory in Afghanistan's violent south. As one Western ambassador remarked to me: "We can clear territory, but we can't hold it. There aren't sufficient numbers of NATO or Afghan forces."[54] During Operation Medusa in 2006, for example, Canadian and other NATO forces had cleared Panjwai district from Taliban forces, but the Canadians and Afghans couldn't hold the district. The Canadian military established a forward operating base in Panjwai and worked with local Afghan National Police, Afghan National Auxiliary Police, and some Afghan National Army soldiers to prevent a Taliban return. But their numbers were insufficient, and the Afghan police were unwilling to confront Taliban forces as they gradually reinfiltrated. By the summer of 2007, the Taliban were back in Panjwai at levels comparable to when Operation Medusa began.[55]

Reinfiltration was a persistent problem, especially across the south, where one NATO general told me that in mid-2007, "NATO and Afghan forces control at most 20 percent of the southern provinces of Nimroz, Helmand, Kandahar, Oruzgan, Day Kundi, and Zabol. The rest are controlled by Taliban, groups allied to the Taliban, or local commanders."[56]

Writing on the Walls

By 2007, there were growing signs of NATO's distress. Too few NATO forces and crippling national caveats impacted the organization's ability to stem the rising violence, especially in southern Afghanistan. In December, Paddy Ashdown, a former member of the British Parliament and High Representative for Bosnia and Herzegovina, who was being considered to head civilian reconstruction efforts in Afghanistan, wrote to Prime Minister Gordon Brown and Foreign Secretary David Miliband, warning: "We do not have enough troops, aid or international will to make Afghanistan much different from what it has been for the last 1,000 years. . . . And even if we had all of these in sufficient quantities, we would not have them for sufficient time . . . to make the aim of fundamentally altering the nature of Afghanistan, achievable."[57]

If Afghanistan was supposed to be NATO's first opportunity to show its new *raison d'être*, the result was underwhelming. "One of the lessons of NATO's involvement in Afghanistan," General Eikenberry told me, "is the need to fulfill minimal requirements *before* deploying forces. If minimal requirements are not filled, then perhaps NATO shouldn't go in."[58] There were other lessons as well. One of the most salient was the lesson of securing neighboring countries. The history of recent insurgencies demonstrates that the ability of insurgents to gain sanctuary and support in adjacent states significantly increases their probability of success over the long run. This brings us to Pakistan.

CHAPTER FIFTEEN

The Water Must Boil

SEPTEMBER 22, 2005, was a crisp night in Shkin, Afghanistan, a small Pashtun village four miles from the Pakistan border in the eastern province of Paktika. With the exception of a few apple orchards, there is little agricultural activity because the soil is too poor. Several dirt roads snake through the area, but virtually none are paved. The landscape is strangely reminiscent of Frederic Remington or C. M. Russell's paintings of the American West. Gritty layers of dust sap the life from a parched landscape. Shkin lies just south of the setting for Rudyard Kipling's "Ballad of the King's Jest," which notes:

> *When spring-time flushes the desert grass,*
> *Our kafilas wind through the Khyber Pass.*
> *Lean are the camels but fat the frails,*
> *Light are the purses but heavy the bales,*
> *As the snowbound trade of the North comes down*
> *To the market-square of Peshawur town.*[1]

There was an Afghan National Army observation post in Shkin. Four miles away was a U.S. firebase, which that night housed fewer than a dozen Americans, including two U.S. Marines and a handful of CIA personnel. It looked like a Wild West cavalry fort, ringed with coils of razor wire. A U.S. flag rippled above the three-foot-thick mud walls. In the watchtower, a guard scanned the expanse of ridges, rising to 8,000 feet, that marked the border between Afghanistan and Pakistan. At 1 a.m., approximately forty insurgents came over the mountain passes from Pakistan and assaulted the Afghan observation post. Pakistani military observation posts to the east and southeast, at distances of a quarter- and a half-mile, provided supporting fire of heavy machine guns and rocket-propelled grenades. RPGs from the Pakistani posts struck the Afghan post and hit an ammunition storage area, igniting an uncontrollable fire. The compound was quickly surrounded. An Afghan Army Quick Reaction Force had already been dispatched to move into an assault position a thousand feet from the compound and retake it with support from artillery fire located at Firebase Shkin.

CIA personnel at the firebase worked furiously to contact Pakistani military authorities, who successfully reduced the artillery barrage coming from the Pakistani military posts. The small CIA and U.S. Marine contingent then began to direct artillery fire at the insurgent forces, shooting thirty-eight 105-millimeter rounds and scoring several direct hits. The insurgents made a hasty retreat. Using their Joint Land Attack Cruise Missile Defense Elevated Netted Sensor (JLENS), an aerostat with radars to provide over-the-horizon surveillance for defense against air threats, U.S. forces tracked the insurgents retreating across the Pakistan border. Although the insurgent assault was eventually repelled, it succeeded in killing two Afghan National Army soldiers, seriously wounding three others, and destroying an ammunition dump that housed machine guns, AK-47s, recoilless rifles, radios, and ammunition rounds.

Earlier that day, a 5th Special Forces Group operational detachment had departed from the Afghan observation post after conducting training with indigenous forces. The timing of the nighttime attack thus was suspicious, suggesting that the Pakistani military, the insurgents, or both had monitored their departure. The U.S. military after-action report noted that the Pakistani military's direct engagement was an integral part of the insurgent attack. "The Pakistani military actively supported the enemy assault on the [observation post] despite past assurances of cooperation with Afghan and Coalition forces. . . . major damage to the [observation post] and friendly casualties would likely have been avoided had the enemy maneuver element been acting alone." Moreover, it concluded that "[t]he past reluctance of U.S. forces to fire on Pakistani checkpoints when American personnel are not directly engaged likely emboldened the Pakistani military to blatantly support the enemy assault."[2]

This incident was not isolated but rather part of a much broader pattern of attacks along Afghanistan's eastern border with Pakistan. Many of these attacks were supported directly or indirectly by Pakistan agencies—especially the ISI and the Frontier Corps. "The border is our albatross," one 82nd Airborne officer lamented.[3] Pakistan's leaders had long been motivated to become involved in Afghanistan's affairs—including through military engagement—to promote its national-security interests. As Pakistani dictator General Zia-ul-Haq remarked in 1979 to the head of the ISI, Lieutenant-General Akhtar Abdul Rehman Khan, "the water in Afghanistan must boil at the right temperature."[4]

One of the major reasons why the insurgency began and strengthened in Afghanistan was that insurgent groups were able to acquire outside support. After the Taliban overthrow, surviving senior leaders from the Taliban and other groups relocated to Pakistan. Over the next several years, they received increasingly large amounts of support from a variety of state actors. While Afghan government officials had a tendency to blame all of Afghanistan's ills on Pakistan, the ability of insurgent groups to operate from Pakistani soil was integral to their success.

The advantages of outside support for an insurgency are intuitive. It can significantly bolster the capabilities of insurgent groups by giving them more money, weapons, logistics, and other aid. States are usually the largest external donors during insurgencies, since they have the most significant resources. Their motivations tend to be selfish and based on efforts to increase their own security. Policymakers and their populations want to be secure from external threats, and they seek to influence others to ensure that security. This was certainly true with some members of the Pakistani government, which viewed the Taliban as an important proxy group that could push into Afghanistan and undermine the Karzai government's power and authority.

In 2006, PBS *Frontline* producer Martin Smith traveled to the Afghanistan-Pakistan border region to analyze the consequences for U.S. policy. "After the fall of the Taliban," his documentary concluded, "some experts warned of a nightmare scenario in which the Taliban and al Qa'ida would escape from Afghanistan into neighboring Pakistan and set up new command centers far out of America's reach. That nightmare scenario has now come true."[5]

Operation Al Mizan

Beginning in 2002, the U.S. strategy in Pakistan's border areas had two major components. First, a major goal was to capture key al Qa'ida leaders. By 2005 and 2006, U.S. officials also began to pressure Pakistan to deal more harshly with Taliban and other insurgent leaders in Pakistan's border regions. But al Qa'ida was the main focus. Second, no matter the outcome, the United States expected the Pakistani government to conduct the bulk of the operations. The United States provided assistance and occasionally targeted strikes, but it relied on Pakistan to take action.

Consequently, the U.S. government provided more than $1 billion per year to Pakistan's key national-security agencies to conduct counterterrorist and counterinsurgency operations: the Pakistani Army, the Frontier Corps, the Frontier Constabulary, and the ISI. The Frontier Corps—the largest of the civil forces, with just under 100,000 personnel—is charged with securing Pakistan's 3,800-mile western border. The Frontier Constabulary is a federal force assigned specifically to the boundary between the Federally Administered Tribal Areas (FATA) and the rest of Pakistan. Some Frontier Constabulary units, however, were deployed for internal-security purposes to other areas of Pakistan such as Quetta, Karachi, and Islamabad. The U.S. government channeled money and aid through the Department of Defense, including Coalition support funds, other military aid (including the provision of helicopters and air-assault training), and counternarcotics assistance. The United States also sent funds through the Department of State, the CIA, and other government agencies.[6]

The Coalition support funds were a particular point of contention. David Rohde and David Sanger reported in the *New York Times* that the United States was making the annual $1 billion payments for what it called "reimbursements" to the country's military for conducting counterterrorism efforts along the border with Afghanistan. But they also discovered that despite the additional funding, Pakistan's president had decided to slash patrols through the area where al Qa'ida and Taliban fighters were most active. Over five years, Pakistan received more than $5.6 billion, more than half of the total aid the United States sent to the country since the September 11, 2001, attacks, not counting covert funds. Rohde and Sanger also reported that some American military officials in the region had recommended that the money be tied to Pakistan's performance in pursuing al Qa'ida and keeping the Taliban from gaining a haven from which to attack Afghanistan, but this advice was not followed.[7]

Beginning in 2002, Pakistan conducted counterinsurgency campaigns under what became known as Operation Al Mizan. At that time, a number of senior U.S. officials viewed Pakistan as a reliable ally. "The Pakistanis were part of the solution, not the problem," said Pentagon comptroller Dov Zakheim. "Musharraf was very helpful. He was definitely opposed to radicalization in Pakistan."[8]

Pakistan's army had limited experience in counterinsurgency operations. Prior to 2002, it had last done that sort of work in Eastern Pakistan (now Bangladesh) in 1971 and 1972, and in Baluchistan between 1973 and 1977. Both campaigns had relied heavily on firepower and had inflicted significant collateral damage. But the major focus of Pakistani Army training had been geared toward a conventional war with India. During Operation Al Mizan, Pakistan deployed between 70,000 and

80,000 forces to the tribal areas. Despite their limited experience, however, the Pakistan military and intelligence services helped capture or kill such important al Qa'ida leaders as Khalid Sheikh Muhammad, Abu Faraj al-Libbi, Abu Zubeida, and Abu Talha al-Pakistani.[9] The government also deployed the Pakistani Army and the Frontier Corps against foreign fighters in the Kurram and Khyber Agencies in December 2001. It continued deployments between 2002 and 2005, mainly in Baluchistan, just south of the FATA, and in North and South Waziristan.[10] Hundreds and perhaps thousands of Pakistani soldiers died during these incursions. In early 2004, for example, Pakistan's intelligence services had been gathering reports of al Qa'ida activities in the Wana Valley of South Waziristan. In March, the Pakistani Frontier Corps launched an operation to disrupt them, but when the troops reached Wana, they were ambushed. It was a typical al Qa'ida operation. Just as they had done to U.S. forces in 2002 during Operation Anaconda, the insurgents occupied the surrounding hills and mountains, leaving the Frontier Corps troops exposed in the low-lying area.[11]

A barrage of firepower from entrenched positions in the mountains delivered heavy casualties to the Pakistan troops. The Pakistan Army was called in to retrieve the trapped Frontier Corps soldiers. Nearly 6,000 troops immediately moved in, including 600 lifted by helicopters. They set up a cordon around the ambush site and sent out a search operation. After sustained fighting, the army launched an attack on the ridge and cleared it, killing sixty-three militants, including thirty-six foreigners. They also disrupted a major al Qa'ida command-and-control center and a network of tunnels containing sophisticated electronic equipment.

In June 2004, Pakistani forces conducted an attack in the Shakai Valley after a series of alarming intelligence reports claimed that a force of more than 200 Chechens and Uzbeks, some Arabs, and several hundred local supporters were gathering in the area. On June 10, the government deployed 10,000 Pakistan Army troops along with Pakistani Special Operations Task Force and Frontier Corps troops. Nearly 3,000 soldiers established an outer cordon before the Pakistan Air

Force struck at dawn, using precision weapons against nine compounds. Pakistan Army forces used indirect artillery fire and precision
rocket attacks by helicopter gunships. Other helicopters dropped off
Pakistani Special Operations Task Force troops to search the compounds, and infantry troops initiated a simultaneous operation to clear
the valley and link up with the Special Operations Task Force. Later,
another 3,000 troops were brought into the area to clear more of the
valley. During the operation, four soldiers were killed and twelve
injured, while more than fifty militants were killed.

The Pakistani military, with help from U.S. Special Operations
Forces and CIA assets, had just eliminated a major propaganda base
and militant stronghold, which also included a facility for manufacturing improvised explosive devices. The haul from a large underground cellar in one of the compounds included two truckloads of
TV sets, computers, laptops, disks, tape recorders, and tapes.[12] But
it was only a tactical, short-term success, since militant groups afterward developed an increasingly robust sanctuary in Waziristan.

Besides this type of organized assault, Pakistani security services also
provided clandestine assistance. In March and April 2007, the army
covertly supported Taliban commander Mullah Nazir against Uzbek
militants. Nazir was a charismatic man in his midthirties who spouted
a religious fervor far beyond his minimal credentials. Several months
earlier, he had been endorsed by Mullah Omar as the Taliban "emir" of
South Waziristan. The Uzbeks had been extended *memastia* (Pashtun
hospitality) by Nazir's tribal rivals, the Ahmadzai, but they had become
unpopular among locals for their criminality and viciousness.

One Pakistan government official said there was "a groundswell of
support for action against Uzbeks and any attempt by the government
to intervene in support of the tribal action would actually discredit
it."[13] The Pakistan Army largely stayed out of the fighting, using Nazir's
forces as a proxy. But it eventually sent military and paramilitary forces
into the area to seize strategic hilltops and ridges and to help establish
law and order once the fighting stopped. In the end, Nazir's forces
were largely successful in pushing the Uzbeks out of Wazir areas.

Operation Al Mizan included several major operations, and Pakistani forces successfully killed or captured several local and foreign militants. But it ultimately failed to clear the area of militant groups, including al Qa'ida. There were several reasons for this failure.

First, Pakistan's unresolved tensions with India meant that Pakistan's national-security establishment, including the ISI, had a vested interest in supporting some militant groups directed at the Afghanistan and Kashmir fronts. Second, Pakistan's operations were not sustained over time. Their efforts were marked by sweeps, searches, and occasionally bloody battles, but none of these operations employed a sufficient number of forces to clear and hold territory. Third, the government's initiatives were hindered by religious conservative parties operating in the Federally Administered Tribal Areas. These groups considered Pakistan government efforts against al Qa'ida and other militants an "American war." Fourth, there was considerable local support for militant groups. Public-opinion polls indicated that even after the September 11, 2001, attacks, significant portions of the Pakistani population supported their government's links to the Taliban and "favored by a wide margin increasing support for Mullah Omar's regime."[14] In sum, Pakistan could not muster the political will to maintain the necessary operational tempo of counterinsurgency operations in the face of opposition within the country.

The United States Debates Pakistan

The debate in the U.S. government about Pakistan was a lively one. Deputy Secretary of State Richard Armitage said, "We had some information that there was assistance from the Pakistan government to the Taliban between 2002 and 2004. The question was how high up it went. Was it official Pakistan government policy?"[15]

Robert Grenier, the CIA station chief in Islamabad, was similarly blunt: "I never believed that government ties with these groups had been irrevocably cut."[16] A CIA operative deployed to Afghanistan further acknowledged that as early as 2001 and 2002, "ISID advisors were supporting the Taliban with expertise and material and, no doubt, sending a steady stream of intelligence back to Islamabad."[17] This caused some officials, both inside and outside of the government, to push for swift action. In an October 2003 memo to Defense Secretary Rumsfeld, retired general James B. Vaught urged the secretary to "stop playing two faced games with Saudi Arabia, Pakistan and Syria. All three are supporting both sides to some degree." He advised Rumsfeld: "Give them a choice, join and support the war against terrorism, no holding back, or we will neutralize them."[18]

But U.S. government assessments were not uniform. When Lieutenant General Karl Eikenberry took over as head of the Combined Forces Command—Afghanistan in 2005, he said the evidence of Pakistan's complicity was not clear: "I was not initially convinced that Pakistan presented a grave problem. But that changed."[19]

The confusion stemmed, in part, from the bifurcated nature of dealing with the insurgent threat in Afghanistan and Pakistan. Insurgents used both sides of the border, but the U.S. government had no joint Afghan-Pakistan strategy. In fact, there frequently were tensions between U.S. officials in Kabul and Islamabad. The CIA was virtually at war with itself. Agency personnel based in Islamabad argued that the Pakistani government, including the ISI, was still helpful in supporting U.S. efforts against al Qa'ida. They pointed to the capture of such targets as Khalid Sheikh Muhammad, Abu Faraj al-Libbi, and Abu Zubeida. But CIA officials in Kabul were frustrated with what they viewed as slow efforts to target al Qa'ida, Taliban, and other insurgents in Pakistan.[20] There was some concern among U.S. military officials, especially those based in Afghanistan, that the Pakistani Army had blundered in a number of operations in the Federally Administered Tribal Areas and thus were extremely risk-averse.

There were also different command-and-control arrangements for U.S. "white" and "black" Special Operations Forces, most of which were based in Afghanistan. Black forces focused on high-value targets; their operations were covert. In contrast, white forces initially took on a variety of missions to build the capacity of Afghan security forces (what is often called "foreign internal defense") and to conduct strikes against insurgents, though they increasingly focused on the latter over the course of the insurgency. Their efforts were thwarted by an increasingly questionable ally across the border in Pakistan.

A Stab in the Back

The Pakistani government often insisted that it was not providing assistance to the Taliban. Some U.S. analysts agreed. After a trip to Pakistan and Afghanistan to meet with top U.S., NATO, Afghan, and Pakistani officials, retired general Barry McCaffrey concluded: "The Pakistanis are not actively supporting the Taliban—nor do they have a strategic purpose to destabilize Afghanistan."[21] But the evidence to the contrary was overwhelming. Some Pakistani forces—including individuals within the ISI and the Frontier Corps—abetted insurgents who would go on to fight U.S. and NATO forces in Afghanistan. There was considerable disagreement about whether ISI support was directed by senior Pakistani government officials, at least until mid-2008, when the United States collected fairly solid evidence of senior-level complicity.[22] But many U.S. officials, especially at the CIA, found it highly unlikely that ISI units would be able to carry out missions in support of groups like the Taliban without approval from senior ISI and military leaders.

ISI assistance, especially from Directorate S, which was charged with external operations, appeared to take several forms. One was a willingness to provide sanctuary to Pashtun militant groups and their senior leadership. Some ISI officials sent money and logistical supplies to insurgents, as they had previously done. As Husain Haqqani, who became Pakistan's ambassador to the United States, acknowledged during the 1990s, "Pakistani support for the Taliban was crucial."[23] In addition, ISI agents based in Peshawar, Quetta, and other areas kept in regular contact with militant leaders, including Mullah Omar, Jalaluddin Haqqani, and Siraj Haqqani.

At the end of his tenure as U.S. ambassador in Afghanistan, Zalmay

Khalilzad quipped: "[Mullah Akhtar] Usmani, who is one of the Taliban leaders, spoke to Pakistan's Geo TV at a time when the Pakistani intelligence services claimed that they did not know where they were. If a TV company could find him, how is it that the intelligence service of a country which has nuclear bombs and a lot of security and military forces cannot find them?"[24]

Khalilzad was among those most frustrated with U.S. policy toward Pakistan. As the ambassador to Afghanistan, and later as U.S. ambassador to the United Nations, he complained in person and in video teleconferences about the growing sanctuary in Pakistan. "We had the data and the intelligence estimates," said one adviser to Khalilzad in Kabul, "but senior officials in the U.S. government were unwilling to put pressure on Pakistan and President Musharraf, especially to go after the Taliban."[25]

Indeed, some individuals in the ISI were helpful in providing strategic and operational advice to three main Afghan groups active on different fronts along the Afghanistan-Pakistan border: Mullah Omar's Taliban, based in Quetta; the Haqqani network, based in North Waziristan; and Gulbuddin Hekmatyar's Hezb-i-Islami, based in the northern parts of Pakistan's tribal agencies and in the North West Frontier Province.

ISI officials helped train some Taliban and other insurgents destined for Afghanistan and Kashmir in Quetta, Mansehra, Shamshattu, Parachinar, and other areas in Pakistan. In order to minimize detection, the ISI also supplied indirect assistance—including financial assistance—to Taliban training camps. Some ISI officials also used former operatives to collaborate with Afghan insurgents to ensure deniability. One NATO document concluded that "external/local elements trained in Pakistan (Taliban/Hezb-i-Islami Haqqani/ISI) enter through the Paktika border."[26]

United States and NATO officials uncovered several instances in which the ISI provided intelligence to Taliban and other insurgents (such as the Haqqani network) at the tactical, operational, and strategic levels. They tipped off Taliban forces about the location and movement of Afghan and Coalition forces, which undermined several anti-Taliban military operations. ISI operatives were highly aggressive in collecting intelligence on the movement and activity of Afghan, U.S., and other NATO forces in eastern and southern Afghanistan. ISI members then shared some of this information with the Taliban and other insurgent groups.[27] Most shockingly, some Pakistani intelligence officials were also involved in suicide attacks, including the Indian Embassy bombing in Kabul in July 2008.

The majority of the ISI's assistance appeared to come directly from individuals in the middle and lower levels of the organization, but there were some reports that senior officials of the ISI and the Pakistani government were aware of the ISI's role and were actively encouraging it. It was even reported that General Ashfaq Kayani, the chief of army staff, had referred to Jalaluddin Haqqani as a "strategic asset."[28] Pakistani military officials (especially from the Frontier Corps) regularly failed to cooperate on stemming cross-border activity, and, in some cases, they actively helped insurgents cross the border. David Kilcullen, who served as a counterinsurgency adviser to Condoleezza Rice and General David Petraeus, remarked that some militants moved into Afghanistan "with direct assistance from Pakistani Frontier Corps troops."[29] Officials such as General Hamid Gul (former head of the ISI) and Sultan Amir (former ISI member also known as Colonel Imam) gave speeches at Pakistani government and military institutions calling for jihad against the United States and the Afghan government.[30] Pakistan's Frontier Corps also supported insurgent offensive operations. Interviews with U.S. soldiers indicated that there were dozens of incidents in 2006, for example, where Pakistani military posts—especially Frontier Corps posts—provided supporting fire for insurgent offensive operations.[31] One joint paper by the United Nations and the European Union offered a grim assessment:

> Given the wide-ranging nature of ISI involvement, [the ISI] would need to endorse any talks with the Taliban. Anyone negotiating without their sanction would have to do so covertly, or face heavy consequences. It was not clear President Musharraf could be persuaded to

control the ISI in this regard, which was not even obviously in his interest. His direction to the formal side was explicit, but forward and informal elements, retired generals with extremist views (e.g. Hamid Gul, Aziz Khan, Ehsan), retired Taliban liaison staff (e.g. Imam, Afridi) and many in a variety of services below the rank of major were more difficult to make accountable.[32]

The U.S. government found that Pakistan largely refrained from conducting operations against the Taliban leadership structure.[33] As one Pakistani journalist pointed out, the Pakistan government "plunges into action when they know they can lay their hands on a foreign militant but they are still reluctant to proceed against the Taliban."[34] The reluctance was even true of some key Taliban leaders who were arrested by Pakistani security forces. For example, Mullah Ubaidullah Akhund, who was captured by Pakistani forces in February 2007, continued to communicate with Taliban leaders even after his capture.[35]

The Pakistani government negotiated several agreements with tribal leaders, including those allied with—or even members of—the Taliban. In April 2004, the government established an agreement, known as the Shakai Agreement, with the Taliban and local tribal leaders, including Nek Muhammad. Nek Muhammad was an upstart jihadi born in 1975. He had a youthful handsomeness, a thick black beard, and long, wavy hair, but it was his extraordinary confidence and tribal mien that catapulted him to power in South Waziristan. "Nek never had an intellectual mind but some other traits of his personality became evident during his stay at the Darul Uloom" seminary, recalled one of his teachers. "He showed himself to be a hard-headed boy, endowed with an impenetrable soul and an obstinate determination to carry out his will no matter how mindless it might be."[36] He was mercurial and cavalier but also extremely charismatic, and the Pakistan government made a deal with him.

The Shakai Agreement included several provisions: Pakistan Army troops would not interfere in internal tribal affairs and agreed to stay in their cantonment areas; local insurgents would not attack Pakistan government personnel or infrastructure; and all foreigners would have to register with the government.[37] But Nek Muhammad quickly violated the agreement and refused to hand over any foreigners, while also publicly humiliating the Pakistan government, boasting to reporters, "I did not go to them, they came to my place. That should make it clear who surrendered to whom."[38] He ultimately paid a hefty price. In June 2004, he was killed by a CIA Predator strike near Wana.[39] His successor, Maulvi Abbas, agreed not to attack Pakistani government positions if the government allowed him to run the affairs of his tribe without interference.

In September 2006, the governor of the North West Frontier Province, Lieutenant General (ret.) Ali Muhammad Jan Orakzai, reached an agreement in Miramshah with a tribal grand *jirga* whose members were drawn from the Federally Administered Tribal Areas. As part of the agreement, the Taliban promised that it would not use the area to conduct attacks against the Afghan or Pakistani governments; it would stop targeted killings of pro-government *maliks* (tribal elders); and it would not impose its lifestyle on others by force. It also permitted the Taliban to retain their administrative and political position, allowed them to retain their weapons, and permitted foreigners to remain without any registration on promise of good conduct. In return, the Pakistan Army agreed to withdraw from most areas.[40]

But the agreement had the exact opposite impact: It strengthened the power of the mullahs at the expense of the *maliks*. A Pakistan Ministry of Interior document informed President Pervez Musharraf that "Talibanisation has not only unfolded potential threats to our security, but is also casting its dark shadows over FATA and now in the settled areas adjoining the tribal belt. The reality is that it is spreading." The document summarized the situation by affirming that there was "a general policy of appeasement towards the Taliban, which has further emboldened them."[41] A U.S. government assessment came to a similar conclusion, arguing that cross-border infiltration increased by 300 to 400 percent in some districts after the 2006 agreement in Miramshah. It found that the "Federally Administered Tribal Areas (FATA) constitute an active sanctuary, along with Quetta and other parts of Baluchistan."[42] Local Taliban groups gradually became a parallel government in the tribal areas and a sanctuary for insurgent groups operating in Afghanistan. The traditional *jirga* was formally banned by the Taliban. In its place, aggrieved parties had to seek the intervention of their village Taliban representative, who performed the functions of police officer, administrator, and judge. The Taliban banned music stores, videos, and televisions and issued edicts that men had to grow beards. In 2005, the Taliban and other militants carried out a sustained campaign and killed more than 100 pro-government tribal elders. Other *maliks* fled from the tribal areas.[43]

In 2006, President Musharraf acknowledged that the Pakistani tribal agreements "didn't prove effective" and contributed to "the spread of Talibanization" in Pakistan's tribal areas.[44] This had been the Taliban's intention all along, and they did not hesitate to reinforce it in public statements.[45]

Strategic Rationale

A group of U.S. officials, including General David Barno, thought that one reason Pakistan increased support to the Taliban was that the United States was discussing downsizing forces in Afghanistan. The trigger point was in 2005, when discussions had become intense about a U.S. drawdown and a handover to NATO. Pakistani and Afghan government officials interpreted this as a signal that the U.S. commitment to Afghanistan was waning. It encouraged Afghan government officials increasingly to look toward India as its long-term strategic partner, which in turn encouraged Pakistani government officials to support the Taliban.[46]

In February 2007, General Barno testified before the House Committee on Foreign Affairs. "It is my personal opinion," he said, "that since mid-2005, Pakistan has also calculated its position vis-à-vis Afghanistan in light of concerns for a diminished and less aggressive U.S. presence in the nation that lies in Pakistan's backyard."[47] Barno continued:

In mid-summer 2005, shortly after my departure from Afghanistan, the U.S. announced that NATO was assuming control from the U.S.-led coalition for the entire Afghan mission—and shortly thereafter, we also announced we were withdrawing over 1,000 U.S. troops from the combat zone. This, in my personal estimation, sent a most unfortunate and misinterpreted signal to friend and foe alike—that the U.S. was leaving and turning the mission over to some largely unknown (in that part of the world) organization of 26 countries directed from Europe. Tragically, I believe that this misunderstood message caused both friends and enemies to re-calculate their options—with a view toward the U.S. no longer being a lead actor in Afghanistan. The truth, of course, is much different but many of the shifts in enemy activity and even the behavior of Afghanistan's neighbors, I believe, can be traced to this period.[48]

The Indian Angle

The Indian threat was much more important for the Pakistani government than its commitments to the United States. An Indian intelligence official told me: "After the fall of the Taliban, India took advantage of a window of opportunity to develop close ties with Hamid Karzai's government in Afghanistan and counter Pakistan in the region."[49] Of course, Pakistan and India have long been involved in a balance-of-power struggle in South Asia; both laid claim to the Kashmir region and they have fought three major wars over Kashmir since 1947.

After September 11, 2001, India provided hundreds of millions of dollars in financial assistance to Afghanistan and sent money to Afghan political candidates during the 2004 presidential elections and 2005 parliamentary elections. India also helped fund construction of the new Afghan Parliament building, as well as provide financial assistance to elected legislators.[50] India built roads near the Pakistan border—projects that were run by India's state-owned Border Roads Organisation, whose publicly acknowledged mission was to "support the [Indian] armed forces [to] meet their strategic needs."[51] When India established consulates in the Afghan cities of Jalalabad, Kandahar, and Herat, Pakistan accused India of using these consulates as bases for "terrorist activities" inside Pakistan, especially in the province of Baluchistan. One Pakistani Army official argued that these Indian consulates soon became a "hub of intelligence activities. Indian covert activities—under the guise of intelligence gathering and sharing information with the Coalition Forces—have been rampant along the Durand Line in Pashtun dominant areas."[52]

India pushed other projects that were clearly provocative. In the eastern Afghanistan province of Kunar, India built several schools within spitting distance of Pakistan. The Indian government signed a subnational local governance initiative with the minister of reconstruction and rural development in Kabul. Kunar Governor Sayed Fazlullah Wahidi—a man with a plump build, a bushy white beard, and a striking resemblance to Santa Claus—joked that he should start a bidding war between Pakistan and India to build infrastructure in the province.[53]

The Indian-Afghan axis left Pakistan isolated and exposed in South Asia. In 2001, Pakistan had a close relationship with the Taliban government in Afghanistan, which it had nurtured since the Soviet War. But after the September 11 attacks, India's growing relationship with the Afghan government shifted the balance of power in Afghanistan. Some Pakistan government officials discerned that India had several objectives in Afghanistan: destabilize Pakistan as a quid pro quo for Pakistan's actions in Kashmir by supporting Baluch and other insurgents; create a two-front threat scenario for Pakistan; deny Pakistan direct economic, trade, and energy linkages to Central Asia; and prevent the rise of a radical Sunni regime in Kabul that would permit sanctuary for jihadi groups who threatened India.[54] Feroz Hassan Khan, brigadier general in the Pakistani Army, noted: "Pakistan perceives India seeking a 'strategic envelopment,' a policy of manipulating events in Afghanistan and Iran to elicit anti-Pakistan responses so as to cause political and security problems for Pakistan. The foremost objective of Pakistan has been to establish a friendly government in Kabul that at the minimum does not pose a second front in the event of a war with India."[55]

Consequently, assistance to insurgents in Afghanistan was a way for some Pakistani officials to counter the growing Indian influence in Afghanistan. At the very least, it maximized Pakistan's strategic depth. As President Musharraf had explained in 2001 to U.S. Ambassador Wendy Chamberlin, Pakistan needed "strategic depth" in Afghanistan to protect its western flank.[56] But Pakistan also knew that the United States and NATO eventually would withdraw from Afghanistan, just as the United States had done after the Soviet withdrawal in 1989. During the 1990s, Pakistani support to the Taliban was extensive. In the absence of Soviet resistance and U.S. support, Pakistan provided arms, training, intelligence, vehicles, ammunition, fuel, and spare parts. In the back of every Pakistani official's mind was the possibility that they once again would have to pick up the pieces in the region after the inevitable U.S. withdrawal.

Other State Supporters

In addition to Pakistan, U.S. and other NATO troops had to contend with interference from Iran. Iranian interest in Afghanistan, especially in the west, dated back thousands of years. Part of the ancient Persian Achaemenid Empire became Afghanistan, and the Persian Samanid dynasty reincorporated Afghanistan as a Persian-ruled domain in the ninth century. In the fifteenth century, Jahan Shah briefly established Herat as the capital of his Iranian domains. In the early sixteenth century, the Safavid Shah Tahmasp drove the Uzbeks from Herat for a short time, but by the turn of that century, Shah Abbas had reasserted Iranian dominance over the city and all of western Afghanistan. In the early nineteenth century, the Qajar dynasty ruler Muhammad Shah tried to reassert Iran's claim to Herat by marching on the city in 1837, but the international landscape had changed.

British policymakers, who believed India was vulnerable to an overland invasion from Russia, worried that the Iranian shah might welcome Russian transit, so they resolved to keep Afghanistan under informal British influence. Pressured by the British, Muhammad Shah withdrew his army, and Iranian troops seized Herat in October 1856. A few weeks later, British authorities in Bombay dispatched forty-five ships carrying almost 6,000 troops, seized the Iranian port of Bushehr, and pushed inland. The shah sued for peace and, in the 1857 Treaty of Paris, he relinquished all claim to Afghanistan. In return, the British forces withdrew.[57] But western Afghanistan has always remained an area of strategic interest to Iranian leaders.

After the overthrow of the Taliban regime in 2001, the Iranians employed what was known as a "hedging strategy" in Afghanistan. The logic was that if Iran could demonstrate an ability to undermine U.S. efforts on a variety of fronts, such as in Iraq and Afghanistan, the United States might be deterred from conducting an attack against Iranian nuclear facilities. On top of an array of patron-client relationships with powerful Shi'ite groups in Lebanon and Iraq, Tehran developed partnerships with some Sunni jihadists across the region, including the Taliban. General Dan McNeill, the top NATO commander in Afghanistan until mid-2008, acknowledged that NATO forces had tracked supply convoys from Iran into Afghanistan.

McNeill, a stockily built man with gray hair and slight southern accent, described an incident in 2007 in which several vehicles were monitored crossing from Iran into western Afghanistan. A straight shooter who spoke bluntly in both public and private, McNeill said that NATO forces, after engaging the vehicles, found that one contained small-arms ammunition, mortar rounds, and more than 300 kilograms of C4 demolition charges. Other convoys from Iran carried rocket-propelled grenades, 107-millimeter rockets, and improvised explosive devices.[58]

Some of these shipments may have come from international arms dealers. But NATO and Afghan officials claimed that elements of the Iranian government, especially the Iranian Revolutionary Guards Corps, provided small arms and limited advanced-technology weapons to the Taliban and other insurgent groups.[59] One of the most disturbing trends was the export of a handful of explosively formed penetrators (EFPs), which send a semimolten copper slug through the armor of a Humvee and then create a deadly spray of hot metal inside the vehicle. EFPs were used against Israeli forces in Lebanon in 2006 and against U.S. forces in Iraq beginning in 2005.[60] In addition, there is some evidence that units of the Iranian government may have assisted—or knowingly allowed—the transit of jihadists moving between the Pakistan-Afghanistan front and the broader Middle East, especially Iraq.[61]

Though Iran had a strategic motive, its support for the Taliban was somewhat surprising, since Iran's historical relationship with the Taliban was not a good one. Iran, which is predominantly Shi'ite, viewed with deep concern the rise of the Sunni Taliban in the 1990s. In October 1998, for instance, nearly 200,000 regular Iranian troops massed along the border with Afghanistan, and the Taliban mobilized thousands of fighters to thwart an expected Iranian invasion. Only a last-minute effort by the United Nations prevented a war between the Taliban and Iran. Despite those tensions, however, Iran had a fairly close relationship with the Afghan government.[62] Iran and Afghanistan cooperated on drug enforcement across their shared border and conducted trade, energy, investment, cultural, and scientific exchanges. Iran also played a helpful role at the 2001 Bonn Conference. According to UN Secretary-General Kofi Annan, the UN worked well with Iran in Afghanistan after the overthrow of the Taliban regime.[63]

But the prospect of conflict with the United States appeared to temporarily change Iran's strategic calculations. And there was some precedent for Iranian support to Sunni extremist groups. According to Defense Intelligence Agency estimates, for example, Iran joined the United States in providing rifles, land mines, shoulder-fired anti-tank rockets, heavy machine guns, and nonlethal assistance to Gulbuddin Hekmatyar and other Sunni leaders against the Soviet Union in the 1980s.[64] Former U.S. Under Secretary of State for Political Affairs Nicholas Burns was quoted as saying that there was "irrefutable evidence" of arms "from the government of Iran."[65] In addition, the Iranian government provided aid to Tajik, Hazara, and Uzbek commanders in northern, central, and western Afghanistan, as they had done during the 1980s and 1990s.

But Iran and Pakistan weren't the only external supporters of the insurgency. There were reports that China sent arms to the Taliban, including ammunition and small arms.[66] The EFPs that seem to have arrived from Iran also may have included Chinese technology. Yet the Chinese government's role was not entirely clear. One NATO soldier, who specialized in information operations, told me that China's most important role in Afghanistan was more accidental than purposeful. "Virtually every soccer ball or toy that I purchase and hand out to Afghan kids," he noted, "says 'Made in China.' How's that for information operations?"[67] China's historical role in Afghanistan was minimal compared with that of many of Afghanistan's other neighbors, though China did provide small arms such as AK-47s and 60-millimeter mortars to Afghan mujahideen during the 1980s.[68]

Finally, there were reports that wealthy donors from Saudi Arabia, the United Arab Emirates (UAE), and other Gulf states provided support to insurgents and other militants in Pakistan and Afghanistan, though it was not entirely clear to what degree these governments were directly involved. At least one European Union and UN assessment held that "[c]urtailing Taliban financing—from Saudi Arabia and UAE—was also key."[69] Saudi Arabia had been among the first countries to recognize the Taliban regime in May 1997, despite the fact that Osama bin Laden, a committed enemy of the Saudi regime, had returned to Afghanistan a year earlier.[70] But after the Saudi government's fallout with Osama bin Laden and then the Taliban in the late 1990s, its support for Taliban fighters dwindled. After the overthrow of the Taliban regime in 2001, *zakat* (almsgiving) was a key funding source for the Taliban and its allies. Saudi money was especially important for the Taliban because it helped fund mosques and *madrassas* in Pakistan and Afghanistan, the most important centers of community support and recruitment for the Taliban.

The Razor's Edge

The challenge of borders had perhaps best been evoked by Lord Curzon of Kedleston, who served as viceroy of India and British foreign secretary in the early twentieth century. While riding horseback as a teenager, he incurred a spinal injury that required him to wear a metal corset under his clothes. This gave him a formal air of rigidity and haughtiness. In January 1899, he was appointed viceroy of India and had to deal with insurrection in the tribal areas, along the border with Afghanistan. In a 1907 lecture at All Souls College, Oxford University, that regal bearing was on display during his speech, in which he famously remarked: "Frontiers are indeed the razor's edge on which hang suspended the modern issues of war and peace, of life and death to nations."[71]

As for the most recent insurgency, external frontiers and support were critical at the onset. Of particular significance was the use of Pakistan by insurgent groups; after the overthrow of the Taliban regime, there was a massive exodus of Taliban, al Qa'ida, and other fighters across the snow-capped Hindu Kush mountains. Over the next several years, these fighters regrouped and began their sustained insurgency to overthrow the Afghan government. The solution to this problem was to have the Pakistani government, or tribal proxies—with U.S. support—target groups operating out of this sanctuary. A U.S. State Department document averred that the United States needed to "move against the Taliban in Quetta" and other areas of Pakistan:

> Actions to support this would include detaining Taliban leaders, financiers and operational support cells; pressing Pakistan to close madrassas whose students participated in the recent Pashmul/Panjwai fighting; seizing Taliban-linked financial assets in Quetta; interdicting courier movement between Quetta, the FATA, and Afghanistan and closing arms bazaars in the Quetta area. While Pakistani-led action is ideal, we may need to consider unilateral action, or the threat of it, to encourage a sufficiently energetic Pakistani response.[72]

Most of these steps, however, did not occur. In 2007, for example, an American military proposal outlined an intensified effort to enlist FATA tribal leaders in the fight against al Qa'ida and the Taliban. It was part of a broader effort to bolster Pakistani forces against an expanding militancy. The proposal came in a strategy paper prepared by staff members of the U.S. Special Operations Command (SOCOM). The planning at SOCOM had intensified after Admiral Eric Olson, the SOCOM commander, met with President Pervez Musharraf and senior Pakistani military leaders in late August 2007 to discuss how the U.S. military could increase cooperation in Pakistan's fight against the extremists. The briefing stated that U.S. forces would not be involved in any conventional combat in Pakistan but that elements of the Joint Special Operations Command, an elite counterterrorism unit, might be involved in strikes against militant leaders under specific conditions.[73]

But there were no sustained operations. The vast majority of U.S. planning was on paper, not in practice. The United States refused to take concerted action against the Taliban and other insurgents in Pakistan—especially in Baluchistan Province, where the Taliban's inner *shura* was located—or to put serious pressure on Pakistan to do it. At least one White House official acknowledged that the U.S. government did not place any serious conditions on its assistance to Pakistan. It did not request a quid pro quo in which the United States provided money and equipment and Pakistan helped capture or kill key Taliban and other militants.[74] Several Western ambassadors— especially those from countries whose troops were fighting and dying in Afghanistan—became frustrated at America's apparent unwillingness to confront Pakistan.[75] At the same time, a resurgent al Qa'ida on Pakistani soil became an increasingly acute threat.

CHAPTER SIXTEEN

Al Qa'ida: A Force Multiplier

SINCE ITS CREATION IN 1973, the National Intelligence Council (NIC) has provided U.S. policymakers with assessments on current and future threats to U.S. national security. Located at the CIA's wooded headquarters near the Potomac River in northern Virginia, the NIC meets on a regular basis to craft perhaps its most important official assessments: National Intelligence Estimates (NIEs). These documents contain the judgments and predictions of the U.S. intelligence community on a wide range of issues. In 2007, representatives from U.S. intelligence agencies met to hone and coordinate the full text of a document on the terrorist threat to the U.S. homeland. The directors of the CIA, National Security Agency, National Geospatial-Intelligence Agency, and Defense Intelligence Agency, as well as the assistant secretary of the State Department's Bureau of Intelligence and Research, submitted formal assessments that highlighted the strengths, weaknesses, and overall credibility of their sources in developing the document's key judgments. In other words, it had been thoroughly vetted by the U.S. intelligence community.

The conclusions of the document, titled *The Terrorist Threat to the U.S. Homeland*, were grim: "Al-Qa'ida is and will remain the most serious terrorist threat to the Homeland." Although many commentators in the United States had looked to Iraq as the center of international terrorism, the report revealed that the core al Qa'ida threat

279

emanated from the Pakistan-Afghanistan border regions. "We assess
the group has protected or regenerated key elements of its Homeland attack capability, including: a safehaven in the Pakistan Federally
Administered Tribal Areas (FATA), operational lieutenants, and its
top leadership."[1] The best and brightest minds in the American intelligence community had effectively discovered that since the September 11, 2001, attack, al Qa'ida had barely moved from its base in
eastern Afghanistan. Scarcely 100 miles separated al Qa'ida's Darunta
camp complex near Jalalabad—one of bin Laden's most significant
training complexes before September 11—from North Waziristan, a
key al Qa'ida haven after September 11. American military action,
then, had succeeded in moving senior al Qa'ida leaders only the distance between New York City and Philadelphia.

The significance of the 2007 NIE was clear: al Qa'ida presented an
imminent threat to the United States, and it enjoyed a sanctuary in
Pakistan. Another U.S. intelligence assessment unambiguously
concluded:

> Al-Qa'ida has been able to retain a safehaven in Pakistan's Federally
> Administered Tribal Areas (FATA) that provides the organization
> many of the advantages it once derived from its base across the bor-
> der in Afghanistan, albeit on a smaller and less secure scale. The FATA
> serves as a staging area for al-Qa'ida's attacks in support of the Tali-
> ban in Afghanistan as well as a location for training new terrorist
> operatives, for attacks in Pakistan, the Middle East, Africa, Europe
> and the United States.[2]

The FBI came to a similar conclusion, warning in a June 2008
report: "A large number of terrorists have escaped from prisons
around the world, raising the threat these terrorist escapees might
pose to U.S. interests." FBI officials were particularly concerned
about several operatives in Pakistan, including Abu Yahya al-Libi and
Rashid Rauf. "Al-Libi is arguably the most dangerous," the FBI concluded, "because of his demonstrated ability to spread al-Qa'ida ideology" and to target the United States.[3]

The Return of al Qa'ida

By 2007, if not before, it was clear that al Qa'ida had enjoyed a resurgence in Pakistan's tribal belt and that it remained committed to conducting attacks on a global scale, not just in Afghanistan and Pakistan. Al Qa'ida had launched successful attacks and had been foiled in other plots, including the successful attack in London in July 2005 and the thwarted transatlantic plot in the summer of 2006 to detonate liquid explosives aboard several airliners flying from Britain to the United States and Canada. In 2007, officials drew worldwide attention when they broke up an al Qa'ida cell in Denmark and an Islamic Jihad Union cell in Germany led by Fritz Gelowicz. In 2008, police and intelligence forces uncovered several terrorist plots in Europe (including in Spain and France) linked to militants in Pakistan's tribal areas. People taking part in each of these operations received training and other assistance in Pakistan.

The July 2005 terrorist attack in London serves as a useful example. British authorities initially believed that the attacks were the work of purely "home grown" British Muslims. However, subsequent evidence compiled by British intelligence agencies indicated that key participants, including Mohammad Sidique Khan and Shahzad Tanweer, between November 2004 and February 2005 visited Pakistani terrorist camps, where they were trained by al Qa'ida operatives. In September 2005, Ayman al-Zawahiri said that al Qa'ida "was honoured to launch" the London attacks. "In the Wills of the hero brothers, the knights of monotheism," Zawahiri remarked, "may God have mercy on them, make paradise their final abode and accept their good deeds."[4]

A year earlier, British and American authorities had foiled a plot by a London-based al Qa'ida cell, led by Dhiren Barot, to carry out suicide attacks on the New York Stock Exchange and the Citi-Group Building in New York City; the Prudential Center in Newark, New Jersey; and the International Monetary Fund and World

Bank headquarters in Washington, DC. The trail similarly led back to Pakistan.[5]

Al Qa'ida was also involved in the infamous 2006 transatlantic plot.[6] One of the controllers of the operation, which the British MI5 code-named Operation Overt, was Abu Ubaydah al-Masri, a senior al Qa'ida operative. What surprised U.S. intelligence analysts, however, was how little they knew about some of the individuals involved. "When the British government handed us the names of the individuals they believed were involved in the 2006 translatlantic plot," remarked Bruce Riedel, a longtime CIA officer who was at NATO, "we had no idea who many of them were. They were complete unknowns."[7]

Al Qa'ida was involved in more terrorist attacks after September 11, 2001, than during the previous six years. It averaged fewer than two attacks per year between 1995 and 2001, but it averaged more than ten major international attacks per year between 2002 and 2006 (excluding in Afghanistan and Iraq).[8] Between 1995 and 2001, al Qa'ida launched approximately a dozen terrorist attacks—beginning on November 13, 1995, when they detonated an explosive device outside the office of the program manager of the Saudi Arabian National Guard in Riyadh, killing five Americans and two Indian government officials. The Saudi government arrested four perpetrators, who admitted connections with Osama bin Laden.[9] Over the next several years, al Qa'ida conducted attacks in Kenya, Tanzania, and Yemen, among other places. In 1996, bin Laden issued a declaration of jihad against the United States, in part because he felt that the "presence of the USA Crusader military forces on land, sea and air of the states of the Islamic Gulf is the greatest danger threatening the largest oil reserve in the world." Consequently, America's oppression of the Holy Land "cannot be demolished except in a rain of bullets."[10]

In 1998, bin Laden called specifically for the murder of any American, anywhere on earth, as the "individual duty for every Muslim who can do it in any country in which it is possible to do it."[11] A growing number of extremists all over the world sought training from al Qa'ida in Afghanistan and other countries. A British House of Commons report noted that, as "Al Qaida developed in the 1990s, a number of extremists in the UK, both British and foreign nationals— many of the latter having fled from conflict elsewhere or repressive regimes—began to work in support of its agenda, in particular, radicalising and encouraging young men to support jihad overseas."[12]

After 2001, as al Qa'ida significantly increased its number of attacks, it continued to operate most actively in Saudi Arabia. But the group also expanded operations into North Africa (Tunisia and Algeria), Asia (Bangladesh, Indonesia, and Pakistan), the Middle East (Jordan and Turkey), and Europe (the United Kingdom). Most of these attacks were located in the area that had been controlled by the Caliphate, notably the Umayyad Caliphate from 661 to 750 AD, the land in which al Qa'ida wanted to establish its own pan-Islamic empire.[13]

An Apostate Regime

Al Qa'ida leaders based in Pakistan had three main objectives in Afghanistan. First, they wanted to overthrow the "apostate" regime of Hamid Karzai. In their mind, Karzai was doubly guilty of failing to establish a "true" Islamic state and of cooperating with the infidel Western governments. Second, al Qa'ida leaders wanted to replace the Afghan regime with one that followed a radical version of *sharia* law envisioned by Sayyid Qutb and other Islamist thinkers. Al Qa'ida leaders appeared content with the prospect of another Taliban victory in Afghanistan and the establishment of a Taliban-style interpretation of Islam, including *sharia* law—even though the Taliban had objectives that were largely parochial and limited to Afghanistan. The third objective was to wage a war of attrition against the United States and other Western governments, with the hope of weakening them and ultimately pushing them out of Muslim lands.

All of these goals were interconnected and consistent with the philosophy of bin Laden, Zawahiri, and others—an ideology that had been forged in the Afghan jihad against the Soviet Union and the struggle against Egypt, Saudi Arabia, and other "apostate regimes." They wanted to unite Muslims to fight the United States and its allies (the far enemy) and to overthrow Western-friendly regimes in the Middle East (the near enemy).[14] Ultimately, they envisioned the establishment of an "Islamic belt" that connected Pakistan to Central Asia, cut through the Caucasus, and then moved into Turkey and the Middle East.[15]

In an audio message in 2007, bin Laden rhetorically asked the people of Europe: "So what is the sin of the Afghans due to which you are continuing this unjust war against them? Their only sin is that they are Muslims, and this illustrates the extent of the Crusaders' hatred of Islam and its people."[16] Westerners brought with them such concepts as democracy, which Islamists considered *nizam al-kufr* (a deviant system). They viewed democracy—as evidenced by the free elections in Afghanistan in 2004 and 2005—as supplanting the rule of God with that of a popular majority. Jihadis were obsessed with controlling state bureaucracies and using them to advance their Islamic project.[17]

Al Qa'ida leaders were also quick to draw parallels between the United States and the Soviet Union in Afghanistan. The Afghan jihad, Zawahiri argued, was an extension of the struggle against the Soviets. The rhetoric was very much the same. Discussing the necessity of attacking the United States, he wrote that it is "of the utmost importance to prepare the Muslim mujahideen to wage their awaited battle against the superpower that now has sole dominance over the globe, namely, the United States."[18]

Al Qa'ida's Organizational Structure

After the overthrow of the Taliban, al Qa'ida evolved a fairly decentralized and nonlinear network based out of Pakistan. Terrorism expert Bruce Hoffman divided the group into four categories, or a series of concentric circles: al Qa'ida central, affiliated groups, affiliated cells, and the informal network.[19]

Al Qa'ida central included the remnants of the pre-9/11 al Qa'ida organization. Despite the death or capture of key al Qa'ida figures, such as Khalid Sheikh Muhammad, the core leadership included many old faces, such as bin Laden and Zawahiri.[20] Much of the founding core was scattered across Pakistan. After the death of his wife and two children during U.S. attacks in Afghanistan, Zawahiri married a woman from the Mahmund tribe in Bajaur Agency. This enabled him to develop even stronger tribal links to the leadership of militant Deobandi groups, such as Mullah Faqir Muhammad, the leader of Tehreek-e-Nafaz-e-Shariat-e-Mohammadi (TNSM).[21]

As we have seen, al Qa'ida central was directly or indirectly involved in a number of terrorist efforts outside of Pakistan, such as in London in July 2005 and the foiled transatlantic plot in 2006. In some cases, this included direct command and control, such as commissioning attacks and planning operations. Relative freedom to operate in Pakistan enabled al Qa'ida to maintain operational capabilities, conduct training, and arrange meetings among operational planners and foot soldiers, recruiters, and others in relative safety. It also gave al Qa'ida's leaders the space to focus on future attacks rather than to waste effort trying to hide from U.S. or Pakistani forces. Hoffman writes that this freedom allowed them the same latitude to operate as when they planned the 1998 East African embassy bombings and the September 11 attacks. Such attacks were entrusted only to al Qa'ida's professional cadre—the most committed and reliable individuals in the movement—though locals were usually critical to executing the operation.[22]

The *affiliated groups* included formally established insurgent or terrorist groups that cooperated with al Qa'ida. They benefited from bin Laden's financial assistance and inspiration and received training, arms, money, and other support. In some cases, such as al Qa'ida in Iraq, burgeoning groups also funneled funds back to al Qa'ida central. Al Qa'ida in Iraq sent money to al Qa'ida in Pakistan—funds they had raised from donations as well as kidnappings and other criminal activity.[23] These affiliated groups hailed from countries as disparate as Pakistan, Iraq, Uzbekistan, Indonesia, Morocco, and the Philippines, as well as Kashmir. Among them were al Qa'ida in Iraq, Ansar al-Islam, the Islamic Movement of Uzbekistan, Moro Islamic Liberation Front, and the various Kashmiri Islamic groups based in Pakistan, such as Jaish-e-Muhammad and Lashkar-e-Taiba. The Salafist Group for Preaching and Combat (GSPC) officially merged with al Qa'ida in September 2006, changed its name to al Qa'ida in the Islamic Maghreb (AQIM), and attacked a U.S. contractor bus in December 2006 in greater Algiers, marking its first attack against a U.S. entity.[24]

The *affiliated cells* were small, dispersed groups of adherents who enjoyed some direct connection with al Qa'ida, though it was often tenuous and transitory. These units were not large insurgent organizations attempting to overthrow their local government but often self-organized and radicalized small groups, much like the Hamburg cell that helped plan and execute the September 11 attacks in the United States. That cell included Muhammad Atta, Marwan al Shehhi, and Ziad Jarrah. In some cases, they comprised individuals who had some prior terrorism experience in previous jihadi campaigns in Algeria, the Balkans, Chechnya, Afghanistan, or perhaps Iraq. Others were individuals who had recently traveled to camps in Pakistan and other locations for training, as with the British Muslims responsible for the July 2005 London bombings.[25]

Finally, the *informal network* included individuals who had no direct contact with al Qa'ida central but were outraged by Western attacks in Iraq, Afghanistan, Chechnya, and the Palestinian territories and thus were inspired to join the jihadi cause. Without direct support, these networks tended to be amateurish and clumsy. The four men charged in June 2007 with plotting to blow up fuel tanks, terminal buildings, and the web of fuel lines running beneath John F. Kennedy International Airport (which was code-named Chicken Farm by the plotters) belong in this category. They had no direct connections with al Qa'ida but were prepared to conduct attacks in solidarity with it.[26]

Though less reliable, the informal network could occasionally be lethal. The terrorist cells that conducted the Madrid train bombings in March 2004 emerged from a loose association of Islamic extremists. What links there were to al Qa'ida and other groups were tangential at best. According to court documents from the case, the terrorists "were part of a cell that was formed, both locally and internationally, to operate in Spain (Catalonia and Madrid) and outside the country (Belgium, the Netherlands, Turkey, Morocco, Syria, and Iraq)."[27] In December 2003, intelligence officials discovered an al Qa'ida Internet strategy document that showed the Madrid attack to have been motivated by Spain's unpopular involvement in the Iraq War. "In order to force the Spanish government to withdraw from Iraq," it said, "the resistance should deal painful blows to its forces."[28] Another example of this category included the so-called Hofstad Group in the Netherlands, of which a member (Mohammed Bouyeri) murdered the Dutch filmmaker Theo van Gogh in Amsterdam in November 2004.[29]

Musical Chairs

In 2008, Osama bin Laden and Ayman al-Zawahiri still ran al Qa'ida's Pakistan contingent. But security concerns prohibited many of al Qa'ida's operational commanders from gaining daily access to bin Laden and Zawahiri. For security purposes, al Qa'ida adopted a four-tiered courier system to communicate. There was an administrative courier network designed for communication pertaining to the movement of al Qa'ida members' families and other administrative activities. Another courier network dealt with operational instructions. Where possible, unwitting couriers were substituted for knowledgeable people in order to minimize detection. A media-support courier network was used for propaganda. Messages were sent in the form of CDs, videos, and leaflets to television networks such as Al Jazeera. Finally, a separate courier network was used only by al Qa'ida's top leadership, who usually did not pass written messages to each other. Often, their most trusted couriers memorized messages and conveyed them orally.

By 2008, there had been some recent successful apprehensions of senior al Qa'ida operatives by Pakistani and American intelligence forces. One was Abd al-Hadi al-Iraqi, whose real name was Nashwan Abd al-Razzaq Abd al-Baqi. He was born in Mosul, Iraq, in 1961, served in the Iraqi military, and was one of al Qa'ida's highest-ranking and most experienced senior operatives. Abd al-Hadi served on al Qa'ida's ruling Shura Council—a ten-person advisory body to Osama bin Laden—as well as on the group's military committee, which oversaw terrorist and guerrilla operations and paramilitary training. The U.S. Department of Defense said, "He had been one of the organization's key paramilitary commanders in Afghanistan from the late 1990s and, during 2002–04, was in charge of cross-border attacks in Afghanistan against Coalition forces." It continued: "Abd al-Hadi was known and trusted by Bin Ladin and Ayman al-Zawahiri. Abd al-Hadi was in direct communication with both leaders and, at one point, was Zawahiri's caretaker."[30]

Abd al-Hadi also served as a conduit between al Qa'ida in Iraq, the Taliban, and al Qa'ida senior commanders operating inside Pakistan, and he was involved in the foiled 2006 transatlantic-aviation plot. According to a report compiled by the Joint Terrorism Analysis Center, based at MI5's London headquarters, Abd al-Hadi "stressed the need to take care to ensure that the attack was successful and on a large scale."[31] He was captured in 2006 in Turkey.

In 2007, al Qa'ida appointed a new leader to run operations in Afghanistan: Mustafa Ahmed Muhammad Uthman Abu al-Yazid. Abu al-Yazid was born in Egypt's al-Sharqiyah governorate in the Nile Delta in 1955; in his youth, he became a member of the country's radical Islamist movement. In 1981, he took part in the assassination of Egyptian President Anwar Sadat and spent three years in prison, where he became a member of Ayman al-Zawahiri's Egyptian Islamic Jihad. Abu al-Yazid left Egypt for Afghanistan in 1988 and accompanied bin Laden from Afghanistan to Sudan in 1991. While there, he served as the accountant for bin Laden's

Sudan-based businesses, including his holding company, Wadi al-Aqiq.[32] He also may have arranged the funding for the June 1995 failed assassination attempt by the Egyptian Islamic Group against Egyptian President Hosni Mubarak in Addis Ababa. Convicted in absentia in several trials in Egypt, he was sentenced to both life imprisonment and the death penalty.

Abu al-Yazid apparently returned to Afghanistan with bin Laden in 1996. By that time, he was a confidant of bin Laden, a senior al Qa'ida leader, a member of its Shura Council, and a key manager of the organization's finances. He was reported to have supplied the requisite funding for Muhammad Atta—the leader of the September 11, 2001, attackers—and to have received from Atta the return of surplus funds just before the attacks occurred. In 2002, the U.S. government placed Abu al-Yazid's name on the list of terrorists and organizations subject to having their financial accounts frozen. Pakistan's *Daily Times* (Lahore) reported in December 2004 that Abu al-Yazid had some unspecified duties in maintaining the relationship between al Qa'ida and the Islamic Movement of Uzbekistan.[33] One of his daughters married the son of the incarcerated Egyptian Islamic Group spiritual leader, Sheikh Omar Abd al-Rahman. The daughter and her husband, Muhammad Abd al-Rahman, were captured by U.S. forces in Afghanistan in early 2003.

There were a number of other senior al Qa'ida leaders operating out of Pakistan, such as Abu Ubaydah al-Masri, an Egyptian who died of hepatitis in 2007. Al-Masri served as one of al Qa'ida's senior external-operations figures after the death of Abu Hamza Rabi'a, who was killed by a missile strike in Pakistan in 2005. He was implicated in the 2006 transatlantic-aircraft plot, which was to be carried out by a terrorist cell operating in London, but which involved al Qa'ida's central leadership. Another operative, Fahid Muhammad Ally Msalam, a Kenyan, served as a facilitator for communication between Osama bin Laden and the East Africa network and was located for a time with senior al Qa'ida leaders based in Waziristan. He was reported as killed in a U.S. missile strike on January 1, 2009.

Despite the loss of these key leaders, however, al Qa'ida remained capable of conducting lethal attacks regionally and globally. According to a CIA assessment of al Qa'ida, "the group's cadre of seasoned, committed leaders has allowed it to remain fairly cohesive and stay focused on its strategic objectives."[34] In fact, they began opening new channels of communication by issuing propaganda directed specifically at American audiences, either in translation or given directly by English-speaking al Qa'ida members based in Pakistan. One of the spokesmen most visible to the West was Adam Gadahn, an American raised in Southern California who converted to Islam at the age of seventeen and moved to Pakistan in 1998. With his head wrapped in a black turban and sporting a jet-black beard, he expressed profound rage in his video exposés on YouTube. "We love nothing better than the heat of battle, the echo of explosions, and slitting the throats of the infidels," he thundered in one video. In another, he callously quipped: "It's hard to imagine that any compassionate person could see pictures, just pictures, of what the Crusaders did to those children and not want to go on a shooting spree at the Marines' housing facilities at Camp Pendleton."[35]

A Force Multiplier in Afghanistan

Afghanistan remained the most important strategic component for al Qa'ida. According to a Defense Intelligence Agency analysis, "Al-Qa'ida remains committed to reestablishing a fundamentalist Islamic government in Afghanistan and has become increasingly successful in defining Afghanistan as a critical battleground against the West and its regional allies." Al Qa'ida was also able to leverage its resources through its "increasingly cooperative relationship with insurgent networks."[36] Al Qa'ida personnel met with wealthy Arab businessmen during the Tablighi Jamaat annual meeting in Raiwind, Pakistan, which attracted one of the largest concentrations of Muslims after the *hajj*.[37] Appealing to the international jihadi network was consistent with historical patterns. During the rise of the Taliban, an important source of funding was the "Golden Chain," an informal financial network of prominent Saudi and Gulf individuals established to support Afghan fighters. This network collected funds through Islamic charities and other nongovernmental organizations. Bin Laden also drew on the network of Islamic charities, nongovernmental organizations, and educational institutions to recruit volunteers.[38]

The Golden Chain provided financial backing, but bin Laden offered Afghan fighters much more than financial assistance. Afghan groups were able to tap into the broad international jihadi network. For example, al Qa'ida was instrumental in improving the communications capabilities of Afghan groups. These groups leveraged Al-Sahab, al Qa'ida's media enterprise, to distribute well-produced video propaganda and recruit supporters. "Al-Qa'ida spreads its propaganda through taped statements," a CIA assessment reported, "sometimes featuring relatively sophisticated production values."[39] A UN report similarly found that there was an "increasing level of professionalism achieved by Al-Sahab, the main Al-Qaida media production unit." It continued by noting that Osama bin Laden's September 2007 video was "expertly produced and, like previous videos, was subtitled in English and uploaded almost simultaneously onto hundreds of servers by what must be a large group of volunteers."[40] In January 2007, federal prosecutors in Chicago indicted Rockford, Illinois, resident Derrick Shareef (also known as Talib Abu Salam Ibn Shareef) on one count of attempting to damage or destroy a building by fire or explosion and one count of attempting to use a weapon of mass destruction. He had been inspired by watching one of Adam Gadahn's propaganda videos that justified killing women and children.[41]

Senior Afghan leaders began to appear in videos produced with the help of al Qa'ida, reciting passages of the Qur'an and outlining their ideology. Taliban leaders such as Mullah Omar increasingly adopted al Qa'ida's global rhetoric. In a statement in December 2007, for example, Omar turned to Muslims across the globe: "We appeal to Muslims to help their Mujahideen brothers against the international invader economically. . . . Now you know both religion and country are in danger, you follow the way of good and religious leaders and leave the way of bad and dishonest and do Jihad."[42] And jihadi Websites with links to al Qa'ida, such as those run by Azzam Publications (including www.azzam.com and www.qoqaz.net, which were eventually shut down), helped raise funds for the Taliban.[43] Some solicited military items for the Taliban, including gas masks and night vision goggles.[44]

Insurgent groups also used al Qa'ida support to construct increasingly sophisticated improvised explosive devices (IEDs), including remotely controlled detonators.[45] For example, al Qa'ida ran a handful of manufacturing sites in the Bush Mountains, the Khamran Mountains, and the Shakai Valley in Pakistan's Federally Administered Tribal Areas. They ranged from small facilities hidden within compounds that built IEDs, to much larger "IED factories" that doubled as training centers and labs where recruits experimented with IED technology. Some of this explosives expertise came from Iraqi groups that provided information on making and using various kinds of remotely controlled devices and timers. In return for this assistance, al Qa'ida received operational and financial support from local clerics and Taliban commanders in Waziristan. They recruited young Pashtuns from the local *madrassas* and financed their activities through "religious racket"—forced religious contribution, often accompanied by death threats.

There is even evidence of cooperation between insurgents in Iraq and Afghanistan. Islamic militants in Iraq apparently provided information through the Internet and face-to-face visits with Taliban members, Hezb-i-Islami forces, and foreign fighters from eastern and southern Afghanistan and Pakistan's tribal areas. In addition, there is some evidence that a small number of Pakistani and Afghan militants received military training in Iraq, and Iraqi fighters met with Afghan and Pakistani extremists in Pakistan. It is clear that militants in Afghanistan had great success with homemade bombs, suicide attacks, and other tactics honed in Iraq.[46]

One effective IED was the "TV bomb," which was pioneered by Iraqi groups. The bomb was a "shaped"-charge mechanism that could be hidden under brush or debris on a roadside and set off by remote control from 300 yards or more. It was useful for focusing the energy of a bomb toward a specific target. Taliban commanders learned from Iraqi groups to disassemble rockets and rocket-propelled-grenade rounds, remove the explosives and propellants, and repack them with high-velocity shaped charges—thus creating armor-penetrating weapons. In addition, Afghan groups occasionally adopted brutal terrorist tactics, such as beheadings, used by Iraqi groups. In December 2005, insurgents posted a video of the decapitation of an Afghan hostage on al Qa'ida–linked Websites. This was the first published video showing the beheading of an Afghan hostage, and it sent the message that the Taliban was no less serious about repelling the Americans than Iraqi insurgent groups were.[47] The Taliban also developed or acquired new commercial communications gear and field equipment from the Iraqi insurgents, and they appeared to have received good tactical, camouflage, and marksmanship training, too. Some Taliban units even included al Qa'ida members or other Arab fighters, who brought experience from jihadi campaigns in Iraq and Chechnya.[48]

Perhaps most troubling, insurgents increasingly adopted suicide tactics, especially in such major cities as Kandahar and Kabul.[49] Afghan National Police were common targets of suicide bombers. Al Qa'ida leaders in Pakistan encouraged the use of such attacks. Ayman al-Zawahiri argued that "suicide operations are the most successful in inflicting damage on the opponent and the least costly in terms of casualties among the fundamentalists."[50] Al Qa'ida's involvement was particularly important in this regard because Afghan insurgent groups were surprisingly inept at suicide attacks. Even a UN study of suicide bombing led by Christine Fair acknowledged: "Employed by the Taliban as a military technique, suicide bombing—paradoxically—has had little military success in Afghanistan."[51]

Despite their initial reluctance, Afghan insurgents began to use suicide attacks for a variety of reasons.[52] First, the Taliban had begun to rely more and more on the expertise and training of the broader jihadi community, especially the international al Qa'ida network, which advocated and condoned such attacks. These militants—with al Qa'ida's assistance—helped supply a steady stream of suicide bombers. Second, al Qa'ida and the Taliban saw the success of such groups as Hamas in the Palestinian territories, Hizbullah in Lebanon, the Tamil Tigers in Sri Lanka, and Iraqi groups, and they concluded this was an effective method for disrupting Coalition actions.[53] Suicide attacks allowed insurgents to achieve maximum impact with minimal resources, and the chance of killing people and instilling fear increased exponentially with suicide attacks.[54] Third, al Qa'ida and the Taliban believed that suicide attacks raised the level of insecurity among the Afghan population. This caused some Afghans to question the government's ability to protect them and further destabilized the authority of local government institutions. Consequently, the distance widened between the Afghan government and the population in specific areas. Fourth, suicide attacks provided renewed visibility for the Taliban and al Qa'ida, which previous guerrilla attacks did not generate. Because each attack was spectacular and usually lethal, every suicide bombing was reported in the national and international media.

Most of the bombers were Afghans or Pakistanis, though some foreigners were also involved.[55] Many were recruited from Afghan refugee camps and *madrassas* in Pakistan, where they were radicalized and immersed in extremist ideologies. Taliban-affiliated Deobandi *madrassas* in Pakistan afforded ready access to bombers, and the Taliban prevailed on some teachers and administrators to help recruit them.[56] Al Qa'ida continued to play an important role by funding suicide bombers, and they paid as much as several thousand dollars to the families of suicide bombers.

Al Qa'ida's role in Afghanistan can be accurately summed up by the advertising slogan used by the German-based chemical giant BASF: "We don't make a lot of the products you buy. We make a lot of the products you buy better." Al Qa'ida leaders improved the tactical and operational competence of Afghan and Pakistani groups, who were able to manufacture a better array of products—from improvised explosive devices to videos. Al Qa'ida strengthened the competence of insurgent groups, although its leaders generally shied away from direct involvement in ground operations in Afghanistan, leaving the dirty work to local Afghans. Instead, it operated as a force multiplier, improving the groups' capabilities. Even as al Qa'ida enjoyed a resurgence in the Federally Administered Tribal Areas, however, some U.S. military forces began to make limited progress in eastern Afghanistan in late 2007 and early 2008.

CHAPTER SEVENTEEN

In the Eye of the Storm

AS IT BECAME CLEAR that the U.S. military would have to shift its focus from military operations to counterinsurgency tactics, new personnel were given a different set of responsibilities. U.S. Navy Commander Larry Legree was one of those new faces. Legree's preparation for counterinsurgency operations in landlocked Afghanistan was, somewhat ironically, serving aboard an aircraft carrier, a destroyer, and an amphibious ship. It was not exactly standard training for participating on the front line of a major ground war. "I was a nuclear-trained surface warfare officer," Legree told me, almost apologetically. "The four and a half months I spent at Fort Bragg in North Carolina before deploying to Afghanistan was about the only preparation I had. I learned how to wear body armor and shoot, move, and communicate, but didn't learn any real fundamentals about counterinsurgency." Most of that had to come on the fly.

Legree also didn't have the stereotypical disposition of a warfighter. His congenial, unassuming temperament, honed during his childhood in western Michigan, and his extraordinary politeness seemed oddly suited for Afghanistan's bloody front lines. He was also something of an academic. Legree attended the prestigious U.S. Naval Academy in Annapolis, Maryland, and then went on to get three master's degrees at George Washington University, Duke, and North Carolina State.

But he was a critical cog in the U.S. military's transition in eastern Afghanistan from a purely war-fighting machine to a counterinsurgency force through 2008. Legree was sent to Kunar Province in eastern Afghanistan, only a few miles from the Pakistan border, to become the commander of a U.S. Provincial Reconstruction Team. Insurgent groups had dug into the impenetrable terrain and created extensive cave networks along the province's border with Pakistan's North West Frontier Province. They had done the same thing during the Soviet era. Legree's job was to show locals that the United States could provide reconstruction and development assistance. "Our primary contributions were building roads and bridges," Legree said, "as well as helping establish a health care network. They brought concrete change to local Afghans." The roads and bridges paid off: Legree and his colleagues helped build extensive infrastructure across the province, transforming the dynamics of the local economy. As commerce began to flow more rapidly and into new areas, Legree became a powerful and popular figure.

"I was almost never targeted," Legree said, somewhat nonplussed, since Kunar was one of Afghanistan's most violent provinces. "My view is that the locals were pragmatic. They wanted the money and they knew I was the checkbook. The message got out: Don't mess with the Provincial Reconstruction Team."[1] And Afghans in Kunar felt increasingly secure. A 2008 Asia Foundation poll indicated that Afghans in the province felt relatively secure, despite violence in isolated pocket like the Korengal Valley.[2]

An Epiphany

Legree was not alone in his efforts. The U.S. military gradually improved its counterinsurgency capabilities over the course of its tenure in Afghanistan, though it still faced an entrenched and dedicated enemy. Among the most successful contingents were those led by Major General David M. Rodriguez, commander of the 82nd Airborne Division, Coalition Joint Task Force 82. Rodriguez is tall and immensely polite but somewhat uncomfortable in front of large crowds. He had served as deputy director of regional operations on the joint staff at the Pentagon, where he was responsible for synchronizing and monitoring U.S. military operations abroad.

The 82nd Airborne's previous tours in Afghanistan in 2002 and 2004 had been marred by controversy, earning them a reputation as "doorkickers." "We were good at one thing," said Colonel Martin Schweitzer, commander of the 4th Brigade Combat Team, 82nd Airborne Division. "Killing bad guys." This ultimately proved counterproductive. Schweitzer was a gregarious, affable colonel with short-cropped hair, bushy eyebrows, and dark sunglasses that clung to his neck like a necklace. "What we needed to do was to spend more time separating the enemy from the population. That meant engaging in non-kinetic operations," Schweitzer continued. In U.S. military lingo, "non-kinetic" referred to reconstruction and development activities, such as building health clinics, roads, and schools.[3]

In August 2002, the 82nd Airborne conducted Operation Mountain Sweep, which involved a weeklong hunt for al Qa'ida and Taliban fugitives in eastern Afghanistan. During the operation, a U.S. Special Forces team knocked at the door of a mud compound in the Shah-i-kot Valley, near the Afghanistan-Pakistan border. An elderly Pashtun farmer let the soldiers inside. When they asked if there were any weapons in the house, he led them to his only firearm, a decrepit hunting rifle. The Special Forces team thanked him and walked toward the next house. Not long after the Special Forces left, six paratroopers, also from the 82nd Airborne, also part of Operation Mountain Sweep, kicked in the door. Terrified, the farmer tried to run but was grabbed by one of the soldiers, while others tried to frisk the women. "The women were screaming bloody murder," recalled Mike, one of the Special Forces soldiers who was present during the confusion. "The guy was in tears. He had been completely dishonored." It was a strategic blunder, recalled another soldier. "After Mountain Sweep," he noted, "for the first time since we got here, we're getting rocks thrown at us on the road in Khowst."[4]

This and other experiences had marred the 82nd Airborne's reputation. But through the end of its rotation in early 2008, the 82nd Airborne had worked assiduously to change the general impression of the division, embracing the three core principles of counterinsurgency: clear, hold, and build. Colonel Schweitzer declared: "The Taliban and other groups tell locals: don't send your kids to school, don't take advantage of the medical care provided, and don't support the government by helping with security. We say the opposite. Send your kids to school and we'll build them, seek the available medical care, and the government will support you through the construction of roads, schools, dams, and infrastructure that will stimulate the economy."[5]

Building on counterinsurgency lessons from the British, French, and American historical experiences, the 82nd Airborne increasingly focused its efforts on "soft power." This translated into a greater focus on reconstruction and development projects and less emphasis on combat operations. At the core of this strategy was an assumption that local Afghans were the center of gravity, a basic tenet of counterinsurgency warfare. The French counterinsurgency expert Roger Trinquier summed this up lucidly: "The *sine qua non* of victory in modern warfare is the unconditional support of a population."[6]

Many Afghans had been frustrated by the lack of development over the previous several years, and unhappy with poor governance. To address these concerns, the 82nd Airborne worked with tribal leaders to identify local needs and to develop projects that helped address those needs. Thus, in Khowst Province, for example, Colonel Schweitzer and provincial governor Arsala Jamal teamed up to build infrastructure and hospitals. In Paktia Province and in Kunar, where Larry Legree was stationed, locals saw newly paved roads, electricity, and reliable water projects move toward swift completion. A sizable chunk of the money came from the Commander's Emergency Response Program (CERP), which enabled U.S. military commanders to dole out aid quickly. Another strategic component was hiring local Afghans to perform and evaluate the work.[7]

Against all odds, eastern Afghanistan appeared to rebound in 2008. In Khowst Province, the number of children in school quadrupled—from 38,000 in 2004 to more than 160,000 in 2008. Roughly 10 percent of Afghans in the east had access to basic health care in 2004, while more than 75 percent had access in 2008.[8] And, perhaps one of the most revealing metrics of progress in a country where cell phones were a primary method of communication for those who could afford them, there suddenly seemed to be service throughout the region. It was a shock when my BlackBerry worked almost everywhere I visited in eastern Afghanistan, including in remote border outposts.

The 82nd Airborne Division's efforts created a bit of defensiveness among some U.S. allies. In May 2008, the British government circulated a paper in response to "suggestions that U.S. successes in their counter-insurgency campaign in eastern Afghanistan should be migrated to the south," where British forces were located. The paper asked whether there were any lessons that might be applied to British operations in Helmand Province. The British pointed out that U.S. forces had been present in eastern Afghanistan much longer than British forces had in Helmand; U.S. military tours of duty were longer than British tours; and the United States provided significantly more funding through its CERP and the U.S. Agency for International Development (USAID) than Britain had in the south. Also, there were important differences between the east and the south in geography, population density, tribal structure, and types of jihadi groups. The result, British analysts concluded, was that "the east is easier terrain for counter-insurgency" and that "differences of geography, of resources, and of campaign timing suggest that many of the American approaches . . . are not transferable to Helmand."[9]

Building on Success?

Despite an innovative strategy, inadequate resources once again thwarted U.S. efforts. "We're like the Pacific theatre in World War II," a U.S. civil-affairs officer in eastern Afghanistan complained. "We will get more resources after we defeat Berlin," he said, alluding to the U.S. focus on Iraq.[10]

There were too few American and Coalition military forces, and there was too little American civilian expertise to ensure the permanence of this progress. By 2008, some 56,000 Coalition forces were stationed in Afghanistan, compared with more than three times that number in Iraq. American troop strength was even more disproportionate. U.S. military force levels in Iraq were frozen at 140,000 personnel, while just over 30,000 were deployed to Afghanistan. Thus, as during the earlier periods of the campaign, the U.S. military, other Coalition forces, and the Afghan National Army could clear territory but generally could not hold it. In June 2008, General David McKiernan became commander of ISAF; several months later, his staff completed the ISAF campaign plan, which was fairly blunt about the lack of forces to hold territory, noting that NATO had to resort to an "economy of force and special operations" effort to make up for the shortfalls and "to disrupt the insurgency and shape future operations."[11] Troops involved in reconstruction work could have been reallocated to combat operations, but there were still too few civilians in the field from the State Department and USAID. The rough living conditions and acute security concerns meant that the U.S. military had to shoulder most of the burden for governance and economic development activities, which in more normal circumstances would have fallen to officials in the Department of State, Commerce, Agriculture, or USAID.

U.S. and other NATO forces also had trouble "building" in some areas. In his book *Modern Warfare: A French View of Counterinsurgency*, Roger Trinquier argued that counterinsurgency requires "an interlocking system of actions—political, economic, psychological, military—that aims at the [insurgents' intended] overthrow of the established authority in a country and its replacement by another regime."[12] One of the most innovative aspects of the Afghan counterinsurgency campaign was the cooperation between civil and military programs, especially the use of Provincial Reconstruction Teams.[13]

The "building" that the Americans were able to accomplish almost always happened through these PRTs.

Each PRT consisted of roughly 60 to 100 personnel. Soldiers, who made up the bulk of each team, were divided into civil-affairs units, Special Forces, force-protection units, and psychological operations personnel. In most cases, more than 90 percent of the personnel were soldiers because of the struggle to get civilian personnel.[14] According to Larry Legree, "recruiting civilians was a tremendous challenge" in Kunar Province. "A number of U.S. agencies, such as the U.S. Agency for International Development, were simply not optimized to operate in an insurgency."[15] Legree was fortunate, however, since he managed to recruit a handful of competent civilians to assist in development and reconstruction. One was Alison Blosser, a sharp, young foreign service officer who spoke Pashto and was instrumental in dealing with Kunar's governor, Sayed Fazlullah Wahidi.

Both U.S. and NATO Provincial Reconstruction Teams faced significant staffing hurdles. Short tours of duty—including some for as little as three months—made it difficult for PRT members to understand local politics and culture. There were also too few of the teams. Five years after the overthrow of the Taliban regime, the United States and other NATO countries were able to put PRTs in virtually all major Afghan cities, but they had little operational reach into rural areas.[16] Colonel John Agoglia, director of the Counterinsurgency Training Center on Afghanistan, bluntly acknowledged that "many Coalition forces do not actively and consistently patrol their areas of responsibility or, when they do patrol, they sally forth from Forward Operating Bases (FOBs) for a quick-order patrol that has very little enduring effect."[17]

USAID faced serious challenges in adapting to the new environment. According to one official involved, USAID's initial attitude was to treat Afghanistan as a post-conflict environment. It wasn't. It was an insurgency. USAID did not prioritize reconstruction aid geographically and focus specifically on the south and east until 2006.[18]

NATO countries also faced deep challenges in linking military operations with reconstruction efforts. In a series of briefings in 2008 at NATO headquarters in Kabul, for example, key military officials from Regional Command South expressed growing frustration with the failure to meld reconstruction efforts with military operations. Despite oral commitments to focus on development and not combat operations, these officers reported: "By the time we get to executing plans, most of our operations are kinetic." There was little comprehensive NATO activity on economic development in rural areas of the south, and no systematic coordination between the military and such civilian agencies as USAID, the Canadian International Development Agency, and the UK's Department for International Development. "The biggest problem we have," the briefers concluded, "is consolidating military gains with development."[19]

Civilian Casualties

In addition to reconstruction challenges, civilian casualties— "collateral damage"—from NATO airstrikes created an uproar among Afghans, even though the Taliban and other groups killed a larger number of civilians. In 2008, U.S. military data indicated that the number of civilian casualties caused by NATO and Taliban fighting increased by somewhere between 39 and 54 percent from 2007 levels.[20] Over the course of the war, however, improvements in intelligence minimized the number of civilian casualties when the U.S. military planned airstrikes in advance. Rules were written to prevent major catastrophes. Targeters were required to obey strict procedures to minimize collateral damage. They had to make a positive identification of any target, and they were expected to alter the angle, depth, and type of bombs dropped, depending on the context. In addition, targeters were required to make a thorough assessment of who lived in a particular structure or area before calling in an airstrike. Problems sometimes emerged, however, when ground forces were ambushed in the field or came under unexpected fire. In such "troops-in-contact" situations, NATO and Afghan forces required immediate support, leaving little time to complete a formal collateral-damage assessment and increasing the possibility of faulty intelligence and civilian casualties. It was in these situations that the close air support—AH-64 Apache attack helicopters, A-10 and F-14 fighters, B-52 bombers, and AC-130 Spectre gunships—could lead to heavy civilian casualties. To make matters worse, the Taliban and other insurgent groups frequently fired from homes and other buildings near civilian populations, retreated into civilian areas, and concealed themselves as civilians while firing on NATO and Afghan forces. Their goal, of course, was to trick NATO forces into killing civilians, a nihilistic and horrifying tactic that has nevertheless worked in previous insurgencies.[21]

Not all civilian casualties were caused by airstrikes, however. One of the most widely publicized incidents took place on March 4, 2007, when nineteen civilians were killed in the eastern province of Nangarhar, a farming region known for its plump oranges, rice, and sugarcane. An explosives-rigged minivan had targeted a convoy of Marines from Marine Corps Forces Special Operations Command (MARSOC), who were traveling along the road between Torkham and Jalalabad. Some local Afghans insisted that the Americans fired on civilian cars and pedestrians as they sped away. U.S. officials said insurgents shot at the Marines and may have caused some of the civilian casualties. But a U.S. investigation of the incident concluded that the Marines' response was "out of proportion to the threat that was immediately there." Lieutenant Colonel Paul Montanus, commander of 2nd Marine Special Operations Battalion, after consultation with Major General Dennis Hejlik, MARSOC commander, pulled the Marine company out of Afghanistan days after the incident. He had "lost trust and confidence in the MARSOC leadership" in Afghanistan.[22] The U.S. military formally apologized, telling the families of the victims that they were "deeply, deeply ashamed" about the incident and describing it as a "terrible, terrible mistake."[23] The local response was swift and intense. Angry demonstrations erupted in Nangarhar and other provinces, with locals chanting antigovernment and anti-American slogans.

On August 22, 2008, U.S. and Afghan forces in the Shindand district of Herat Province were ambushed during an operation against a Taliban commander named Mullah Sidiq, who was planning to attack a nearby American base. Pinned down under small-arms fire and rocket-propelled grenades, U.S. Special Forces engaged Taliban forces with small-arms fire, crew-served weapons, and close air support. Just after midnight, an AC-130H Spectre gunship opened fire with 20-millimeter guns and 105-millimeter howitzers on several compounds that were believed to house a large contingent of Taliban. But the airstrikes also killed civilians. The U.S. military initially reported that only seven civilians were killed in the attack while the strikes killed nearly three dozen Taliban insurgents, including Mullah Sidiq.[24]

A United Nations report on the incident, however, claimed that ninety civilians had been killed, including sixty children, fifteen women, and fifteen men.[25] The Afghan Ministry of Interior released a statement blaming the United States and announcing that "seventy-six civilians, most of them women and children, were martyred today in a coalition force operation in Herat Province."[26] President Karzai, who rarely left the Presidential Palace in Kabul, made an unprecedented trip to Shindand and "strongly condemned the unilateral operation of the Coalition Forces in Shindand district of Herat Province."[27] On August 25, Karzai held an emotional meeting at the palace in which cabinet members vented about the U.S. actions. That same day, Karzai held a meeting with approximately fifty legislators, including speaker Yunus Qanooni, who harshly criticized the attack and pressed Karzai to condemn the U.S. actions.

American officials, including U.S. Ambassador to Afghanistan William Wood, complained that these were cursory assessments and that there was no physical evidence to support the higher death tolls. They said that the UN and Afghan reports had relied on the word of villagers who either supported or were cowed by Taliban fighters. Ambassador Wood sent a memo to Secretary of Defense Robert Gates prior to his September visit to Afghanistan, warning that President Karzai would express his outrage to Gates and would push for rethinking "the proportionality of air strikes, U.S. coordination with Afghan security forces, the violation of Afghan homes during night raids on residential compounds, and the detention of Afghans without prior approval of the government."[28] A subsequent U.S. military investigation, led by Brigadier General Michael Callan of the U.S. Air Force, concluded that thirty-three civilians had died, not the seven that U.S. commanders had initially announced. The report concluded that the United Nations, Afghan government, and other assessments were wrong because they relied primarily on "villager statements, limited forensics, and no access to a multi-disciplined intelligence architecture."[29]

Regardless of what the actual number was, the attack had a searing impact on Afghans, who grew increasingly angry about the civilian casualties caused by U.S. airstrikes. An assessment for U.S. Central Command said American credibility had dropped "sharply" and found "that civilian casualties and security are strongly linked to attitudes to the U.S. military."[30] And an opinion poll in 2008 found that 40 percent of Afghans who sympathized with the Taliban were at least partly motivated by resentment about civilian casualties from NATO airstrikes.[31] In a war over the hearts and minds of Afghans, civilian casualties undermined the gains made with infrastructure and other projects and increasingly pushed locals toward the Taliban and other insurgent groups.

A Regional War

In 2008, U.S. military data showed a stark increase in violence from 2007 levels. There was a 32 percent increase in insurgent-related violence, a 25 percent increase in attacks from improvised explosive devices, a 56 percent increase in kidnappings and assassinations, and a 300 percent increase in attacks on district centers. In addition, violence was up in several provinces, such as Helmand and Wardak, and along major highways. Highway 4, which connects Kandahar City and Spin Boldak, experienced a 400 percent spike in violence.[32] A leaked 2008 United Nations security report showed that insurgent violence had increased that year to the highest levels since the U.S. invasion in 2001.[33] Afghan National Police and Afghan civilians took the brunt of insurgent attacks. Between January 2007 and July 2008, nearly two-thirds of the security forces killed were Afghan National Police, rather than Afghan National Army or Coalition forces.[34]

The Taliban and other insurgent groups also conducted a number of audacious attacks against U.S. and other NATO forces. On July 13, about 200 militants raided a U.S. base in Nuristan Province, using machine guns, crew-served weapons, rocket-propelled grenades, and mortars. They breached the walls of the base before eventually being driven back by U.S. forces, but the defense required the support from AH-64 Apache helicopters, a Predator drone with Hellfire missiles, and eventually B-1B, A-10, and F-15s. Afghan and U.S. reports indicated that the militants received assistance from locals in the village of Wanat, as well as the district governor, Zul Rachman. As a U.S. Army after-action report concluded, "post-attack intelligence indicates that both the District Police Chief and District Governor were complicit in supporting the AAF [Anti-Afghan Force] attack."[35]

On August 18, the Taliban ambushed a French patrol east of Kabul, killing ten French soldiers and wounding another twenty-one. A NATO after-action report found that "the French platoon had only one radio," making it difficult to call for air support, and the Afghan National Army "performed very poorly. . . . The ANA force spent much of the time lounging on the battlefield. When they finally dispersed, most left their military equipment [including] weapons, ID cards, and other items for the enemy."[36] The French soldiers' bodies were not recovered until the following day; and insurgents had stripped most of the bodies and taken their equipment.

The irony of even the limited U.S. progress was that while such forces as the 82nd and 101st Airborne Divisions had made great gains in counterinsurgency actions, they were hamstrung by militant groups crossing the border on a daily basis. "The problem," one military intelligence officer candidly noted, is obvious: "We recognize the border. They don't."[37]

What had started out as a U.S.-led war in Afghanistan developed into a regional insurgency. In nuclear-armed Pakistan, militant groups were destabilizing the North West Frontier Province, the Federally Administered Tribal Areas, Baluchistan Province, and urban areas. The U.S. ambassador to Pakistan, Anne Patterson, circulated a memo in early 2008 warning that "militant extremists in Pakistan have sharply increased attacks, both in tribal areas along the Pak-Afghan border and into settled areas." These attacks were "undermining regional stability and effective prosecution of the war on terror by Coalition Forces in Afghanistan," and the Pakistan military was "hindered by significant capability gaps and fears of civilian casualties, which could undercut already weak public support for offensive operations."[38] Consequently, some U.S. officials advocated overhauling U.S. assistance to Pakistan and called for providing additional airmobile capacity, combat logistics and sustainment, counter-IED capability, and night operations.

But America's biggest challenge was impacting the *will* of Pakistan's security agencies. Efforts to bolster Pakistani security capabilities were significantly undermined by the political and security chaos in Pakistan. Pervez Musharraf, who had established a close relationship with Washington, resigned from the presidency on August 18, 2008, in the midst of impeachment proceedings. And a weak civilian government led by Asif Ali Zardari, widower of the assassinated presidential candidate Benazir Bhutto, tried to pick up the pieces.

In the fall of 2008, the government of Pakistan shuffled its way to the brink with a severe balance-of-payments crisis. The new civilian government, reluctant to jeopardize its popularity, maintained price controls on food and fuel, financing the difference from the budget. Pakistan's trade deficit widened alarmingly because of higher global oil prices. The capital market upheavals on Wall Street triggered a flight toward less risky assets, and Pakistani and foreign investors fled the rupee. In its 2008 *Monetary Policy Statement,* the State Bank of Pakistan noted that government borrowing from the central bank— which it had earlier described as having reached "alarming levels" during 2007 and 2008—was "unsustainable." The State Bank also concluded that inflationary pressures were "alarming," and inflation continued to be stoked by "aggregate demand pressures" and a "fall in the productive capacity of the economy."[39]

On September 9, Pakistan Army and Frontier Corps forces, supported by aerial bombing sorties, conducted operations in the Bajaur Agency and Swat district against several militant groups, including Tehreek-e-Nafaz-e-Shariat-e-Mohammadi. The effort was code-named Operation Sher Dil. They were met with staunch resistance from heavily armed militants reinforced by fighters who had come from Afghanistan. The conflict triggered significant population displacement within Pakistan, and some residents even fled to Afghanistan. The U.S. Agency for International Development's Office of Transition Initiatives provided humanitarian relief, delivering nonfood items and engaging in reconstruction once the fighting stopped. USAID was also involved in governance and development projects in Pakistan's tribal areas, including Bajaur. But as one senior State Department official remarked, "Pakistan has not employed a clear, hold, build counterinsurgency strategy," making sustained reconstruction work virtually impossible.[40]

On September 20, a truck bomb exploded outside the Marriott Hotel in Islamabad, killing more than fifty people, including two Americans. It left a crater forty feet wide and twenty-five feet deep, mangling cars and charring trees in the blast zone. "All roads lead to FATA," said Interior Minister Rehman Malik, explaining where the terrorists came from.[41] The Marriott bombing damaged a nearby office building (the Evacuee Trust Complex, also known as Software Technology Park 2), which housed local offices of American and multinational information-technology companies, including Microsoft, Cisco Systems, Motorola, and Kestral (the local representative of Lockheed Martin).

Escalation Among "Allies"

American and Pakistani forces engaged in several firefights in 2008, escalating tensions along the border—often referred to as the "zero line" by U.S. military and CIA forces. During a June 10 firefight, U.S. forces killed about a dozen Pakistani Frontier Corps soldiers who were targeting them. One villager from Suran Dara, a few hundred yards from the fighting on the Pakistan side, remarked: "When the Americans started bombing the Taliban, the Frontier Corps started shooting at the Americans. . . . They were trying to help the Taliban. And then the American planes bombed the Pakistani post."[42]

On July 29, NATO, Afghan, and Pakistani military commanders met at Nawa Pass in eastern Afghanistan to discuss cross-border issues. Afghanistan's border police central-zone commander, Colonel Qadir-Gul, represented the Afghan side; Brigadier General Adamcyn Khan and Lieutenant Colonel Ahmed headed the Pakistani delegation. According to a senior NATO official involved in the meeting, "the Pakistanis wanted to recuperate their weapons and equipment," which they claimed had been taken from their border posts during a firefight a few months earlier. During the fighting, the Frontier Corps had abandoned several positions along the border to insurgents, who then directed fire against Afghan forces. The Afghans counterattacked and seized the border posts, occupying the positions for seventy-two hours before Afghan and Pakistani commanders could negotiate their withdrawal. In a provocative move, Afghan troops then posed for the press with the captured equipment. But the July 29 meeting degenerated into finger-pointing. As the NATO official remarked, "sentiment on both sides of the Durand Line is coloring border units' ability to cooperate. Afghan claims that Pakistani units are complicit in cross-border attacks and have undermined the two sides' relationship." Part of the problem was that Afghan and Pakistani officials disagreed about the exact location of the border. "The Durand Line underlies much of the argument; the two sides will not openly disagree about where territory lies, but appear to be under orders not to concede anything."[43]

A defining moment for U.S.-Pakistan relations came in late July 2008, following the July 7 bombing of the Indian Embassy in Kabul. U.S. intelligence assessments, which were based on intercepted communications, concluded that ISI agents were involved in planning the attack, which killed fifty-four people, including an Indian defense attaché.[44] The attack destroyed the embassy's protective blast walls and front gates and tore into civilians waiting outside for visas.

After being briefed on the situation by U.S. intelligence officials, President Bush lost his temper. He approved orders that allowed U.S. Special Operations Forces to conduct ground operations in Pakistan without the approval of Pakistan's weak civilian government or the ISI. "We had no other option," said a senior White House official I interviewed. "A range of high-value targets were operating at will in Pakistan, and conducting attacks in Afghanistan and Pakistan. Security in Afghanistan and Pakistan, as well as at home in the United States, was in serious jeopardy."[45]

In early September, U.S. Navy SEALs working for a Joint Special Operations Command task force, supported by AC-130 Spectre gunships, launched a ground assault from Afghanistan into South Waziristan against members of al Qa'ida and the Haqqani network. These and other cross-border U.S. attacks raised the ire of Pakistani officials. General Ashfaq Parvez Kayani, Pakistan's chief of army staff, responded that the "right to conduct operations against the militants inside our own territory is solely the responsibility of the [Pakistani] armed forces."[46] President Zardari and Prime Minister Yousuf Raza Gilani supported Kayani's statement, as did the Pakistani press. The English-language *Daily Times* front page ran side-by-side headlines: "Boots on Ground: Bush" and "No Way, Says Kayani."

Between June 20 and July 20, 2008, there had been more than sixty insurgent attacks against Afghan or Coalition forces along the Paktika and Khowst border with North and South Waziristan. There were also twenty attacks along the Kunar and Nangarhar border with Pakistan's Bajaur, Mohmand, and Khyber Agencies.[47] On September 25, U.S. OH-58 Kiowa helicopters flying near the Afghanistan-Pakistan border came under small-arms fire from a Pakistani military checkpoint near Tanai district in Khowst Province. A ground-based American patrol then returned fire with the checkpoint. What had begun in September 2001 as a U.S.-led war in Afghanistan had gradually transitioned into a regional struggle involving the United States and all major countries in the region. The Great Game was alive and well.

CHAPTER EIGHTEEN

Back to the Future

JUST SOUTH OF KABUL, nestled on the western slope of the jagged Sher-i-Darwaza mountain, lies a series of serene walled gardens built in the mid-sixteenth century by the first Mughal emperor, Babur. Among the dozen or so gardens that he built around Kabul, this was his favorite, and he chose it as his final resting place. The layout is rectangular, with a system of pools, channels, and distinctive waterfalls. The main entrance to the gardens from the Sarak-e-Chilsitun road leads to a gentle climb up the mountainside that becomes noticeably steeper near the eastern cusp of the gardens. The gardens fell into disrepair during the decline of the Mughal Empire in the eighteenth century, and over the next several centuries they went through several cycles of decrepitude and rehabilitation.

During the Afghan civil war in the early 1990s, the gardens served as a temporary refuge for civilians fleeing the fighting. Most of the trees in the gardens were either destroyed by the rain of rockets or cut down and used for firewood. The pavilion, built for the entertainment of royal guests, was looted in 1993. So was the *Harmesarai* (Royal Residence), which was burned and left cluttered with unexploded ordnance. Bullet holes are still visible in several of the remaining trees and buildings, which look like pockmarks from Afghanistan's violent past.

Yet the gardens have demonstrated an almost surreal ability to regenerate. With the aid of the Aga Khan Trust for Culture and other donors, the gardens experienced a rebirth after the 2001 overthrow of the Taliban regime. They now include ten terraces that are part of the central axis descending westward toward the Kabul River, which meanders through the city before eventually joining the Indus River in Pakistan. The central axis has been reconstructed after extensive archaeological excavation and research, and water is again flowing down the length of the garden, as it did during Babur's time. Yellow, red, and pink roses welcome visitors near the entrance of the gardens, and an avenue of trees has been planted to provide shade along the terraces of the central axis.

Tucked away on the upper terrace is the tomb of Babur. His body, moved here in 1540, lies next to those of his son Hindal and one of his grandsons. Around 1507, Babur penned the following lines, which illustrate the hardships faced by all Afghans:

> There is no violence or injury of fortune
> That I have not experienced
> This broken heart has endured them all.
> Alas, is there one left that I have not encountered?[1]

Today, Babur's grave lies open to the sky, encircled by a carved marble screen surrounded by fruit trees. Just below the grave is an exquisite mosque layered in marble and built by Babur's successor, Shah Jahan, in the mid-seventeenth century. Shah Jahan's reign proved to be the height of Mughal splendor—his lasting monument is the Taj Mahal—and it is fitting that these two great historical figures left their mark on the gardens of Kabul.

For me, the gardens illustrate serenity and mystique, both literally and symbolically, in the midst of chaos. Their evolution—from destruction to rejuvenation—over the centuries reminds Afghans and foreigners alike that this is an ancient land that has seen terrible bloodshed and revived itself time and again. There is hope that the region will eventually stabilize and prosper, as it did during the first half of the twentieth century. To get there, however, requires completely rethinking America's involvement in the region.

The Tragedy of Afghanistan

The U.S. experience in Afghanistan, like that of the great powers that came before it, will not soon be forgotten. Before launching the 2001 campaign, few Americans had an appreciation for the country's history and subtle complexities, despite the U.S. involvement in the Soviet Union's disastrous defeat in the 1980s. U.S. policymakers had to relearn that building a government in a fractured, xenophobic country is almost infinitely more challenging than overthrowing one.

The rise of the insurgency in the wake of the U.S. victory over the Taliban was deeply unfortunate. But it was not inevitable. Indeed, the irony of the U.S. experience is that some of America's most seasoned diplomats and military commanders in Afghanistan *did* understand the country, but they could not get through to their leaders, who were initially uninterested in nation-building and distracted by Iraq. Zalmay Khalilzad, who had grown up in Afghanistan, and Ronald Neumann, whose first expedition to Afghanistan was in 1967, had a keen appreciation for the historic challenges they faced in Afghanistan. But despite their calls for greater resources and attention, and those of several of their colleagues, such support never came.

In order to restore peace in Afghanistan, we must first understand the causes of war. Afghanistan's insurgency was caused by a supply of disgruntled villagers unhappy with their government, and a demand for recruits by ideologically motivated leaders. Too little outside support for the Afghan government and too much support for insurgents further undermined governance. This combination proved deadly for the onset—and continuation—of the insurgency.

The existence of a weak and ineffective government was a critical precondition to the rise of violence in Afghanistan. In the past, insurgencies have been likely to develop and acquire local support where state control has declined or collapsed. Afghan leaders at all levels failed to provide good governance. National and local officials were unable to manage resources effectively and implement sound policies. In rural areas of the country, such as the southern provinces of

Kandahar and Helmand, there was virtually no improvement in the provision of key services, such as electricity and water, from the Taliban period to the Karzai era.

"Reconstruction efforts" in Afghanistan's violent south, one Provincial Reconstruction Team commander told me, "have largely been relegated to urban areas because security conditions are so dangerous."[2] This created grievances among the local population, who turned to the Taliban and other groups for order and justice. Institutions such as the Afghan National Police were unable to contain a monopoly of violence because of corruption and incompetence, as well as the power of local warlords. Police checkpoints were sometimes used to shake down local Afghans, and they regularly took bribes to allow licit and illicit goods to pass along routes they controlled.

Outside support to the Afghan government was strikingly insufficient as U.S. policymakers began their sojourn into Afghanistan. "I recommended reassuring the Pashtuns that 'nation-building is *not* our key strategic goal,'" acknowledged Under Secretary of Defense Douglas Feith. "Rumsfeld was determined not to do 'nation-building' as the United States typically did it in the 1990s."[3] Indeed, the United States adopted a "light footprint" approach. But they ultimately would be forced to engage in nation-building to save a country that lacked the basic government institutions necessary to prevent a return of the Taliban, al Qa'ida, and other militant groups. But they did it on the cheap. The number of international troops per capita in Afghanistan was significantly less than virtually every nation-building operation since World War II. By 2003, U.S. financial resources that could have been devoted to Afghanistan were going to Iraq, squandering a momentous opportunity.

In addition, insurgents were also able to gain significant assistance from the international jihadi network and neighboring states, such as Pakistan and Iran. In one of his final reports before leaving Afghanistan in 2008 as the European Union's special representative, Francesc Vendrell reflected on his decade in Afghanistan and remarked that "we blinded ourselves to growing evidence that Pakistan, contrary to assurances, was condoning the presence of, and probably providing assistance to, the Taliban in keeping with its old policy of supporting extreme Islamist groups as the best means of installing a pliable government in Kabul." Ironically, Pakistan was not immune to the spreading militancy. "The monster that elements in the ISI . . . intended to send to Afghanistan has turned against Pakistan itself."[4]

Like Babur's gardens, peace in Afghanistan has been cyclical. Despite several decades of war beginning with the Soviet invasion, the reign of Zahir Shah, which lasted from 1933 to 1973, included the longest period of peace and prosperity in Afghanistan's recent history. During that period, the king found a balance between the central government in Kabul and the local tribal officials who mistrusted national leaders. French social scientist Olivier Roy reminds us that the "history of Afghanistan is one of revolts against the central power and of resistance to the penetration of the countryside by state bureaucracy."[5]

Based on these challenges and the country's history, the United States should follow several critical steps to achieve security: It must confront corruption, partner with local (not just national) entities, and undermine the sanctuary in Pakistan. The goal of an effective strategy should be to improve the competence and legitimacy of national and local Afghan institutions to provide security and services to the local population. Success in any counterinsurgency hinges on the support of the local population.

Undermining Corruption

The first step must be to address the massive corruption at the national and local levels, which has steadily alienated the local population and fueled support for insurgent groups. While corruption is endemic in many societies, several forms of corruption appear to have specifically contributed to the Afghan insurgency: drug trafficking, bribery among senior officials, and pervasive extortion among Afghan police and judges. While the central government in Afghanistan has historically been weak, especially in rural areas, it needs to be viewed as legitimate by Afghans. At a bare minimum, Afghans should respect the central government enough that they don't want to overthrow it.

Ironically, corruption was a major undermining factor for Zahir Shah's regime. In a private conversation with Zahir Shah in 1971, U.S. Ambassador Robert Neumann pleaded with the king to fix the "widespread corruption" that was angering the local population. "In my four and one-half years here," Neumann acknowledged, asking forgiveness for his blunt tone, "I had never heard so many expressions at all levels of society about a feeling of hopelessness that [the] new government could accomplish anything."[6]

While there are no universally applicable anticorruption strategies, there are a number of insightful lessons from successful cases in Singapore, Liberia, Botswana, and Estonia. Effective efforts have generally included the immediate firing of corrupt officials, bolstering of the justice system, professionalization of new staff, and incentive and performance assessment programs. Even then, broader reforms have frequently played an important role. In Uganda, for example, Yoweri Museveni's government, which came to power in 1986, implemented a strategy that involved passing economic reforms and deregulation, reforming the civil service, strengthening the auditor general's office, empowering a reputable inspector general to investigate and prosecute corruption, and implementing an anticorruption public-information campaign.

Corrupt Afghan government officials, including those involved in the drug trade, need to be prosecuted and removed from office. Ambassador Thomas Schweich, who served as U.S. coordinator for counternarcotics and justice reform in Afghanistan, revealed that "a lot of intelligence . . . indicated that senior Afghan officials were deeply involved in the narcotics trade. Narco-traffickers were buying off hundreds of police chiefs, judges and other officials. Narco-corruption went to the top of the Afghan government."[7] The United States and other NATO countries also have intelligence on who many of these officials are, though a substantial amount of information is kept at the classified level. Senior officials within the Afghan government have

thus far been unwilling to target government officials involved in corruption, partly because they do not want to alienate powerful political
figures in the midst of an insurgency. President Karzai's efforts to
establish a High Office of Oversight and Anti-Corruption and create
special anticorruption units in the Office of the Attorney General and
in the Judiciary were largely window dressing.

The United States and others in the international community
should encourage Afghan leaders to draft sweeping anticorruption
legislation, arrest and prosecute corrupt officials at the national and
local levels, create inspector general offices in key ministries, provide
support to the justice system (including protecting judges, prosecutors, and witnesses involved in corruption trials), and conduct a
robust public-information campaign. Undermining high-level corruption in Afghanistan is just as much about finding the *political will*
to implement effective anticorruption programs as it is about developing them. And the strategic goal should be a sense of legitimacy
among local Afghans.

Bottom-Up Efforts

A second step is for the United States and other countries to find a
better balance between top-down efforts to build a viable central
government and bottom-up efforts to support local actors. Both are
critical for establishing security and providing public services. Governance in Afghanistan has never been just about the central government. During the reign of Zahir Shah, security was established using
a combination of Afghan national forces—police, intelligence, and
military—and local entities. Much has changed since then. But the
historical weakness of the Afghan state, the local nature of politics,
and a population deeply intolerant of outside forces require that
strong local governance complement national-level efforts. The
United States and its allies have thus far focused almost exclusively on
top-down nation-building efforts to establish a viable central government. There must be a balance between the central and the local to

build a government that can deliver services to its population and protect them with national security forces. Such a task is too much to expect of a weak central government in a tribal society.

One of the most serious problems has been the inability of international and Afghan forces to "hold" territory once it was cleared of insurgent groups. British forces operating in the southern province of Helmand complained that they were simply "mowing the lawn." With insufficient numbers of troops to clear and hold territory, the insurgency seemed to grow back, forcing British soldiers to clear the same territory repeatedly. And they weren't alone. All across Afghanistan, U.S. and other NATO forces repeatedly had to "mow" areas that had been reinfiltrated by insurgents. Part of the answer is to increase the number of international forces, Afghan soldiers, and Afghan police to help clear and hold territory—and to get closer to the ratio of twenty soldiers per thousand inhabitants that has often been considered a minimum troop density for effective counterinsurgency.[8]

Yet tribes, subtribes, and clans have historically played an important role in establishing order in Afghanistan, especially in rural areas where the government's reach is minimal or nonexistent. Unfortunately, there has never been a well-coordinated tribal engagement strategy. Pashtun tribes have historically resolved most disputes through *shuras* and *jirgas*. The rules of dispute resolution, called *narkh*, are unwritten and based on precedent.[9] Bottom-up strategies require supporting and empowering legitimate tribal leaders and providing them with security and aid, since they are bound to be targets of insurgents and criminal networks. International and Afghan national forces can help locals by providing a rapid-reaction force in case tribes come under attack by insurgents. Tribes have also needed assistance in providing services in their areas. In practical terms, this means gaining the support of tribes that have not always supported the government, such as the Alikozai in the south or the Achakzai in the west.

The U.S. reliance on militias to hunt down al Qa'ida terrorists after the overthrow of the Taliban, as well as the effort to build the Afghan National Auxiliary Police, suggest several problems to avoid.

The focus of bottom-up efforts should be on tribal leaders and their *shuras* and *jirgas,* not individuals. The rise of warlords and their private militias has alienated Afghans, since many of these warlords have subsequently terrorized the local population and become involved in criminal activity. A 2008 opinion poll by the Asia Foundation indicated that most Afghans did not trust warlords, and only 4 percent said they would turn to a local warlord to deal with a crime.[10] In addition, assistance should avoid strengthening some tribes over others and thus unnecessarily reigniting tribal rivalries. In general, security in rural areas must come from local Afghan institutions, especially tribal ones, since foreign armies have never succeeded in establishing law and order in Afghanistan. There is little reason to believe the United States will be able to reverse this trend.

Eliminating the Safe Haven

A third step is addressing the sanctuary in Pakistan, which has been fundamental to the success of every successful insurgency and counterinsurgency in Afghanistan's recent history. Mohammad Yousaf, the head of ISI's Afghan Bureau during much of the Soviet war, noted that "a safe haven—a secret base area to which the guerrilla could withdraw to refit and rest without fear of attack" was necessary for winning the insurgency in Afghanistan, and "Pakistan provided the Mujahideen with such a sanctuary."[11] Afghanistan, by reason of its poverty and geography, has always been a weak state at the mercy of its more powerful neighbors, including Pakistan. Unlike during previous periods, however, Pakistan has suffered considerable blowback from its support of proxy organizations like the Taliban after the 2001 U.S. invasion, as the country became infected by an insurgency that spread into its border regions and urban areas. By spring 2009, Deobandi militants successfully pushed into the Swat District of Pakistan, forcing the Pakistan government to negotiate.

Stabilizing Pakistan requires tackling the structural gap that exists in the country's border regions, including the Federally Administered

Tribal Areas. Government institutions in the tribal areas are weak, and social and economic conditions are among the bleakest in the world. Security options will be limited unless the Pakistan government provides tangible benefits to disaffected local communities. Political steps may also be important, including rethinking the Political Parties Act, which regulates the activities of Pakistan's political parties and their members. Under its strictures, the major parties are not authorized to campaign or hold rallies or meetings in the tribal areas. Religious parties thus are at a distinct advantage, since they don't need to conduct "party" gatherings—they have ready access to religious institutions from which they can run their political campaigns and associated political outreach. Though it would require an enormous lobbying effort, it may also be worth integrating the Federally Administered Tribal Areas—which are only nominally controlled by Islamabad—more fully into Pakistan.

While confronting these social, political, and economic challenges is important, any impact will be limited unless there is a focus on Pakistan's strategic interests, which support the use of proxy organizations to help execute its foreign policy in neighboring countries. Pakistan and India follow the political truism outlined by George Kennan, the father of America's containment strategy against the Soviet Union, and academics such as Hans Morgenthau of the University of Chicago. In simple terms, states balance against more powerful ones. As the German-born Morgenthau wrote, the balance of power is a "natural and inevitable outgrowth of the struggle for power" that is "as old as political history itself."[12] Security competition between India and Pakistan, which has triggered several wars and countless skirmishes, creates the impetus for each to check the power of the other. And Afghanistan has served as a key battleground state, much as Poland did for European powers in the eighteenth, nineteenth, and twentieth centuries—a country that historian Norman Davies referred to as "God's playground."[13]

After September 11, 2001, senior U.S. policymakers—such as Secretary of State Colin Powell, Deputy Secretary of State Richard Armitage, and U.S. Ambassador to Pakistan Wendy Chamberlin—presented then-President Pervez Musharraf with a stark choice: Support the United States *or* militant groups. There was no middle ground. This choice put Musharraf in a difficult position, since it meant overthrowing the very Taliban government that Pakistan had painstakingly supported for nearly a decade. But the combination of blunt threats and promises of economic assistance altered Musharraf's cost-benefit calculation. By 2002, however, the United States quickly lost interest in the Taliban, who fled to Pakistan, deferring to Islamabad. Instead, the United States fixated first on al Qa'ida in Pakistan and then on prosecuting the war in Iraq. Ironically, the United States continued to give substantial amounts of assistance to Pakistan, even as individuals in the ISI, the Frontier Corps, and other organizations provided support to militant groups such as the Taliban and the Haqqani network, who were attacking U.S. forces in Afghanistan.

Pakistan has historically used militant groups operating in Kashmir, India, and Afghanistan to pursue its interests. It has legitimate security interests in its region, and its key neighbors—India and Afghanistan—have frequently shown resolute disinterest in accommodating Pakistan's security concerns. Until the appointment of U.S. regional envoy Richard Holbrooke in 2009, the United States demonstrated little inclination to promote regional solutions that would help resolve Pakistan's territorial tensions with its neighbors. This was unfortunate, since Musharraf had agreed to cooperate with the United States because he believed America would help protect its regional interests. After joining hands with Washington, most of Pakistan's key security challenges worsened rather than improved, long after Musharraf left office.

Pakistan's security interests, however, do not justify the use of militant proxies. It is imperative that the United States persuade Pakistani military and civilian leaders to conduct a sustained campaign against militants mounting attacks in Afghanistan and the region (including India), plotting attacks in the United States and European capitals, and, most important, threatening the foundation of the nuclear-armed Pakistani state. This requires that Washington identify pressure points that raise the costs of stalling. Perhaps the most significant is tying current assistance to cooperation. Since the United States annually gives Pakistan more than $1 billion in military and economic assistance, it could link assistance to achieving specific benchmarks in targeting key groups such as Mullah Omar's Taliban, the Haqqani network, and al Qa'ida.

In addition, Washington needs to make a concerted effort to engage both Pakistan and India, which have competing interests in Afghanistan. Transforming regional security perceptions among the Afghans, Pakistanis, and Indians has always been a monumental challenge, especially in light of such events as the November 2008 terrorist attacks in India's financial hub, Mumbai, which were perpetrated by militants operating from Pakistani soil and tied to the Pakistani group Lashkar-e-Taiba. But regional cooperation constitutes the only way to stabilize and secure Afghanistan so that it does not again become a terrorist sanctuary. Otherwise, the Afghan population will continue to pay a heavy price for the conflict between New Delhi and Islamabad, on the one hand, and Kabul and Islamabad, on the other.

Paradise on Earth?

In Babur's gardens, the inscription on his tomb serves as a source of inspiration for those who pay tribute: "If there is a paradise on earth, it is this, it is this, it is this!" Afghanistan can be deceptive. It has a beautiful, dramatic landscape with villages and district centers that look much as they did hundreds of years ago, untouched by modern technology. But the country has also been a quagmire for invading armies, which have torn the country apart even as they wasted themselves in the high mountain sands.

On the outskirts of Kabul, in an area called Asmai Heights, lies the Kabre Ghora graveyard, which was established by British forces during the second Anglo-Afghan War. The name is taken from the term used by Afghans to describe British soldiers (*ghora*), and the cemetery is believed to contain the graves of 158 British soldiers, diplomats, and their families who died in the city during the occupations of 1839–1842 and 1879–1880. The original British gravestones have mostly disappeared, leaving only the remnants of ten grave markers, now relocated against the southern wall of the cemetery. But a new memorial has been erected and new names have been added, honoring soldiers from the United States, Canada, and Europe who have died here from 2001 to the present day.

Perhaps the most extraordinary thing about Afghanistan is its continuity. The NATO memorial may be brand new, but soon it will feel as ancient and totemic as the British graveyard, another artifact from empires past. Like the gardens of Babur, Afghans have shown an uncanny ability to regenerate. Time has a rather curious way of slowing down here. "You have the watches," one Taliban detainee told his American interrogators, "but we have the time."[14] Most Afghans have never asked for much. They have longed for security and hope, and perhaps something to make their difficult lives more bearable. After decades of constant war, they deserve it.

ACKNOWLEDGMENTS

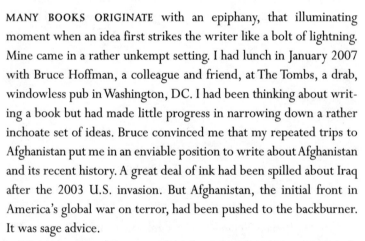

MANY BOOKS ORIGINATE with an epiphany, that illuminating moment when an idea first strikes the writer like a bolt of lightning. Mine came in a rather unkempt setting. I had lunch in January 2007 with Bruce Hoffman, a colleague and friend, at The Tombs, a drab, windowless pub in Washington, DC. I had been thinking about writing a book but had made little progress in narrowing down a rather inchoate set of ideas. Bruce convinced me that my repeated trips to Afghanistan put me in an enviable position to write about Afghanistan and its recent history. A great deal of ink had been spilled about Iraq after the 2003 U.S. invasion. But Afghanistan, the initial front in America's global war on terror, had been pushed to the backburner. It was sage advice.

Writing any book is a struggle, what John Mearsheimer, my graduate school adviser, likened to getting up every day and wrestling with a bear. This book was no different. But the process was facilitated by the kindness and help of countless individuals. Several read drafts of the manuscript and provided excellent comments, including Peter Bergen, Daniel Byman, James Dobbins, Bruce Hoffman, Arturo Munoz, Ronald Neumann, David Phillips, and Obaid Younossi. Several others served as explicit or implicit tutors on Afghanistan, Pakistan, and their respective histories, especially Barnett Rubin and Ahmed Rashid. Still others were helpful in broader discussions on counterinsurgency, including Austin Long, Christine Fair, Steve Hosmer, William Rosenau, and John Gordon. And Peter Crowley educated me on the finer points of Alexander the Great's incursion into Afghanistan.

Several key people served behind the scenes but had extraordinary input in the book. One of the most significant was Tom Mayer, my editor, who put the manuscript through a grist mill and turned the research and ideas into something digestible. My agent, Eric Lupfer, was patient, tirelessly helpful, and excited from the beginning about the book. Kathleen Brandes copyedited the book from her perch in Spruce Head, Maine, not far from my undergraduate alma mater. Don Rifkin and Devon Zahn gave the book careful attention and should be applauded for getting this complicated project done under tight deadlines. My assistants, Nathan Chandler and Joya Laha, were extraordinarily helpful throughout the research, writing, and editing phases.

The book would not have been possible without the ability to interview a range of policymakers, including Secretary of State Colin Powell, Deputy Secretary of State Richard Armitage, Comptroller and Under Secretary of Defense Dov Zakheim, Under Secretary of Defense for Policy Douglas Feith, U.S. Ambassador to Pakistan Wendy Chamberlin, CIA Station Chief in Islamabad Robert Grenier, CIA Station Chief in Afghanistan Graham Fuller, commander of U.S. forces in Afghanistan Lieutenant General Karl Eikenberry, U.S. Ambassador to Afghanistan Ronald Neumann, U.S. Ambassador to Afghanistan Zalmay Khalilzad, commander of U.S. forces in Afghanistan Lieutenant General David Barno, and countless others. I also owe a debt of gratitude to those Afghanistan officials that I interviewed—such as Foreign Minister Abdullah Abdullah, Minister of Interior Ali Jalali, and Afghan Ambassador to the United States Said Jawad—who worked tirelessly for their country during such trying times.

One of the most fruitful parts of the book was presenting drafts and ideas to a range of academic and U.S. government audiences, as well as those from foreign countries and international organizations. Within the United States, I gave presentations to audiences at the

Massachusetts Institute of Technology, Georgetown University, New York University, Heritage Foundation, Naval Postgraduate School's Center for Homeland Defense and Security, RAND Corporation, and George Washington University. Students in my summer 2008 Georgetown University course on counterinsurgency were particularly helpful in pointing out problems with the manuscript.

I would also like to thank those individuals who gave me their precious time and energy from the U.S. Department of Defense, State Department, Federal Bureau of Investigation, White House, and U.S. intelligence community. Others from Canada, the Netherlands, Germany, Italy, United Kingdom, Pakistan, India, United Nations, European Union, and NATO were also generous with their time and knowledge. Many requested that I not thank them by name, so they remain anonymous.

Finally, I would like to thank my family. My parents (Alec and Sethaly) and three brothers (Alex, Josh, and Clark) have been supportive during the writing process and jumped to my wife's defense whenever I had to travel to Afghanistan or other war-torn places. I owe a particularly heartfelt debt of gratitude to my wife, Suzanne, and daughters, Elizabeth and Alexandra. They have been my daily solace and joy, and I dedicate this book to them.

NOTES

Introduction

1. Central Intelligence Agency, *CIA World Factbook 2007* (Washington, DC: Central Intelligence Agency, 2006).

2. Edward Walsh, "Staff Sgt. Robert J. Paul Killed Sept. 8 in Afghanistan," *The Oregonian*, September 12, 2006, p. B1.

3. Cecilia Rasmussen, "Army Reserve Sgt. 1st Class Merideth Howard, 52, Alameda, Killed in Blast," *Los Angeles Times*, October 1, 2006, p. 14.

4. Alexander Downer, Minister for Foreign Affairs of Australia, Address to the 61st Session of the United Nations General Assembly, September 21, 2006 (New York: Australian Mission to the United Nations, 2006).

5. President Karzai Calls the Terrorist Attack on the Funeral Ceremony of Hakim Taniwal an Animosity Against Islam and the People of Afghanistan (Kabul: Office of the President, Islamic Republic of Afghanistan, September 11, 2006).

6. President George W. Bush, Address to a Joint Session of Congress and the American People, United States Capitol, Washington, DC, September 20, 2001 (Washington, DC: White House Press Office, 2001).

7. David M. Walker, *Global War on Terrorism: Observations on Funding, Costs, and Future Commitments* (Washington, DC: U.S. Government Accountability Office, 2006), p. 7.

8. Central Intelligence Agency, *CIA World Factbook 2007* (Washington, DC: Central Intelligence Agency, 2006). Figures were in purchasing-power parity. Only 27 out of 229 countries had a gross domestic product over $430 billion.

9. Transcript of Combatant Status Review Tribunal Hearing for ISN 10024 (Khalid Sheikh Muhammad), March 10, 2007, U.S. Naval Base Guantánamo Bay, Cuba, pp. 17–18.

10. On the overthrow of the Taliban regime, see Gary Schroen, *First In: An*

Insider's Account of How the CIA Spearheaded the War on Terror in Afghanistan
(New York: Ballantine Books, 2005); Stephen Biddle, *Afghanistan and the
Future of Warfare: Implications for Army and Defense Policy* (Carlisle, PA: Strate-
gic Studies Institute, U.S. Army War College, November 2002); Gary
Berntsen and Ralph Pezzullo, *Jawbreaker: The Attack on Bin Laden and Al Qa'ida*
(New York: Crown Publishers, 2005); Bob Woodward, *Bush at War* (New
York: Simon and Schuster, 2002).

11. Henry A. Crumpton, "Intelligence and War: Afghanistan 2001–2002," Jen-
    nifer E. Sims and Burton Gerber, eds., *Transforming U.S. Intelligence* (Wash-
    ington, DC: Georgetown University Press, 2005), p. 177.

12. Berntsen and Pezzullo, *Jawbreaker*, p. 312.

13. On the definition of insurgency, see Central Intelligence Agency, *Guide to
    the Analysis of Insurgency* (Washington, DC: Central Intelligence Agency,
    n.d.), p. 2; *Department of Defense Dictionary of Military and Associated Terms*,
    Joint Publication 1–02 (Washington, DC: U.S. Department of Defense,
    2001), p. 266.

14. I use *insurgency* as roughly synonymous with what is often called *civil war*,
    which can be defined as "armed conflict that pits the government and
    national army of an internationally recognized state against one or more
    armed opposition groups able to mount effective resistance against the
    state." Michael W. Doyle and Nicholas Sambanis, *Making War and Building
    Peace* (Princeton, NJ: Princeton University Press, 2006), p. 31. Also see,
    for example, Stathis N. Kalyvas, *The Logic of Violence in Civil War* (New York:
    Cambridge University Press, 2006), p. 5; James D. Fearon and David D.
    Laitin, "Ethnicity, Insurgency, and Civil War," *American Political Science
    Review*, vol. 97, no. 1, February 2003, pp. 75–90.

15. RAND-MIPT Terrorism Incident Database. Following are the yearly figures
    on insurgent-initiated attacks in Afghanistan: 2002 (65 attacks); 2003 (148
    attacks); 2004 (146 attacks); 2005 (207 attacks); 2006 (353 attacks). Fol-
    lowing are the fatalities during the same period: 2002 (79 deaths); 2003
    (133 deaths); 2004 (230 deaths); 2005 (288 deaths); 2006 (755 deaths). A
    comparison of the RAND-MIPT data with U.S. and European government
    data shows that the RAND-MIPT data significantly understate the number
    of attacks and deaths, since most improvised-explosive-device and armed
    attacks were never reported in the press. Nevertheless, the trend in the
    RAND-MIPT data is consistent with U.S. and European government data.

16. Pamela Constable, "Gates Visits Kabul, Cites Rise in Cross-Border Attacks,"
    Washington Post, January 17, 2007, p. A10.

17. The data come from Admiral Michael Mullen, Chairman of the Joint Chiefs
    of Staff. See, for example, Ed Johnson, "Gates Wants NATO to Reorganize
    Afghanistan Mission," *Bloomberg News*, December 12, 2007.

18. Sarah Chayes, *The Punishment of Virtue: Inside Afghanistan After the Taliban*
    (New York: Penguin Press, 2006), pp. 105–6.

19. Amrullah Saleh, *Strategy of Insurgents and Terrorists in Afghanistan* (Kabul, Afghanistan: National Directorate of Security, 2006), p. 4.

20. Rudyard Kipling, *Rudyard Kipling's Verse: Inclusive Edition, 1885–1926* (New York: Doubleday, 1931), p. 479.

21. Winston S. Churchill, *The Story of the Malakand Field Force: An Episode of Frontier War*, 2nd ed. (London: Longmans, Green, 1901), p. 274.

22. Ahmed Rashid, *Taliban: Militant Islam, Oil and Fundamentalism in Central Asia* (New Haven, CT: Yale University Press, 2000), p. 13; Barnett R. Rubin, *The Search for Peace in Afghanistan: From Buffer State to Failed State* (New Haven, CT: Yale University Press, 1995), p. 7; Lester Grau, ed., *The Bear Went Over the Mountain: Soviet Combat Tactics in Afghanistan* (Washington, DC: National Defense University Press, 1996), p. xix.

23. Ann Scott Tyson, "British Troops, Taliban in a Tug of War over Afghan Province," *Washington Post*, March 30, 2008, p. A1.

24. General Tommy Franks, *American Soldier* (New York: Regan Books, 2004), p. 324.

25. Author interview with senior U.S. cabinet official, January 15, 2008.

26. United Nations Office on Drugs and Crime, *Afghanistan Opium Survey 2007: Executive Summary* (Kabul: United Nations Office on Drugs and Crime, 2007), p. iv.

27. For other variants of the weak-state argument, see Antonio Giustozzi, *Koran, Kalashnikov, and Laptop: The Neo-Taliban Insurgency in Afghanistan* (London: Hurst & Company, 2007), pp. 7, 15–21.

28. Amartya Sen, *Development as Freedom* (New York: Anchor Books, 2000), p. 11.

29. James Michener, *Caravans* (New York: Fawcett Crest, 1963), p. 7.

30. See, for example, Saleh, *Strategy of Insurgents and Terrorists in Afghanistan*; Afghanistan National Security Council, *National Threat Assessment* (Kabul: Afghanistan National Security Council, 2005); Afghanistan Ministry of Defense, *The National Military Strategy* (Kabul: Afghanistan Ministry of Defense, October 2005).

31. George Crile, *Charlie Wilson's War: The Extraordinary Story of the Largest Covert Operation in History* (New York: Atlantic Monthly Press, 2003), p. 4.

32. Mohammad Yousaf and Mark Adkin, *Afghanistan—The Bear Trap: The Defeat of a Superpower* (Havertown, PA: Casemate, 1992), p. 1.

Chapter One

1. Stephen Tanner, *Afghanistan: A Military History from Alexander the Great to the Fall of the Taliban* (Cambridge, MA: Da Capo Press, 2002), pp. 17–18.

2. Quintus Curtius Rufus, *History of Alexander*, book 2, vol. 6, translated by John C. Rolfe (Cambridge, MA: Harvard University Press, 1946), pp. 25–29.

3. Rufus, *History of Alexander*, book 2, vol. 6, p. 29.

4. Rufus, *History of Alexander*, book 2, vol. 7, p. 147. Also see, for example, Lewis V. Cummings, *Alexander the Great* (Boston: Houghton Mifflin Company, 1940), pp. 280–81.

5. Eric Newby, *A Short Walk in the Hindu Kush* (London: Martin Secker, 1958), p. 243.

6. See, for example, Frank L. Holt, *Into the Land of Bones: Alexander the Great in Afghanistan* (Berkeley, CA: University of California Press, 2005).

7. Marco Polo, *The Travels of Marco Polo*, translated by Ronald Latham (New York: Penguin Books, 1958), p. 77.

8. Sir George Lawrence, *Reminiscences of Forty-Three Years in India* (Lahore, Pakistan: Sang-e-Meel Publications, 1981), pp. 308–9. The appendix includes a copy of William Brydon's account, provided on arrival in Jalalabad in 1842.

9. Holt, *Into the Land of Bones*, p. 4.

10. Holt, *Into the Land of Bones*, pp. 4–5.

11. Author interview with Ambassador Ronald Neumann, April 16, 2008.

12. Rory Stewart, *The Places in Between* (Orlando, FL: Harcourt, 2006).

13. Marco Polo, *Travels of Marco Polo*, p. 80.

14. Author interview with Ambassador Ronald Neumann, March 25, 2008.

15. Henry Kissinger, Memorandum for the President, "Private Conversations with the King and Prime Minister of Afghanistan," January 26, 1970. Released by the National Security Archive.

16. U.S. Department of State, Bureau of Intelligence and Research, Research Study, "Afghanistan: Both Government and Political System Face Trial," March 30, 1973. Also see U.S. Embassy Kabul to Department of State, Airgram A-90, "King Zahir's Experiment: Some End-of-Tour Observations," August 1, 1970. Released by the National Security Archive.

17. U.S. Embassy Kabul to Department of State, Cable 4745, August 2, 1971, "Audience with King Zahir." Released by the National Security Archive.

18. U.S. Embassy Kabul to Department of State, Airgram A-77, "Afghanistan's Clerical Unrest: A Tentative Assessment," June 24, 1970. Released by the National Security Archive.

19. Ambassador Ronald Neumann, Airgram A-90, "King Zahir's Experiment: Some End-of-Tour Observations," August 1, 1970. Released by the National Security Archive.

20. U.S. Embassy Kabul to Department of State, Cable 1806, March 21, 1972, "Afghanistan—Political Uncertainties." Released by the National Security Archive.

21. Department of State to U.S. Embassy Kabul, Cable 74767, April 29, 1972, "Political Situation." Also see, for example, Memorandum from Robert A. Flaten, NEA/PAB (Bureau of Near Eastern Affairs, Office for Pakistan, Afghanistan, and Bangladesh), to Bruce Laingen, Office Director, NEA/

PAB, "Afghan Politics—the Creeping Crisis," May 21, 1972. Released by the National Security Archive.

22. The KGB in Afghanistan—Geographical Volume 1, Vasili Mitrokhin Archive. Released by the Cold War International History Project.

23. U.S. Embassy Kabul to Department of State, Cable 4728, "King Zaher Travel to London for Medical Therapy," June 26, 1973. Released by the National Security Archive.

24. Memorandum, Harold H. Saunders and Henry A. Appelbaum, National Security Council Staff, to Dr. Kissinger, "Coup in Afghanistan," July 17, 1973. Released by the National Security Archive.

25. Author interview with Graham Fuller, August 19, 2008.

26. Decree of the Secretariat of the CC CPSU—An Appeal to the Leaders of the PDPA Groups "Parcham" and "Khalq," January 8, 1974; CC CPSU Information for the Leaders of the Progressive Afghan Political Organizations "Parcham" and "Khalq" Concerning the Results of the Visit of Mohammed Daud to the USSR, June 21, 1974. Released by the Cold War International History Project.

27. Barnett R. Rubin, *The Fragmentation of Afghanistan: State Formation and Collapse in the International System*, 2nd ed. (New Haven, CT: Yale University Press, 2002), p. 115.

28. The Delivery of Special Equipment to the DRA, CC CPSU Politburo meeting, April 21, 1978. Released by the Cold War International History Project.

29. Author interview with Graham Fuller, August 19, 2008.

30. Quoted in David B. Edwards, *Before Taliban: Genealogies of the Afghan Jihad* (Berkeley, CA: University of California Press, 2002), p. 36.

31. Alexander Lyakhovskiy, *Plamya Afgana* (Moscow: Iskon, 1999). Released by the Cold War International History Project.

32. Eric Pace, "Babrak Karmal, Afghanistan's Ex-President, Dies at 67," *New York Times*, December 6, 1996.

33. Anatoly Dobrynin, *In Confidence: Moscow's Ambassador to America's Six Cold War Presidents (1962–1986)* (New York: Times Books, 1995), p. 435.

34. Zbigniew Brzezinski, *Power and Principle: Memoirs of the National Security Adviser, 1977–1981* (New York: Farrar, Straus and Giroux, 1983), p. 413.

35. CC CPSU Politburo Session March 17–18, 1979, Deterioration of Conditions in the Democratic Republic of Afghanistan and Possible Responses from Our Side. Released by the National Security Archive.

36. Transcript of Telephone Conversation between Soviet Premier Alexei Kosygin and Afghan Prime Minister Nur Mohammad Taraki, March 18, 1979; Conversation of the chief of the Soviet military advisory group in Afghanistan, Lt. Gen. Gorelov, with H. Amin, August 11, 1979. Released by the Cold War International History Project.

37. Transcript of A. N. Kosygin–A. A. Gromyko–D. F. Ustinov–B. N. Pono-marev–N. M. Taraki Conversation on March 20, 1979. Released by the National Security Archive.

38. CPSU CC Politburo Decision and Instruction to Soviet Ambassador in Afghanistan, May 24, 1979. Released by the Cold War International History Project.

39. Excerpt from Politburo meeting, March 18, 1979. Released by the Cold War International History Project.

40. Tanner, *Afghanistan*, pp. 231–32.

41. Andropov–Gromyko–Ustinov–Ponomarev Report to CC CPSU on the Situation in Afghanistan, June 28, 1979. Released by the Cold War International History Project.

42. On the Soviet Union's dossier on Amin, see Alexander Lyakhovskiy, *Plamya Afgana*.

43. Andropov–Gromyko–Ustinov–Ponomarev Report to the CC CPSU on the Situation in Afghanistan, October 29, 1979. Released by the National Security Archive.

44. Dobrynin, *In Confidence*, p. 436. Personal Memorandum from Andropov to Brezhnev, December 1, 1979. Released by the Cold War International History Project.

45. Author interview with Graham Fuller, August 19, 2008.

46. Alexander Lyakhovskiy's account of the meeting from Alexander Lya-khovskiy, *The Tragedy and Valor of the Afghani* (Moscow: GPI Iskon, 1995), pp. 109–12. Released by the Cold War International History Project. Lya-khovskiy was a major general in the Russian Army. During the war in Afghanistan, he served as assistant to the commander of the Operative Group of the USSR Defense Ministry.

47. Georgy Kornienko's Account of the Politburo Decision to Send Soviet Troops into Afghanistan, from Georgy M. Kornienko, *The Cold War: Testimony of a Participant* (Moscow: Mezhdunarodnye otnosheniya, 1994). Released by the National Security Archive.

48. Lyakhovskiy, *The Tragedy and Valor of the Afghani*, pp. 109–12.

49. Georgy Kornienko's Account of the Politburo Decision to Send Soviet Troops into Afghanistan.

50. On growing concerns of Islam in Afghanistan, see Soviet Communication to the Hungarian Leadership on the Situation in Afghanistan, March 28, 1979. Released by the Cold War International History Project.

51. Directive No. 312/12/001 of December 24, 1979, signed by Ustinov and Ogarkov, December 24, 1979. U.S. President Jimmy Carter sent a letter to Brezhnev arguing that the Afghan government—especially Amin—had not requested Soviet assistance. On Brezhnev's response, see Reply to an appeal of President Carter about the issue of Afghanistan through the direct

communications channel (Excerpt from the Minutes of the CC CPSU Politburo Meeting, December 29, 1979). Released by the Cold War International History Project.

52. Dobrynin, *In Confidence*, p. 440.

53. Ibid., p. 439.

54. Author interview with Ambassador Ronald Neumann, April 16, 2008.

55. Tanner, *Afghanistan*, pp. 235–36.

56. Christopher Andrew and Vasili Mitrokhin, *The Sword and the Shield: The Mitrokhin Archive and the Secret History of the KGB* (New York: Basic Books, 1999), p. 11. Also see, for example, USSR Ministry of Defense and General Staff Operations Groups in the DRA. Released by the Cold War International History Project.

57. Tanner, *Afghanistan*, p. 237.

58. Brzezinski, *Power and Principle*, p. 427.

59. Robert M. Gates, *From the Shadows: The Ultimate Insider's Story of Five Presidents and How They Won the Cold War* (New York: Simon & Schuster, 1996), pp. 143–45.

60. Gates, *From the Shadows*, pp. 145–46.

61. Brzezinski, *Power and Principle*, p. 427.

62. Gates, *From the Shadows*, pp. 147–48.

63. Rubin, *Fragmentation of Afghanistan*, pp. 104–5.

64. Ibid., p. 121.

Chapter Two

1. Jon Lee Anderson, "American Viceroy: Zalmay Khalilzad's Mission," *The New Yorker*, December 19, 2005, p. 60.

2. See, for example, Albert Wohlstetter, "The Delicate Balance of Terror," *Foreign Affairs*, vol. 37, no. 2, January 1959. A slightly different version of the article was published by RAND as P-1472 in December 1958.

3. University of Chicago, "Ambassador Zalmay M. Khalilzad, PhD '79: President Bush's choice to become the next United States Ambassador to the United Nations," Alumni in the News, 2007.

4. Samuel P. Huntington, *The Clash of Civilizations and the Remaking of World Order* (New York: Simon and Schuster, 1996), pp. 246–48; National Commission on Terrorist Attacks Upon the United States, *The 9/11 Commission Report* (New York: W. W. Norton, 2004), pp. 63–67; 371–74; Ahmed Rashid, *Taliban: Militant Islam, Oil and Fundamentalism in Central Asia* (New Haven, CT: Yale University Press, 2000), pp. 48, 54; *SIPRI Yearbook 1991: World Armaments and Disarmament* (New York: Oxford University Press, 1991), p. 199.

5. Central Intelligence Agency, Directorate of Intelligence, "The Costs of Soviet Involvement in Afghanistan," February 1987, p. 5. Released by the National Security Archive.

6. Rashid, *Taliban*, p. 13; Barnett R. Rubin, *The Search for Peace in Afghanistan: From Buffer State to Failed State* (New Haven, CT: Yale University Press, 1995), p. 7; Lester Grau, ed., *The Bear Went Over the Mountain: Soviet Combat Tactics in Afghanistan* (Washington, DC: National Defense University Press, 1996), p. xix; Mohammad Yousaf and Mark Adkin, *Afghanistan—The Bear Trap: The Defeat of a Superpower* (Havertown, PA: Casemate, 2001), pp. 215–16.

7. Joseph Brodsky, *Sochineniia Iosifa Brodskogo* (Sankt-Peterburg: Pushkinskiĭ fond, 1997), pp. 118–19.

8. Cynthia L. Haven, ed., *Joseph Brodsky: Conversations* (Jackson: University Press of Mississippi), p. 97.

9. Barnett R. Rubin, *The Fragmentation of Afghanistan: State Formation and Collapse in the International System*, 2nd ed. (New Haven, CT: Yale University Press, 2002), pp. 122–23.

10. Central Intelligence Agency, National Foreign Assessment Center, "Afghanistan: Ethnic Diversity and Dissidence," March 1, 1980. Released by the National Security Archive.

11. Defense Intelligence Agency, Directorate for Research, "The Economic Impact of Soviet Involvement in Afghanistan," May 1983. Released by the National Security Archive.

12. Rubin, *Fragmentation of Afghanistan*, p. 130.

13. Central Intelligence Agency, Directorate of Intelligence, "The Soviet Invasion of Afghanistan: Five Years After," May 1985, p. 9. Released by the National Security Archive.

14. Yousaf and Adkin, *Afghanistan—The Bear Trap*, p. 58. On the desertion estimates, see page 57.

15. Stephen Tanner, *Afghanistan: A Military History from Alexander the Great to the Fall of the Taliban* (Cambridge, MA: Da Capo Press, 2002), p. 244.

16. Defense Intelligence Agency, Directorate for Research, "Afghan Resistance," November 5, 1982. Released by the National Security Archive. Also see Session of CC CPSU Politburo, November 13, 1986. Released by the Cold War International History Project.

17. Yousaf and Adkin, *Afghanistan—The Bear Trap*, p. 48.

18. Tanner, *Afghanistan*, p. 239.

19. *Pravda* Correspondent Schedrov's Letter to the CC CPSU on the Situation in Afghanistan, November 12, 1981. Released by the National Security Archive.

20. Report of Military Leaders to D. F. Ustinov, May 10, 1981. Released by the Cold War International History Project.

21. Tanner, *Afghanistan*, p. 248.

22. On a Soviet analysis of Massoud, see, for example, Dossiers of Rebel Field Commanders. Released by the Cold War International History Project.

23. Sebastian Junger, *Fire* (New York: W. W. Norton, 2001), p. 199.

24. On the lethality of the Mi-24s during the Soviet War, see Central Intelligence Agency, Directorate of Intelligence, "The Costs of Soviet Involvement in Afghanistan," February 1987, p. 4. Released by the National Security Archive. Also see Yousaf and Adkin, *Afghanistan—The Bear Trap*, pp. 177–78.

25. Tanner, *Afghanistan*, p. 255; Robert M. Gates, *From the Shadows: The Ultimate Insider's Story of Five Presidents and How They Won the Cold War* (New York: Simon and Schuster, 1996), p. 348.

26. Central Intelligence Agency, Directorate of Intelligence, "The Soviet Invasion of Afghanistan: Five Years After," May 1985, p. 2. Released by the National Security Archive.

27. Sir Morrice James, *Pakistan Chronicle* (Karachi: Oxford University Press, 1993), p. 25.

28. Yousaf and Adkin, *Afghanistan—The Bear Trap*, p. 113.

29. Sean P. Witchell, "Pakistan's ISI: The Invisible Government," *International Journal of Intelligence and Counter-Intelligence*, vol. 16, no. 1, Spring 2003, pp. 374–88.

30. Alexander Lyakhovskiy, *Plamya Afgana* (Moscow: Iskon, 1999). Released by the Cold War International History Project.

31. Yousaf and Adkin, *Afghanistan—The Bear Trap*, p. 40.

32. On the importance of Islamic fundamentalism, see, for example: "Some Ideas About Foreign Policy Results of the 1970s (Points)" of Academician O. Bogomolov of the Institute of the Economy of the World Socialist System, sent to the CC CPSU and the KGB, January 20, 1980. Released by the Cold War International History Project.

33. Yousaf and Adkin, *Afghanistan—The Bear Trap*, p. 117.

34. Milt Bearden and James Risen, *The Main Enemy: The Inside Story of the CIA's Final Showdown with the KGB* (New York: Random House, 2003), pp. 236, 283.

35. Quoted in Steve Coll, *Ghost Wars: The Secret History of the CIA, Afghanistan, and Bin Laden, from the Soviet Invasion to September 10, 2001* (New York: Penguin Press, 2004), p. 120.

36. See, for example, Bearden and Risen, *The Main Enemy*, pp. 236, 281–82.

37. Thomas H. Johnson, "Financing Afghan Terrorism: Thugs, Drugs, and Creative Movement of Money," in Jeanne K. Giraldo and Harold A. Trinkunas, *Terrorism Financing and State Responses: A Comparative Perspective* (Stanford, CA: Stanford University Press, 2007), p. 107.

38. On Soviet information on Hekmatyar, see Dossiers of Alliance–7 Rebel Leaders. Released by the Cold War International History Project.

39. Author interview with Graham Fuller, August 19, 2008.

40. Quoted in Coll, *Ghost Wars*, p. 119.

41. See, for example, Olivier Roy, *Islam and Resistance in Afghanistan*, 2nd ed. (New York: Cambridge University Press, 1986), p. 128.

42. Coll, *Ghost Wars*, p. 17.

43. Yousaf and Adkin, *Afghanistan—The Bear Trap*, p. 1.

44. Grau, ed., *The Bear Went Over the Mountain*; Grau, *Artillery and Counterinsurgency: The Soviet Experience in Afghanistan* (Fort Leavenworth, KS: Foreign Military Studies Office, 1997).

45. Pierre Allan and Albert A. Stahel, "Tribal Guerrilla Warfare Against a Colonial Power," *Journal of Conflict Resolution*, vol. 27, December 1983, pp. 590–617.

46. Central Intelligence Agency, Directorate of Intelligence, "The Soviet Invasion of Afghanistan: Five Years After," May 1985. Released by the National Security Archive.

47. See, for example, Andropov's comments that the situation in Afghanistan is "stabilizing now," in CC CPSU Politburo Transcript, February 7, 1980. Released by the Cold War International History Project.

48. Anatoly Chernyaev's Notes from the Politburo of the CC CPSU Session of October 17, 1985. Released by the National Security Archive.

49. Session of CC CPSU Politburo, November 13, 1986. Released by the Cold War International History Project.

50. Ibid.

51. Colonel Tsagolov's Letter to USSR Minister of Defense Dmitry Yazov on the Situation in Afghanistan, August 13, 1987. Released by the National Security Archive.

52. Minutes of the Politburo of the CC CPSU Session of February 23–26, 1987. Released by the National Security Archive.

53. Tanner, *Afghanistan*, p. 266.

54. Christopher Andrew and Vasili Mitrokhin, *The World Was Going Our Way: The KGB and the Battle for the Third World* (New York: Basic Books, 2005), p. 408.

55. Agreements on the Settlement of the Situation Relating to Afghanistan (Geneva Accords), April 14, 1988.

56. Rashid, *Taliban*, p. 13; Rubin, *Search for Peace in Afghanistan*, p. 7; Grau, ed., *The Bear Went Over the Mountain*, p. xix.

57. Central Intelligence Agency, Directorate of Intelligence, "The Soviet Invasion of Afghanistan: Five Years After," May 1985. Released by the National Security Archive.

58. Rashid, *Taliban*, p. 18; Rubin, *Fragmentation of Afghanistan*, p. 20; Henry S. Bradsher, *Afghanistan and the Soviet Union* (Durham, NC: Duke University Press, 1985), pp. 24–25.

59. George Crile, *Charlie Wilson's War: The Extraordinary Story of the Largest Covert Operation in History* (New York: Atlantic Monthly Press, 2003), p. 262.

60. Gates, *From the Shadows*, pp. 251, 319–21, 348–49. Also see Crile, *Charlie Wilson's War*.

61. Yousaf and Adkin, *Afghanistan—The Bear Trap*, pp. 78–112; Gates, *From the Shadows*, p. 349.

62. Gates, *From the Shadows*, pp. 349–50.

63. Yousaf and Adkin, *Afghanistan—The Bear Trap*, p. 184.

64. Anderson, "American Viceroy: Zalmay Khalilzad's Mission," p. 61.

65. Huntington, *Clash of Civilizations*, pp. 246–48; National Commission on Terrorist Attacks Upon the United States, *The 9/11 Commission Report* (New York: W. W. Norton, 2004), pp. 63–67, 371–74; Rashid, *Taliban*, pp. 48, 54; *SIPRI Yearbook 1991: World Armaments and Disarmament* (New York: Oxford University Press, 1991), p. 199.

66. Session of CC CPSU Politburo, January 28, 1980; Gromyko–Andropov–Ustinov–Ponomarev Report to CC CPSU on the Situation in Afghanistan, January 27, 1980. Released by the Cold War International History Project.

67. Report by Soviet Defense Minister Ustinov to CPSU CC on "Foreign Interference" in Afghanistan, January 2, 1980. Also see Information from the CC CPSU to Erich Honecker, June 21, 1980; Report of Military Leaders to D. F. Ustinov, May 10, 1981. Released by the Cold War International History Project.

68. Intelligence Note Concerning Actions by the US in Aiding the Afghanistan Rebel Fighters, September 1, 1980; A Report by Soviet Military Intelligence, September 1, 1981. Released by the Cold War International History Project.

69. Excerpt from KGB USSR and General Staff Report of December 1982. Released by the National Security Archive.

70. Session of CC CPSU Politburo, November 13, 1986. Released by the Cold War International History Project.

Chapter Three

1. Robert M. Gates, *From the Shadows: The Ultimate Insider's Story of Five Presidents and How They Won the Cold War* (New York: Simon and Schuster, 1996), p. 431.

2. Author interview with Ambassador Robert Oakley, February 1, 2008.

3. Defense Intelligence Agency, Defense Intelligence Appraisal, "Afghanistan: Soviet Withdrawal Scenario," May 9, 1988. Released by the National Security Archive.

4. Central Intelligence Agency, Special National Intelligence Estimate 11/37/88, "USSR: Withdrawal from Afghanistan," March 1988, p. 1. Also see, for example, Central Intelligence Agency, Special National Intelligence Estimate 37-89, "Afghanistan: The War in Perspective," November 1989. Released by the National Security Archive.

5. Zalmay Khalilzad, "Ending the Afghan War," *Washington Post*, January 7, 1990, p. B4.

6. CPSU CC Politburo Decision of January 24, 1989, With Attached Report of January 23, 1989. Released by the Cold War International History Project.

7. Barnett R. Rubin, *The Fragmentation of Afghanistan: State Formation and Collapse in the International System*, 2nd ed. (New Haven, CT: Yale University Press, 2002), p. 179.

8. Rubin, *Fragmentation of Afghanistan*, p. 165.

9. Stephen Tanner, *Afghanistan: A Military History from Alexander the Great to the Fall of the Taliban* (Cambridge, MA: Da Capo Press, 2002), pp. 272–73.

10. Zalmay Khalilzad, *Prospects for the Afghan Interim Government* (Santa Monica, CA: RAND, 1991), pp. v, vi.

11. "Profile: General Rashid Dostum," *BBC News,* September 25, 2001.

12. On the 1988 Geneva Accords, which failed to establish peace in Afghanistan, see Barnett R. Rubin, *The Search for Peace in Afghanistan: From Buffer State to Failed State* (New Haven, CT: Yale University Press, 1995).

13. U.S. Embassy (Islamabad), Cable, "Afghanistan: [Excised] Briefs Ambassador on his Activities. Pleads for Greater Activism by U.N.," August 27, 1997. Released by the National Security Archive.

14. Quoted in Neamatollah Nojumi, "The Rise and Fall of the Taliban," in Robert D. Crews and Amin Tarzi, eds., *The Taliban and the Crisis of Afghanistan* (Cambridge, MA: Harvard University Press, 2008), p. 99.

15. Human Rights Watch, *Human Rights Watch World Report 1993* (New York: Human Rights Watch, 1993).

16. U.S. Department of State, Cable, "Discussing Afghan Policy with the Pakistanis," December 22, 1995. Released by the National Security Archive.

17. Ibid.; U.S. Embassy (Islamabad), Cable, "Afghanistan and Sectarian Violence Contribute to a Souring of Pakistan's Relations with Iran," March 13, 1997. Released by the National Security Archive.

18. U.S. Embassy (Islamabad), Cable, "Afghanistan and Sectarian Violence Contribute to a Souring of Pakistan's Relations with Iran," March 13, 1997. Released by the National Security Archive.

19. U.S. Embassy (Islamabad), Cable, "Afghanistan: Taliban Seem to Have Less Funds and Supplies This Year, But the Problem Does Not Appear to Be that Acute," February 17, 1999. Released by the National Security Archive.

20. U.S. Embassy (Islamabad), Cable, "Afghanistan: Russian Embassy Official Claims Iran Interfering more than Pakistan," November 30, 1995. Released by the National Security Archive.

21. U.S. Intelligence Assessment, [date and title unknown] Mori DocID: 800277, U.S. Central Command. Released by the National Security Archive.

22. U.S. Department of State, Cable, "Discussing Afghan Policy with the Pakistanis," December 22, 1995. Released by the National Security Archive.

23. Ibid.

24. U.S. Department of State, Cable, "A/S Raphel's October 4 Meeting with Assef All on Afghanistan," October 13, 1995. Released by the National Security Archive.

25. U.S. Department of State, Cable, "Discussing Afghan Policy with the Pakistanis," December 22, 1995. Released by the National Security Archive.

26. Khalilzad, *Prospects for the Afghan Interim Government*, p. 2.

27. Author interview with Ambassador Robert Oakley, February 1, 2008.

28. Quoted in Steve Coll, *GhostWars: The Secret History of the CIA, Afghanistan, and Bin Laden, from the Soviet Invasion to September 10, 2001* (New York: Penguin Press, 2004), p. 239.

29. Author interview with Ambassador Robert Oakley, February 1, 2008.

30. Peter R. Blood, ed., *Afghanistan: A Country Study* (Washington, DC: U.S. Government Printing Office, 2001).

31. Rubin, *Search for Peace in Afghanistan*.

32. Mountstuart Elphinstone, *An Account of the Kingdom of Caubul and Its Dependencies in Persia, Tartary, and India* (Graz, Austria: Akademische Druck, 1969), p. 434.

33. Zalmay Khalilzad, "Afghanistan: Time to Reengage," *Washington Post*, October 7, 1996, p. A21.

Chapter Four

1. Central Intelligence Agency, *Biography of Mohammad Omar*, December 21, 1998. Released by the National Security Archive.

2. Gilles Kepel, *Jihad: The Trail of Political Islam* (Cambridge, MA: Harvard University Press, 2002), p. 54.

3. Ahmed Rashid, *Taliban: Militant Islam, Oil and Fundamentalism in Central Asia* (New Haven, CT: Yale University Press, 2000), p. 20.

4. Ayman al-Zawahiri, *Knights Under the Prophet's Banner*, translated by Laura Mansfield (Old Tappan, NJ: TLG Publications, 2002), p. 130.

5. Ayman al-Zawahiri, "Supporting the Palestinians," Statement released June 2006.

6. Osama bin Laden, "Message to the Peoples of Europe," Released November 2007.

7. Olivier Roy, *Islam and Resistance in Afghanistan*, 2nd ed. (New York: Cambridge University Press, 1990), p. 57; Kepel, *Jihad*, p. 58.

8. S. V. R. Nasr, *The Vanguard of the Islamic Revolution: The Jamaat-i Islami of Pakistan* (London: I. B. Tauris, 1994), p. 7. Also see, for example, Syed Abul Ala Maudoodi, *A Short History of the Revivalist Movement in Islam* (Lahore, Pakistan: Islamic Publications, 1972); Sayyid Abūlā'lá Maudūdī, *Al-Jihād fī al-Islām* (Dihlī: Markazī Maktabah-yi Islāmī, 1988).

9. Mariam Abou Zahab and Olivier Roy, *Islamist Networks: The Afghan-Pakistan Connection*, translated by John King (New York: Columbia University Press, 2004), pp. 22–23.

10. Kepel, *Jihad*, pp. 224–25.

11. S. V. R. Nasr, "Islamic Opposition to the Islamic State: The Jama'at-i Islami 1977–1988," *International Journal of Middle East Studies*, vol. 25, no. 2, May 1993, p. 267; Kepel, *Jihad*, pp. 100–1.

12. Jamal Malik, *Colonialization of Islam: Dissolution of Traditional Institutions in Pakistan* (New Delhi: Vanguard Books, 1996).

13. Zahab and Roy, *Islamist Networks*, pp. 22–23.

14. Rashid, *Taliban*, p. 17.

15. Ibid., pp. 22–23.

16. Zahab and Roy, *Islamist Networks*, p. 13.

17. U.S. Embassy (Islamabad), Cable, "Afghanistan and Sectarian Violence Contribute to a Souring of Pakistan's Relations with Iran," March 13, 1997. Released by the National Security Archive.

18. U.S. Embassy (Islamabad), Cable, "Afghanistan: [Excised] Describes Pakistan's Current Thinking," March 9, 1998. Released by the National Security Archive.

19. Abdulkader Sinno, "Explaining the Taliban's Ability to Mobilize the Pashtuns," in Robert D. Crews and Amin Tarzi, eds., *The Taliban and the Crisis of Afghanistan* (Cambridge, MA: Harvard University Press, 2008), pp. 59–89.

20. Jason Burke, *Al-Qa'ida: Casting a Shadow of Terror* (London and New York: I. B. Tauris, 2003), p. 111.

21. Decree Announced by the General Presidency of Amr Bil Maroof Wa Nahi An al-Munkar, Religious Police, Kabul, November 1996.

22. U.S. Embassy (Islamabad), Cable, "Scenesetter for Your Visit to Islamabad: Afghan Angle," January 16, 1997. Released by the National Security Archive. The document was a background note for an upcoming visit of Assistant Secretary of State for South Asia Robin Raphel. The cable summarizes the political and military state of affairs in Afghanistan.

23. Zalmay Khalilzad and Daniel Byman, "Afghanistan: The Consolidation of a Rogue State," *Washington Quarterly*, vol. 23, no. 1, Winter 2000, p. 65.

24. Decree Announced by General Presidency of Amr Bil Maruf, Religious Police, Kabul, December 1996.

25. Privy Council Office (PCO) [Ottawa, Canada] [Released by the U.S. National Security Agency], "IAC Intelligence Assessment—IA 7/96," "Afghanistan: Taliban's Challenges, Regional Concerns, October 18, 1996." Released by the National Security Archive.

26. Rashid, *Taliban*, pp. 68–76.

27. Quoted in Rashid, *Taliban*, p. 50.

28. Ibid., pp. 119–20.

29. Quoted in Ahmed Rashid, *Descent into Chaos: The United States and the Failure of Nation-Building in Pakistan, Afghanistan, and Central Asia* (New York: Viking, 2008), p. 317.

30. U.S. Department of State, Cable, "Osama bin Laden: Taliban Spokesman Seeks New Proposal for Resolving bin Laden Problem," November 28, 1998. Released by the National Security Archive.

31. U.S. Embassy (Islamabad), Cable, "Scenesetter for Your Visit to Islamabad: Afghan Angle," January 16, 1997. Released by the National Security Archive.

32. U.S. Department of State, Cable, "Discussing Afghan Policy with the Pakistanis," December 22, 1995. Released by the National Security Archive.

33. U.S. Embassy (Islamabad), Cable, "Afghanistan: Pakistanis to Regulate Wheat and Fuel Trade to Gain Leverage Over Taliban," August 13, 1997; U.S. Embassy (Islamabad), Cable, "Scenesetter for Your Visit to Islamabad: Afghan Angle," January 16, 1997; U.S. Embassy (Islamabad), Cable, "Afghanistan: [Excised] Briefs Ambassador on his Activities. Pleads for Greater Activism by U.N." August 27, 1997. Released by the National Security Archive.

34. U.S. Embassy (Islamabad), Cable, "Bad News on Pak Afghan Policy: GOP Support for the Taliban Appears to Be Getting Stronger," July 1, 1998. Released by the National Security Archive.

35. U.S. Department of State, From Ron McMullen (Afghanistan Desk), "Developments in Afghanistan," December 5, 1994. Released by the National Security Archive.

36. U.S. Embassy (Islamabad), Cable, "Afghanistan: [Excised] Criticizes GOP's Afghan Policy; Says It Is Letting Policy Drift," June 16, 1998. Released by the National Security Archive.

37. From [Excised] to DIA, Washington, DC, Cable, "Pakistan Interservice Intelligence/Pakistan (PK) Directorate Supplying the Taliban Forces," October 22, 1996. Released by the National Security Archive.

38. Ibid.; U.S. Consulate (Peshawar), Cable, "Afghan-Pak Border Relations at Torkham Tense," October 2, 1996. Released by the National Security Archive.

39. Declan Walsh, "As Taliban Insurgency Gains Strength and Sophistication, Suspicion Falls on Pakistan," The Guardian, November 13, 2006.

40. Zahab and Roy, Islamist Networks, pp. 55–56.

41. U.S. Department of State, Cable, From Ron McMullen (Afghanistan Desk), "Developments in Afghanistan," December 5, 1994. Released by the National Security Archive.

42. U.S. Department of State, Action Cable from Karl F. Inderfurth to Embassy, Islamabad, "Pakistan Support for Taliban," September 26, 2000. Released by the National Security Archive.

43. From [Excised] to DIA, Washington, DC, "IIR [Excised] Pakistan Involvement in Afghanistan," November 7, 1996. Released by the National Security Archive.

44. U.S. Embassy (Islamabad), Cable, "Bad News on Pak Afghan Policy: GOP Support for the Taliban Appears to Be Getting Stronger," July 1, 1998. Released by the National Security Archive.

45. US Mission to the UN (USUN New York), Cable, "Letter of GOP Permrep to SYG on Afghanistan," November 1, 1995; U.S. Embassy (Islamabad), Cable, "Afghanistan: Taliban Seem to Have Less Funds and Supplies This Year, But the Problem Does Not Appear to Be that Acute," February 17, 1999; U.S. Embassy (Islamabad), Cable, "In Bilateral Focussed [sic] on Afghanistan, GOP Reviews Pak/Iran Effort; A/S Inderfurth Expresses U.S. Concerns About the Taliban," July 23, 1998. Released by the National Security Archive.

46. U.S. Embassy (Islamabad), Cable, "Afghanistan: Foreign Secretary Mulls over Afghanistan," October 10, 1996. Released by the National Security Archive.

47. The report indicated that the ISI provided at least $30,000—and possibly as much as $60,000—per month to Harakat ul-Ansar. Central Intelligence Agency, "Harakat ul-Ansar: Increasing Threat to Western and Pakistani Interests," August 1996. Also see, for example, U.S. Embassy (Islamabad), Cable, "Afghanistan: British Journalist Visits Site of Training Camps; HUA Activity Alleged," November 26, 1996; U.S. Embassy (Islamabad), Cable, To Assistant Secretary of State Robin Raphel, "Scenesetter for Your Visit to Islamabad: Afghan Angle," January 16, 1997. Released by the National Security Archive.

48. Ali A. Jalali, "Afghanistan: The Anatomy of an Ongoing Conflict," *Parameters*, vol. XXXI, no. 1, Spring 2001, pp. 86–89.

49. U.S. Embassy (Islamabad), Cable, To Assistant Secretary of State Robin Raphel, "Scenesetter for Your Visit to Islamabad: Afghan Angle," January 16, 1997. Released by the National Security Archive.

50. Rashid, *Taliban*, p. 1.

51. Quoted in Steve Coll, *Ghost Wars: The Secret History of the CIA, Afghanistan, and Bin Laden, from the Soviet Invasion to September 10, 2001* (New York: Penguin Press, 2004), p. 521.

52. Memorandum from Richard A. Clarke to Condoleezza Rice, Subject: Presidential Policy Initiative / Review—The Al-Qida Network, January 25, 2001. Released by the National Security Archive.

53. See, for example, Coll, *Ghost Wars*, pp. 520–21.

54. U.S. Department of State, Cable, "Osama bin Laden: Taliban Spokesman Seeks New Proposal for Resolving bin Laden Problem," November 28, 1998. Released by the National Security Archive.

55. National Commission on Terrorist Attacks Upon the United States, *The 9/11 Commission Report* (New York: W. W. Norton, 2004); Coll, *Ghost Wars*, pp. 327–44, 363–65, 379–86, 400–15.

Chapter Five

1. See, for example, Neil MacFarquhar, "Tapes Offer a Look Beneath the Surface of Bin Laden and Al Qaeda," *New York Times*, September 11, 2008.

2. Ayman al-Zawahiri, *Knights Under the Prophet's Banner*, translated by Laura Mansfield (Old Tappan, NJ: TLG Publications, 2002), p. 23.

3. Ibid., p. 38.

4. Gilles Kepel, *Jihad: The Trail of Political Islam* (Cambridge, MA: Harvard University Press, 2002), pp. 61–80.

5. Chris Suellentrop, "Abdullah Azzam: The Godfather of Jihad," *Slate*, April 16, 2002.

6. Quoted in Kepel, *Jihad*, p. 145.

7. Abdullah Anas, *The Birth of the Afghan Arabs* (London: Dar al-Saqi, 2002), p. 36; Mohammed Salah, *Narratives of the Jihad Years: The Journey of the Arab Afghans* (Cairo, 2001), pp. 43–62, 65–84.

8. Weekly Compilation of Presidential Documents (Washington, DC: U.S. Government Printing Office), vol. 16, no. 4, January 28, 1980, pp. 194–96.

9. Zbigniew Brzezinski, *Power and Principle: Memoirs of the National Security Adviser, 1977–1981* (New York: Farrar, Straus and Giroux, 1983), p. 485.

10. On the differences between defensive and offensive jihad, see Alfred Morabia, *Le gihâd dans l'islam médiéval: Le combat sacré des origines au douzième siècle* (Paris: Albin Michel, 1993); Rudolf Peters, *Islam and Colonialism: The Doctrine of Jihad in Modern History* (The Hague: Mouton, 1979); Ramadan al-Bouti, *Le jihad en islam: Comment le comprendre? Comment le pratiquer?* (Damascus: Dar el-Fikr, 1996).

11. Mariam Abou Zahab and Olivier Roy, *Islamist Networks: The Afghan-Pakistan Connection*, translated by John King (New York: Columbia University Press, 2004), pp. 14–15.

12. Imtiaz Hussein, "Usama Prepares a List of Arab Martyrs of Afghan Jihad," *The Frontier Post*, May 13, 2000.

13. Basil Mohammed, *Al-Ansar al-Arab fi Afghanistan* (Jeddah: House of Learning, 1991), p. 241.

14. Peter Bergen, *The Osama bin Laden I Know: An Oral History of Al Qa'ida's Leader* (New York: Free Press, 2006); Lawrence Wright, *The Looming Tower: Al-Qaeda and the Road to 9/11* (New York: Knopf, 2006), p. 133.

15. The quotes are from the exhibit of "Tareekh Osama" (Osama's history), document presented in United States of America v. Enaam M. Arnaout, United States District Court, Northern District of Illinois, Eastern Division.

16. Quoted in Wright, *The Looming Tower*, p. 157.

17. U.S. Department of State Bureau of Intelligence and Research (INR), Intelligence Assessment, "Bin Ladin's Jihad: Political Context," August 28, 1998. Released by the National Security Archive.

18. Kepel, *Jihad*, pp. 213–14.

19. Ibid., pp. 159–84, 237–53, 254–75.

20. Central Intelligence Agency, *Usama bin Ladin: Islamic Extremist Financier*, 1996. Released by the National Security Archive.

21. Central Intelligence Agency, "Harakat ul-Ansar: Increasing Threat to Western and Pakistani Interests," August 1996. Released by the National Security Archive.

22. Zahab and Roy, *Islamist Networks*, pp. 51–52.

23. On conflict between the Taliban and al Qa'ida, see U.S. Embassy (Islamabad), Cable, "TFX01: SITREP 5: Pakistan/Afghanistan Reaction to U.S. Air Strikes," August 24, 1998. Released by the National Security Archive. Also see Fawaz A. Gerges, *The Far Enemy: Why Jihad Went Global* (New York: Cambridge University Press, 2005), p. 83.

24. Gerges, *The Far Enemy*, pp. 38–40; Zahab and Roy, *Islamist Networks*, pp. 48–52.

25. U.S. Department of State, Cable, "Message to the Taliban on Bin Laden," August 23, 1998. Also see, for example, U.S. Embassy (Islamabad), Cable, "Usama Bin Ladin: Bin Ladin Uses Recent Interviews to Assert Right to WMD, and to Threaten U.S. and U.K. Over Iraq," December 28, 1998. Released by the National Security Archive.

26. Laura Mansfield, *His Own Words: A Translation of the Writings of Dr. Ayman al Zawahiri* (Old Tappan, NJ: TLG Publications, 2002), pp. 314–15.

27. Gerges, *The Far Enemy*.

28. "UK's Arabic Paper Interviews bin Laden's Former 'Bodyguard,'" *BBC Monitoring International Reports,* March 30, 2005. "Interview of Bin Ladin's Former Body Guard, Abu Jandal," *Al-Quds al-Arabi* (London), August 25, 2005.

29. Alan Cullison stumbled upon several al Qa'ida computers in Kabul shortly after the overthrow of the Taliban regime. Alan Cullison, "Inside al-Qa'ida's Hard Drive," *Atlantic Monthly*, vol. 294, no. 2, September 2004, p. 67.

30. Sayyid Qutb, *Ma'alim fi-l-Tariq [Milestones]* (Karachi: International Islamic Publishers, 1981).

31. The Qur'an, 5:50.

32. On Qutb's work, see Gilles Kepel, *The Prophet and Pharaoh: Muslim Extremism in Egypt* (Berkeley: University of California Press, 1985); Olivier Carré, *Mystique et politique* (Paris: Presses de la FNSP et Cerf, 1984); Ibrahim M. Abu Rabi, *Intellectual Origins of Islamic Resurgence in the Muslim Arab World* (Albany, NY: SUNY Press, 1996).

33. See, for example, Qutb, *Ma'alim fi-l-Tariq*, p. 57.

34. See, for example, Kepel, *Jihad*, pp. 25–27.

35. Coll, *Ghost Wars*, p. 113.

36. Qutb, *Ma'alim fi-l-Tariq*.

37. The Qur'an, 5:50.

38. Ayman al-Zawahiri, *Knights Under the Prophet's Banner*, translated by Laura Mansfield (Old Tappan, NJ: TLG Publications, 2002), p. 61.

39. Osama Rushdi, "How Did the Ideology of the 'Jihad Group' Evolve?" *Al Hayat*, January 30, 2002; Gerges, *The Far Enemy*, p. 97.

40. Gerges, *The Far Enemy*, p. 101.

41. On the establishment of a caliphate, see, for example, Abu Bakr Naji, *The Management of Savagery: The Most Critical Stage Through Which the Umma Will Pass*, translated and published by the John M. Olin Institute for Strategic Studies at Harvard University, May 23, 2006.

42. Zawahiri, *Knights Under the Prophet's Banner*, p. 201.

43. Mansfield, *In His Own Words*, p. 47.

44. ABC Television News interview, "Terror Suspect: An Interview with Osama bin Laden," December 22, 1998 (conducted in Afghanistan by ABC News producer Rahimullah Yousafsai).

45. See, for example, Wright, *The Looming Tower*, p. 48; Gerges, *The Far Enemy*, pp. 3–4.

46. *United States of America v. Zacarias Moussaoui*, Transcript of Jury Trial Before the Honorable Leonie M. Brinkema, United States District Court for the Eastern District of Virginia, Alexandria, VA, March 6, 2006.

47. The Qur'an, 4:29–30.

48. On paradise, see, for example, The Qur'an, 56:12–39.

49. See, for example, Memorandum from the Rendon Group to J5 CENT-COM Strategic Effects, "Polling Results—Afghanistan Omnibus May 2007," June 15, 2007.

50. Mohammed el-Shafey, "Al-Zawahiri's Secret Papers," Part 6, *Al-Sharq al-Awsat*, December 18, 2002.

51. Zawahiri, *Knights Under the Prophet's Banner*, p. 200.

52. Sayyid Qutb, "Letter to Tewfig al-Hakeem," in al-Khaledi, *Amrika min al-dahkhil*, p. 39.

53. Zawahiri argued: "Jerusalem will not be liberated unless the battle for Egypt and Algeria is won and unless Egypt is liberated." See, for example, Montasser al-Zayat, *Ayman Zawahiri as I Knew Him* (Cairo, 2002), pp. 113–36; Salah, *Narratives of the Jihad Years*, chapter 5.

54. Zawahiri, *Knights Under the Prophet's Banner*, p. 199.

55. Osama bin Laden, video clip released in September 2007.

56. Abdullah Azzam, *Defense of Muslim Lands: The Most Important Personal Duty* (Amman, Jordan: Modern Mission Library, 2005), chapter 1.

57. Quoted in Bergen, *The Osama bin Laden I Know*, p. 35.

58. Zawahiri, *Knights Under the Prophet's Banner*, p. 128.

59. Ibid., p. 111.

60. Samuel P. Huntington, *The Clash of Civilizations and the Remaking of World Order* (New York: Simon and Schuster, 1996), pp. 209–18.

61. Ayman al-Zawahiri, *Al Walaa wa al Baraa*, obtained by *Al Hayat*, January 14, 2003.

62. Zawahiri, *Knights Under the Prophet's Banner*, p. 113.

63. Ibid., p. 111.

64. The text is the second *fatwa* originally published on February 23, 1998, to declare a holy war, or jihad, against the West and Israel. It was signed by Osama bin Laden, head of al Qa'ida; Ayman al-Zawahiri, head of al-Jihad; Rifa'i Ahmad Taha, leader of the Egyptian Islamic Group; Sheikh Mir Hamzah, secretary of the Jamiat Ulema-e-Pakistan; and Fazlur Rehman, leader of the Jihad Movement in Bangladesh.

65. See, for example, Sandia National Laboratories, U.S. Department of Energy, Dr. Gary W. Richter, *Osama bin Laden: A Case Study,* December 6, 1999. Released by the National Security Archive.

66. U.S. Embassy (Islamabad), Cable, "TFXX01: Afghanistan: Reaction to U.S. Strikes Follows Predictable Lines: Taliban Angry, Their Opponents Support U.S.," August 21, 1998.

67. U.S. Embassy (Islamabad), Cable, "Afghanistan: Reported Activities of Extremist Arabs and Pakistanis Since August 20 U.S. Strike on Khost Terrorist Camps," September 9, 1998. Released by the National Security Archive.

68. Executive Order 13129 of July 4, 1999, Blocking Property and Prohibiting Transactions With the Taliban.

69. Ahmed Rashid, *Taliban: Militant Islam, Oil and Fundamentalism in Central Asia* (New Haven, CT: Yale University Press, 2000), pp. 98–100.

70. On Saudi Arabia's historical role in Afghanistan, see National Commission on Terrorist Attacks Upon the United States, *The 9/11 Commission Report* (New York: W. W. Norton, 2004), pp. 371–74.

71. U.S. Embassy (Islamabad), Cable, "Afghanistan: Tensions Reportedly Mount Within Taliban as Ties With Saudi Arabia Deteriorate Over Bin Ladin," September 28, 1998. Released by the National Security Archive.

72. U.S. Embassy (Islamabad), Cable, "Afghanistan: Taliban Seem to Have Less Funds and Supplies This Year, But the Problem Does Not Appear to Be that Acute," February 17, 1999. Released by the National Security Archive.

73. Memorandum from Richard A. Clarke to Condoleezza Rice, Subject: Presidential Policy Initiative / Review—The Al-Qida Network, January 25, 2001. Released by the National Security Archive.

74. Zawahiri, *Knights Under the Prophet's Banner*, pp. 38–39.

75. Mohammad Yousaf and Mark Adkin, *Afghanistan—The Bear Trap: The Defeat of a Superpower* (Havertown, PA: Casemate, 2001).

76. Wright, *The Looming Tower*, p. 110. Gilles Kepel also argues that "the Arabs seem to have played only a minor part in fighting the Red Army. Their feats of arms were largely perpetrated after the Soviet withdrawal in February 1989 and were highly controversial." Kepel, *Jihad*, p. 147. And Fawaz Gerges notes: "There exists no evidence pointing to any vital role played by foreign veterans in the Afghan victory over the Russians." Gerges, *The Far Enemy*, pp. 83–84.

77. See, for example, ABC reporter John Miller's interview with bin Laden in

May 1998, a little over two months before the U.S. Embassy bombings in Tanzania and Kenya. Part of the transcript was played at the trial of Zacarias Moussaoui, who was arrested in August 2001, shortly before the September 11, 2001, attacks in the United States. *United States of America v. Zacarias Moussaoui,* Transcript of Jury Trial Before the Honorable Leonie M. Brinkema, United States District Court for the Eastern District of Virginia, Alexandria, VA, March 6, 2006.

78. Memorandum from Richard A. Clarke to Condoleezza Rice, January 25, 2001.

Chapter Six

1. Jon Lee Anderson, "American Viceroy: Zalmay Khalilzad's Mission," *The New Yorker,* December 19, 2005, p. 63.

2. On the overthrow of the Taliban regime, see Gary Schroen, *First In: An Insider's Account of How the CIA Spearheaded the War on Terror in Afghanistan* (New York: Ballantine Books, 2005); Stephen Biddle, *Afghanistan and the Future of Warfare: Implications for Army and Defense Policy* (Carlisle, PA: Strategic Studies Institute, U.S. Army War College, November 2002); Gary Berntsen and Ralph Pezzullo, *Jawbreaker: The Attack on Bin Laden and Al Qa'ida* (New York: Crown Publishers, 2005); Bob Woodward, *Bush at War* (New York: Simon and Schuster, 2002).

3. Author interview with Ambassador Wendy Chamberlin, August 27, 2008.

4. Ibid.

5. Transcript of Martin Smith interview with Richard Armitage, July 20, 2006. I received a copy of the transcript from *Frontline.*

6. Woodward, *Bush at War,* p. 47.

7. Author interview with Ambassador Wendy Chamberlin, August 27, 2008.

8. Woodward, *Bush at War,* p. 59.

9. Author interview with Ambassador Wendy Chamberlin, August 27, 2008.

10. Ibid.

11. Woodward, *Bush at War,* p. 51.

12. George Tenet, *At the Center of the Storm: My Years at the CIA* (New York: HarperCollins, 2007), p. 207.

13. Douglas J. Feith, *War and Decision: Inside the Pentagon at the Dawn of the War on Terrorism* (New York: HarperCollins, 2008), pp. 75–76.

14. Schroen, *First In,* p. 28.

15. Andrew J. Birtle, *Afghan War Chronology* (Washington, DC: U.S. Army Center of Military History Information Paper, March 22, 2002), pp. 2–3.

16. Biddle, *Afghanistan and the Future of Warfare,* pp. 8–10.

17. Michael DeLong and Noah Lukeman, *Inside CENTCOM: The Unvarnished Truth about the Wars in Afghanistan and Iraq* (Washington, DC: Regnery Publishing, 2004), p. 46.

18. U.S. Army Military History Institute: Tape 032602p, CPT M. int.; Tape 032802p, CPT D. int. This information comes from deposits at the U.S. Army Military History Institute's archive at Carlisle Barracks, Pennsylvania. See also Dale Andrade, *The Battle for Mazar-e-Sharif, October–November 2001* (Washington, DC: U.S. Army Center of Military History Information Paper, March 1, 2002), pp. 2–3. Roadbound Taliban and al Qa'ida reserves moving from Sholgerah were decimated by American air interdiction as they moved south to reinforce the defenses of Bai Beche and Ac'capruk, then as they fled north toward Mazar after November 5. See U.S. Army Military History Institute: Memorandum for the Record, COL J. int., July 2002; Tape 032602p, CPT M. int.

19. Biddle, *Afghanistan and the Future of Warfare*, p. 10.

20. Ibid., p. 9.

21. Ahmed Rashid, *Descent into Chaos: The United States and the Failure of Nation Building in Pakistan, Afghanistan, and Central Asia* (New York: Viking, 2008), pp. 3–6.

22. U.S. Army Military History Institute: Tape 032802a, MAJ D. int.; Tape 032802p, MAJ C. int.; Tape 032602a, CPT H. et al. int. Also see John Carland, *The Campaign Against Kandahar* (Washington, DC: U.S. Army Center of Military History Information Paper, March 4, 2002), pp. 2–5.

23. U.S. Army Military History Institute: Tape 032602p, CPT M. int.

24. United Nations Security Council Resolution 1383, December 6, 2001, S/RES/1383 (2001).

25. On Operation Anaconda, see *Operation Anaconda: An Air Power Perspective* (Washington, DC: Headquarters United States Air Force AF/XOL, February 2005); Paul L. Hastert, "Operation Anaconda: Perception Meets Reality in the Hills of Afghanistan," *Studies in Conflict and Terrorism*, vol. 28, pp. 11–20; Sean Naylor, *Not a Good Day to Die: The Untold Story of Operation Anaconda* (New York: Berkley Books, 2005).

26. Author interview with Ambassador Wendy Chamberlin, August 27, 2008.

27. Author interview with Robert Grenier, November 6, 2007.

28. Author interview with Lieutenant Colonel Ed O'Connell (ret.), July 8, 2007.

29. Pervez Musharraf, *In the Line of Fire: A Memoir* (New York: Free Press, 2006), p. 217.

30. Philip Smucker, *Al Qa'ida's Great Escape: The Military and the Media on Terror's Trail* (Washington, DC: Brassey's, 2004); Berntsen and Pezzullo, *Jawbreaker*, pp. 255–64; Mary Anne Weaver, "Lost at Tora Bora," *New York Times*, September 11, 2005.

31. Weaver, "Lost at Tora Bora."

32. Author interview with U.S. intelligence operative who was in the vicinity

of Tora Bora at the time, March 6, 2009. Berntsen and Pezzullo, *Jawbreaker*, pp. 314–15.

33. Brigadier Muhammad Ijaz Chaudry, "Pakistan's Counterterrorism Strategy," Paper presented at National Defense University, Washington, DC, July 27, 2007, p. 12.

34. Berntsen and Pezzullo, *Jawbreaker*, pp. 307–8.

35. Author interview with Robert Grenier, November 6, 2007.

36. European Union and UNAMA, *Discussion of Taliban and Insurgency* (Kabul: European Union and UNAMA, April 30, 2007), p. 1.

37. Stephen T. Hosmer, *The Army's Role in Counterinsurgency and Insurgency* (Santa Monica, CA: RAND, 1990), pp. 30–31; Daniel Byman et al., *Trends in Outside Support for Insurgent Movements* (Santa Monica, CA: RAND, 2001); Byman, *Deadly Connections: States that Sponsor Terrorism* (New York: Cambridge University Press, 2005).

38. Data are from the Population Census Organization, Statistics Division, Ministry of Economic Affairs and Statistics, Government of Pakistan, 2007. The Population Census Organization estimated that 15.42 percent of a total population of 160,612,500 had Pashto as their mother tongue.

39. David Galula, *Counterinsurgency Warfare: Theory and Practice* (St. Petersburg, FL: Hailer Publishing, 1964), pp. 23–24.

40. James D. Fearon and David D. Laitin, "Ethnicity, Insurgency, and Civil War," *American Political Science Review*, vol. 97, no. 1, February 2003, pp. 75–90; Galula, *Counterinsurgency Warfare: Theory and Practice*, pp. 35–37.

41. Agreement between His Highness Amir Abdur Rahman Khan G.C.S.I., Amir of Afghanistan and its Dependencies on the one part and Sir Henry Mortimer Durand K.C.I.C.S.I., Foreign Secretary to the Government of India representing the Government of India, on the other part. Signed in Kabul, Afghanistan, on November 12, 1893.

42. Ralph Peters, "Blood Borders: How a Better Middle East Would Look," *Armed Forces Journal*, June 2006.

43. Author interview with senior Afghanistan government official, Kabul, Afghanistan, September 2006.

44. Pakistani officials frequently denied this assertion. As one Pakistani senator noted in testimony before Pakistan's Senate Foreign Relations Committee: "Pakistan has arrested over 500 Taliban this year from Quetta and 400 of them have been handed over to Afghans." Pakistan Senate Foreign Relations Committee, *Pakistan–Afghanistan Relations*, Report 13 (Islamabad: Pakistan Senate Foreign Relations Committee, March 2007), p. 38.

45. Author interview with Ambassador Wendy Chamberlin, August 27, 2008.

46. Author interview with Richard Armitage, October 17, 2007.

47. Author interview with Robert Grenier, November 6, 2007.

48. Joint Paper by the Government of Afghanistan, UNAMA, CFC-A, ISAF, Canada, Netherlands, UK, and U.S. Governments, *Assessment of Factors Contributing to Insecurity in Afghanistan* (Kabul: Government of Afghanistan, 2006), p. 1.

49. See, for example, "Al Jazeera Airs Hikmatyar Video," Al Jazeera TV, May 4, 2006.

50. Amrullah Saleh, *Strategy of Insurgents and Terrorists in Afghanistan* (Kabul: National Directorate of Security, 2006), p. 2.

51. European Union and UNAMA, *Discussion of Taliban and Insurgency*, p. 2.

52. Mahomed Ali Jinnah, *Quaid-i-Azam Mahomed Ali Jinnah: Speeches as Governor-General of Pakistan, 1947–1948* (Karachi: Pakistan Publications, 1960), p. 133.

53. Dossiers of Rebel Field Commanders, date unknown. Released by the Cold War International History Project.

54. Steve Coll, *Ghost Wars: The Secret History of the CIA, Afghanistan, and Bin Laden, from the Soviet Invasion to September 10, 2001* (New York: Penguin Press, 2004), pp. 201–3.

55. Milt Bearden and James Risen, *The Main Enemy: The Inside Story of the CIA's Final Showdown with the KGB* (New York: Random House, 2003), p. 289.

56. On Pakistan raids against Haqqani, see Iqbal Khattak, "40 Militants Killed in North Waziristan," *Daily Times* (Pakistan), September 30, 2005; "Pakistani Law Enforcers Intensify Hunt for Haqqani," *Pajhwok Afghan News*, March 7, 2006. On Haqqani's historical role, also see Charles Dunbar, "Afghanistan in 1986: The Balance Endures," *Asian Survey*, vol. 27, no. 2, pp. 127–42.

57. Coll, *Ghost Wars*, pp. 131, 167, 202.

58. European Union and UNAMA, *Discussion of Taliban and Insurgency*, p. 2.

59. Rahimullah Yousufzai interview with Sirajuddin Haqqani, July 2008.

60. John D. Negroponte, Annual Threat Assessment of the Director of National Intelligence for the Senate Armed Services Committee, Statement to the Senate Armed Services Committee, February 28, 2006.

61. "Al Jazeera Reveals New Al Qa'ida Leader," *Washington Times*, May 25, 2007, p. 17.

62. Mariam Abou Zahab, "Changing Patterns of Social and Political Life Among the Tribal Pashtuns in Pakistan," Paper presented at the U.S. Naval Postgraduate School, Monterey, CA, September 2006.

63. On Ismail, see "Taliban Claim Shooting Down U.S. Helicopter," *The News* (Islamabad), June 29, 2005. On Wana, see Intikhab Amir, "Whose Writ Is It Anyway?" *The Herald* (Pakistan), April 2006, pp. 80–82.

64. On al Qa'ida in the tribal areas, see Musharraf, *In the Line of Fire*, pp. 264–81.

65. U.S. Department of State, *Afghanistan, Autumn 2006: A Campaign at a Crossroads* (Washington, DC: Office of the Coordinator for Counterterrorism, U.S. Department of State, 2006), p. 2. Unclassified document.

66. Antonio Giustozzi, *Koran, Kalashnikov, and Laptop: The Neo-Taliban Insurgency in Afghanistan* (London: Hurst & Company, 2007), p. 13.

67. Quoted in Selig S. Harrison, "Ethnicity and the Political Stalemate in Pakistan," in Ali Banuazizi and Myron Weiner, eds., *The State, Religion, and Ethnic Politics* (Syracuse, NY: Syracuse University Press, 1986), p. 285.

68. Statement of Karen P. Tandy, Administrator, U.S. Drug Enforcement Agency, Testimony before the House Armed Services Committee, Washington, DC, June 28, 2006.

Chapter Seven

1. Author interview with Richard Armitage, October 17, 2007.

2. Author interview with Colin Powell, January 15, 2008.

3. David Rohde and David E. Sanger, "How the 'Good War' in Afghanistan Went Bad," *New York Times*, August 12, 2007, p. A1.

4. Author interview with Ambassador James Dobbins, October 4, 2007.

5. See, for example, Vernon Loeb, "Franks Supports an Afghan Army," *Washington Post*, February 26, 2002, p. A16; Tim Friend, "U.S. Hints It Will Back More Peacekeepers," *USA Today*, February 25, 2002, p. 1A.

6. Agreement on Provisional Arrangements in Afghanistan Pending the Re-Establishment of Permanent Government Institutions, Annex I, Paragraph 3. The agreement, commonly referred to as the Bonn Agreement, was signed on December 5, 2001.

7. United Nations, *Daily Press Briefing by the Office of the Spokesman for the Secretary-General* (New York: United Nations, February 6, 2002). Also see, for example, William M. Reilly, "Brahimi: Expand, Extend Afghan Force," United Press International, February 6, 2002.

8. Author interview with Ambassador James Dobbins, October 4, 2007.

9. Author interview with Richard Armitage, October 17, 2007; author interview with Douglas Feith, November 4, 2008.

10. Author interview with senior U.S. administration official, Washington, DC, January 15, 2008.

11. Douglas J. Feith, *War and Decision: Inside the Pentagon at the Dawn of the War on Terrorism* (New York: HarperCollins, 2008), pp. 101–2.

12. In the October 11, 2000, debate between George W. Bush and Al Gore, Bush noted: "I don't think our troops ought to be used for what's called nation-building. I think our troops ought to be used to fight and win wars." See Commission on Presidential Debates, Debate Transcript: The Second Gore-Bush Presidential Debate, Winston-Salem, North Carolina, October 11, 2000.

13. Todd Purdum, "Bush Offers Afghanistan U.S. Help for Training of Military and Police," *New York Times*, January 29, 2002, p. A13. On opposition from Pentagon officials, see Bill Gertz, "Rumsfeld Takes Dim View of U.S. Peacekeeping Role," *Washington Times*, February 27, 2002, p. A8; Loeb, "Franks Supports an Afghan Army."

14. Press Briefing by Ari Fleischer (Washington, DC: White House Office of the Press Secretary, February 25, 2002).

15. Author interview with Ambassador James Dobbins, October 4, 2007. See Michael Gordon, "A Nation Challenged: Policy Divisions," *New York Times*, February 21, 2002, p. A1. On the divisions between the State and Defense Departments, also see Ben Barber, "U.S. Considers Force Expansion," *Washington Times*, February 22, 2002, p. A13; Alan Sipress, "White House May Support Peacekeeping Force Growth," *Washington Post*, February 28, 2002, p. A16.

16. Author interview with Ambassador James Dobbins, October 4, 2007.

17. Author interview with Richard Armitage, October 17, 2007.

18. The account of the NSC meeting was courtesy of the author's interview with Ambassador James Dobbins, October 4, 2007.

19. On the Marshall Plan, see, for example, Melvyn A. Leffler, *A Preponderance of Power: National Security, The Truman Administration, and the Cold War* (Stanford, CA: Stanford University Press, 1992), pp. 157–65, 173, 178; John Lewis Gaddis, *Strategies of Containment: A Critical Appraisal of Postwar American National Security Policy* (New York: Oxford University Press, 1982), pp. 54–88; Gaddis, *We Now Know: Rethinking Cold War History* (New York: Oxford University Press, 1997), pp. 37–43; Marc Trachtenberg, *A Constructed Peace: The Making of the European Settlement, 1945–1963* (Princeton, NJ: Princeton University Press, 1999), pp. 62–63, 74.

20. George W. Bush, Speech at Virginia Military Institute, Lexington, Virginia (Washington, DC: White House Office of the Press Secretary, April 17, 2002).

21. Author interview with Ambassador Said Jawad, October 5, 2007. In early 2002, Jawad had returned to Afghanistan to serve as President Karzai's press secretary, chief of staff, and director of the Office of International Relations before becoming the ambassador to the United States.

22. Author interview with Ambassador James Dobbins, September 21, 2004; Richard Clarke, *Against All Enemies: Inside America's War on Terror* (New York: Free Press, 2004); Afghanistan Stabilization and Reconstruction: A Status Report, Hearing Before the Committee on Foreign Relations, United States Senate, S.Hrg. 108–460, January 27, 2004, pp. 14, 17–18; Seymour M. Hersh, "The Other War: Why Bush's Afghanistan Problem Won't Go Away," *The New Yorker*, April 12, 2004; *Report of the Secretary-General on the Situation in Afghanistan and Its Implications for International Peace and Security*, UN doc A/56/875-S/2002/278, para. 98.

23. General Tommy Franks with Malcolm McConnell, *American Soldier* (New York: Regan Books, 2004), p. 324.

24. Ibid.

25. Author interview with Daoud Yaqub, January 2, 2008.

26. United Nations, *Daily Press Briefing by the Office of the Spokesman for the Secretary-General* (New York: United Nations, February 6, 2002).

27. Barry Posen, "The Security Dilemma and Ethnic Conflict," in Michael E. Brown, ed., *Ethnic Conflict and International Security* (Princeton, NJ: Princeton University Press, 1993); Stephen Stedman, "Spoiler Problems in Peace Processes," *International Security*, vol. 22, no. 2, Fall 1997, pp. 5–53; Rui de Figueiredo and Barry Weingast, "The Rationality of Fear: Political Opportunism and Ethnic Conflict," in Barbara Walter and Jack Snyder, eds., *Civil Wars, Insecurity, and Intervention* (New York: Columbia University Press, 1999), pp. 261–302; Michael W. Doyle and Nicholas Sambanis, "International Peacebuilding: A Theoretical and Quantitative Analysis," *American Political Science Review*, vol. 94, no. 4, December 2000, p. 780.

28. Robert M. Perito, *Where Is the Lone Ranger When We Need Him? America's Search for a Postconflict Stability Force* (Washington, DC: U.S. Institute of Peace, 2004); Perito, *The American Experience with Police in Peace Operations* (Clementsport, Canada: The Canadian Peacekeeping Press, 2002); Robert B. Oakley, Michael J. Dziedzic, and Eliot M. Goldberg, *Policing the New World Disorder: Peace Operations and Public Security* (Washington, DC: National Defense University Press, 1998).

29. James T. Quinlivan, "Force Requirements in Security Operations," *Parameters*, vol. 25, no. 4, Winter 1995–96, pp. 59–69; James Dobbins, *America's Role in Nation-Building: From Germany to Iraq* (Santa Monica, CA: RAND, 2003); Dobbins, *The UN's Role in Nation-Building: From the Congo to Iraq* (Santa Monica, CA: RAND, 2005).

30. James Dobbins, Seth G. Jones et al., *Europe's Role in Nation-Building: From the Balkans to the Congo* (Santa Monica, CA: RAND, 2008).

31. Dobbins, *America's Role in Nation-Building*; Dobbins, *The UN's Role in Nation-Building*.

32. Vincenzo Coppola, "Briefing on the Multinational Specialized Unit," Paper presented at the U.S. Army Peacekeeping Institute, Carlisle Barracks, PA, June 16, 1999; Paolo Valpolini, "The Role of Police-Military Units in Peacekeeping," *Jane's Europe News*, July/August 1999.

33. Author interview with Colonel Domenico Libertini, commander of the Multinational Specialized Unit, Pristina, Kosovo, April 2007. Also see Multinational Specialized Unit, *MSU Concept* (Pristina, Kosovo: Multinational Specialized Unit, 2007).

34. These numbers include local police, sheriff, primary state, special jurisdiction, constable/marshal, and federal. Department of Justice, *Law Enforcement Statistics* (Washington, DC: Department of Justice, Office of Justice Programs, Bureau of Justice Statistics, 2004).

35. The CIA comes with significant historical baggage in working with foreign police. By the early 1970s, the U.S. Congress became deeply concerned that U.S. assistance to police abroad frequently strengthened the recipient government's capacity for repression. Congress was particularly concerned

about the role of the CIA, which trained foreign police in countersubversion, counterguerrilla, and intelligence-gathering techniques. Consequently, Congress in 1974 adopted Section 660 of the Foreign Assistance Act, which prohibited the United States from providing internal-security assistance to foreign governments. In addition, the CIA does not have a viable policing arm. The CIA's Special Activities Division is primarily a paramilitary organization—not a policing one. See, for example, Seth G. Jones et al., *Securing Tyrants or Fostering Reform? U.S. Internal Security Assistance to Repressive and Transitioning Regimes* (Santa Monica, CA: RAND, 2006), pp. 9–22.

36. Dobbins, *Europe's Role in Nation-Building.*

37. William I. Zartman, *Collapsed States: The Disintegration and Restoration of Legitimate Authority* (Boulder, CO: Lynne Rienner, 1995), pp. 267–73; Doyle and Sambanis, "International Peacebuilding."

38. Seth G. Jones, Jeremy Wilson, Andrew Rathmell, and Jack Riley, *Establishing Law and Order After Conflict* (Santa Monica, CA: RAND, 2005); Dobbins, *America's Role in Nation-Building*; Dobbins, *The UN's Role in Nation-Building.*

39. Author interview with Ambassador James Dobbins, September 21, 2004; Hersh, "The Other War."

40. Dobbins, *Europe's Role in Nation-Building.*

41. Author interview with Dov Zakheim, January 30, 2008.

42. Ibid.

43. Author interview with senior White House official, Washington, DC, January 15, 2008.

44. Letter from Rangin Dadfar Spanta to Adamantios Vassilakis, Permanent Representative of Greece to the United Nations, September 20, 2006.

45. Colin L. Powell, "U.S. Forces: Challenges Ahead," *Foreign Affairs*, vol. 72, no. 5, Winter 1992/93, pp. 32–45. On the Weinberger Doctrine, see Caspar W. Weinberger, *Fighting for Peace: Seven Critical Years in the Pentagon* (New York: Warner Books, 1990); Thomas R. Dubois, "The Weinberger Doctrine and the Liberation of Kuwait," *Parameters*, vol. XXI, no. 4 (Winter 1991–1992), pp. 24 38. The Weinberger Doctrine and the Powell Doctrine are named after Caspar Weinberger, Ronald Reagan's secretary of defense, and Colin Powell, most recently George W. Bush's first secretary of state.

46. Powell, "U.S. Forces," p. 40.

47. Speech by Caspar Weinberger, "The Uses of Military Power," November 28, 1984, Reprinted in *Defense Issues*, January 1985, p. 35.

48. Seth G. Jones, "Averting Failure in Afghanistan," *Survival*, vol. 48, no. 1, Spring 2006, pp. 111–28.

49. Interview with Major General Craig P. Weston, Chief, Office of Military Cooperation–Afghanistan, June 23, 2004, Kabul, Afghanistan.

50. Author interview with Richard Armitage, October 17, 2007.

51. Feith, *War and Decision*, pp. 14–15.

52. Ibid., pp. 51–52.

53. Author interview with senior U.S. official present at the September 2001 Camp David meetings, Washington, DC, January 15, 2008. Also see, for example, Bob Woodward, *Bush at War* (New York: Simon and Schuster, 2002), pp. 74–92.

54. Author interview with senior U.S. official present at the September 2001 Camp David meetings, Washington, DC, January 15, 2008.

55. See, for example, Michael R. Gordon and General Bernard E. Trainor, *Cobra II: The Inside Story of the Invasion and Occupation of Iraq* (New York: Pantheon Books, 2006), pp. 21–23.

56. Author interview with Lieutenant Colonel Edward O'Connell (ret.), October 4, 2007.

57. Author interview with Richard Armitage, October 17, 2007.

58. Gary C. Schroen, *First In: An Insider's Account of How the CIA Spearheaded the War on Terror in Afghanistan* (New York: Ballantine Books, 2005), p. 360.

59. See, for example, Seymour Hersh, *Chain of Command* (New York: Harper-Collins, 2004), p. 188; George Packer, *The Assassins' Gate: America in Iraq* (New York: Farrar, Straus and Giroux, 2006), p. 45.

60. Author interview with Robert Grenier, November 6, 2007.

61. Author interview with Lieutenant General Karl Eikenberry, October 27, 2007.

62. Author interview with Dov Zakheim, January 30, 2008.

63. Sarah Chayes, *The Punishment of Virtue: Inside Afghanistan After the Taliban* (New York: Penguin Press, 2006), p. 155.

64. Ahmed Rashid, "Afghanistan: Progress Since the Taliban," *Asian Affairs*, vol. 37, no. I, March 2006, p. 33.

65. L. Paul Bremer III, *My Year in Iraq: The Struggle to Build a Future of Hope* (New York: Simon and Schuster, 2006), p. 143.

66. Letter from Jeb Mason to Ambassador Bremer, Talking Points: Progress in the War on Terror, September 17, 2003.

67. Ali Jalali, "The Future of Afghanistan," *Parameters*, vol. 36, no. 1, Spring 2006, p. 5.

68. Andrew M. Roe, "To Create a Stable Afghanistan," *Military Review*, November–December 2005, p. 21.

69. David L. Buffaloe, *Conventional Forces in Low-Intensity Conflict: The 82d Airborne in Firebase Shkin,* Landpower Essay 04-2 (Arlington, VA: Association of the United States Army, 2004), p. 12.

70. On a firsthand account of the Battle for Deh Chopan, see Michael McInerney, "The Battle for Deh Chopan, Part 1," *Soldier of Fortune*, August 2004; McInerney, "The Battle for Deh Chopan, Part 2," *Soldier of Fortune*, September 2004.

71. Anne Evans et al., *A Guide to Government in Afghanistan* (Washington, DC: World Bank Publications, 2004), p. 14.

72. On warlords and Afghanistan, see Roe, "To Create a Stable Afghanistan," pp. 20–26; Government of Afghanistan, *Security Sector Reform: Disbandment of Illegal Armed Groups Programme (DIAG) and Disarmament, Demobilisation, and Reintegration Programme (DDR)* (Kabul: Government of Afghanistan, October 2005); Mark Sedra, *Challenging the Warlord Culture: Security Sector Reform in Post-Taliban Afghanistan* (Bonn: Bonn International Center for Conversion, 2002).

73. Several warlords were reassigned as provincial governors, including Sher Muhammad Akhundzada of Helmand (2005), Ismail Khan of Herat (2004), Gul Agha of Kandahar (2004), Haji Din Muhammad of Nangarhar, Muhammad Ibrahim of Ghor (2004), Gul Ahmad of Badghis (2003), and Syed Amin of Badakshan (2003).

74. Combined Forces Command—Afghanistan and Altai Consulting, *Afghan National Development Poll* (Kabul: Combined Forces Command, 2005).

75. Afghanistan National Security Council, *National Threat Assessment* (Kabul: Afghanistan National Security Council, 2005), p. 4. Also see Afghanistan Ministry of Defense, *The National Military Strategy* (Kabul: Afghanistan Ministry of Defense, October 2005).

76. Evans et al., *A Guide to Government in Afghanistan*, p. 14.

77. Feith, *War and Decision*, p. 123.

78. Lester Grau, ed., *The Bear Went Over the Mountain: Soviet Combat Tactics in Afghanistan* (Washington, DC: National Defense University Press, 1996), p. 201.

79. Steve Coll, *Ghost Wars: The Secret History of the CIA, Afghanistan, and bin Laden, from the Soviet Invasion to September 10, 2001* (New York: Penguin Books, 2004), pp. 131, 167, 202.

80. Ibid., p. 89.

81. Francesc Vendrell, *EUSR Vendrell's Valedictory Report* (Kabul: European Union, 2008).

Chapter Eight

1. Author interview with Ambassador Zalmay Khalilzad, February 22, 2008.

2. Mountstuart Elphinstone, *An Account of the Kingdom of Caubul and Its Dependencies in Persia, Tartary, and India* (Graz, Austria: Akademische Druck, 1969), p. 489.

3. Radek Sikorski, "The Devil You Know," *Newsweek*, August 9, 2004, p. 31.

4. Author interview with Ambassador James Dobbins, July 27, 2007.

5. Ibid.

6. United Nations Security Council Resolution 1383, December 6, 2001, S/RES/1383 (2001).

7. "Agreement on Provisional Arrangements in Afghanistan Pending the Reestablishment of Permanent Government Institutions," December 2001, Annex II.

8. Ahmed Rashid, *Descent into Chaos: The United States and the Failure of Nation Building in Pakistan, Afghanistan, and Central Asia* (New York: Viking, 2008), p. 184.

9. Author interview with Daoud Yaqub, January 2, 2008.

10. David Rohde and David E. Sanger, "How the 'Good War' in Afghanistan Went Bad," *New York Times*, August 12, 2007, p. A1.

11. Author interview with Lieutenant General David Barno, September 4, 2007.

12. Author interview with Ambassador Zalmay Khalilzad, February 22, 2008; Statement of Zalmay Khalilzad Before the U.S. Senate Committee on Foreign Relations, October 29, 2003.

13. Author interview with Ambassador Zalmay Khalilzad, February 22, 2008.

14. Statement of Zalmay Khalilzad Before the U.S. Senate Committee on Foreign Relations, October 29, 2003.

15. Author interview with Ambassador Zalmay Khalilzad, February 22, 2008.

16. Ali Ahmad Jalali and Lester W. Grau, *The Other Side of the Mountain: Mujahideen Tactics in the Soviet-Afghan War* (Quantico, VA: U.S. Marine Corps, Studies and Analysis Division, 1995).

17. Ali A. Jalali, "Rebuilding Afghanistan's National Army," *Parameters*, vol. 32, no. 3, Autumn 2002, p. 79.

18. Author interview with Ambassador Zalmay Khalilzad, February 22, 2008.

19. Author interview with Lieutenant General David Barno, September 4, 2007.

20. Michael O'Hanlon and Adriana Lins de Albuquerque, *Afghanistan Index: Tracking Variables of Reconstruction and Security in Post-Taliban Afghanistan* (Washington, DC: Brookings Institution, September 15, 2005).

21. Author interview with Lieutenant General David Barno, January 17, 2008.

22. Lieutenant General David W. Barno, "Fighting 'The Other War': Counterinsurgency Strategy in Afghanistan, 2003–2005," *Military Review*, September–October 2007, p. 36.

23. Memorandum from Donald L. Evans to the President, Subject: "Recent Visit to Baghdad, Iraq, and Kabul, Afghanistan," October 24, 2003. Secretary of Defense Donald Rumsfeld subsequently wrote a memo to Evans noting that "your report to the President on your visit to Iraq and Afghanistan was excellent. Thanks so much for going. I appreciate it a great deal. Thanks also for letting other folks know what you found." Letter from Donald Rumsfeld to the Honorable Donald L. Evans, October 29, 2003.

24. Author interview with Lieutenant General David Barno, September 4, 2007.

25. George W. Bush, *State of the Union Address* (Washington, DC: White House, 2004).

26. Author interview with Lieutenant General David Barno, January 17, 2008.

27. See, for example, International Crisis Group, *Countering Afghanistan's Insurgency: No Quick Fixes* (Kabul: International Crisis Group, 2006).

28. ABC News/BBC/ARD Poll, *Afghanistan—Where Things Stand* (Kabul: ABC News/BBC/ARD Poll, December 2007), p. 6.

29. Frank Newport, *Bush Job Approval at 28%, Lowest of His Administration* (Washington, DC: Gallup, April 11, 2008). The poll included Bush's job-approval average each year from 2001 to 2008.

30. Info Memo from Ronald Neumann to the Administrator, Subject: Highlights of the June 24th MCNS Meeting, June 24, 2004.

31. E-mail from Paul Bremer to Jaymie Durnan, Subject: Message for SecDef, June 30, 2003.

32. Coalition Provisional Authority, Summary: Bomb-Making Tips, Mukhabarat Habits, Views from the Street, July 15, 2003.

33. E-mail from Paul Bremer to Jaymie Durnan, Subject: Message for SecDef, June 30, 2003.

34. Brief on Iraq Security and Military Issues, NSC Meeting, July 1, 2003.

35. Coalition Provisional Authority, Security Update for Ambassador Bremer, July 18, 2003.

36. Office of Research, Bureau of Intelligence and Research, Department of State, *Iraqis Offer Dim Evaluation of Reconstruction Effort Thus Far*, August 22, 2003.

37. Iraqi Impressions of Coalition Forces and the Security Situation in Iraq: Office of Research Survey Results from 7 Cities in Iraq & Preliminary Results from Gallup Baghdad Survey, September 30, 2003.

38. Memo from James Ellery to Ambassador Bremer, Subject: Read Ahead for Ambassador Bremer: Infrastructure Security Strategy, January 11, 2004.

39. Infrastructure Security Planning Group, Infrastructure Security Strategy, January 12, 2004.

40. Info Memo from Bill Miller to the Administrator, Subject: Security Town Hall, March 18, 2004. Also see Memorandum from L. Paul Bremer to Regional and Governorate Coordinators, Subject: Safety and Security, March 19, 2004.

41. Memo from L. Paul Bremer to Hon. Chris Shays, April 16, 2004; Memo from L. Paul Bremer to Hon. Brian Baird, April 1, 2004; Memo from L. Paul Bremer to Hon. Jim Kolbe, April 1, 2004.

42. Some have argued that the insurgency began in earnest in June 2004. But Taliban offensive operations two years earlier suggest that it was in the spring of 2002. Colonel Walter M. Herd et al., *One Valley at a Time* (Fort Bragg, NC: Combined Joint Special Operations Task Force–Afghanistan, 2005), p. 121.

43. "Country Risk Assessment: Afghanistan," *Jane's Intelligence Review*, vol. 16,

no. 5, May 2004, pp. 38–41; Michael Bhatia, Kevin Lanigan, and Philip Wilkinson, *Minimal Investments, Minimal Results: The Failure of Security Policy in Afghanistan* (Kabul: Afghanistan Research and Evaluation Unit, June 2004), pp. 1–8; Anthony Davis, "Afghan Security Deteriorates as Taliban Regroup," *Jane's Intelligence Review*, vol. 15, no. 5, May 2003, pp. 10–15.

44. *ANSO Security Situation Summary*, Weekly Report 039, September 24–30, 2004, p. 15.

45. Carlotta Gall, "21 Killed in Afghanistan Attacks Directed at Provincial Governor," *New York Times*, August 15, 2004; *ANSO Security Situation Summary*, Weekly Report 039, September 24–30, 2004, p. 7; *ANSO Security Situation Summary*, Weekly Report 036, September 3–9, 2004, p. 5; *ANSO Security Situation Summary*, Weekly Report 038, September 17–23, 2004, pp. 7–8.

46. Author interview with Daoud Yaqub, January 2, 2008.

47. Author interview with Lieutenant General David Barno, January 17, 2008.

48. Memo from Donald Rumsfeld to General Dick Myers, Paul Wolfowitz, General Pete Pace, and Doug Feith, Subject: Global War on Terrorism, October 16, 2003.

49. On Afghan numbers, see Seth G. Jones et al., *Establishing Law and Order After Conflict* (Santa Monica, CA: RAND, 2005), pp. 89–91.

50. The Asia Foundation, *Voter Education Planning Survey: Afghanistan 2004 National Elections* (Kabul: The Asia Foundation, 2004), p. 106.

51. International Republican Institute, *Afghanistan: Election Day Survey*, October 9, 2004, slide 13.

52. Arno J. Mayer, *The Furies: Violence and Terror in the French and Russian Revolutions* (Princeton, NJ: Princeton University Press, 2000), p. 323.

Chapter Nine

1. Mao Tse-tung, *On Guerrilla Warfare*, translated by Samuel B. Griffith II (Urbana: University of Illinois Press, 1961), p. 93.

2. William Cullen Bryant, *Poems* (Philadelphia: Henry Altemus, 1895), p. 79.

3. On the definition of insurgency, see Central Intelligence Agency, *Guide to the Analysis of Insurgency* (Washington, DC: Central Intelligence Agency, n.d.), p. 2; *Department of Defense Dictionary of Military and Associated Terms*, Joint Publication 1-02 (Washington, DC: U.S. Department of Defense, 2001), p. 266.

4. David Galula, *Counterinsurgency Warfare: Theory and Practice* (St. Petersburg, FL: Hailer Publishing, 1964), p. 3.

5. *Department of Defense Dictionary of Military and Associated Terms*, Joint Publication 1-02, defines unconventional warfare as: "A broad spectrum of military and paramilitary operations, normally of long duration, predominantly

conducted through, with, or by indigenous or surrogate forces who are organized, trained, equipped, supported, and directed in varying degrees by an external source. It includes, but is not limited to, guerrilla warfare, subversion, sabotage, intelligence activities, and unconventional assisted recovery." U.S. Department of Defense, *Department of Defense Dictionary of Military and Associated Terms*, Joint Publication 1-02 (Washington, DC: U.S. Department of Defense, 2001), p. 574.

6. Roger Trinquier, *Modern Warfare: A French View of Counterinsurgency*, translated by Daniel Lee (Westport, CT: Praeger, 2006), p. 6.

7. Daniel Siegel and Joy Hackel, "El Salvador: Counterinsurgency Revisited," in Michael T. Klare and Peter Kornbluh, eds., *Low-Intensity Warfare: Counterinsurgency, Proinsurgency, and Antiterrorism in the Eighties* (New York: Pantheon Books, 1988), p. 119.

8. Bruce Hoffman, *Insurgency and Counterinsurgency in Iraq* (Santa Monica, CA: RAND, 2004); U.S. Marine Corps, *Small Wars Manual* (Washington, DC: U.S. Government Printing Office, 1940); Julian Paget, *Counter-Insurgency Campaigning* (London: Faber and Faber, 1967); Charles Simpson, *Inside the Green Berets: The First Thirty Years* (Novato, CA: Presidio Press, 1982); Robert J. Wilensky, *Military Medicine to Win Hearts and Minds: Aid to Civilians in the Vietnam War* (Lubbock, TX: Texas Tech University Press, 2004).

9. Daniel Byman, *Understanding Proto-Insurgencies* (Santa Monica, CA: RAND, 2007), p. 1.

10. Trinquier, *Modern Warfare*, p. 8; Galula, *Counterinsurgency Warfare: Theory and Practice*, pp. 7-8.

11. Kimberly Marten Zisk, *Enforcing the Peace: Learning from the Imperial Past* (New York: Columbia University Press, 2004); Amitai Etzioni, "A Self-Restrained Approach to Nation-Building by Foreign Powers," *International Affairs*, vol. 80, no. 1 (2004); Etzioni, *From Empire to Community: A New Approach to International Relations* (New York: Palgrave Macmillan, 2004); Stephen T. Hosmer, *The Army's Role in Counterinsurgency and Insurgency* (Santa Monica, Calif,: RAND Corporation, R-3947-A, 1990), pp. 30-31.

12. Seth G. Jones, *Counterinsurgency in Afghanistan* (Santa Monica, CA: RAND, 2008). On time, also see Galula, *Counterinsurgency Warfare*, p. 10.

13. David M. Edelstein, "Occupational Hazards: Why Military Occupations Succeed or Fail," *International Security*, vol. 29, no. 1 (Summer 2004), p. 51.

14. See, for example, James D. Fearon and David D. Laitin, "Ethnicity, Insurgency, and Civil War," *American Political Science Review*, vol. 97, no. 1, February 2003, pp. 83, 85; Paul Collier, Anke Hoeffler, and Nicholas Sambanis, "The Collier-Hoeffler Model of Civil War Onset and the Case Study Project Research Design," in Paul Collier and Nicholas Sambanis, eds., *Understanding Civil War, Vol. 2: Europe, Central Asia, and Other Regions* (Washington, DC: World Bank, 2005), pp. 1-34; Galula, *Counterinsurgency Warfare*, pp. 37-38.

15. Galula, *Counterinsurgency Warfare*, p. 38.

16. Ann Hironaka, *Neverending Wars: The International Community, Weak States, and the Perpetuation of Civil War* (Cambridge, MA: Harvard University Press, 2005); Fearon and Laitin, "Ethnicity, Insurgency, and Civil War," pp. 75–90. On the importance of building institutions, see Roland Paris, *At War's End: Building Peace After Civil Conflict* (New York: Cambridge University Press, 2004).

17. Stathis N. Kalyvas, *The Logic of Violence in Civil War* (New York: Cambridge University Press, 2006), p. 218.

18. Nelson Manrique, "The War for the Central Sierra," in Steve J. Stern, ed., *Shining and Other Paths: War and Society in Peru, 1980–1995* (Durham, NC: Duke University Press, 1998), p. 204.

19. Jeffrey Race, *War Comes to Long An: Revolutionary Conflict in a Vietnamese Province* (Berkeley, CA: University of California Press, 1973), p. 199.

20. Richard Berman, *Revolutionary Organization: Institution-Building within the People's Liberation Armed Forces* (Lexington, MA: D. C. Heath, 1974), pp. 4–5.

21. Adrian H. Jones and Andrew R. Molnar, *Internal Defense against Insurgency: Six Cases* (Washington, DC: Center for Research in Social Systems, 1966), p. 47.

22. Max Weber, "Politics as a Vocation," in H. H. Gerth and C. Wright Mills, eds., *From Max Weber: Essays in Sociology* (New York: Oxford University Press, 1958), p. 78.

23. Jane Stromseth, David Wippman, and Rosa Brooks, *Can Might Make Rights? Building the Rule of Law After Military Interventions* (New York: Cambridge University Press, 2006), pp. 137–140.

24. William R. Easterly, *The Elusive Quest for Growth: Economists' Adventures and Misadventures in the Tropics* (Cambridge, MA: MIT Press, 2001); Robert E. Klitgaard, *Institutional Adjustment and Adjusting to Institutions* (Washington, DC: World Bank, 1995); Nicolas van de Walle, *African Economies and the Politics of Permanent Crisis, 1979–1999* (Cambridge, UK: Cambridge University Press, 2001); Judith Tendler, *Good Government in the Tropics* (Baltimore, MD: Johns Hopkins University Press, 1997).

25. Mohammed Ayoob, "State Making, State Breaking, and State Failure," in Chester Crocker, Fen Osler Hampson, and Pamela Aall, eds., *Turbulent Peace: The Challenges of Managing International Conflict* (Washington, DC: U.S. Institute of Peace Press, 2001), p. 130.

26. Hironaka, *Neverending Wars*, pp. 42–46.

27. Stromseth, Wippman, and Brooks, *Can Might Make Rights?* pp. 137–40; Francis Fukuyama, *State-Building: Governance and World Order in the 21st Century* (Ithaca, NY: Cornell University Press, 2004), pp. 92–118; Ayoob, "State Making, State Breaking, and State Failure."

28. Fearon and Laitin, "Ethnicity, Insurgency, and Civil War," pp. 75–76.

29. Hironaka, *Neverending Wars*, p. 45.

30. See, for example, Jeffrey Herbst, "Responding to State Failure in Africa," *International Security*, vol. 21, no. 3, Winter 1996/1997, pp. 120–44.

31. David D. Laitin and Said S. Samatar, *Somalia: Nation in Search of a State* (Boulder, CO: Westview Press, 1987); I. M. Lewis, *A Modern History of Somalia: Nation and State in the Horn of Africa* (Boulder, CO: Westview Press, 1988); Michael W. Doyle and Nicholas Sambanis, *Making War and Building Peace* (Princeton, NJ: Princeton University Press, 2006), pp. 145–61.

32. Patrick Brogan, *World Conflicts* (Lanham, MD: Scarecrow Press, 1998), p. 99.

33. Hussein M. Adam, "Somalia: A Terrible Beauty Being Born?" in I. William Zartman, ed., *Collapsed States: The Disintegration and Restoration of Legitimate Authority* (Boulder, CO: Lynne Rienner, 1995), p. 78.

34. Richard J. Kessler, *Rebellion and Repression in the Philippines* (New Haven, CT: Yale University Press, 1989), p. 140.

35. William Chapman, *Inside the Philippine Revolution* (New York: W. W. Norton, 1987).

36. Samir Makdisi and Richard Sadaka, "The Lebanese Civil War, 1975–1990," in Collier and Sambanis, eds., *Understanding Civil War, Vol. 2*, pp. 59–85.

37. Michael Clodfelter, *Warfare and Armed Conflicts: A Statistical Reference* (Jefferson, NC: McFarland, 1992).

38. Thomas A. Marks, *Maoist Insurgency since Vietnam* (Portland, OR: Frank Cass, 1996), p. 261.

39. Crawford Young, *Politics in the Congo: Decolonization and Independence* (Princeton, NJ: Princeton University Press, 1965), p. 56.

40. William Minter, *Apartheid's Contras* (Atlantic Highlands, NJ: Zed Books, 1994); Leonid L. Fituni, "The Collapse of the Socialist State: Angola and the Soviet Union," in I. William Zartman, ed., *Collapsed States*, pp. 143–56.

41. Mwangi S. Kimenyi and Njuguna S. Ndung'u, "Sporadic Ethnic Violence: Why Has Kenya Not Experienced a Full-Blown Civil War?" in Paul Collier and Nicholas Sambanis, eds., *Understanding Civil War, Vol. 1: Africa* (Washington, DC: World Bank, 2005), pp. 123–56.

42. See, for example, Stephen Saideman, *The Ties That Divide: Ethnic Politics, Foreign Policy, and International Conflict* (New York: Columbia University Press, 2001); Saideman, "Explaining the International Relations of Secessionist Conflicts," *International Organization*, vol. 51, no. 4, 1997, pp. 721–53; Tatu Vanhanen, "Domestic Ethnic Conflict and Ethnic Nepotism: A Comparative Analysis," *Journal of Peace Research*, vol. 36, no. 1, 1999, pp. 55–73; Chaim Kaufmann, "Possible and Impossible Solutions to Ethnic Civil Wars," *International Security*, vol. 20, no. 4, Spring 1996, pp. 136–75.

43. Donald L. Horowitz, *Ethnic Groups in Conflict* (Berkeley: University of California Press, 1985).

44. Kaufmann, "Possible and Impossible Solutions to Ethnic Civil Wars," pp. 136–75.

45. There is no definitive assessment of ethnic breakdowns in Afghanistan, since there has been no census since 1979. Even the 1979 census was partial and incomplete. For estimates, see, for example, Central Intelligence Agency, *The World Factbook 2007* (Washington, DC: Central Intelligence Agency, 2006).

46. On Pashtuns and the Taliban, see Olivier Roy, *Islam and Resistance in Afghanistan*, 2nd ed. (New York: Cambridge University Press, 1990); Ahmed Rashid, *Taliban: Militant Islam, Oil and Fundamentalism in Central Asia* (New Haven, CT: Yale University Press, 2000); William Maley, ed., *Fundamentalism Reborn? Afghanistan and the Taliban* (New York: New York University Press, 2001).

47. Gary Berntsen and Ralph Pezzullo, *Jawbreaker: The Attack on Bin Laden and Al Qa'ida* (New York: Crown Publishers, 2005), p. 219.

48. Thomas H. Johnson and M. Chris Mason, "Understanding the Taliban and Insurgency in Afghanistan," *Orbis*, vol. 51, no. 1, Winter 2007, p. 86. Also see Thomas H. Johnson, "Afghanistan's Post-Taliban Transition: The State of State-Building After War," *Central Asian Survey*, vol. 25, nos. 1–2, March–June 2006, pp. 1–26.

49. Johnson, "Afghanistan's Post-Taliban Transition," pp. 7, 14.

50. The election results are from Afghanistan's Joint Electoral Management Body.

51. International Republican Institute, *Afghanistan: Election Day Survey* (Washington, DC: International Republican Institute, October 9, 2004).

52. U.S. State Department, *Afghanistan: Closer to One Nation than a House Divided* (Washington, DC: Office of Research, U.S. Department of State, January 29, 2007), pp. 1, 3.

53. Memorandum from the Rendon Group to J5 CENTCOM Strategic Effects, "Polling Results—Afghanistan Omnibus May 2007," June 15, 2007.

54. Asia Foundation, *Voter Education Planning Survey: Afghanistan 2004 National Elections* (San Francisco: Asia Foundation, 2004).

55. Asia Foundation, *A Survey of the Afghan People: Afghanistan in 2006* (San Francisco: Asia Foundation, 2006).

56. Author interview with Ambassador James Dobbins, July 11, 2007.

57. S. Frederick Starr, "Sovereignty and Legitimacy in Afghan Nation-Building," in Francis Fukuyama, ed., *Beyond Afghanistan and Iraq* (Baltimore, MD: Johns Hopkins University Press, 2006), pp. 107–24; Starr, *U.S. Afghanistan Policy: It's Working* (Washington, DC: Central Asia–Caucasus Institute, Johns Hopkins University, 2004).

58. On ideology and insurgency, see, for example, Michael F. Brown and Eduardo Fernández, *War of Shadows: The Struggle for Utopia in the Peruvian Amazon* (Berkeley: University of California Press, 1991), p. 98.

59. *Military Teachings: For the Preparation of Mujahideen*, n.d. The Taliban manual was leaked to the press in 2007. See, for example, Isambard Wilkinson, "How To Be A Jihadi: Taliban's Training Secrets," *Daily Telegraph* (London), August 16, 2007.

60. Trinquier, *Modern Warfare*, p. 43; Galula, *Counterinsurgency Warfare*, p. 31.

61. As David Galula argues: "[C]onventional operations by themselves have at best no more effect than a fly swatter. Some guerrillas are bound to be caught, but new recruits will replace them as fast as they are lost." Galula, *Counterinsurgency Warfare*, p. 72.

62. Stromseth, Wippman, and Brooks, *Can Might Make Rights?* pp. 137–40.

Chapter Ten

1. Gary C. Schroen, *First In: An Insider's Account of How the CIA Spearheaded the War on Terror in Afghanistan* (New York: Ballantine Books, 2005), p. 358.

2. Amrullah Saleh, *Strategy of Insurgents and Terrorists in Afghanistan* (Kabul, Afghanistan: National Directorate of Security, May 2006).

3. German Federal Ministry of the Interior (2004), p. 6; Asian Development Bank and World Bank, *Afghanistan: Preliminary Needs Assessment for Recovery and Reconstruction* (Kabul: Asian Development Bank and World Bank, January 2002), p. 7.

4. German Federal Foreign Office and Federal Ministry of the Interior, *Assistance in Rebuilding the Police Force* (Bonn: Federal Foreign Office and Federal Ministry of the Interior, 2004), p. 6.

5. Author interview with Jochen Rieso, Training Branch, German Project for Support of the Police in Afghanistan, June 27, 2004.

6. Author interview with senior U.S. official, White House, September 2004. This view was corroborated by multiple interviews with U.S. officials in Washington and Afghanistan in 2004 and 2005.

7. German Federal Foreign Office and Federal Ministry of the Interior, *Assistance in Rebuilding the Police Force*, p. 3.

8. Letter from Donald Rumsfeld to Jerry Bremer and General John Abizaid (cc to General Dick Myers, Paul Wolfowitz, and Doug Feith), Assistance from Germany, September 29, 2003.

9. Author interviews with members of DynCorp International, Kabul and Gardez, June 2004 and November 2005.

10. Author interview with Interior Minister Ali Jalali, September 4, 2007.

11. Author interview with Lieutenant General David Barno, September 4, 2007.

12. Author interviews with senior U.S. Defense Department official involved in the discussions, August 21 and October 4, 2007.

13. Author interview with Nora Bensahel, May 7, 2008.

14. Author interview with Major General Robert Durbin, January 3, 2008.

15. Central Intelligence Agency, *CIA World Factbook 2007* (Washington, DC: Central Intelligence Agency, 2006). The list included small, poor countries such as East Timor, Djibouti, and Liberia.

16. Author interview with Major General Robert Durbin, January 3, 2008.

17. Author interview with U.S. Army general, Washington, DC, January 10, 2008.

18. Author interviews with members of the Office of Security Cooperation—Afghanistan, Kabul, December 2005.

19. Offices of Inspector General of the Departments of State and Defense, *Interagency Assessment of Afghanistan Police Training and Readiness* (Washington, DC: Offices of Inspector General of the Departments of State and Defense, 2006), p. 1.

20. Colonel Rick Adams, *Police Reform Directorate: Overview—Current Operations and Strategic Initiatives* (Kabul: Combined Security Transition Command—Afghanistan, 2006), slide 6.

21. Author interview with Minister Ali Jalali, September 4, 2007; author interviews with Shahmahmood Miakhel, August 29 and September 14, 2007.

22. Author interview with Minister Ali Jalali, September 4, 2007.

23. Atos Consulting, *Afghanistan Stabilisation Programme: Summary Project Completion Report* (Kabul, Afghanistan: Atos Consulting, May 2007).

24. Combined Security Transition Command—Afghanistan, *RC South–ANP Efforts to Increase Security* (Kabul: Combined Security Transition Command—Afghanistan, 2006), p. 2.

25. General Barry R. McCaffrey (ret.), Trip to Afghanistan and Pakistan, Memorandum from General McCaffrey to Colonel Mike Meese and Colonel Cindy Jebb, United States Military Academy, June 2006; McCaffrey, Trip to Afghanistan and Pakistan, Memorandum from General McCaffrey to Colonel Mike Meese and Colonel Cindy Jebb, United States Military Academy, February 2007.

26. Combined Security Transition Command—Afghanistan, *Better Distribution of Afghan Uniformed Police—"Close the Gap"* (Kabul: Combined Security Transition Command—Afghanistan, 2006), slide 9.

27. Quoted in Chris Sands, "Bring Back Taliban to End Police Corruption, Say Afghan Truckers," *The Independent* (London), May 10, 2007.

28. Author interviews with U.S. and German police officials, Afghanistan, 2004, 2005, 2006, and 2007.

29. Author interview with Minister Ali Jalali, September 4, 2007; author interviews with Shahmahmood Miakhel, August 29 and September 14, 2007.

30. Colonel Rick Adams, *Police Reform Directorate: Overview—Current Operations*

and Strategic Initiatives (Kabul: Combined Security Transition Command—Afghanistan, 2006), slide 16.

31. Transitional Islamic Government of Afghanistan, *Securing Afghanistan's Future: Accomplishments and the Strategic Path Forward, National Police and Law Enforcement* (Kabul: Transitional Islamic Government of Afghanistan, January 2004), p. 10.

32. Author interviews with U.S. State and Defense Department officials, 2004, 2005, and 2006.

33. Author interviews with Office of Security Cooperation—Afghanistan officials, Kabul, Afghanistan, November and December 2005.

34. *Afghan National Police Program* (Kabul: Ministry of Interior, 2005); Barnett R. Rubin, *Afghanistan's Uncertain Transition from Turmoil to Normalcy* (New York: Council on Foreign Relations, 2006); U.S. Government Accountability Office, *Afghanistan Security: Efforts to Establish Army and Police Have Made Progress, but Future Plans Need to Be Better Defined* (Washington, DC: GAO, 2005).

35. Government of Germany, *Doha II Conference on Border Management in Afghanistan: A Regional Approach* (Berlin: Government of Germany, 2006). Also see U.S. Department of State, *Border Management Initiative: Information Brief* (Kabul: Afghanistan Reconstruction Group, U.S. Department of State, 2005).

36. Ali Jalali, "The Future of Afghanistan," *Parameters*, vol. 36, no. 1, Spring 2006, p. 10.

37. Afghan Non-Governmental Organization Security Office, *Security Incident—Armed Clash: ANP Was Disarmed* (Kabul: Afghan Non-Governmental Organization Security Office, March 2006).

38. Combined Security Transition Command—Afghanistan, *Better Distribution of Afghan Uniformed Police—"Close the Gap"* (Kabul: Combined Security Transition Command—Afghanistan, 2006), slide 17.

39. Author interview with Lieutenant General David Barno, September 4, 2007.

40. Author interviews with U.S. State Department and Defense Department officials involved in police training, Afghanistan, 2004, 2005, 2006, and 2007.

41. Author interview with Ambassador Ronald Neumann, September 7, 2007.

42. Author correspondence with Ambassador Ronald Neumann, October 29, 2008. On policing during counterinsurgency and stability operations, see Robert B. Oakley, Michael J. Dziedzic, and Eliot M. Goldberg, eds., *Policing the New World Disorder: Peace Operations and Public Security* (Washington, DC: National Defense University Press, 1998); Seth G. Jones, Jeremy M. Wilson, Andrew Rathmell, and K. Jack Riley, *Establishing Law and Order After Conflict* (Washington, DC: RAND, 2005); Robert M. Perito, *Where Is*

the Lone Ranger When We Need Him? America's Search for a Postconflict Stability Force (Washington, DC: United States Institute of Peace, 2004); David H. Bayley, *Democratizing the Police Abroad:What to Do and How to Do It* (Washington, DC: National Institute of Justice, June 2001).

43. Author interview with Richard Armitage, October 17, 2007.

44. Author interview with Minister Ali Jalali, September 4, 2007.

45. Author interview with Ambassador Ronald Neumann, September 7, 2007.

46. Author interview with Major General Robert Durbin, January 3, 2008.

47. Author interview with Ambassador Ronald Neumann, September 7, 2007.

48. Author correspondence with Ambassador Ronald Neumann, October 29, 2008.

49. Author interview with Lieutenant General Karl Eikenberry, October 27, 2007.

50. The author visited the Office of Military Cooperation—Afghanistan in 2004 and the Office of Security Cooperation—Afghanistan in 2005, as well as regional training centers, to assess the U.S. and Coalition efforts to rebuild the Afghan National Army and the Afghan National Police. On training of the ANA, also see Anja Manuel and P. W. Singer, "A New Model Afghan Army," *Foreign Affairs*, vol. 81, no. 4, July/August 2002, pp. 44–59; Luke Hill, "NATO to Quit Bosnia, Debates U.S. Proposals," *Jane's Defence Weekly*, vol. 40, no. 23, December 10, 2003, p. 6.

51. Anthony Davis, "Kabul's Security Dilemma," *Jane's Defence Weekly*, vol. 37, no. 24, June 12, 2002, pp. 26–27; Mark Sedra, *Challenging the Warlord Culture: Security Sector Reform in Post-Taliban Afghanistan* (Bonn, Germany: Bonn International Center for Conversion, 2002), pp. 28–30.

52. Author interview with Lieutenant General Karl Eikenberry, October 27, 2007.

53. Ibid.

54. Attrition was caused by a number of factors, such as low pay rates and apparent misunderstandings between ANA recruits and the U.S. military. For example, some Afghan soldiers believed they would be taken to the United States for training. On attrition rates, see *Securing Afghanistan's Future: Accomplishments and the Strategic Path Forward, National Army* (Kabul: Ministry of Defense, 2004); *Capitol Hill Monthly Update, Afghanistan* (Washington, DC: United States Department of State, June 2004); *Rebuilding Afghanistan* (Washington, DC: The White House, 2004). Also, author interviews with U.S. Department of Defense officials, May 2006.

55. Author interview with U.S. Army general involved in police and army training in Afghanistan, January 3, 2008.

56. Author interview with Minister of Defense Abdul Rahim Wardak, November 13, 2008.

57. Author interview with Daoud Yaqub, January 2, 2008.

58. "Fighting in Afghanistan Leaves 40 Insurgents Dead," *American Forces Press Service*, June 22, 2005.

59. "Coalition Launches 'Operation Mountain Lion' in Afghanistan," *American Forces Press Service*, April 12, 2006.

60. U.S. Air Force F-15Es, A-10s, and B-52s provided close air support to troops on the ground engaged in rooting out insurgent sanctuaries and support networks. Royal Air Force GR-7s also provided close air support to Coalition troops in contact with enemy forces. U.S. Air Force Global Hawk and Predator aircraft provided intelligence, surveillance, and reconnaissance, while KC-135 and KC-10 aircraft provided refueling support.

61. Neil Chandler and Billy Labrum, "Apache Apocalypse," *Sunday Star* (UK), March 16, 2008.

62. Major Robert W. Redding, "19th SF Group Utilizes MCA Missions to Train Afghan National Army Battalions," *Special Warfare*, vol. 17, February 2005, pp. 22–27.

63. *Afghanistan: Managing Public Finances for Development* (Washington, DC: World Bank, 2005), p. 24.

64. General Barry R. McCaffrey (ret.), Trip to Afghanistan and Pakistan, Memorandum from General McCaffrey to Colonel Mike Meese and Colonel Cindy Jebb, United States Military Academy, June 2006.

65. National Ground Intelligence Center, *Afghanistan: Anti-Coalition Militia (ACM) Tactics, Techniques, and Procedures* (Charlottesville, VA: U.S. Army, National Ground Intelligence Center, 2004).

66. Amrullah Saleh, *Strategy of Insurgents and Terrorists in Afghanistan* (Kabul, Afghanistan: National Directorate of Security, 2006), p. 8.

67. Presidential Office of National Security, *National Threat Assessment 2004* (Kabul: Presidential Office of National Security, April 2004), p. 5.

68. Author interview with Ambassador Said Jawad, August 24, 2007.

69. Combined Forces Command—Afghanistan, *Afghan National Development Poll* (Kabul: Combined Forces Command—Afghanistan, 2005), p. 46.

70. International Security Assistance Force, *Nationwide Research and Survey on Illegal State Opposing Armed Groups (ISOAGS): Qualitative and Quantitative Surveys* (Kabul: International Security Assistance Force, 2006), p. 120.

Chapter Eleven

1. Lieutenant General David W. Barno, *Counter-Insurgency Strategy* (Kabul, Afghanistan: Combined Forces Command—Afghanistan, 2005), slide 14.

2. World Bank, *Afghanistan—State Building, Sustaining Growth, and Reducing Poverty* (Washington, DC: World Bank, 2005), p. 153.

3. Author interview with Ambassador Ronald Neumann, April 16, 2008.

4. Ibid.

5. The Asia Foundation, *Voter Education Planning Survey: Afghanistan 2004 National Elections* (Kabul: The Asia Foundation, July 2004), p. 105.

6. The question posed to Afghans was: "What is the biggest problem in your local area?" I combined the similar issues of unemployment, poverty, and poor economy into one category. See The Asia Foundation, *Afghanistan in 2006: A Survey of the Afghan People* (Kabul: The Asia Foundation, 2006), p. 97.

7. U.S. Department of State, *In Their Own Words: Afghan Views of the U.S., Karzai and the Taliban* (Washington, DC: U.S. Department of State, Bureau of Intelligence and Research, 2006), slides 13 and 16.

8. World Bank, *Afghanistan: State Building*, p. xxvi.

9. Anne Evans et al., eds., *A Guide to Government in Afghanistan* (Kabul: World Bank, and Afghanistan Research and Evaluation Unit, 2004), p. 145.

10. World Bank, *Afghanistan: State Building*, p. 83.

11. Ibid., p. 86.

12. Ibid., pp. 133–34.

13. Other countries also exported electricity to Afghanistan. In May 2003, Tajikistan resumed supplying electricity to the northern Afghanistan province of Kunduz, although power supplies were expected to halt in October 2003. Iran also supplies electricity to Afghanistan, in some areas directly adjacent to the Afghan-Iranian border in Herat, Farah, and Nimroz Provinces. See, for example, U.S. Department of Energy, *Afghanistan Fact Sheet 2004* (Washington, DC: U.S. Department of Energy, 2004); U.S. Department of Energy, *Afghanistan Fact Sheet 2006* (Washington, DC: U.S. Department of Energy, 2006).

14. Author interview with Dr. Abdullah Abdullah, September 14, 2007.

15. Andrew S. Natsios, "The Nine Principles of Reconstruction and Development," *Parameters*, vol. 35, no. 3, Autumn 2005, pp. 4–20.

16. Ron Synovitz, "Afghanistan: Workers Still Await Security Clearance to Repair Kajaki Dam," *Radio Free Europe/Radio Liberty*, June 12, 2007.

17. Author interview with Michelle Parker, August 15, 2007. She had previously managed the USAID Jalalabad Field Office, where she served as the USAID representative in Nangarhar and Laghman Provinces and as the development lead in the Jalalabad Provincial Reconstruction Team from 2004 to 2006.

18. Author correspondence with Ambassador Ronald Neumann, October 29, 2008.

19. Author interview with Michelle Parker, August 15, 2007.

20. Author interview with senior official, Canadian International Development Agency, Kandahar, Afghanistan, January 14, 2007.

21. Combined Forces Command—Afghanistan, *ANSF Operational Primacy Process Planning Group* (Kabul, Afghanistan: Combined Forces Command—Afghanistan, June 2006), slide 16.

22. Combined Forces Command—Afghanistan, *Update to LTG Eikenberry: ANSF Operational Primacy Process Planning Group IPR #3* (Kabul, Afghanistan: Combined Forces Command—Afghanistan, July 15, 2006), slide 10.

23. Joint Center for Operational Analysis, *Provincial Reconstruction Teams in Afghanistan: An Interagency Assessment* (Suffolk, VA: U.S. Department of Defense, Joint Center for Operational Analysis, 2006), p. 12.

24. Author interviews with senior U.S. Defense Department official with knowledge of the assessment, August 21 and October 4, 2007.

25. Denis D. Gray, "Afghan Village 'On the Fence,' " *Washington Times*, April 30, 2007, p. 12.

26. United Nations Assistance Mission in Afghanistan, *UNAMA Assessment of the Effects of the Musa Qala Agreement* (Kabul: United Nations Assistance Mission in Afghanistan, January 2007), p. 3.

27. Author interview with Michael Semple, September 14, 2007.

28. Author interviews with Shahmahmood Miakhel, and August 29 and September 14, 2007.

29. Author interviews with Royal Canadian Mounted Police and U.S. police trainers, Kandahar, Afghanistan, September 18, 2007.

30. Joint Paper by the Government of Afghanistan, UNAMA, CFC—A, ISAF, Canada, Netherlands, UK, and U.S. Governments, *Assessment of Factors Contributing to Insecurity in Afghanistan* (Kabul: Government of Afghanistan, 2006), p. 3.

31. United Nations, *A Review of the Taliban and Fellow Travelers as a Movement: Concept Paper Updating PAG Joint Assessment of June 2006* (Kabul: United Nations Assistance Mission in Afghanistan, August 2007), pp. 5, 8.

32. Afghan Ministry of Defense, *The National Military Strategy, 2005* (Kabul: Afghan Ministry of Defense, 2005), p. 3.

33. Statement of Lieutenant General Karl W. Eikenberry, Testimony Before the U.S. House Armed Services Committee, February 13, 2007, p. 5.

34. United Nations Office on Drugs and Crime, *Afghanistan Opium Survey 2008* (Vienna: United Nations Office on Drugs and Crime, 2008).

35. Author interview with Doug Wankel, director of the Office of Drug Control, Kabul, Afghanistan, November 23, 2005.

36. Ibid.

37. Jon Lee Anderson, "Letter from Afghanistan: The Taliban's Opium War," *The New Yorker*, July 9, 2007.

38. Interview with Doug Wankel, director of the Office of Drug Control, Kabul, Afghanistan, November 23, 2005.

39. Correspondence with former Afghan Minister of Interior Ali Jalali, September 5, 2006.

40. Coalition Provisional Authority and Interim Ministry of Interior, *Talking Points: Drug-Trafficking Trends and Forecast for Iraq, Prepared for Ambassador L.*

Paul Bremer (Baghdad: Coalition Provisional Authority and Interim Ministry of Interior, July 17, 2003), p. 1.

41. Statement of Karen P. Tandy, Administrator, U.S. Drug Enforcement Agency, Testimony Before the House Armed Services Committee, Washington, DC, June 28, 2006.

42. Author interview with intelligence officer, 82nd Airborne Division, Bagram, Afghanistan, March 7, 2008.

43. Author interview with Doug Wankel, January 11, 2007. Statement of Karen P. Tandy, Administrator, U.S. Drug Enforcement Agency, Testimony Before the House Armed Services Committee, Washington, DC, June 28, 2006.

44. Thomas H. Johnson, "Financing Afghan Terrorism: Thugs, Drugs, and Creative Movement of Money," in Jeanne K. Giraldo and Harold A. Trinkunas, *Terrorism Financing and State Responses: A Comparative Perspective* (Stanford, CA: Stanford University Press, 2007), p. 98.

45. Ahmed Rashid, *Taliban: Militant Islam, Oil and Fundamentalism in Central Asia* (New Haven, CT: Yale University Press, 2000), p. 118.

46. Author interview with Ambassador Said Jawad, August 24, 2007.

47. "U.S. Military Links Karzai Brother to Drugs," *ABC World News Tonight,* June 22, 2006. Also see, for example, Ron Moreau and Sami Yousafzai, "A Harvest of Treachery," *Newsweek,* January 9, 2006, p. 32.

48. James Risen, "Reports Link Karzai's Brother to Afghanistan Heroin Trade," *New York Times,* October 4, 2008, p. A1.

49. Author interview with two U.S. intelligence operatives, March 3, 2009.

50. Anthony Loyd, "Corruption, Bribes and Trafficking: A Cancer That Is Engulfing Afghanistan," *The Times* (London), November 24, 2007, p. 55. On other accusations of corruption in the Afghan government, see, for example, Philip Smucker, "Afghan Opium Crop Booms: More People Doing Illicit Trade, Corruption Cited," *Washington Times,* March 16, 2007, p. A17.

51. Sakayi, "Hidden Hands for Damaging the Government," *Daily Afghanistan,* February 25, 2007. It was reprinted in English by the BBC. See "Afghan Daily Says Government Under Attack from Within," *BBC Monitoring South Asia,* February 26, 2007.

52. Author interview with Michelle Parker, August 15, 2007.

53. United Nations Office on Drugs and Crime, *Afghanistan: Opium Survey 2005* (Kabul and Vienna: United Nations Office on Drugs and Crime, 2005), p. 29.

54. Author interview with Doug Wankel, November 23, 2005; *Afghanistan: Opium Survey 2005,* p. iii.

55. *Afghanistan: Opium Survey 2005,* pp. iii–iv.

56. World Bank, *Governance Matters 2008: Worldwide Governance Indicators, 1996–2007* (Washington, DC: World Bank, 2008).

57. Author interview with Deputy Minister of Justice Muhammad Qasim Hashimzai, June 26, 2004. Rama Mani, *Ending Impunity and Building Justice in Afghanistan* (Kabul: Afghanistan Research and Evaluation Unit, 2003), p. 2.

58. Amrullah Saleh, *Strategy of Insurgents and Terrorists in Afghanistan* (Kabul, Afghanistan: National Directorate of Security, 2006), p. 15.

59. Asia Foundation, *Afghanistan in 2006*, pp. 14–16.

60. Stephen Weber et al., *Afghan Public Opinion Amidst Rising Violence* (College Park, MD: Program on International Policy Attitudes, University of Maryland, December 2006), p. 6.

61. U.S. Department of State, *In Their Own Words*, slides 11 and 12.

62. Presidential Office of National Security, *National Threat Assessment 2004* (Kabul: Presidential Office of National Security, April 2004), p. 3.

63. Presidential Office of National Security, *National Threat Assessment 2005* (Kabul: Presidential Office of National Security, April 2005), p. 5.

64. European Union and UNAMA, *Discussion of Taliban and Insurgency* (Kabul: European Union and UNAMA, April 30, 2007), p. 3.

65. Saleh, *Strategy of Insurgents and Terrorists in Afghanistan*, p. 11.

66. Joint Paper by the Government of Afghanistan, UNAMA, CFC-A, ISAF, Canada, Netherlands, UK, and U.S. Governments, *Assessment of Factors Contributing to Insecurity in Afghanistan* (Kabul: Government of Afghanistan, 2006), p. 2.

67. Author interview with Dr. Abdullah Abdullah, September 14, 2007.

68. Author interview with Ambassador James Dobbins, May 7, 2008.

69. Loyd, "Corruption, Bribes and Trafficking," p. 55.

70. Author interview with Ambassador Ronald Neumann, September 7, 2007.

71. Author interview with senior NDS officials, Kabul, Afghanistan, September 22, 2007. The purpose of the interview was to review NDS conclusions on support for the Taliban and other insurgent groups. We reviewed NDS conclusions based on detainee interviews and intelligence reports.

72. Somini Sengupta, "For Afghans, Voting May Be a Life-and-Death Decision," *New York Times*, September 16, 2005, p. A10.

73. World Bank, *Afghanistan: State Building, Sustaining Growth, and Reducing Poverty, 2004*, p. 105.

74. European Union and UNAMA, *Discussion of Taliban and Insurgency*, p. 4.

Chapter Twelve

1. Author interview with Ambassador Ronald Neumann, April 16, 2008.

2. Author interview with Lieutenant General Karl Eikenberry, October 27, 2007.

3. Author interview with Dr. Abdullah Abdullah, September 14, 2007.

4. Rowan Scarborough, "NATO Shrugs Off Afghan Violence," *Washington Times*, March 7, 2006, p. A6.

5. General James L. Jones, USMC (Retired) and Ambassador Thomas R. Pickering, Co-Chairs, *Afghanistan Study Group Report: Revitalizing Our Efforts, Rethinking Our Strategies* (Washington, DC: The Center for the Study of the Presidency, January 2008), p. 7.

6. General Tommy Franks with Malcolm McConnell, *American Soldier* (New York: Regan Books, 2004), p. 277.

7. World Bank, *Afghanistan At a Glance* (Washington, DC: World Bank, 2007), p. 1.

8. International Monetary Fund, *Islamic Republic of Afghanistan: Second Review Under the Three-Year Arrangement Under the Poverty Reduction and Growth Facility—Staff Report* (Washington, DC: International Monetary Fund, July 2007), p. 26.

9. World Bank, *Afghanistan: Rehabilitating the Telecom Sector* (Washington, DC: World Bank, 2006).

10. Secretary of Defense Robert M. Gates, Statement to the House Armed Services Committee, December 11, 2007.

11. Author interview with Abdul Salam Rocketi, September 4, 2006.

12. Pamela Constable, "Gates Visits Kabul, Cites Rise in Cross-Border Attacks," *Washington Post*, January 17, 2007, p. A10.

13. The data come from Admiral Michael Mullen, chairman of the Joint Chiefs of Staff. See, for example, Ed Johnson, "Gates Wants NATO to Reorganize Afghanistan Mission," *Bloomberg News*, December 12, 2007.

14. Antonio Giustozzi, *Koran, Kalashnikov, and Laptop: The Neo-Taliban Insurgency in Afghanistan* (London: Hurst & Company, 2007), p. 102.

15. The Asia Foundation, *Afghanistan in 2006: A Survey of the Afghan People* (Kabul: Asia Foundation, 2006), p. 96. Data on regions are courtesy of the Asia Foundation.

16. Memorandum from the Rendon Group to J5 CENTCOM Strategic Effects, Polling Results—Afghanistan Omnibus May 2007, June 15, 2007.

17. ABC News/BBC/ARD Poll, *Afghanistan—Where Things Stand* (Kabul: ABC News/BBC/ARD Poll, December 2007), p. 12.

18. White House, *President Bush Participates in Joint Press Availability with President Karzai of Afghanistan* (Washington, DC: White House Office of the Press Secretary, August 6, 2007).

19. Afghanistan National Security Council, *National Threat Assessment 2004* (Kabul: Afghanistan National Security Council, April 2004), p. 3.

20. Afghanistan National Security Council, *National Threat Assessment 2005* (Kabul: Afghanistan National Security Council, September 2005), p. 4.

21. Afghanistan National Security Council, *The National Security Policy: The*

Islamic Republic of Afghanistan (Kabul: Afghanistan National Security Council), p. 10.

22. General Michael V. Hayden, *The Current Situation in Iraq and Afghanistan* (Washington, DC: Central Intelligence Agency, 2006), p. 2. The document, which was unclassified, was given to the Senate Armed Services Committee in November 2006.

23. Lieutenant General Michael D. Maples, *The Current Situation in Iraq and Afghanistan* (Washington, DC: Defense Intelligence Agency, 2006), p. 6. The document, which was unclassified, was given to the Senate Armed Services Committee in November 2006.

24. United Nations Department of Safety and Security, *Half-Year Review of the Security Situation in Afghanistan* (Kabul: United Nations, August 2007), p. 1.

25. Author interview with Ambassador Ronald Neumann, September 7, 2007.

26. Author interview with Lieutenant General David Barno, September 4, 2007.

27. Author interview with U.S. intelligence operative, March 8, 2009.

28. Jim Landers, "U.S. Should Double Afghan Aid in Elections' Wake, Envoy Says," *Dallas Morning News*, October 29, 2005.

29. See, for example, White House, *Request for Fiscal Year 2006 Supplemental Appropriations* (Washington, DC: White House, February 16, 2006), p. 63. The State Department was given $43 million for unanticipated requirements in Afghanistan, including $11 million for the subsidy cost of 100 percent debt reduction for Afghanistan. And $32 million went for power-sector projects. This included aid for the replacement of crucial emergency generating equipment, and critical early stage components of the Northeast Transmission Project, a $500 million effort, which was funded primarily by other bilateral and multilateral donors.

30. Author interview with Ambassador Ronald Neumann, September 7, 2007.

31. L. Paul Bremer III, *My Year in Iraq: The Struggle to Build a Future of Hope* (New York: Simon and Schuster, 2006), p. 114.

32. Memo from Ambassador L. Paul Bremer to Secretary Rumsfeld, "Moving Faster: A Problem or Two," July 7, 2003.

33. John Hamre, Memorandum for the Secretary of Defense and the Administrator, Coalition Provisional Authority, "Preliminary Observations Based on My Recent Visit to Baghdad," June 2003.

34. Commander British Forces, *Counterinsurgency in Helmand: Task Force Operational Design*, January 2008, p. 5.

35. Andrew Feickert, *U.S. and Coalition Military Operations in Afghanistan: Issues for Congress* (Washington, DC: Congressional Research Service, June 9, 2006), pp. 4–5.

36. Warren Chin, "British Counter-Insurgency in Afghanistan," *Defense & Security Analysis*, vol. 23, no. 2, June 2007, pp. 201–25; Andrew Feickert, *U.S.*

and Coalition Military Operations in Afghanistan: Issues for Congress (Washington, DC: Congressional Research Service, December 11, 2006), p. 3.

37. Richard K. Kolb, " 'We Are Fighting Evil': Canadians in Afghanistan," *VFW Magazine*, March 2007, p. 26.

38. Adnan R. Khan, "I'm Here to Fight: Canadian Troops in Kandahar," *Maclean's*, April 5, 2006.

39. Author interviews with Canadian soldiers, Kandahar, Afghanistan, January 13–17, 2007.

40. United Nations Assistance Mission in Afghanistan, *A Review of the Taliban and Fellow Travelers as a Movement: Concept Paper Updating PAG Joint Assessment of June 2006* (Kabul: United Nations, August 2007), p. 9.

41. Captain Edward Stewart, *Op MEDUSA—A Summary* (London, Ontario: The Royal Canadian Regiment, 2007). Captain Stewart was the forward public affairs officer for Operation Medusa, from the Task Force 3-06 Battle Group.

42. Board of Inquiry Minutes of Proceedings, Convened by LGen J. C. M. Gauthier, Commander CEFCOM, 22 September 2006, A-10A Friendly Fire Incident 4 September 2006, Panjwayi District, Afghanistan, p. 14.

43. Author interviews with Canadian soldiers, Kandahar, Afghanistan, January 13–17, 2007.

44. Captain Edward Stewart, *Op MEDUSA—A Summary*.

45. Board of Inquiry Minutes of Proceedings, p. 14; Captain Edward Stewart, *Op MEDUSA—A Summary*.

46. Author interviews with Canadian soldiers, Kandahar, Afghanistan, January 13–17, 2007.

47. Board of Inquiry Minutes of Proceedings, p. 14.

48. Alex Dobrota and Omar El Akkad, "Friendly Fire Claims Former Olympic Athlete," *Globe and Mail* (Canada), September 5, 2006.

49. Board of Inquiry Minutes of Proceedings.

50. Captain Edward Stewart, *Op MEDUSA—A Summary*.

51. Captain Edward Stewart, *Op MEDUSA—A Summary*.

52. Patrick Dickson and Sandra Jontz, "Discovering What Makes a Hero," *Stars and Stripes*, June 14, 2005.

53. Inspector General, United States Department of Defense, *Review of Matters Related to the Death of Corporal Patrick Tillman, U.S. Army* (Washington, DC: United States Department of Defense, March 2007).

54. United States House of Representatives Committee on Oversight and Government Reform, *Misleading Information from the Battlefield: The Tillman and Lynch Episodes* (Washington, DC: United States House of Representatives, July 2008), pp. 5, 49. Also see Mary Tillman with Narda Zacchino, *Boots on the Ground by Dusk: My Tribute to Pat Tillman* (New York: Modern Times, 2008).

55. Author interviews with Canadian soldiers, Kandahar, Afghanistan, January 13–17, 2007.

56. Captain Edward Stewart, *Op MEDUSA—A Summary*.

57. Captain Edward Stewart, *Op MEDUSA—A Summary*.

58. Author interviews with Canadian soldiers, Kandahar, Afghanistan, January 13–17, 2007.

59. General James L. Jones, *Allied Command Operations*, slide 6.

60. Letter from Brad Adams, Executive Director of Human Rights Watch's Asia Division, to NATO Secretary General, Subject: Summit in Latvia, October 30, 2006.

61. Author interview with Lieutenant Colonel Simon Hetherington, commanding officer of the Canadian Forces Provincial Reconstruction Team in Kandahar, Kandahar, Afghanistan, January 16, 2007.

62. Michael Smith, "British Troops in Secret Truce with the Taliban," *The Times* (London), October 1, 2006.

63. United Nations Assistance Mission in Afghanistan, *UNAMA Assessment of the Effects of the Musa Qala Agreement* (Kabul: United Nations Assistance Mission in Afghanistan, January 2007), p. 2.

64. Author interview with senior White House official, Washington, DC, November 28, 2007. Also see, for example, Karen DeYoung, "U.S. Notes Limited Progress in Afghan War," *Washington Post*, November 25, 2007, p. A1.

65. Julian E. Barnes, "U.S. Military Says Iraq Is the Priority," *Los Angeles Times*, December 12, 2007.

66. Author interviews with senior U.S. Marine Corps officials, Washington, DC, December 10, 2007.

67. Thom Shanker, "Gates Decides Against Marines' Offer to Leave Iraq for Afghanistan," *New York Times*, December 6, 2007, p. A16.

Chapter Thirteen

1. PBS *Frontline*, "The Return of the Taliban," Written, produced, and reported by Martin Smith. Airdate: October 3, 2006.

2. See, for example, Murray Gell-Mann, *The Quark and the Jaguar* (New York: Henry Holt and Company, 1994); John Holland, *Hidden Order* (Reading, MA: Addison-Wesley, 1995); Kevin Dooley, "A Complex Adaptive Systems Model of Organization Change," *Nonlinear Dynamics, Psychology, and Life Science*, vol. 1, no. 1, 1997, pp. 69–97.

3. Author interview with Commander Larry Legree, June 10, 2008.

4. Joby Warrick, "CIA Places Blame for Bhutto Assassination," *Washington Post*, January 18, 2008, p. A1.

5. Author interview with U.S. intelligence officer, Bagram, Afghanistan, March 8, 2008.

6. On cooperation among insurgents, see Barnett R. Rubin, *Afghanistan and the International Community: Implementing the Afghanistan Compact* (New York: Council on Foreign Relations, 2006); "Afghan Taliban Say No Talks Held with U.S., No Differences with Hekmatyar," *Karachi Islam*, February 24, 2005, pp. 1, 6; "Pajhwok News Describes Video of Afghan Beheading by 'Masked Arabs,' Taliban," *Pajhwok Afghan News*, October 9, 2005; "Spokesman Says Taliban 'Fully Organized,' " *Daily Ausaf* (Islamabad), June 23, 2005, pp. 1, 6; "UK Source in Afghanistan Says al Qa'ida Attacks Boost Fear of Taliban Resurgence," *The Guardian*, June 20, 2005; "Taliban Military Chief Threatens to Kill U.S. Captives, Views Recent Attacks, Al-Qa'ida," Interview with Al Jazeera TV, July 18, 2005.

7. David Galula, *Counterinsurgency Warfare: Theory and Practice* (St. Petersburg, FL: Hailer Publishing, 2005), pp. 11–12, 78–79.

8. On terrorism and learning, see Brian A. Jackson, *Aptitude for Destruction, Vol. 1: Organizational Learning in Terrorist Groups and Its Implications for Combating Terrorism* (Santa Monica, CA: RAND, 2005); Jackson, *Aptitude for Destruction, Vol. 2: Case Studies of Organizational Learning in Five Terrorist Groups* (Santa Monica, CA: RAND: 2005).

9. United Nations Assistance Mission in Afghanistan, *A Review of the Taliban and Fellow Travelers as a Movement: Concept Paper Updating PAG Joint Assessment of June 2006* (Kabul: United Nations, August 2007), p. 3.

10. United States Marine Corps, *After Action Report on Operations in Afghanistan* (Camp Lejeune, NC: United States Marine Corps, August 2004); *Operation Enduring Freedom: Tactics, Techniques, and Procedures* (Fort Leavenworth, KS: U.S. Army Training and Doctrine Command, December 2003); United Nations Department of Safety and Security, *Half-Year Review of the Security Situation in Afghanistan* (Kabul: United Nations, August 2007).

11. Amnesty International, *Amnesty International Contacts Taliban Spokesperson, Urges Release of Hostages* (New York: Amnesty International, August 2, 2007).

12. See, for example, Action Memo from Steven Casteel (Senior Adviser to the Iraq Ministry of Interior) to L. Paul Bremer (Administrator of the Coalition Provisional Authority), Ransom Payments for Hostages, April 21, 2004. According to the memo, the Japanese government paid $750,000 per hostage for the release of three Japanese hostages captured on April 8, 2004, near Fallujah, and the French government paid $600,000 for the release of journalist Alexandre Jordanov.

13. Letter from L. Paul Bremer (Administrator of the Coalition Provisional Authority) to Foreign Embassies in Iraq, Ransom Payments for Hostages, April 21, 2004.

14. See, for example, Ian Fisher, "Italy Paid Ransom for Journalist, It Confirms," *International Herald Tribune*, March 22, 2007, p. 1; Peter Kiefer, "Italian Leader Faces New Attack on Prisoner Swap After Reported Death of Jour-

nalist's Aide," *New York Times*, April 10, 2007, p. A12; Massoud Ansari, "Taliban Funds Blitz on British Troops with Hostage Cash," *The Sunday Telegraph* (London), October 14, 2007; Saeed Ali Achakzai, "Korea Pays Taliban $24m for Hostages," *The Sunday Mail* (Australia), September 2, 2007, p. 46.

15. "Taliban Military Chief Threatens to Kill U.S. Captives."

16. Lester Grau, ed., *The Bear Went Over the Mountain: Soviet Combat Tactics in Afghanistan* (Washington, DC: National Defense University Press, 1996); Grau, *Artillery and Counterinsurgency: The Soviet Experience in Afghanistan* (Fort Leavenworth, KS: Foreign Military Studies Office, 1997); U.S. Army Training and Doctrine Command, *Operation Enduring Freedom: Tactics, Techniques, and Procedures* (Fort Leavenworth, KS: U.S. Army Training and Doctrine Command, December 2003).

17. Statement of Lieutenant General Karl Eikenberry, Commander, Combined Forces Command—Afghanistan, Testimony before the House Armed Services Committee, Washington, DC, June 28, 2006; Memorandum from General Barry R. McCaffrey (ret.) to Colonel Mike Meese and Colonel Cindy Jebb, United States Military Academy, "Trip to Afghanistan and Pakistan," June 2006, p. 4; *Operation Enduring Freedom: Tactics, Techniques, and Procedures*; *Opposing Militant Forces: Elections Scenario* (Kabul: ISAF, 2005).

18. "The Rule of Allah," Video by Al Qa'ida in Afghanistan, produced in 2006; "Taliban Execute Afghan Woman on Charges of Spying for U.S. Military," *Afghan Islamic Press*, August 10, 2005; "Afghan Taliban Report Execution of Two People on Charges of Spying for U.S.," *Afghan Islamic Press*, July 12, 2005.

19. "Taliban Says Responsible for Pro-Karzai Cleric's Killing, Warns Others," *The News* (Islamabad), May 30, 2005; "Taliban Claim Responsibility for Killing Afghan Cleric," Kabul Tolo Television, May 29, 2005. Also see the killings of other clerics, such as Mawlawi Muhammad Khan, Mawlawi Muhammad Gol, and Mawlawi Nur Ahmad in " 'Pro-Karzai' Cleric Killed by Bomb in Mosque in Khost Province," *Pajhwok Afghan News*, October 14, 2005; "Karzai Condemns Murder of Clerics," *Pajhwok Afghan News*, October 18, 2005. Also see Antonio Giustozzi, *Koran, Kalashnikov, and Laptop: The Neo-Taliban Insurgency in Afghanistan* (London: Hurst & Company, 2007), p. 46.

20. "Taliban Threatens Teachers, Students in Southern Afghan Province," *Pajhwok Afghan News*, January 3, 2006. Also see "Gunmen Set Fire to Schools in Ghazni, Kandahar Provinces," *Pajhwok Afghan News*, December 24, 2005.

21. Afghan Islamic Press interview with Mofti Latifollah Hakimi, August 30, 2005.

22. Olivier Roy, *Islam and Resistance in Afghanistan*, 2nd ed. (New York: Cambridge University Press, 1990); Ahmed Rashid, *Taliban: Militant Islam, Oil and Fundamentalism in Central Asia* (New Haven, CT: Yale University Press, 2000); William Maley, ed., *Fundamentalism Reborn? Afghanistan and the Taliban* (New York: New York University Press, 2001).

23. Commander British Forces, *Counterinsurgency in Helmand: Task Force Operational Design*, January 2008.

24. Estimates of insurgents are notoriously difficult for two reasons. First, it is difficult to count the number of insurgents, since they hide in urban and rural areas to evade foreign and domestic intelligence and security forces. Second, the number of insurgents is often fluid. Some are full-time fighters but many are not. In addition, there is a significant logistics, financial, and political support network for insurgent groups, making it virtually impossible to reliably estimate the total number of guerrillas and their support base. These reasons make it more difficult to estimate the number of insurgents than to estimate the size of state military forces. On the Taliban numbers, the author interviewed U.S., European, and Afghan officials on numerous occasions throughout 2004, 2005, and 2006.

25. United Nations, *A Review of the Taliban and Fellow Travelers as a Movement: Concept Paper Updating PAG Joint Assessment of June 2006* (Kabul: United Nations Assistance Mission in Afghanistan, August 2007), p. 3.

26. Amrullah Saleh, *Strategy of Insurgents and Terrorists in Afghanistan* (Kabul: National Directorate of Security, 2006), p. 2.

27. Mariam Abou Zahab and Olivier Roy, *Islamist Networks: The Afghan-Pakistan Connection*, translated by John King (New York: Columbia University Press, 2004), p. 13.

28. Al Jazeera interview with Mullah Dadullah, February 2006. Also see, for example, "Taliban Spokesman Condemns Afghan Parliament as 'Illegitimate,' " Sherberghan Aina Television, December 19, 2005.

29. "Spokesman Rejects Afghan Government's Amnesty Offer for Taliban Leader," *Afghan Islamic Press*, May 9, 2005.

30. See, for example, "Al Jazeera Airs Hikmatyar Video," Al Jazeera TV, May 4, 2006.

31. Gulbuddin Hekmatyar, May 2007, recorded DVD response to Agence France Presse questions. Also see, for example, Sardar Ahmad, "Afghan Insurgency Here for a Long Time: Rebel Leader," Agence France Presse, May 6, 2007.

32. Parts of the video clip were released in such Pakistan newspapers as *Dawn*. See, for example, "US Can't Stay for Long in Afghanistan: Hekmatyar," *Dawn* (Pakistan), February 22, 2007.

33. The video clip was released in 2003. See, for example, Aileen McCabe, "Attack Seen as 'Payback' for Drug Raid," *National Post* (Canada), January 28, 2004, p. A2. Hekmatyar's comments were regularly anti-American. In an address to U.S. President George W. Bush, he noted: "You must have realized that attacking Afghanistan and Iraq was a historic mistake. You do not have any other option but to take out your forces from Iraq and Afghanistan and give the Iraqis and Afghans the right to live their own way." Zarar Khan, "Afghan Warlord Splits with Taliban, Hints at Talks with Karzai Government," Associated Press, March 8, 2007.

34. Roy, *Islam and Resistance in Afghanistan*, pp. 77–78.

35. Gilles Kepel, *Jihad: The Trail of Political Islam* (Cambridge, MA: Harvard University Press, 2002), pp. 141–43.

36. Author interview with Ambassador Said Jawad, August 24, 2007.

37. United Nations, *A Review of the Taliban and Fellow Travelers as a Movement: Concept Paper Updating PAG Joint Assessment of June 2006* (Kabul: United Nations Assistance Mission in Afghanistan, August 2007), p. 4.

38. Author interview with Robert Grenier, November 6, 2007.

39. See, for example, Zahab and Roy, *Islamist Networks*, p. 1.

40. The term *salafi jihadist* initially began to occur in the literature of the Islamic Armed Group in Algeria. See, for example, Alain Grignard, "La littérature politique du GIA, des origines à Djamal Zitoun—Esquisse d'une analyse," in F. Dassetto, ed., *Facettes de l'Islam belge* (Louvain-la-Neuve, Belgium: Academia-Bruylant, 2001).

41. Video clip of Abu Laith al-Libi, released in September 2007.

42. Zahab and Roy, *Islamist Networks*, p. 14

43. See, for example, Thomas H. Johnson, "The Taliban Insurgency and an Analysis of Shabnamah (Night Letters)," *Small Wars and Insurgencies*, vol. 18, no. 3, September 2007, pp. 317–44.

44. "Taliban Military Chief Threatens to Kill U.S. Captives."

45. Saleh, *Strategy of Insurgents and Terrorists in Afghanistan*, p. 8.

46. "Religious Scholars Call on Taliban to Abandon Violence," *Pajhwok News Agency*, July 28, 2005.

47. "Taliban Claim Killing of Pro-Government Religious Scholars in Helmand," *Afghan Islamic Press*, July 13, 2005.

48. The Asia Foundation, *Voter Education Planning Survey: Afghanistan 2004 National Elections* (Kabul: The Asia Foundation, 2004); pp. 107–8.

49. Author interview with Ambassador Ronald Neumann, September 7, 2007.

Chapter Fourteen

1. The North Atlantic Treaty, Washington, DC, April 4, 1949.

2. Eric V. Larson, "U.S. Air Force Roles Reach Beyond Securing the Skies," *RAND Review*, vol. 26, no. 2, Summer 2002.

3. Author interview with NATO military official, Kandahar, Afghanistan, September 16, 2007.

4. Douglas J. Feith, *War and Decision: Inside the Pentagon at the Dawn of the War on Terrorism* (New York: HarperCollins, 2008), p. 154.

5. Author interview with Daoud Yaqub, January 2, 2008.

6. UNDP, *Rebuilding the Justice Sector of Afghanistan* (Kabul: United Nations Development Program, January 2003), p. IA.

7. The Bonn Agreement (2001), article II, paragraph 2.

8. Author interviews with Carlos Batori, counselor and deputy head of mission, Italian Government, Kabul, June 22, 2004, and Colonel Gary Medvigy, Office of Military Cooperation—Afghanistan, June 24, 2004.

9. J. Alexander Thier, *Reestablishing the Judicial System in Afghanistan* (Stanford, CA: Center on Democracy, Development, and the Rule of Law, Stanford University, September 2004), p. 13.

10. Feith, *War and Decision*, pp. 153–55.

11. World Bank, *Governance Matters 2007:Worldwide Governance Indicators, 1996–2006* (Washington, DC: World Bank, 2007).

12. Transparency International, *Corruption Perceptions Index 2007* (Berlin, Germany: Transparency International, 2007).

13. World Bank, *Governance Matters 2007*.

14. Author interview with Daoud Yaqub, January 2, 2008.

15. Author interview with Lieutenant General Karl Eikenberry, October 27, 2007.

16. United Nations Security Council Resolution 1510, October 13, 2003, S/RES/1510. Resolution 1510 specifically authorized "expansion of the mandate of the International Security Assistance Force to allow it, as resources permit, to support the Afghan Transitional Authority and its successors in the maintenance of security in areas of Afghanistan outside of Kabul and its environs, so that the Afghan Authorities as well as the personnel of the United Nations and other international civilian personnel engaged, in particular, in reconstruction and humanitarian efforts, can operate in a secure environment, and to provide security assistance for the performance of other tasks in support of the Bonn Agreement."

17. Hans-Jürgen Leersch, "Deutsche Soldaten werden im Norden Afghanistans patrouillieren," *Die Welt,* October 16, 2003; Halima Kazem, "Germany Pushes to Extend Security Beyond Kabul," *Christian Science Monitor*, October 7, 2003, p. 7.

18. Author interview with Lieutenant General David Barno, September 4, 2007; North Atlantic Treaty Organization, *NATO in Afghanistan: How Did This Operation Evolve?* (Brussels: NATO, 2008).

19. Map courtesy of NATO.

20. Author interview with Lieutenant General David Barno, September 4, 2007.

21. Anne Barnard and Neil Swidey, "U.S. Commander's Background Considered a Strength in War with Iraq," *Boston Globe*, March 27, 2003, p. A28.

22. Lieutenant General Ricardo S. Sanchez with Donald T. Phillips, *Wiser in Battle: A Soldier's Story* (New York: HarperCollins, 2008), p. 50.

23. United Nations Security Council Resolution 1623, September 13, 2005, S/RES/1623.

24. Eric Schmitt and David S. Cloud, "U.S. May Start Pulling Out of Afghanistan Next Spring," *New York Times*, September 14, 2005, p. 3; Bradley Graham, "U.S. Considering Troop Reduction in Afghanistan," *Washington Post*, September 14, 2005, p. A26.

25. See, for example, Eric Schmitt, "U.S. to Cut Force in Afghanistan," *New York Times*, December 20, 2005, p. A19.

26. See, for example, Christopher Layne, "America as European Hegemon," *National Interest*, no. 72, Summer 2003, pp. 17–29.

27. Elizabeth Pond, *Friendly Fire: The Near-Death of the Transatlantic Alliance* (Washington, DC: Brookings Institution Press, 2004), pp. 56–62; Laurent Cohen-Tanugi, *An Alliance at Risk: The United States and Europe Since September 11* (Baltimore, MD: Johns Hopkins University Press, 2004), p. 82.

28. Claire Trean, "La guerre contre l'Irak se fera sans le feu vert des Nations unies," *Le Monde*, March 12, 2003; Luc de Barochez, "Alors que la date du prochain vote du Conseil de securité n'est pas encore fixée," *Le Figaro*, March 11, 2003; "Paris rejetera une deuxième resolution au conseil de securité," *La Tribune*, March 11, 2003, p. 4.

29. See, for example, the speech by Foreign Minister Frank-Walter Steinmeier to the German Bundestag, Berlin, December 14, 2005: "Speech by Foreign Minister Steinmeier in the German Bundestag" (Berlin: Federal Foreign Office, December 2005). Also see Chancellor Angela Merkel's objections to the U.S. prison at Guantánamo Bay in Jens Tartler and Olaf Gersemann, "Merkel fordert Ende von Guantánamo," *Financial Times Deutschland*, January 9, 2006.

30. Henry A. Kissinger, "Role Reversal and Alliance Realities," *Washington Post*, February 10, 2003, p. A21.

31. Patrick E. Tyler, "Threats and Responses: Old Friends," *New York Times*, February 12, 2003, p. A1.

32. Ivo H. Daalder, "The End of Atlanticism," *Survival*, vol. 45, no. 2, Summer 2003, pp. 147–48. Also see Samuel F. Wells, "The Transatlantic Illness," *Wilson Quarterly*, vol. XXVII, no. 1, Winter 2003, pp. 40–46; James B. Steinberg, "An Elective Partnership: Salvaging Transatlantic Relations," *Survival*, vol. 45, no. 2, Summer 2003, pp. 113–46; Philip H. Gordon and Jeremy Shapiro, *Allies at War: America, Europe, and the Crisis Over Iraq* (New York: McGraw-Hill, 2004), p. 2.

33. Eric Schmitt, "NATO Troops Will Relieve Americans in Fighting the Taliban," *New York Times*, December 31, 2005, p. A3.

34. Jason Beattie, "5,000 British Troops to Root Out the Taliban," *The Evening Standard* (London), September 13, 2005, p. 8.

35. Doug Saunders, "NATO Chief Defends Afghan Mission," *The Globe and Mail*, March 7, 2006, p. A12.

36. Author interview with Lieutenant General Karl Eikenberry, October 27, 2007.

37. UK House of Commons Select Committee on Defence, *Thirteenth Report* (London: HMSC, 2007), para. 46.

38. Author interview with NATO official, NATO ISAF Headquarters, Kabul, Afghanistan, September 15, 2007.

39. Judy Dempsey and David S. Cloud, "Europeans Balking at New Afghan Role," *International Herald Tribune*, September 14, 2005, p. 1.

40. UK House of Commons Select Committee on Defence, *Thirteenth Report*, para. 43.

41. German Marshall Fund of the United States and the Compagnia di San Paolo (Italy), *Transatlantic Trends: Key Findings 2007* (Washington, DC: German Marshall Fund of the United States and the Compagnia di San Paolo, 2007), p. 33.

42. Author interview with General Markus Kneip, September 6, 2006.

43. John D. Banusiewicz, " 'National Caveats' Among Key Topics at NATO Meeting," *American Forces Press Service*, February 9, 2005.

44. Author interview with Ambassador David Sproule, January 10, 2007.

45. Author interviews with senior German military officials in Mazar-e-Sharif and Kunduz, September 6–7, 2006; September 2007.

46. Memorandum from General Barry R. McCaffrey (ret.) to Colonel Mike Meese and Colonel Cindy Jebb, United States Military Academy, "Trip to Afghanistan and Pakistan," June 2006, p. 4.

47. Quoted in Hy S. Rothstein, *Afghanistan and the Troubled Future of Unconventional Warfare* (Annapolis, MD: Naval Institute Press, 2006), p. 111.

48. Secretary of Defense Robert M. Gates, Statement to the House Armed Services Committee, December 11, 2007.

49. Peter Spiegel, "Gates Says NATO Force Unable to Fight Guerrillas," *Los Angeles Times*, January 16, 2008, p. A1.

50. David Galula, *Counterinsurgency Warfare: Theory and Practice* (St. Petersburg, FL: Hailer Publishing, 2005), p. 77.

51. The clear, hold, and expand section draws extensively from Joseph D. Celeski, *Operationalizing COIN, JSOU Report 05-2* (Hurlburt Field, FL: Joint Special Operations University, 2005).

52. Celeski, *Operationalizing COIN*.

53. Colonel Bruce Burda, *Operation Enduring Freedom Lessons Learned* (Hurlburt Field, FL: Air Force Special Operations Command, 2003).

54. Author interview with Western ambassador, Kabul, Afghanistan, September 13, 2007.

55. Author interviews with Canadian soldiers, Kandahar, Afghanistan, September 16–19, 2007. See also, for example, United Nations Assistance Mission

in Afghanistan, *A Review of the Taliban and Fellow Travelers as a Movement: Concept Paper Updating PAG Joint Assessment of June 2006* (Kabul: United Nations, August 2007).

56. Author interview with senior NATO military official, Kandahar, Afghanistan, September 16, 2007.

57. Letter from Paddy Ashdown to Gordon Brown and David Miliband, December 2007.

58. Author interview with Lieutenant General Karl Eikenberry, October 27, 2007.

Chapter Fifteen

1. Rudyard Kipling, *Verses, 1889–1896*, vol. 11 (New York: Charles Scribner, 1899), p. 79.

2. "Enemy Assault on North OP in VIC BCP 213 Shkin," U.S. After Action Report, September 22, 2005. I interviewed one of the U.S. officials present at Shkin that night (he wished to remain anonymous) on February 7 and February 11, 2007. I also interviewed nearly a dozen U.S. soldiers with similar reports along the Afghanistan-Pakistan border in 2006, 2007, and 2008.

3. Author interview with senior officer, 82nd Airborne Division, March 7, 2008.

4. Quoted in Mohammad Yousaf and Mark Adkin, *Afghanistan—The Bear Trap: The Defeat of a Superpower* (Havertown, PA: Casemate, 2001), p. 20.

5. PBS *Frontline,* "The Return of the Taliban," Written, Produced, and Reported by Martin Smith, Airdate: October 3, 2006.

6. On U.S. aid to Pakistan, see C. Christine Fair and Peter Chalk, *Fortifying Pakistan: The Role of U.S. Internal Security Assistance* (Washington, DC: United States Institute of Peace Press, 2006); Craig Cohen and Derek Chollet, "When $10 Billion Is Not Enough: Rethinking U.S. Strategy toward Pakistan," *Washington Quarterly*, vol. 30, no. 2, Spring 2007, pp. 7–19.

7. David E. Sanger and David Rohde, "U.S. Pays Pakistan to Fight Terror, but Patrols Ebb," *New York Times*, May 20, 2007, p. 1. There were a number of additional *New York Times* investigative pieces on the Coalition support funds. See, for example, David Rohde, Carlotta Gall, Eric Schmitt, and David E. Sanger, "U.S. Officials See Waste in Pakistan Aid," *New York Times*, December 24, 2007, p. A1.

8. Author interview with Dov Zakheim, January 30, 2008.

9. On the capture of these al Qa'ida figures, see Pervez Musharraf, *In the Line of Fire: A Memoir* (New York: Free Press, 2006), pp. 222–63.

10. See, for example, Intikhab Amir, "Waziristan: No Man's Land?" *The Herald* (Pakistan), vol. 37, no. 4, April 2006, pp. 74–79; Amir, "Whose Writ Is It Anyway?" *The Herald* (Pakistan), vol. 37, no. 4, April 2006, pp. 80–82;

Iqbal Khattak, "40 Militants Killed in North Waziristan," *Daily Times* (Pakistan), September 30, 2005.

11. On Operation Anaconda, see, for example, U.S. Air Force, Office of Lessons Learned (AF/XOL), *Operation Anaconda: An Air Power Perspective* (Washington, DC: Headquarters United States Air Force AF/XOL, February 2005); Paul L. Hastert, "Operation Anaconda: Perception Meets Reality in the Hills of Afghanistan," *Studies in Conflict and Terrorism*, vol. 28, no. 1, January–February 2005, pp. 11–20; Sean Naylor, *Not a Good Day to Die: The Untold Story of Operation Anaconda* (New York: Berkley Books, 2005).

12. Musharraf, *In the Line of Fire*, pp. 269–70.

13. Ismail Khan and Alamgir Bhittani, "42 Uzbeks among 58 Dead: Fierce Clashes in S. Waziristan," *Dawn* (Pakistan), March 21, 2007.

14. Assistant Secretary of State for Intelligence and Research Carl W. Ford, Jr. to Secretary of State Colin Powell, "Pakistan—Poll Shows Strong and Growing Public Support for Taleban," November 7, 2001. Released by the National Security Archive.

15. Author interview with Richard Armitage, October 17, 2007.

16. Author interview with Robert Grenier, November 6, 2007.

17. Gary Berntsen and Ralph Pezzullo, *Jawbreaker: The Attack on Bin Laden and Al Qa'ida* (New York: Crown Publishers, 2005), p. 241.

18. Letter from Lieutenant General James B. Vaught (U.S. Army Retired) to Secretary Rumsfeld, October 28, 2003.

19. Author interview with Lieutenant General Karl Eikenberry, October 27, 2007.

20. Author interview with Robert Grenier, November 6, 2007.

21. General Barry R. McCaffrey USA (ret.), *After Action Report*, February 26, 2007.

22. The rest of this section relies on extensive author interviews with American, European, Canadian, Afghan, and Pakistani government officials between 2003 and 2008. The interviews—which took place throughout Afghanistan and in Washington, London, Brussels, The Hague, and Ottawa—were conducted with military, political, and intelligence officials.

23. Husain Haqqani, *Pakistan: Between Mosque and Military* (Washington, DC: Carnegie Endowment for International Peace, 2005), p. 240.

24. "Outgoing U.S. Envoy Enthusiastic about Afghanistan's Future," Sherberghan Aina Television, June 18, 2005. Ambassador Khalilzad's comments were supported by President Karzai's office in "Afghan Spokesman Calls on Pakistan to Curb Taliban Activities," Kabul Tolo Television, June 21, 2005.

25. Author interview with senior adviser to Ambassador Zalmay Khalilzad, Kabul, Afghanistan, June 24, 2004.

26. International Security Assistance Force, *Nationwide Research and Survey on*

Illegal State Opposing Armed Groups (ISOAGS): Qualitative and Quantitative Surveys (Kabul: International Security Assistance Force, 2006).

27. Author interviews with three U.S. soldiers from 7th Group Special Forces, Washington, DC, May 10, 2007.

28. Author interviews with senior U.S. officials, U.S. Embassy, Kabul.

29. David Kilcullen, *The Accidental Guerrilla: Fighting Small Wars in the Midst of a Big One* (New York: Oxford University Press, 2009), p. 57.

30. Barnett R. Rubin, *Afghanistan and the International Community: Implementing the Afghanistan Compact* (New York: Council on Foreign Relations, 2006), p. 24.

31. Author interviews with three U.S. soldiers from 7th Group Special Forces, Washington, DC, May 10, 2007.

32. European Union and UNAMA, *Discussion of Taliban and Insurgency* (Kabul: European Union and UNAMA, April 30, 2007), p. 4.

33. Pakistani officials frequently denied this assertion. As one Pakistani senator noted in testimony before Pakistan's Senate Foreign Relations Committee: "Pakistan has arrested over 500 Taliban this year from Quetta and 400 of them have been handed over to Afghans." Pakistan Senate Foreign Relations Committee, *Pakistan–Afghanistan Relations*, Report 13 (Islamabad: Pakistan Senate Foreign Relations Committee, March 2007), p. 38.

34. Amir, "Waziristan: No Man's Land?" p. 78.

35. Author interview with White House official, Washington, DC, June 20, 2007.

36. M. Ilyas Khan, "Profile of Nek Mohammad," *Dawn* (Pakistan), June 19, 2004.

37. Locals denied the existence of the last clause and argued that they did not agree to register all foreigners with the government.

38. Iqbal Khattak, "I Did Not Surrender to the Military, Said Nek Mohammad," *The Friday Times* (Pakistan), April 30–May 6, 2004.

39. Ismail Khan and Dilawar Khan Wazir, "Night Raid Kills Nek, Four Other Militants," *Dawn* (Pakistan), June 19, 2004.

40. See, for example, Peace Pact North Waziristan, September 5, 2006. This agreement was negotiated by a political agent from North Waziristan representing Governor N.W.F.P. Federal Government, and tribal representatives from North Waziristan, Local Mujahideen N.W.F.P., Atmanzai Tribe.

41. Pakistan Ministry of Interior, *The Talibanisation Problem* (Islamabad: Ministry of Interior, 2007). The document was subsequently leaked to the press. See, for example, Ismail Khan, "Talibanisation Imperils Security, NSC Warned: Immediate Action Urged," *Dawn* (Pakistan), June 22, 2007.

42. U.S. Department of State, *Afghanistan, Autumn 2006: A Campaign at a Crossroads* (Washington, DC: Office of the Coordinator for Counterterrorism, U.S. Department of State, 2006), pp. 2–3. Unclassified document.

43. Amir, "Whose Writ Is It Anyway?" pp. 80–82.

44. Transcript of Martin Smith interview with General Pervez Musharraf, Pakistan, June 8, 2006. I received a copy of the transcript from *Frontline*.

45. In one public statement, for example, the Taliban argued that "the situation is augmenting and the Taliban in Waziristan are capturing hearts and minds. We see the tribes who were struggling for tens of years accepting arbitration by Taliban scholars." Taliban Statement on Waziristan, April 13, 2006.

46. Author interviews with Pakistan government officials, Washington, DC, January 2006.

47. Lieutenant General David W. Barno, Testimony Before the Committee on Foreign Affairs, U.S. House of Representatives, February 15, 2007, p. 21.

48. Ibid.

49. Author interview with senior Indian intelligence official, April 4, 2007.

50. David C. Mulford, U.S. Ambassador to India, *Afghanistan Has Made a Remarkable Transition* (New Delhi: U.S. Department of State, February 2006); Amin Tarzi, "Afghanistan: Kabul's India Ties Worry Pakistan," *Radio Free Europe/Radio Liberty*, April 16, 2006.

51. Border Roads Organisation, *Vision, Mission, Role* (Delhi: Border Roads Organisation, 2006).

52. Feroz Hassan Khan, "The Durand Line: Tribal Politics and Pakistan-Afghanistan Relations," Paper Presented at a Conference on Tribalism, U.S. Naval Postgraduate School, Monterey, CA, September 2006, p. 20. As one Pakistan Senate panel concluded, India was more successful at winning Afghan hearts and minds than Pakistan. Pakistan Senate Foreign Relations Committee, *Pakistan—Afghanistan Relations*, Report 13, p. 9.

53. Author interview with Sayed Fazlullah Wahidi, May 20, 2008.

54. See, for example, Aly Zaman, "India's Increased Involvement in Afghanistan and Central Asia: Implications for Pakistan," *Islamabad Policy Research Journal*, vol. 3, no. 2, Summer 2003; Aimal Khan, "Historic Hostility," *The Herald* (Pakistan), vol. 37, no. 4, April 2006, pp. 83–85; Khan, "The Durand Line: Tribal Politics and Pakistan-Afghanistan Relations," p. 20.

55. Feroz Hassan Khan, "Rough Neighbors: Afghanistan and Pakistan," *Strategic Insights*, vol. II, issue 1, January 2003, p. 6.

56. Author interview with Ambassador Wendy Chamberlin, August 27, 2008.

57. Abd Allah Mustawfi, *Shahr-i zindigani-yi man ya tarikh-i ijtima'i va idari-yi dawreh-yi qajariyeh* [*The Town of My Life or the History of Society and Administration of the Qajar Era*] (Tehran: Kitabfurushi-yi Zavvab, 1964).

58. Author interview with General Dan McNeill, May 25, 2008. See, for example, John Ward Anderson, "Arms Seized in Afghanistan Sent From Iran, NATO Says," *Washington Post*, September 21, 2007, p. A12; Tom Coghlan, "Iran 'Arming Taliban with Anti-Armour Roadside Bombs,'" *Daily Telegraph* (London), October 4, 2007, p. 1; Robin Wright, "Iranian

Arms Destined for Taliban Seized in Afghanistan, Officials Say," *Washington Post*, September 16, 2007, p. A19.

59. Author interviews with NATO officials: Washington, DC, June 4, 2007; Kabul, Afghanistan, September 15, 2007; Kandahar, Afghanistan, September 17, 2007.

60. Author interview with Ambassador Said Jawad, August 24, 2007.

61. Author interviews with NATO officials: Washington, DC, June 4, 2007; Kabul, Afghanistan, September 15, 2007; Kandahar, Afghanistan, September 17, 2007.

62. Author interview with Afghan Foreign Minister Rangin Dadfar Spanta, July 2006; author interview with Dr. Zalmai Rassoul, November 23, 2005.

63. Memorandum of Conversation, From L. Paul Bremer III, June 22, 2003 Meeting with Kofi Annan, Amman, Jordan.

64. Defense Intelligence Agency, "Iranian Support to the Afghan Resistance," excerpt from unidentified study, n.d.; Defense Intelligence Agency, "Iranian Support to the Afghan Resistance," 11 July 1985. Released by the National Security Archive.

65. Thom Shanker, "Iran May Know of Weapons for Taliban, Gates Contends," *New York Times*, June 14, 2007, p. 12.

66. Bill Gertz, "China Arming Terrorists," *Washington Times*, June 15, 2007, p. 5.

67. Author interviews with NATO officials, Kandahar, Afghanistan, September 17, 2007.

68. Steve Coll, *Ghost Wars: The Secret History of the CIA, Afghanistan, and Bin Laden, from the Soviet Invasion to September 10, 2001* (New York: Penguin Press, 2004), p. 66.

69. European Union and UNAMA, *Discussion of Taliban and Insurgency*, p. 5.

70. On Saudi Arabia's historical role in Afghanistan, see National Commission on Terrorist Attacks Upon the United States, *The 9/11 Commission Report* (New York: W. W. Norton, 2004), pp. 371–74.

71. Lord Curzon of Kedleston, *Frontiers: The Romanes Lecture 1907* (Westport, CT: Greenwood Press, 1976), p. 7.

72. U.S. State Department, *Afghanistan, Autumn 2006*, p. 17. Unclassified document.

73. Eric Schmitt, Mark Mazzetti, and Carlotta Gall, "U.S. Hopes to Arm Pakistani Tribes Against Al Qa'ida," *New York Times*, November 19, 2007, p. A1.

74. Author interview with White House official, Washington, DC, June 20, 2007.

75. Author interview with Western ambassador, Kabul, Afghanistan, September 13, 2007; author interview with Western ambassador, Kabul, Afghanistan, January 10, 2007.

Chapter Sixteen

1. National Intelligence Council, *The Terrorist Threat to the U.S. Homeland* (Washington, DC: National Intelligence Council, July 2007), p. 1.

2. Office of the Director of National Intelligence, *Annual Threat Assessment of the Director of National Intelligence* (Washington, DC: Office of the Director of National Intelligence, February 2008), pp. 5–6.

3. Author interview with FBI counterterrorism official, July 1, 2008.

4. House of Commons, *Report of the Official Account of the Bombings in London on 7th July 2005*, HC 1087 (London: The Stationery Office, 2006), p. 21.

5. Bruce Hoffman, "Challenges for the U.S. Special Operations Command Posed by the Global Terrorist Threat: Al Qa'ida on the Run or on the March?" Written Testimony Submitted to the House Armed Services Sub-committee on Terrorism, Unconventional Threats and Capabilities, February 14, 2007.

6. On the plot's connection to al Qa'ida, see United States Department of State, *Country Reports on Terrorism 2006*, p. 269.

7. Author interview with Bruce Riedel, Washington, DC, June 5, 2008.

8. Seth G. Jones and Martin Libicki, *How Terrorist Groups End* (Santa Monica, CA: RAND, forthcoming).

9. National Commission on Terrorist Attacks Upon the United States, *The 9/11 Commission Report* (New York: W. W. Norton, 2004), p. 60; Daniel Benjamin and Steve Simon, *The Age of Sacred Terror* (New York: Random House, 2002), pp. 132, 242.

10. "Declaration of Jihad Against the Americans Occupying the Land of the Two Holy Mosques," *Al Islah* (London), September 2, 1996.

11. "Text of World Islamic Front's Statement Urging Jihad Against Jews and Crusaders," *Al-Quds al-Arabi* (London), February 23, 1998.

12. House of Commons, *Report of the Official Account of the Bombings in London on 7th July 2005*, p. 29.

13. See, for example, Bernard Lewis, *The Crisis of Islam* (New York: Random House, 2003), p. xi.

14. On the establishment of a Caliphate, see, for example, Abu Bakr Naji, *The Management of Savagery: The Most Critical Stage Through Which the Umma Will Pass*, translated and published by the John M. Olin Institute for Strategic Studies at Harvard University, May 23, 2006.

15. Ayman al-Zawahiri, *Knights Under the Prophet's Banner*, translated by Laura Mansfield (Old Tappan, NJ: TLG Publications, 2002), p. 132.

16. Osama bin Laden, "Message to the Peoples of Europe," released in November 2007.

17. Fawaz A. Gerges, *The Far Enemy: Why Jihad Went Global* (New York: Cambridge University Press, 2005), p. 49.

18. Zawahiri's reference to the Afghan jihad in this context was the Soviet War in the 1980s. He argued that it provided a critical opportunity for training Arabs against the forthcoming war with the United States. Zawahiri, *Knights Under the Prophet's Banner*, p. 38.

19. This section adopts the framework laid out by Bruce Hoffman. See, for example, Bruce Hoffman, *Inside Terrorism*, 2nd ed. (New York: Columbia University Press, 2006), pp. 285–89; Hoffman, "Challenges for the U.S. Special Operations Command Posed by the Global Terrorist Threat."

20. Indeed, six months after September 11, 2001, al Qa'ida had lost sixteen of twenty-five key leaders on the Pentagon's "Most Wanted" list. Rohan Gunaratna, *Inside Al Qa'ida: Global Network of Terror* (New York: Berkley Books, 2002), p. 303.

21. "Pakistan: Villagers Start Rebuilding Seminary Destroyed in Bajaur Airstrike," *The News* (Pakistan), November 18, 2006.

22. Hoffman, "Challenges for the U.S. Special Operations Command Posed by the Global Terrorist Threat"; Jason Burke, *Al-Qa'ida: The True Story of Radical Islam* (London: Penguin, 2004); Peter L. Bergen, *Holy War, Inc: Inside the Secret World of Osama bin Laden* (New York: Touchstone, 2001); Lawrence Wright, *The Looming Tower: Al-Qaeda and the Road to 9/11* (New York: Knopf, 2006).

23. Greg Miller, "Influx of Al Qa'ida, Money into Pakistan Is Seen," *Los Angeles Times*, May 20, 2007.

24. United States Department of State, *Country Reports on Terrorism 2006* (Washington, DC: United States Department of State), p. 269; Hoffman, "Challenges for the U.S. Special Operations Command Posed by the Global Terrorist Threat."

25. House of Commons, *Report of the Official Account of the Bombings in London on 7th July 2005*, pp. 24–27; Hoffman, "Challenges for the U.S. Special Operations Command Posed by the Global Terrorist Threat."

26. New York Police Department, *Threat Analysis: JFK Airport / Pipeline Plot* (New York: New York Police Department, June 2, 2007).

27. Juzgado Central de Instrucción Numero 5, Audiencia Nacional, Sumario (Proc. Ordinario) 21/2006 L, Madrid, 23 Octubre 2007.

28. The Information Center for the Support of the Iraqi People, *Iraqi Jihad, Hopes and Risks: Analysis of the Reality and Visions for the Future, and Actual Steps in the Path of the Blessed Jihad* (The Information Center for the Support of the Iraqi People, December 2003).

29. Lorenzo Vidino, "The Hofstad Group: The New Face of Terrorist Networks in Europe," *Studies in Conflict and Terrorism*, vol. 30, no. 7, pp. 579–92; Algemene Inlichtingen en Veiligheidsdienst, *From Dawa to Jihad: The Various Threats from Radical Islam to the Democratic Legal Order* (The Hague: Algemene Inlichtingen en Veiligheidsdienst, December 2004).

30. U.S. Department of Defense, *Background and Activities of Abd al-Hadi al-Iraqi* (Washington, DC: U.S. Department of Defense, 2007). Also see U.S.

Department of State, *Wanted Poster for Abd al-Hadi al-Iraqi* (Washington, DC: Rewards for Justice Program, U.S. Department of State, 2006).

31. Dipesh Gadher, "Al-Qa'ida 'Planning Big British Attack,' " *Sunday Times* (London), April 22, 2007.

32. On Wadi al-Aqiq, see, for example, Wright, *The Looming Tower*, pp. 166, 192.

33. See, for example, "Bin Laden's Treasurer Appointed New Afghan Qa'ida Leader," *Daily Times* (Pakistan), May 30, 2007.

34. General Michael V. Hayden, *The Current Situation in Iraq and Afghanistan* (Washington, DC: Central Intelligence Agency, 2006), p. 2.

35. Raffi Khatchadourian, "Azzam the American: The Making of an Al Qa'ida Homegrown," *The New Yorker*, January 22, 2007.

36. Lieutenant General Michael D. Maples, *The Current Situation in Iraq and Afghanistan* (Washington, DC: Defense Intelligence Agency, 2006), p. 6.

37. Alex Alexiev, "Tablighi Jamaat: Jihad's Stealthy Legions," *Middle East Quarterly*, vol. 12, no. 1, Winter 2005. On *zakat* and jihad, also see Marc Sageman, *Understanding Terror Networks* (Philadelphia: University of Pennyslvania Press, 2004).

38. See, for example, Alfred B. Prados and Christopher M. Blanchard, *Saudi Arabia: Terrorist Financing Issues* (Washington, DC: Congressional Research Service, 2004); *The 9/11 Commission Report*, p. 55.

39. General Michael V. Hayden, *The Current Situation in Iraq and Afghanistan* (Washington, DC: Central Intelligence Agency, 2006), p. 2.

40. United Nations Security Council, Letter Dated 15 November 2007 from the Chairman of the Security Council Committee Established Pursuant to Resolution 1267 (1999) Concerning Al-Qaida and the Taliban and Associated Individuals and Entities Addressed to the President of the Security Council, November 29, 2007, S/2007/677, p. 8.

41. *United States of America. v. Hassan Abujihaad, a/k/a Paul R. Hall, Abu-Jihaad,* United States District Court, District of Connecticut, No. 3:07-CR-57, Exhibit 2, Federal Bureau of Investigation FD-302 of William "Jamaal" Chrisman. Interview conducted December 2, 2006.

42. Statement from Mullah Omar, Leader of the Taliban, released December 17, 2007.

43. *United States of America v. Babar Ahmad,* United States District Court, District of Connecticut, No. 3:04-CR-301-MRK, Indictment, Filed October 6, 2004.

44. *United States of America v. Syed Talha Ahsan,* United States District Court, District of Connecticut, No. 3:06-CR-194-JCH, Indictment. Also see *United States of America. v. Hassan Abujihaad, a/k/a Paul R. Hall, Abu-Jihaad,* United States District Court, District of Connecticut, No. 3:07-CR-57, Indictment.

45. Author interviews with European, Afghan, and Pakistani government officials,

Kabul, Afghanistan 2004, 2005, 2006, and 2007. Also see Ali Jalali, "The Future of Afghanistan," *Parameters*, vol. 36, no. 1, Spring 2006, p. 8.

46. Author interviews with U.S. government officials in Shkin, Afghanistan, April 2006. Al Jazeera interview with Mullah Dadullah, July 2005. Also see such press accounts as Sami Yousafzai and Ron Moreau, "Unholy Allies," *Newsweek*, September 26, 2005, pp. 40–42.

47. In what appeared to be a forced confession, Saeed Allah Khan stated: "I worked as a spy for the Americans along with four other people. The group received $45,000 and my share is $7,000." Hekmat Karzai, *Afghanistan and the Globalisation of Terrorist Tactics* (Singapore: Institute of Defence and Strategic Studies, January 2006), p. 2.

48. Author interview with U.S. government officials, Kabul, Afghanistan, December 2005.

49. On the rationale for suicide bombers, see Al Jazeera interview with Mullah Dadullah, February 2006.

50. Zawahiri, *Knights Under the Prophet's Banner*, p. 200.

51. C. Christine Fair et al., *Suicide Attacks in Afghanistan, 2001–2007* (Kabul: United Nations Assistance Mission in Afghanistan, September 2007), p. 10.

52. Hekmat Karzai, *Afghanistan and the Logic of Suicide Terrorism* (Singapore: Institute of Defence and Strategic Studies, March 2006); "Taliban Claim Responsibility for Suicide Bomb Attack in Afghan Kandahar Province," *Afghan Islamic Press*, October 9, 2005; "Pajhwok News Describes Video of Afghan Beheading by 'Masked Arabs,' Taliban," *Kabul Pajhwok Afghan News*, October 9, 2005; "Canadian Soldier Dies in Suicide Attack in Kandahar," *Afghan Islamic Press*, March 3, 2006; "Taliban Claim Attack on Police in Jalalabad, Nangarhar Province," Kabul National TV, January 7, 2006.

53. See, for example, Robert Pape, *Dying to Win: The Strategic Logic of Suicide Terrorism* (New York: Random House, 2005); Mia Bloom, *Dying to Kill: The Allure of Suicide Terror* (New York: Columbia University Press, 2005); Christoph Reuter, *My Life Is a Weapon: A Modern History of Suicide Bombing* (Princeton, NJ: Princeton University Press, 2004); Hoffman, *Inside Terrorism*.

54. Hekmat Karzai and Seth G. Jones, "How to Curb Rising Suicide Terrorism in Afghanistan," *Christian Science Monitor*, July 18, 2006.

55. In its public rhetoric, the Taliban tended to identify the suicide bombers as Afghans, since it suggested there was a significant indigenous component of the insurgency.

56. Fair et al., *Suicide Attacks in Afghanistan*, p. 28.

Chapter Seventeen

1. Author interview with Commander Larry Legree, June 10, 2008.

2. Asia Foundation, *Afghanistan in 2008: A Survey of the Afghan People* (Kabul and San Francisco: Asia Foundation, 2008).

3. Author interview with Colonel Martin Schweitzer, March 7, 2008.

4. Colin Soloway, "I Yelled at Them to Stop," *Newsweek,* October 7, 2002; Hy S. Rothstein, *Afghanistan and the Troubled Future of Unconventional Warfare* (Annapolis, MD: Naval Institute Press, 2006), pp. 141–42.

5. Author interview with Colonel Martin Schweitzer, March 7, 2008.

6. Roger Trinquier, *Modern Warfare: A French View of Counterinsurgency,* translated by Daniel Lee (Westport, CT: Praeger, 2006), p. 6.

7. Author interview with Commander Larry Legree, March 8, 2008; author interview with Colonel Martin Schweitzer, March 7, 2008.

8. Author interview with Colonel Martin Schweitzer, March 7, 2008.

9. British Government, Afghanistan: Countering the Insurgency RC(E) vs. RC (S) Comparative Approaches, May 12, 2008.

10. The quote is from Bruce Hoffman and Seth G. Jones, "Cell Phones in the Hindu Kush," *The National Interest,* No. 96, July/August 2008.

11. International Security Assistance Force, *ISAF Campaign Plan* (Kabul: ISAF, November 2008).

12. Trinquier, *Modern Warfare,* p. 6.

13. Prior to the establishment of the first Provincial Reconstruction Teams, Coalition Humanitarian Liaison Cells and U.S. Army Civil Affairs Teams—Afghanistan supported humanitarian assistance, relief, and reconstruction efforts throughout Afghanistan. These began in 2002.

14. Robert Borders, "Provincial Reconstruction Teams in Afghanistan: A Model for Post-Conflict Reconstruction and Development," *Journal of Development and Social Transformation,* vol. 1, November 2004, pp. 5–12; Michael J. McNerney, "Stabilization and Reconstruction in Afghanistan: Are PRTs a Model or a Muddle?" *Parameters,* vol. 35, no. 4, Winter 2005–06, pp. 32–46.

15. Author interview with Commander Larry Legree, June 10, 2008.

16. McNerney, "Stabilization and Reconstruction in Afghanistan," p. 40.

17. Trent Scott and John Agoglia, "Getting the Basics Right: A Discussion on Tactical Actions for Strategic Impact in Afghanistan," *Small Wars Journal,* November 2008; author interview with John Agoglia, November 13, 2008.

18. Author interview with Michelle Parker, August 15, 2007.

19. Author interviews with NATO officials involved in the meetings, Kabul, Afghanistan, May 2008.

20. Author interview with senior NATO intelligence official, November 13, 2008.

21. J. Alexander Thier and Azita Ranjbar, *Killing Friends, Making Enemies: The Impact and Avoidance of Civilian Casualties in Afghanistan* (Washington, DC: United States Institute of Peace, July 2008); Human Rights Watch, *"Troops in Contact": Airstrikes and Civilian Deaths in Afghanistan* (New York: Human Rights Watch, September 2008).

22. Trista Talton and Robert Burns, "Probe: Spec Ops Marines Used Excessive Force," *Marine Corps Times*, April 13, 2007. Also see Afghanistan Independent Human Rights Commission, *Investigation: Use of Indiscriminate and Excessive Force against Civilians by U.S. Forces Following a VBIED Attack in Nangarhar Province on 4 March 2007* (Kabul: Afghanistan Independent Human Rights Commission, 2007).

23. Josh White, "69 Afghans' Families Get a U.S. Apology," *Washington Post*, May 9, 2007, p. A12.

24. Memorandum from Brigadier General Michael W. Callan to Acting Commander, United States Central Command, Subject: Executive Summary of AR 15-6 Investigation into new information relative to civilian casualties from engagement by U.S. and Afghan Forces on 21–22 AUG 2008 in Azizabad, Shindand District, Herat Province, Afghanistan, October 1, 2008.

25. Statement by the Special Representative of the Secretary-General for Afghanistan, Kai Eide, on Civilian Casualties Caused by Military Operations in Shindand District of Herat Province, August 26, 2008.

26. Jon Boone, "Kabul Accuses Allies of Civilian Deaths," *Financial Times*, August 22, 2008.

27. Office of the President, *President Karzai Condemns Shindand Incident* (Kabul: Office of the President, Islamic Republic of Afghanistan, August 23, 2008).

28. Author interview with senior U.S. State Department official, October 2, 2008.

29. Memorandum from Brigadier General Michael W. Callan to Acting Commander, United States Central Command, Subject: Executive Summary of AR 15-6 Investigation into new information relative to civilian casualties from engagement by U.S. and Afghan Forces on 21–22 AUG 2008 in Azizabad, Shindand District, Herat Province, Afghanistan, October 1, 2008.

30. Memorandum from the Rendon Group to J5 CENTCOM Strategic Effects, Polling Results—Afghanistan Omnibus May 2007, June 15, 2007.

31. Charney Associates, *Afghanistan: Public Opinion Trends and Strategic Implications* (New York: Charney Associates, 2008), slide 20.

32. Author interview with senior NATO intelligence official, November 13, 2008.

33. United Nations Department of Safety and Security, Security Incidents in Afghanistan, July 2008.

34. NATO ISAF, *Afghan National Security Forces Update* (Kabul: NATO ISAF, July 24, 2008), slide 5. Between January 2007 and July 2008, there were 333 Coalition soldiers killed (20 percent), 1,015 Afghan police killed (59 percent), and 369 Afghan soldiers killed (21 percent).

35. Memorandum from Investigating Officer to Commander, Combined Joint Task Force—101, Bagram Airfield, Afghanistan, Subject AR 15–6 Investigation Findings and Recommendations—Vehicle Patrol Base (VPB) Wanat

Complex Attack and Casualties, 13 July 2008, 13 August 2008.

36. The NATO after-action report was leaked to Canada's *Globe and Mail* newspaper. See Graeme Smith, "Taliban Making the Grade in Guerrilla War," *The Globe and Mail*, August 20, 2008.

37. Author interviews with U.S. intelligence officers, Bagram, Afghanistan, March 8, 2008.

38. U.S. Department of State, "Pakistan: Refocusing Security Assistance," January 2008.

39. State Bank of Pakistan, *Monetary Police Statement, July–December 2008* (Islamabad: State Bank of Pakistan, 2008).

40. Author interview with senior State Department official, September 30, 2008.

41. Dexter Filkins, "The Long Road to Chaos in Pakistan," *New York Times*, September 27, 2008.

42. Dexter Filkins, "Right at the Edge," *New York Times Magazine*, September 5, 2008.

43. Author interview with senior NATO official, September 29, 2008.

44. Mark Mazzetti and Eric Schmitt, "Pakistanis Aided Attack in Kabul, U.S. Officials Say," *New York Times*, August 1, 2008, p. A1.

45. Author interview with senior White House official, September 25, 2008.

46. Iftikhar A. Khan, "Kayani Warns US to Keep its Troops Out," *Dawn* (Pakistan), September 11, 2008.

47. Combined Joint Task Force-101, *CJTF-101 Assessment* (Bagram: CJTF-101, 2008), slide 7.

Chapter Eighteen

1. Zehīr-Ed-Dīn Muhammed Bābur, *Memoirs of Zehīr-Ed-Dīn Muhammed Bābur: Emperor of Hindustan*, vol. 2, translated by John Leyden and William Erskine (London: Oxford University Press, 1921), p. 19.

2. Author interview with Lieutenant Colonel Simon Heatherington, Commander, Kandahar Provincial Reconstruction Team, Kandahar, January 16, 2007.

3. Douglas J. Feith, *War and Decision: Inside the Pentagon at the Dawn of the War on Terrorism* (New York: HarperCollins, 2008), pp. 101, 149.

4. Francesc Vendrell, *EUSR Vendrell's Valedictory Report* (Kabul: European Union, 2008).

5. Olivier Roy. *Islam and Resistance in Afghanistan*, 2nd ed. (New York: Cambridge University Press, 1990), p. 10.

6. U.S. Embassy Kabul to Department of State, Cable 4745, August 2, 1971, "Audience with King Zahir." Released by the National Security Archive.

7. Thomas Schweich, "Is Afghanistan a Narco-State?" *New York Times Magazine*, July 27, 2008.

8. See, for example, United States Department of the Army, *Counterinsurgency*, FM 3–24 (Washington, DC: Headquarters, Department of the Army, 2006), pp. 1–13.

9. On the role of tribes, see Shahmahmood Miakhel, "The Importance of Tribal Structures and Pakhtunwali in Afghanistan: Their Role in Security and Governance," in Arpita Basu Roy, ed., *Challenges and Dilemmas of State-Building in Afghanistan: Report of a Study Trip to Kabul* (Delhi: Shipra Publications, 2008), pp. 97–110; David Kilcullen, *The Accidental Guerrilla: Fighting Small Wars in the Midst of a Big One* (New York: Oxford University Press, 2009), pp. 39–114.

10. Asia Foundation, *Afghanistan in 2008: A Survey of the Afghan People* (Kabul and San Francisco: Asia Foundation, 2008).

11. Brigadier Mohammad Yousaf and Mark Adkin, *Afghanistan—The Bear Trap: The Defeat of a Superpower* (Havertown, PA: Casemate, 2001), p. 64.

12. Hans J. Morgenthau, *Politics Among Nations: The Struggle for Power and Peace* (New York: Alfred A. Knopf, 1963), p. 186.

13. Norman Davies, *God's Playground: A History of Poland in Two Volumes* (New York: Oxford University Press, 2005).

14. Author interview with Ambassador Ronald Neumann, September 7, 2007.

INDEX

Page numbers in *italics* refer to maps or graphs.